THE BURNING BUSH

Born in the East End of London of Russian immigrant parentage, Barnet Litvinoff saw active army service throughout the Second World War as a private soldier, in France until Dunkirk then in the Middle East. Captured during the Rommel advance in the Western Desert, he spent three years as a prisoner of war in Italy and Germany.

His earlier books, widely translated, include works of biography, history, contemporary affairs and fiction. He has contributed to numerous magazines and newspapers across the world.

D0878166

THE BURNING BUSH

Antisemitism and World History

BARNET LITVINOFF

Fontana/Collins

First published by William Collins 1988
First issued in Fontana Paperbacks 1989

Copyright © Barnet Litvinoff 1988

Photoset in Linotron Sabon by
Ace Filmsetting Ltd, Frome
Printed and bound in Great Britain by
William Collins Sons and Co. Ltd, Glasgow

And the angel of the Lord appeared
unto him in a flame of fire out of the
midst of a bush: and he looked, and
behold, the bush burned with fire and
the bush was not consumed.

And Moses said, I will now turn
aside, and see this great sight, why the
bush is not burnt.

Exodus 3:2, 3

CONTENTS

ACKNOWLEDGEMENTS

My indebtedness to the many scholars whose works proved of the greatest value in writing this book will be evidenced in the Bibliography, though the interpretation of historical events which they have enabled me to make is naturally my own. I would particularly record my appreciation of the German writer Christian Ferber for his helpful reading of the manuscript and his guidance through various aspects of the subject, and of Bruce Hunter, without whose initial encouragement the work would not have been embarked upon. Finally, I owe thanks to my son, Miles Litvinoff, for many suggestions and his meticulous editing of the text.

INTRODUCTION

Tracing the history and consequences of antisemitism must carry with it the danger of distorting the perspective through isolation of the subject from its general background. The effect would render the thread continuous, and indeed some writers have approached the theme as a story of virtually unbroken persecution. In reality the condition has alternated between periods of quiescence and explosion. During extended periods the Jews lived in harmony with their neighbours, so much so that nothing about them of collective moment was preserved in any permanent record.

Those periods frequently coincided with times of acute distress for other sects, whether religious, political or racial: for example, in the suffering arising from the birth of Protestantism, and in the spread of empire. It is as well, therefore, while the martyrdom of the Jews during the Second World War still casts its shadow, to recall the martyrdom, also within living memory, undergone by other peoples for similar reasons – alienation, prejudice or irrational distrust. This does not detract from the transcending tragedy of the Holocaust. To a certain degree it explains how man's frightening susceptibility to barbarism in times of tension makes such occurrences possible. The Jews were often spared, because of their neutrality, the miseries of violent religious and political conflicts, as during the Thirty Years War in the seventeenth century and the Algerian War in the twentieth. Nor should we forget how Jews could find themselves in situations that gave them a share in the guilt of oppressing others. Their merchants actively participated in the slave traffic to the New World. They formed a part of the white supremacy which kept the indigenous tribes in helotry in southern Africa. The unresolved Middle Eastern crisis leaves them masters of another race in Israel.

Our subject increases in complexity through problems of

definition. What exactly *is* antisemitism? We recognise the evil in the treatment accorded to the Jews by some despotisms since early medieval times, with savage manifestations during the Spanish Inquisition and most recently while Europe was held in the sway of Fascism. Latent antisemitism, both social and economic, most readily came to the surface in countries ruled by a doctrinal authoritarianism. Between these extremes much ambiguity accompanies the diagnosis, so that Jews themselves have been known to discover antisemitism where probably none was intended. As the sociologist Theodor Adorno put it, 'the splinter in your eye is the best magnifying glass'. Discrimination is an injustice rarely absent from human relations, and Jews were sometimes entrapped in a net of persecution designed to contain dissenting individuals irrespective of race or creed. What part did antisemitism play? Zionism was the philosophy of a movement seeking to eliminate its causes, but has added a new dimension to the problem instead.

The playwright Arthur Miller considered he understood the subject sufficiently in 1945 to make it the theme of his novel *Focus*. A visit to the Far East, however, prompted him in 1982 to speak, in an introduction to a new edition of the work, of the hostility towards the Chinese population in Thailand, and towards the Vietnamese inhabitants of Cambodia in the days of Prince Sihanouk. This antipathy towards a minority, Miller discovered, was precisely the same, and drawn from the same motivation, as the prejudice he had encountered as a Jew in the United States. For painful commentary, we have also the recent genocidal catastrophe inflicted upon the Cambodians themselves by the Khmer Rouge.

Thus to isolate the Jews in history so as to make antisemitism an evil *sui generis* leaves too many questions unanswered. Nevertheless, from the time when all our history was made by Europeans – that is, since the termination of the first Jewish commonwealth in Roman times almost to the present – the Jew has been the selected sacrifice of men in power, should they need a sacrifice. The Jew was a European problem, a Christian problem and not least a problem for himself. His individual way of life, preserved through his religion, substituted for a territorial base. He would henceforth be especially vulnerable, in the final reckoning without a shelter on the soil to which all other perse-cuted peoples could repair, either to defend themselves or to await the passing of a storm.

The present work charts antisemitism from its origins in the Crucifixion. This may strike some readers as purely arbitrary: what of antisemitism before Christ? Surely it existed! Yes, but unexceptionably, in the context of primitive societies, when oppression of the weaker by the stronger, no matter the tribe, was in the natural order. Every people practised some form of 'antisemitism', including the Jews themselves, as the Bible vividly illustrates.

The most profound change has taken place in the present century, which divides absolutely into its two halves at the Second World War: new nations arisen, old ones diminished in power, Western Europe and the USA multiracial, a Third World enjoying its newly discovered articulacy. Racial politics are still with us, but so developing as to reduce the distinctiveness of the Jews and placing them in categories that demand a revision of all the assumptions hitherto made about them. Problems the Jews must still have, along with all other peoples, though they are defined in terms other than antisemitism. Perhaps the disease will never die, but it has become one of the lesser ills of mankind.

1

Rome against Jerusalem

With his last agonised breath, the crucified Jesus uttered a cry of reproach to the Lord. 'My God, my God, why hast thou forsaken me?' he sobbed. The Gospel gives it in the actual Aramaic, the language generally spoken by the Jews in the centuries between the birth of Rome as a republic and its zenith as an empire.

Eli, Eli, lama sabachtani?

The cry had been heard before among the descendants of the ancient Israelites. We know it from the Psalmist. And they would have occasion many times more to compel their dying lips to express these words, the saddest in human vocabulary. When Jews suffered torture unto death there must be a divine explanation, for it was God's wrath. Omniscient and omnipotent, he commanded all the actions of man and beast. He was the Jews' personal God. They alone had been chosen to discover him, sealing the Covenant between the Holy One and themselves by circumcision, mutilation of the male flesh. He marched with them, tested them in adversity, guided them from darkness to light, gave them kings and prophets. According to their belief God had caused them to multiply and become a great nation, and their enemies to tremble. Other peoples might have a history, but theirs was History.

The Jews had often suffered defeat and transportation. The blood of countless innocents drenched the soil, and triumphant Rome had planted its standard in their land, but they still looked to their God. Only a Jew would expect this unseen deity, creator of heaven and earth, to answer for his martyrdom. Socrates, cup of hemlock poised, uttered no such cry. Nor Julius Caesar, so much closer in time to the Jew now expiring on Golgotha. They were pagans. He was of the Chosen People.

For all that has been written since, we know little of the

circumstances of the Crucifixion. The records were not, until many centuries later, subjected to analysis or reinterpretation. They inform us that the execution of Jesus was engineered by the religious notables in Jerusalem, much to the bewilderment of the Roman governor of Judea. They wanted Jesus dead as a dangerous rebel against their authority, and Pontius Pilate was induced to pass sentence. Six hours on the Cross, and then the anguished 'Why?'. It happened after the inauguration of the Passover festival, when a ceremonial meal is consumed.

Now the wonderment of it: God had not forsaken his child. The earth trembled on the third day, and Jesus rose from his sepulchre. Then, beginning with the few Jews who had followed him in his earthly state, many people came to believe in the miracle, declaring that Jesus was the Christ-Messiah. But the mass of Jews were unconvinced. Most of them, even those inhabiting Judea, that part of southern Palestine of which Jerusalem was the centre, could not have known of his resurrection for a long time. When told of it they shrank from the report as a shocking blasphemy.

The nature of Jesus remained a domestic argument among different sectaries of Jews, perhaps for years. No doubt disputation was fierce, but in the East diverse cults borrowing each other's practices proliferated, and every man could, by Roman law, have his own god or none. Jews might follow Jesus or reject him, but they still prayed together, kept the same festivals and fasts, drew solace from the Law of Moses inscribed in the same Torah, rested on the seventh day. Pilgrimages to Jerusalem saw them together in the same Temple, that huge edifice, twice the size of St Paul's Cathedral, built by Herod the Great. Its grandeur awed every visitor, heathen and believer alike, to their Holy City.

The Jews walked together in open deference but suppressed hatred of the same alien overlord. But, mindful of an earlier glory, they were sometimes goaded into rebellion by dictatorship from Rome and its insatiable thirst for tribute. On the whole the occupation was not onerous, but savagery could be employed in quelling unrest: when a tumult occurred among the Samaritans, who practised another divergent brand of Judaism (for which they were abhorred by the rest of Jewry), Pontius Pilate's response was so harsh in AD 36 as to bring about his recall from governorship of the province.

Sixty years or so before the birth of Jesus, and thus some ninety years before his Crucifixion, Judea had come under Roman domination. This had transpired less from conquest than by default of opposition. The once great Maccabean priest-kingdom of the Hasmoneans, riven by dynastic rivalries, corrupted (though also enriched) by Greek influences, found itself at the mercy of rapacious neighbours. It had slid into the sorry condition of being unequal to the challenge of independence within the space of a hundred years. While neglectful rulers sought through foreign alliances the authority they could not achieve by personal example, the country fell prey to divisions and conflicts that were inflamed by religious fanaticism. Pompey, a general with the tastes of a potentate, was then securing the Eastern Mediterranean for the Pax Romana. He settled all arguments by marching soldiers of his Tenth Legion into a surprised and resentful Jerusalem.

Roman rule was not without its advantages. Pompey had other preoccupations, and left responsibility for tax collecting to a lackey, Antipater, of an Edomite family converted to Judaism. However, Pompey was falling out of favour in Rome while the star of Julius Caesar rose in the ascendant. Antipater switched sides. He gave valuable support to Caesar, and the Jews were rewarded with a generosity uncommon in the explosive era marking Rome's transition from republic to empire. Caesar absolved them from providing recruits for his campaigns (their insistence on a sabbath rest day impaired their efficiency anyway). In 37 BC Herod, son of Antipater, had secured election by the Roman Senate as king of the vassalised Judea. And so a nominal Jewish commonwealth, hanging by a thread, was sustained, albeit with such pagan refinements as combats between humans and wild animals, borrowed from Herod's masters, and a Hellenistic city culture imported from Alexandria and Antioch.

Jews lived outside Palestine too. Indeed, they were flourishing. Descendants of those Old Testament Judeans led six hundred years earlier with their chained and blinded king Zedekiah into Babylonian exile now constituted an important community among the eastern rivals of Rome. They had kept their religion and culture alive, so that the Temple was not forgotten – in fact, Jerusalem enjoyed the benefits dealt out by rich cousins in the way that it receives them in the present day from the new Babylon across the Atlantic.

The Jews spread themselves westward, by both compulsion and design. A Diaspora was already in the making. The term is Greek, for the Jews learned from the Hellenes, likewise long past their political zenith, that conquest need not entail extinction. Jews could be slaves or free citizens. Congregated in settlements as distant from the Holy Land as Cyrene, Mesopotamia and the Upper Nile, they conserved their identity – rich and poor, towns-folk and peasants, philosophers and brigands. According to con-temporary historians they gave Rome a fairly difficult time, regularly sending deputations with petitions to the Capitol. In Palestine itself quarrels among Herod's numerous progeny (he had ten wives, some of whom he murdered) left the population in a mood alternating between rebelliousness and despair, and ever on the search for a saviour. Moreover, Jews living cheek by jowl with Greeks throughout the realm produced fierce controversies accompanied by mutual contempt, made all the more perplexing by the persistence of the Jews in seeking proselytes, sometimes by force. Dislike the Greeks though they might, the Jews could not hold at bay Greek concepts about the nature of the universe, and this gave the rabbis cause for concern. Jesus of Nazareth made his dramatic entry on to the human stage to become the infinitely complicating factor in this volatile situation.

But what impact did he make on his own time? The classical historians of the early Roman Empire, who have much to say on the subject of Jewish unrest in Palestine, and could before long distinguish between the Jews who clung to Mosaic law and those following a new Messiah, write nothing at all of Jesus or the ferment he caused in Jerusalem, or of his Crucifixion. Suetonius briefly tells how the Jews caused such a disturbance in Rome 'at the instigation of Chrestus' that Claudius expelled them from the city. This occurrence is related also in Acts of the Apostles, though it could hardly have corresponded to the facts, given the emperor's own association with prominent Jews and our know-ledge of their presence in the Eternal City shortly afterwards.

For information regarding Christ's ministry, the fear he is

presumed to have inspired among those refusing to accept him, the struggle to spread the word and the unremitting campaign of hatred launched by the Jews against their Christian defectors, we have only the words of the New Testament. The Dead Sea Scrolls discovered since 1947 at Qumran help very little, except in offering an insight into the ascetic conventicle of Jewish pietists, considered to be Essenes, of which John the Baptist was probably a disciple.

While the Roman historians are silent about Jesus, the Gospels on their side include barely a sentence on the Roman presence in Judea. This is understandable. The narratives have a solitary propagandist objective: to destroy Jewish opposition to the belief in the divinity of Jesus. Extensively revised in their time, the Gospels cast their opponents in the mould of authoritarian bigots, and the Jerusalem populace as ecstatically welcoming the miracle-worker one day and clamouring for his blood the next. As for the pagan masters of them all, it was a case of the least said, soonest mended. One is drawn to a modern parallel in the collaborationist literature published by the French following the German conquest of their country in 1940. Much of it is of the highest quality, with a fiercely ethical tone, but where is the resentment at the loss of freedom, or the rage? French writers too reserved their ire for the latter-day 'Pharisees', which in their case were the 'Jew-dominated' Anglo-American allies belittling their father-figure Marshal Pétain. The three narrative Gospels, as they have come down to us, were written during, or immediately following, the great catastrophe of AD 66–73, that desperate struggle against Roman rule which lost the Jews their Temple, their Holy City and their nationhood.

Concerning these events, the Gospel authors assure us that Jesus foresaw the disasters impending: 'There shall be great distress in the land', he is quoted by Luke as prophesying, 'and wrath upon this people. And they shall fall by the edge of the sword, and shall be led away captive into all nations; and Jerusalem shall be trodden down of the gentiles.'

Whatever the Christians chose to say of Jesus, the manner of his death and the words he was presumed to have uttered, the rabbis chose not to refute but to ignore. In their view executions applied only to humans, and even to refer to the Crucifixion, let alone the charge of its having been instigated by the Jews, brought into profane debate the character of the Eternal. All one needed to know of Creation, and the coming of the Messiah, and the nature of existence, was inscribed in the five books of Moses, or was directly inspired by the Mosaic code. God had not yet chosen to send the Messiah. They would know it, for the time would usher the reunion of heaven and earth, the end of all evil. As a consequence, the Gospels survived to register Jewish calumny unquestioned. Jews refusing to accept Jesus were beyond redemption.

The rabbis decreed all terrestrial happenings following the canonisation of their Bible (the 'Old Testament') as unworthy of record, for the Chosen People were to be in suspended time until the true Messiah's arrival. As Haim Cohn, the eminent contemporary jurist (and a Minister of Justice in the modern State of Israel), has pointed out in speaking of the Crucifixion:

> What the Jews unfortunately failed to do was to meet their Christian challengers on the Christian premise and argue the case for Jewish innocence on the basis of an analysis of the Gospel reports themselves; but then the holy books of the Christians, since the earliest Talmudic times, have been strictly taboo and banned. Not only would no Jewish scholar study them, whether out of intellectual curiosity or in a desire to obtain the necessary intelligence of the adversary's weapons, but there are even pronouncements in the Talmud that these books must be burned.[1]

The practice was destined to continue, keeping the people apart until modern times.

We have a painfully graphic account of the revolt against Rome, which began with sporadic acts of defiance and terminated in self-immolation by the defenders of Massada, through the pen of the Jewish historian Josephus. Again, had his work not been conserved, together with the 'rejected' books of the Apocrypha, by Christian scholars, we would know virtually nothing of the Hasmonean epoch, the Herodian dynasty and daily life

[1] *The Trial and Death of Jesus*, London, 1972, pp. 321–2.

among the Jewish communities under Roman rule. Josephus is the sole contemporary authority from whom we can gain a picture of the Temple edifice and reconstruct the social fabric of the Jews, their struggle to protest their beliefs against pagan inroads, their martial abilities and political ramifications, the public and private lives of their leading personalities. His writings constitute an essential commentary for a fuller understanding of the New Testament.

Yet the extensive literature bearing his name contains but two obscure references to Jesus Christ, with two passages relating to John the Baptist, and nothing at all of the controversies Jesus engendered within Judaism – the religion to which Josephus was, if only nominally, an adherent. These passages, it is now generally accepted, were insinuated in later versions by churchmen searching in vain for some corroboration of the New Testament account of Christian beginnings; a sort of editorial licence, perhaps, in the interests of a higher truth. Of course, in the interests of a higher truth Josephus did not exist at all for the stern upholders of Jewish religious conformity.

Josephus is to be approached with caution. Though without peer as chronicler of his age, he was given to exaggeration, self-advertisement and bias. He claimed membership of a priestly Jerusalem family of Maccabean descent. Apparently destined for a rabbinical career himself, he was austerely educated by the Essenes, spent three years of study in Rome and followed a way of life not untypical of a young Jewish aristocrat. His friends at court included Poppaea, Nero's empress.

On the outbreak of war against Rome the twenty-eight-year-old Josephus was back in Palestine as general in charge of the Jewish forces raised in Galilee. The campaign he describes there, benighted by command-level feuds, ended so disastrously for the Jews as to render him the sole survivor of the siege of Jotapata; and while thousands of his soldiers were either slaughtered or taken into slavery, he saved his skin by personally surrendering to the enemy general Vespasian. Fortuitously, Josephus was able to notify the ambitious Roman of a vision he had been vouchsafed in which Vespasian would emerge triumphant from the civil war then raging in the capital of the empire. Moreover, his son Titus would succeed him as emperor – no small prophecy, given that Rome was burning and three emperors were about to die within a year.[2]

Josephus was then granted safe conduct to Jerusalem, where, standing before the walls of the beleaguered city, he implored the starving populace within to abandon the futile struggle. But Jerusalem was held in the terror-grip of an extremist group known as the Zealots, who fought with a tenacity that nullified human reason. Resistance continued against Titus following Vespasian's hurried return home to proclaim himself. Consoled in love by the Jewish princess Berenice, Titus drove his engines of assault across the hallowed ground in a kind of perplexed frenzy. Stone by stone the city fell to the legionaries clambering over heaps of putrefying bodies. They reached the Temple and put it to flames. Many Jews wished to surrender, but were prevented by the Zealots, who prayed for a miracle and dealt ferociously with every Jew guilty of defeatist talk. In the meantime their own rival factions fought each other without quarter. The Zealots cursed Josephus for his treachery, cursed the Sanhedrin of priestly representatives for its readiness to treat with the enemy, granted no mercy and sought none. In his account, Josephus states that Jerusalem was left a smoking ruin in a holocaust that resulted in a million dead. If the figure is correct, it exceeded the destruction of Carthage in 146 BC.

This was not yet the end. Three years later the Zealots were still holding out, in a final pocket of defiance upon that spur of Judean rock at Massada, Herod's fortress constructed to protect his kingdom from the ambitions of Cleopatra. As its defenders died the cry would surely have been heard once more: 'Oh God! Why hast thou forsaken us?'

Nations in defeat fall into a sullen introspection as they seek to amend with the pen their failure with the sword. Though surviving groups among the Zealots escaped from Palestine and harangued the Jews in Cyrene and Alexandria to renew the struggle from remote parts, the people as a whole left the guard-

[2] Apparently the vision appearing to Josephus was in common circulation. The sage Johanan Ben-Zakkai, allowed by Vespasian to lead his scholars unharmed out of stricken Jerusalem to establish a new centre of learning at Jabneh, is credited in the Talmud with having similarly prophesied the throne to Vespasian.

ianship of their national spirit to the rabbis, their intelligentsia. Theirs was the pressing task now to bring the laws and disciplines up to date and codify them. The Jew must be made to remember Jerusalem in his every waking moment. Not a single regulation, even the most insignificant, dared be forgotten, for on their totality would depend the trust of the Lord in his people. As Jewish political and commercial life decayed in Palestine the religious schools flourished. They shared with schools in Babylonia the charge of holding Judaism aloft, as counterweight to Alexandria's magnetic field in the Hellenisation of Israel and bulwark against the advances of Christianity everywhere. Conversion to Judaism proceeded, but, the doubters asked, if the Jewish God was all powerful why had he abandoned his people? Proselytes still came forward (the Emperor Domitian's nephew, for one) though more rarely. Hopes that Rome itself would one day follow the path to Judaism collapsed.

As for Josephus, he lived grandly within the palace of his benefactors, Vespasian and Titus, whose family name Flavius he incorporated in his own. A retired military figure given over, like so many since, to a life of letters, he sought to justify his egregious past. In adulation of his patrons he stooped to the lowest rungs of servility; in condemnation of those who had insisted upon fighting to the horrific end he ascended to the highest level of abuse. But there is another side to Josephus: defender of his people's faith against any who derided it or spread calumniating notions about their ingratitude, treachery and xenophobia. He compiled a popular version of the Jewish scriptures for a Graeco-Roman readership and isolated the seeds of antisemitism that had been sown by Latin writers even before the birth of Christ.

Jewish belief was rooted in a mystical attachment to the soil of the Holy Land; break the connection and the people would perish. But followers of the Christian variant felt released from any obligation towards a temporal home. Having detached themselves from the great rebellion they did not share in the trauma of its tragic aftermath. For them the Kingdom of God lay within the heart, and salvation was universally available to all who accepted the Son. The two branches of the religion began, after the holocaust in Jerusalem, to correspond to diverging concepts of human purpose. Soon, they would be irreconcilable. Each would entrust its ideals to paper in the form of theological-political tracts; the New Testament on the one side, the Talmud on the other. For a sense of God perceptible in worldly terms the Christians would one day erect a temple of their own, to be called St Peter's, in the hated capital of the conqueror on the banks of the Tiber.

Hated capital? Within the tolerant parameters of Roman rule Jews found that life could be made bearable after the war no less than previously. Of course, their attitudes demonstrated ambivalence, or perhaps the words ascribed to Jesus, as so much else, originally came from them: 'Render unto Caesar the things which are Caesar's, and unto God the things which are God's.' One adjusted. When the Emperor Claudius was embarrassed for funds he went to his friend Alexander, treasurer of the Jewish community in Alexandria; and that man's son Tiberius Julius Alexander played a leading role in the siege of Jerusalem – on the Roman side. The two were kin to the great philosopher Philo Judaeus. A Hellenised aristocrat, Philo was suspected as a heretic by his own people, for he presumed to interpret the Creation allegorically, in Platonist terms. He too was rescued from oblivion by the Christians.[3]

While Rome had its fervid Jewish patriots, others remained determined enemies. Many were located in Parthia, on the eastern periphery of the empire and its running sore. They succoured the efforts of the residue of Zealots, among others, who still refused to accept the humiliation of foreign rule in the Holy Land. They took up the sword again in various provinces of the empire. Within Judea a national hero arose during the reign of Hadrian, early in the second century. He went by the name of Bar-Kochba, which was probably a sobriquet, 'Son of the Star'. He encouraged belief, fostered by the Jews' spiritual leader Rabbi Akiva, that in his person there indeed had arrived, at last, the true Messiah. The early Church Fathers, borrowing a description from the second-century Roman historian Dio Cassius, described Bar-Kochba as a bandit leader and assassin, for in

---

[3] So effective was the ban on nonconformist literature that the great Jewish sage of the Middle Ages, Maimonides, knew nothing of Philo, nor of Josephus.

his reconquest of Palestine he persecuted the Christians for refraining from the struggle and, it was alleged, had them forcibly circumcised.[4]

Gibbon, in his antisemitic (and anti-Christian) *Decline and Fall of the Roman Empire*, borrowed from the same source in his account of the Jews' insurrectionist temper:

> Humanity is shocked at the recital of horrid cruelties which they committed in the cities of Egypt, of Cyprus and Cyrene, where they dwelt in treacherous friendship with the unsuspecting natives. And we are tempted to applaud the severe retaliation which was exercised by the arms of the legions against a race of fanatics whose dire and credulous superstition seemed to render them the implacable enemies not only of the Roman government but of humankind. The enthusiasm of the Jews was supported by the opinion that it was unlawful for them to pay taxes to an idolatrous master, and by the flattering promise which they derived from their ancient oracles, that a conquering Messiah would soon arise, destined to break their fetters, and to invest the favourites of heaven with the empire of the earth.

Then Gibbon, in one of his famous footnotes, retails particulars of Jewish atrocities as bequeathed by Dio Cassius: 'In Cyrene they massacred 220,000 Greeks, in Cyprus 240,000, in Egypt a very great multitude. Many of these unhappy victims were sawn asunder, according to a precedent to which David had given the sanction of his example. The victorious Jews devoured the flesh, licked up the blood and twisted the entrails like a girdle round their bodies.'[5]

Credited in the Talmud with legendary strength, Bar-Kochba gathered a force of two hundred thousand troops under his command. Judean independence was momentarily established, with the minting of coins. His army met with such success that Hadrian, alarmed at the spread of the revolt, summoned Julius Severus from Britain to take over the campaign. It was to require

[4] Eusebius, *Ecclesiastical History*, excerpted in Colm Luibheid (ed.), *The Essential Eusebius*, New York, 1966, p. 122.
[5] *Decline and Fall of the Roman Empire*, London, 1957, Vol. II, pp. 3–4.

three and a half years, from 132 to 135, before the most renowned
Roman general of his time could report victory. According to Dio
Cassius, more than half a million Jews were killed during the
operations, including the 'Son of the Star' himself, now bitterly
demoted to 'Son of Lies' by those of his co-religionists who had
opposed the war from the start. Rabbi Akiva achieved the holy
state of martyrdom in being flayed alive. The people's hopes for a
national renaissance went into repose for some 1800 years.

As retribution, Hadrian determined to paganise the Jews of the
eastern provinces. He forbade circumcision as a form of castration (the edict affected other peoples, particularly in Egypt, who
practised the rite). Jews were not allowed to approach the vicinity of Jerusalem, now transformed into a Roman township, Aelia
Capitolina. It was adorned with a shrine to Jupiter where once
the Temple stood. This also ended the Christian presence there –
all fifteen bishops since the birth of the new faith had been
circumcised Jews, beginning with James, brother of Jesus. Keeping the sabbath day was proscribed, and the maintenance of
religious schools classed as sedition. Anyone discovered in trans-
gression of these edicts was sold into slavery at the price of a
horse. The punishment, however, was short-lived, for Hadrian's
successor abolished all anti-Jewish ordinances except one forbidding the circumcision of proselytes. Gibbon records the tolerance
of Antoninus Pius in this regard with regret and distaste.

Josephus no longer being among the living at the time of
Bar-Kochba, we lack a Jewish account in graphic amplitude,
such as he had made of the earlier war. However, from the works
he left we know of the resentment long borne against the Jews for
their troublesome inclination towards insurgency. What their
neighbours observed was a narrow-minded sect adhering to an
incomprehensible form of worship which demanded strict
attachment to special rules of eating and congress. They saw in
the ordering of a weekly day of rest a mark of their indolence, and
in their refusal to marry outside their faith an example of their
arrogance. Tacitus, in his *Histories*, speaks of the low cunning of
the Jews and their excessive sensuality. With his passionate
determination to sustain the empire as civilisation's model,
Tacitus hated them as one more alien influence undermining
Roman standards of morality.

On his side, Josephus had taken pains to demolish a widespread belief that the Jews were of relatively recent origin, multiplying from Egyptian slave-workers infected by leprosy and other diseases. According to this pagan version they had angered the gods into causing a famine. Banished to desert isolation, the Jews then produced a leader called Moses who led them in revolt against the Egyptian king, to the degree that they held the reins of power for thirteen years. But they were subsequently driven into the Red Sea, where many drowned while the survivors managed to reach dry land and settle in the country subsequently known as Judea. This legend gained widespread credence through an Alexandrian polemicist, Apion, who was prominent in an anti-Jewish movement in his native city. Josephus tells us of Greek–Jew conflicts in Alexandria involving Philo, with both Apion and Philo heading deputations to Rome and bringing their respective grievances to Caligula, who, apparently, was not interested. Apion also gave currency to the earliest known blood-libel against the Jews. He maintained that they sacrificed a Greek stranger every year and consumed his entrails.

Assuming no distinction between those following Christ and those denying him, the Jews numbered about seven millions within the Roman Empire a century after the Crucifixion – perhaps six to nine per cent of the entire population.[6] By this time it was possible even for the pagan outsider, who wished a plague on both houses, to perceive the widening schism within Judaism. Each branch ascribed the other's disasters to divine judgement: Jewish Jews believed God guided the barbarian hand of an emperor when Christians were martyred, while the others found the message of Jesus proven in the punishments meted out to the insurgents in Palestine.

Canonisation of their respective writings rendered their polarisation absolute. The Christians saw no reason to reject the Old Testament record, for it bore witness to their prehistory. They found embedded there prophecies relating to the coming of their Saviour, who was of the lineage of King David. But they preached that Mosaic theology had been superseded by subsequent events.

[6] Michael Grant, *The Jews in the Roman World*, London, 1973, p. xi. Others have estimated as few as four millions.

This was not sufficient for one Christian, Marcion (excommunicated in 144, however). He anathematised the Old Testament entire as the work of unscrupulous forgers, and endeavoured to purge the New Testament of every Jewish influence, to the point of leaving virtually nothing except the Gospel of St Luke and some Epistles of St Paul.

The Talmud, an encyclopaedia twenty generations in the making from the first century almost to the rise of Islam, tells that Jesus, far from being descended from David, was begotten of an adulteress with a Roman soldier named Pandera. The body of 'that man' (mention of him is invariably oblique and contumelious) had been stolen by frauds and traitors so as to stage a 'resurrection'. Not that the Talmud devotes much space to the polemic: references to Christianity are hard to find. To the subordination of all else the Talmud endeavours to enclose the Jews in a uniform mould so as to preserve the people from assimilation and extinction.

Scattered throughout, passages discussing the relationship of Jews with gentiles indicate the strength of animosities in the times encompassed by this voluminous literature. The Talmud treats the gentile with contempt. He is the eternal enemy; he commits crimes against nature. No gentile may be trusted, even the nurse suckling a Jewish child, since she may poison the child unless closely watched. In besieging a gentile city, Jewish soldiers are permitted to desecrate the sabbath. These regulations were reinterpreted by later rabbinical authorities, though the original text survived to furnish the enemies of the Jews with much ammunition.

It is easier to describe what the Talmud excludes rather than what it contains. It tells us nothing of the history of the Jews in a systematic or chronological sense, nothing to enable a reconstruction of their society except by reference to the disciplines through which Jewish law is to be obeyed, with the whole illustrated by lore, parables, commentaries and rabbinical exegesis. It is silent on how the Jews wandered from the Mediterranean into Europe, their triumphs and disasters, their wealth or poverty or, indeed, the kind of political regimes of their location. Such knowledge as has come down to us on these matters derives from alien, and only too frequently inimical, sources.

Everything a Jew needed to know in the husbandry of his land, in his relations with his workers, both slaves and employees, in his conduct towards women – wives, widows and virgins – is laid out in the greatest detail. He would consult the Talmud for guidance in his charity to the deprived, in the mourning of his dead and the keeping of his festivals. It taught him medicine, food and personal hygiene, civil law and the drafting of property contracts. It was as though the Jew existed outside a geographical context pending the moment ordained by God when his exile would terminate in the restitution of his homeland – the Messianic age and a new Garden of Eden where the wolf shall dwell with the lamb. The Jew had a maxim for his every waking moment in the daily miracle that was life itself. Whatever the 'goy' wrote or spoke of him, or of anything else, was of no import. He had no need of it, for here was all wisdom, all literature, all ethics, strung out in six thousand folio pages comprising two and a half million words. Their authority stood next to the Bible, to be held in almost equal veneration.

One can but marvel at the industry of the teachers and scribes labouring in their seminaries, some in Palestine, some in the exile of Mesopotamia. The rabbis travelled between the two centres comparing notes, agreeing doctrine, to produce two separate yet interconnected Hebraicised-Aramaic texts. The Mesopotamian redaction, known as the Babylonian Talmud, is the most expansive. It assumes primacy over the other version, the so-called Jerusalem Talmud, which betrays strong Greek influence in both vocabulary and style.

Studying the Talmud was reckoned a sacred activity and therefore an end in itself, for it was inspired by men blessed with qualities giving them access to the intentions of God. Consequently one studied *with* God, who was presumed to be spending his time in heaven similarly engaged. God had no history, and the Jews did not consider themselves, formally speaking, as having a history either, except in the existential sense.

Cleaving to this immutable pattern of mores and intellectual exercise, the personality of the Jew defied comprehension by the outsider. He inevitably evoked an exasperation leading to suspicion and hatred. In this world but not of it, he might nevertheless walk with kings, die in battle and converse in an alien tongue.

Christianity released itself from the imperatives of such an ideology, which already in the second century received its foundations and core in the codification of oral law, the Mishnah. Christianity was outgrowing its vestigial Judaic inhibitions. It gave forth a radiance where those professing Judaism appeared morose. The Church grasped at opportunities offered by the strains sapping Rome's central vitality and defied official displeasure by preaching the Gospel to an ever-widening public. Baptisms became so numerous that the conversion of an emperor was just a question of time. Spreading from their power base along the shores of the Eastern Mediterranean, the bishops achieved a religious organisation beside which the Jews' rabbinical hierarchy was chaotic. And so the Church flourished despite periodic persecutions, its adherents apparently courting martyrdom as a privilege. 'The buildings of older days could no longer be satisfactory', wrote the historian Eusebius, 'and so in every city churches of spacious dimensions were built. Such was the progress, so great the increase and growth, that no envy could stop them and no wicked spirit cast a spell on them or block them with human devices.'

Such self-assurance could not proceed undeterred. Christianity required an ordered system irrelevant to the Jews, and in Roman eyes it seemed as though the Church harboured political ambitions now that the Jews had been crushed into abandoning theirs. The most fearful repression ensued. Eusebius, who as Bishop of Caesarea had made a study of Josephus and emulated his narrative method, recorded the atmosphere of his times in the Christian interest as his Jewish predecessor had done for his people. He describes how the Emperor Diocletian, in the year 303, attempted to persecute Christianity out of existence. Province by province, city by city, followers of the new faith were subjected to the vilest torments ever to be devised in the barbaric imagination of humankind. Men, women and children, rather than fall captive to their torturers, followed the example of the Jews at Massada and committed suicide. The slaughter continued for ten years. In the end, the Romans themselves grew weary of the killing.

Civil war once again rent the empire, which could no longer be administered as a single entity and had a second emperor in the

East. Pagan Rome was at its last gasp. Constantine's story is well known. A Caesar destined for the greatest glory, he received a vision of Christ while engaged in battle at Milvian Bridge. With so illustrious a convert (though he delayed baptism almost until his death-bed), Christianity stood at the point of triumph.

Restoration of the unity of the empire, so ardently desired by Constantine, depended as much on the unity of doctrine as the elimination of rival contenders for the supreme office. As to the Jews, their rights to a specific (and politically innocuous) cult were not denied. Constantine did not molest them, but they could no longer seek converts among those professing Christianity.

Now in existence for almost three centuries, the newer religion faced dangers through an epidemic of schismatic tendencies principally from Alexandria, stronghold of reason. Here the heresiarch Arius preached that Jesus, being the Son of God, was in essence subordinate to the Father. Unlike God, his attributes could not be expressed in an existence beyond and outside time. Arianism grew apace and generated bitter controversies, sometimes involving the Church fathers in mutual excommunication. Manifestly, speculation leading to a reduction of the divinity of Jesus repudiated the Trinity. The fear arose that Arianism was approaching a form of Judaism, whose Redeemer would be sent by God and must therefore be a creation of God. Christian orthodoxy envisioned the destruction of the Synagogue, yet here came Arius to throw a bridge in its direction.

Constantine personally summoned the presbyters to convocation at Nicaea in 325 and ordered a definite statement of faith so as to terminate the crisis: three hundred learned men, attended by 2,000 lower ecclesiastics, charged with transcribing their distilled collective memory into a creed. Eusebius played a noteworthy if equivocal part in this conclave, for, although he hated contemporary Jewry, he allowed that the Mosaic period had been an essential preparation for the path to holiness. After long debate it was determined that the Son was consubstantial and the equal of God the Father. Jesus had pre-existed his sojourn on earth. He had chosen to reveal himself in temporal guise as a Jew from Galilee because the Jews, a priestly caste, were at that time blessed with the grace of God.

But many had been blinded, refusing the Saviour. In scheming his execution they had, in the words of Eusebius, crucified 'Jesus Christ, the Word of God, God from God, Light of the Light, Life of Life, the only-begotten Son, First-born of all Creation.'[7]

The Nicene Creed thus laid the crime of deicide upon the Jews, a stigma that would survive the current of centuries. They were fallen from grace, an accursed people, agents of Satan. Beyond salvation, they were condemned to wander the earth for ever.

The Church fathers emphasised the separation of the faiths in a reformation of the calendar. To hallow the seventh day they had already chosen a sabbath different from the one on which God had reposed from the labour of Creation. It was to be the next day, Sunday, as belonging to the Resurrection. Nicaea now tore the Christian Passover from the tradition of the synagogue. It fixed the festival to commence on the first Sunday following the full moon of the vernal equinox rather than the fifteenth day of the Hebrew month Nisan. Constantine himself made the pronouncement:

> It is unbecoming beyond measure that on this, the most sacred of festivals, we should follow the custom of the Jews. Henceforward let us have nothing in common with this odious people; our Saviour has shown us another path. It would indeed be absurd if the Jews were able to boast that we are not in a position to celebrate the Passover without the aid of their rules.

Christian communities which continued to follow the Judaic calendar, as did some in the Orient, were branded as heretical. The prohibition before long was extended to the eating of unleavened bread (*matzoth*) and to the rejection of all other Jewish festivals.

Paganism had not yet totally surrendered to the Cross. But it was as good as done. With spiritual and temporal power combined in rulers whose shield was said to reflect a light they could only accord to their own King David, what could be the Jews' response? A few deserted their faith, then and afterwards. But the mass took shelter in their tribal cohesion, and sought solace in

---

[7] Letters to the Church at Caesarea, in Luibheid (ed.), *Essential Eusebius*, p. 218.

their sacred roots. They adopted the secrecy and subterfuge of the hunted animal. Let other nations disappear in their hunger for power. Greece was now gone, and so Rome would go. They, the children of Israel, would remain true to their Covenant and choose survival. The bush might continue to burn, but it would never be consumed.

2

Between the Crescent
and the Cross

Deprived of a geographical base in the loss of their homeland, the Jews might have been expected to dissolve into the tribes among whom they wandered. Instead, they created a spiritual and cultural universe for themselves in their Talmud. Through constant exploration along the endless corridors of thought which constituted this literature, they maintained intimacy with their past. More, the Talmud enforced a social segregation militating against dilution of the genetic strain.

This would prove a constant struggle. The community could not hold itself impenetrable, for mixed marriage would always occur, and of course concubinage brought outside blood, accepted as Jewish, into the stream. But despite the Talmud's limitations, no people could inherit a more inspiring compendium of ethics. It gave the Jews, as it sustained their pride and reaffirmed their corporate existence, both a sense of identity and a feeling of security.

This was a kingdom of God not dissimilar from that proffered in its early evangelical days by Christianity. However, while Judaism resisted modification for centuries, Christianity developed a hundred faces. It assumed a political no less than a spiritual nature, resulting in a proliferation of doctrinal schisms and the birth of national rivalries. The Western Roman imperium, on its extinction in the fifth century, achieved reincarnation in the form of a Christian empire, with its leader, the Great Pontiff, venerated as king of kings, by implication heir to the great Augustus. The Byzantine duplication of Rome in Constantinople, likewise Christian, would survive after a fashion for another thousand years, but it was Oriental rather than European, Greek instead of Latin, politically inept and, after a brief spurt of expansionism, menaced on all sides.

On the other hand, the Jewish kingdom of God, existing as it was on the strength of its own historic memory, was almost hermetically self-contained. So convinced was it of its superiority as a civilisation that no catastrophe, no hardship of a physical order, could break its spirit, uproot its foundations or destroy its belief in a special destiny. The absence of a temporal Zion was mourned, but only in the Jews' prayers. Political aspirations occasionally sparked into a faint presence, but in the main remained dormant.

Jews continued to inhabit Palestine, though under Byzantine rule the country was transformed into a wholly Christian holy land. Shrines, monasteries and conventicles of ascetics marked the landscape wherever tradition might identify a biblical event. So few were the Jews in their ancestral terrain, and so without influence in its affairs, that synagogues fell into decay as churches came to register the sacred associations of every hill and valley, every township from Sinai to Antioch. Constantine himself had begun it all with his search for the 'True Cross'.

If the Jews preserved themselves around a religious life allowing for no deviation (break from the strict rule, as not a few would, and your progeny ceased to be Jewish) they spread widely between those inhabiting the newly born cities of post-Roman Europe and the descendants of the ancient captive settlement still flourishing after the Parthians, in the third century, were succeeded by another Persian dynasty. Palestine lay between these two concentrations, not so much a bridge as a gulf. By the 'rivers of Babylon' in the East a semblance of national form indeed survived, under a Jewish leader recognised as 'Exilarch'. He carried responsibility for his community's concerns and attracted allegiance to his person because of his reputed descent from the royal house of David. The office was therefore hereditary. This 'Prince of the Exile' conducted himself like a minor potentate, and within his fiefdom schools and academies sustained Jewish scholarship through every successive regime, from the early Zoroastrians of the third century to the zenith of the caliphates in the eleventh.

Nothing is known of a parallel Jewish authority in Western Europe. The region as a whole, now semi-barbarous and plague-ridden, in any case lay submerged beneath the weight of its intellectual impoverishment overlaid by political confusion. The Jews nevertheless accommodated themselves conveniently to the collapse of the imperial order there. They entered the early Middle Ages as prominent merchants who travelled vast distances along a golden road. Some were slave-dealers, trading eunuchs, young virgins and consignments of war captives in exchange for spices, silk, sandalwood and horses from India and China. They also had their craftsmen, acknowledged for their skills in glass-making, dyeing and weaving. It was impossible to attend the great trade fairs at Toledo, St Denis and Mainz, throughout Italy and Sardinia and on the Barbary Coast, without jostling against these secretive, alien folk who spoke a smattering of all known languages as they displayed their fine brocades and Crimean furs for sale.

We are, however, leaping centuries, as indeed we must. Contemporary Jewish records are feeble in the extreme. The literature of the time concerned itself with homiletics and simplistic allegory. Like the Talmud, it possessed no feeling for chronology and totally ignored the processes out of which the Jews' medieval society evolved, and how some of them managed to ascend to a scale of mercantile enterprise spanning the continents. We have scant knowledge of synagogue life in the period when Goths, Franks and other northern tribes overran the territories vacated by the Roman legions. We know little of these other peoples either: the social history of the epoch sinks largely into the province of surmise.

Jewish writers, if they deigned at all to create a picture of their environment, spoke mainly of martyrdoms, persecutions and expulsions at the hands of new overlords just embracing Christianity; nothing about when, where or how. Certainly these were savage times, but it is not truly established that Jewish suffering was in any way exceptional among the cruelties invariably perpetrated against defenceless peoples.

The recorded deliberations of the Church councils, still extant, are much more explicit. And they offer evidence in abundance that the Jews, though tolerated, were not admissible to human society. We are told of their sinful practices and congenital venality. The Church, in regular synod from the fifth to the eighth centuries, shaped into juridical language the theologies of earlier ecclesiastics, principally St John Chrysostom of Constantinople and St Augustine of Hippo. The two bishops were contemporaries, born about the year 350, and to them must be accorded the distinction of placing antisemitism into that category of thinking that influenced attitudes to the Jews during the next one thousand five hundred years.

According to John Chrysostom, the Jews were to be eternally accursed, for in crucifying the Saviour they had revealed themselves as carnal devil-worshippers embodying all the forces of evil on earth. Chrysostom's renowned sermons, preached in Antioch, proved too controversial for the more orthodox guardians of Catholic purity, so much we know. But they nevertheless gained for him the utmost veneration among humbler clerics throughout Christendom (his image is shown in sublime pose in a tenth-century mosaic in the cathedral of St Sophia in Istanbul). His influence was exceeded only by Augustine. The latter, nourished in the creed of Manichaeism before his adoption of Christianity, constructed a scheme of Creation wherein Satan wrestles in continuous struggle with God for control of the universe. Satan used the Jews as his instrument, and not before their conversion to the true faith could a state of grace be attained by humankind on earth. In their obstinacy the Jews refused to recognise how the New Testament revealed the truth of the Old, and therefore as 'sons of darkness' they must suffer rejection until they joined the 'sons of light'. They wore the mark of Cain, and thus wandered the earth homeless. The Jews survived because, like Cain, they were not to be killed, for they bore witness to the truth of Christ.[1]

Such theological positions gave birth to innumerable embellishments. Popular belief imagined the Jews as creatures of inexhaustible appetite, sex being a subject of intense interest in the early Middle Ages, with the Devil usually depicted as possessing large genitals.

[1] Augustine, *City of God*, ed. David Knowles, London, 1972, Bk XVIII, Ch. 46. See also Bk XV, Ch. 1. 'I classify the human race into two branches, the one consists of those who live by human standards, the other of those who live according to God's will. I also call these two classes the two cities, speaking allegorically. By two cities I mean two societies of human beings, one of which is predestined to reign with God for all eternity, the other to undergo eternal punishment with the Devil.'

Whatever the Jews wrote concerning their ill-treatment at the hands of Christianity, and the Christians about the Jews as a fallen people, might be taken together as an intellectual propaganda war. It would have its effect as an historical force, but only gradually. The masses of people just then developing into nations, generally illiterate, were for the most part engaged in subsistence farming or other pursuits holding them in vassalage to their soil. They travelled rarely. They would have little contact with Jews, or with their own clergy for that matter.

This propaganda war, conducted from Christian monasteries and Jewish seminaries, could only preoccupy men of intense though blinkered piety. Who beyond the confines of their scriptoria could have read and discussed their works except a privileged few? Nothing seems to have inhibited the Jews from pursuing their daily affairs and, as always, from making their converts. They increased in number, and in prosperity. They did business with kings, and those of adequate wealth maintained great establishments serviced by barbarian slaves as would a neighbouring nobleman.

We do not lack individual examples of Jewish eminence in affairs of state. Bishop Gregory of Tours wrote extensively in his *Historia Francorum* of the influential role played by the Jews in Merovingian Gaul during the latter part of the sixth century.[2] He cites landowners, merchants, physicians and artisans, and was personally involved with one Priscus, who occupied a position of trust at the Frankish court of King Chilperic.

The king had appointed Priscus his commercial agent, and was intent upon having him, with all other Jews, baptised. There took place in 581 one of those theological disputations that were to be held with regularity in the later Middle Ages. The king played referee as Priscus debated the nature of Christ with Bishop Gregory. Priscus is said to have dismissed the story of a virgin birth as a totally unnecessary action for God to perform. Had he not previously sent prophets and inspired other messengers to bring man back to salvation? Gregory, as a true Augustinian, introduced arguments from the Old Testament and Apocrypha

[2] Gregory of Tours, *History of the Franks*, tr. O. M. Dalton, Oxford, 1927; Simon Dubnov, *History of the Jews*, tr. Moshe Spiegel, Vol. II, London, 1968, pp. 498 ff.

to foretell God's intention in this regard. He accused the Jews of having censored out such passages in transcribing the holy text.

Priscus, however, stood his ground. The king then attempted to have him baptised by force, during an episode, described by Gregory, when all the Jews of Paris were ordered to embrace Christianity. The story goes that Priscus was murdered with other members of his family on the way to the synagogue, by a band of ruffians led by a converted Jew. In Gregory's account, the Jews were the pernicious 'liars to God', and had once hurled a baptised Jewish child into a blazing furnace, whereupon it was saved by the Virgin Mary. Another time they had defiled an icon and the visage of Christ began to bleed. Such tales involving blood (Jews drinking it, Christians observing miracles in it) would re-echo in various forms down the ages, right until the twentieth century.

It was mainly through his economic activities that the Jew became best acquainted with his neighbours. And Christian sources, in speaking of their riches, render Jewish money into a coefficient of their character. The chronicles of the Jews, of course, rarely touched upon such matters – who gives away his trade secrets? – so they are meagre in the extreme concerning the paths by which some Jews attained their legendary wealth. Thus the Christians tell us of their predominance in the trafficking of human beings for slavery, and their role in banking and usury, whereas Jewish authors laid emphasis on poverty, and the responsibility of the fortunate few to alleviate the sufferings of the many.

Since the time of Aristotle usury has been condemned as the worst of practices. The Greek philosopher notes in his *Politeia*, 'The most hated form of money-making, and with the greatest reason, is usury. It makes money out of money itself and not from the natural use of it . . . Of all ways of money-making, this is the most unnatural.'

The Pentateuch is clear on lending money for interest: it may be permitted when loaned to a stranger, though not to a fellow-Jew (Deuteronomy 23:20). According to the Talmud, usury is an unqualified sin, though a subtle difference is offered in the case of 'interest', this presumably being a legitimate return on an investment. Christianity took what is now regarded as a mistranslation from a text in Luke 6:35 ('lend, hoping for nothing in return'), as a prohibition against lending money for profit. Some historians speak today of Jewish usury as a product of the Middle Ages, but it was in evidence much earlier.[3]

Though encouraged to become money-lenders, Jews did not hold a monopoly in the trade. The Lombards were famous money-lenders: from their name comes the Russian word for pawnshop. But the Jews were preferred. Kings could claim the property gained by usury on the death of a Jew – several cases are documented – and certainly Christians in need of funds, monarchs and clergy particularly, would invoke the aid of a Jew rather than of a fellow-believer, so as to avoid propelling a virtuous man to damnation. Jews were beyond the pale; later, with the organisation of 'honourable' trade guilds, they had to be excluded by virtue of their refusal to subscribe to Christian rules of association. Thus did the Jewish money-lender become a fact of commercial life.

Slavery was not abhorred in the same way, for society gave Christian sanction to the bondage of serfdom, which was barely a step higher in human dignity. But the Church authorities periodically imposed rules forbidding Jews to own Christian slaves, or to convert pagan slaves (they came mainly from Eastern Europe, hence 'Slavs') to Judaism. Some dealers, Jews included, would sell their slaves to the bishops, who thereupon gave them their freedom.

By utilising the international contacts granted them by their dispersion, the Jews could perform what were manifestly the most ignoble of services, and were readily enlisted for the purpose. It therefore transpired that they could enjoy great influence, even intimacy with their rulers, while being regarded simultaneously as social outcasts for the very practices which made their existence necessary. A rich man is more likely to achieve respect than affection. Rich groups sharing a recognisable identity are frequently hated. And in the case of the Jews, with an intractable religion that enjoined such rituals as circumcision, endogamy and social withdrawal, they were also, in the Christian mind, feared.

●

[3] Koran, Sura IV, London, 1967 edition, p. 373.

Though not universally so. When Christians were in dispute they usually left the Jews in peace. The Goths and Vandals had been converted from paganism to Arian Christianity – the old heresy, refusing to die, surfaced in the most unexpected places – and they fastened their hatreds on to orthodox Catholicism. In the sixth century Theodoric the Ostrogoth gave the Jews protection throughout Italy, earning their gratitude when Byzantium menaced his kingdom. They fought at the siege of Naples in 535 alongside the defenders – in vain, as it happened, for the Ostrogoths were vanquished. Catholicism, emerging triumphant, now assumed total sway over Italy, with the East Roman Emperor Justinian bringing retribution upon all heretics, of whom the Jews were naturally the most conspicuous.

That they should bear arms in the cause of their rulers was taken for granted, nowhere more so than in their second 'homeland', Sassanid Persia. They formed part of the Sassanid force pressing against Byzantine power, where baptism of the Jews was enforced. Justinian's brilliant if repressive reign had given way to weaker successors. This was the Persians' opportunity, and the Jews'. Together they invaded Palestine in the year 611 and seized Jerusalem. A brief span of delirious ecstasy accompanied the conquest. In the process the Jews would surely have joined in the ensuing gruesome massacre of revenge against the Christians.[4]

Would the ancient Jewish kingdom be restored? There was no lack of prophets to announce the wonder. It was not to be. After fifteen years, and the destruction of many sacred Christian sites, the Sassanids were ejected. Punishment was now meted out to the Jews, with an untold number killed. This was the last stroke of Byzantium in the Holy Land, for a new force had entered history. By 640 it had taken possession of Palestine in the name of Muhammad.

Christian Europe failed to recognise the danger. The warriors surging out of Arabia bearing the message of a new messiah could hardly be regarded as a threat to the Visigoths in occupation of Spain and the Franks ruling in Gaul. Or so the descendants of those old Teutonic hunters thought. Alas, they

[4] James Parkes, *A History of Palestine from 135 AD to Modern Times*, London, 1949, pp. 81–2.

were merely resting on their forefathers' laurels: the Visigoths had fragmented into petty rivalling dynasties, while the Merovingians, grown fat in their security, inherited few of the martial virtues of their intrepid ancestor Clovis. Carrying everything before it as it blazed a path westward from Egypt, Islam would soon complete the conquest of North Africa, and reach across the Mediterranean.

Certainly, the Jews had cause to know it. They had scorned Muhammad on his arrival from Mecca to proclaim his mission in Medina. Mecca's fame resided in its possession of the sacred megalith, the Kaaba, while Medina, a partially Jewish city far superior in station, lived by trade. Its Jews had no time for the new prophet, and so paid dearly for their hostility: all their men slain, all their women and children transported into slavery. That was in 627, Year Five of the Hejira. It had been a lesson in the penalties of contempt. Since then the Jews knew the dangers of underestimating the Arabs, even though Christendom continued to regard them as barbarians.

Life under the Visigoths, formerly so congenial, was no longer to their liking. A blunt despotism had supplanted that early tolerance towards the Jews; for, late in the sixth century, King Recarad forswore Arianism for Catholic Christianity, and imported with it the doctrinal rigours forged by the image of God the Son impaled on the Cross in Jewish Jerusalem. The bishops had triumphed in Spain at last. The Council of Toledo, combining the functions of a synod of priests and a house of legislature, pronounced twenty-three articles of anathema upon the Arians and decided to persecute the Jews till they clamoured for conversion. The intention was to unify the entire population under the banner of Catholicism.

Jews were forbidden from taking a Christian wife or concubine, or to acquire slaves, or to occupy any position granting them authority over a member of the Church. Circumcision was prohibited: a mother allowing the rite to be performed on her son had her nose cut off – a frequent punishment of the time. Jews (and pagans) discovered engaged on manual work on the Christian sabbath paid with a hundred lashes and the tearing out of their hair. For these chastisements the bishops found justification in the Old Testament. Finally, Jews refusing to accept Christianity had to leave the country.

These measures, though imposed throughout the realm in varying degrees of intensity, turned the baptised against their brothers and sent many thousands fleeing to new homes. Those who packed their chattels divided almost into separate Jewish civilisations, for some settled in Gaul to inhale the atmosphere of European development while others chose a life among the Moors of North Africa and became Arabised. Baptism purchased tranquillity for some 90,000 remaining in Spain, which is a land where history likes to repeat itself, as we shall observe in the next chapter.

As to the apostates, they were never trusted as true and faithful converts. King Recceswinth addressed the Council of Toledo in 653 as follows:

> I wish to inform you about the life and customs of the Jews, because I am aware of the extent to which the land that I govern is defiled by this pest. At the time that Almighty God had eradicated all kinds of heresy in our country, there remained only this profanity, and it can be corrected either through the steadfastness of our piety or annihilation by the rod of vengeance. I see how some among them cling to the errors of a deceitful tradition and the laws of unbelief, while others, redeemed by the waters of holy baptism, are, to my chagrin, so immersed in the sin of heresy that their blasphemy infuriates even more than in the cases not yet purged through the reviving holy water. Therefore I enjoin you not to be swayed by partiality or promises on the Jews' side.[5]

Abject in their fear of this most fanatical of Visigothic rulers, the Jews gave humiliating undertakings of obedience, as in this letter of 654:

> Our obstinate unbelief, and the inveterate errors of our ancestors, had so overwhelmed us that we could not truly accept the Master, Jesus Christ, or faithfully observe the Catholic religion. Now, however, we voluntarily promise, for ourselves, our wives and our children, that henceforth we will not participate in any Jewish ceremonies and customs, nor have dealings with the con-

[5] Quoted in Dubnov, *History of the Jews*, Vol. II, p. 516.

temptuous society of unbaptised Jews. We shall not, according to our previous custom, enter into lewd marriages with blood kinsmen to the sixth generation, but will marry Christian persons of both sexes. We will not circumcise our flesh, nor celebrate the Passover, the Sabbath or other days holy to the Jewish ritual. We will not observe the dietary laws nor anything of the detestable Jewish customs; but with sincere belief we shall honour Christ, the traditions of the Gospel and the Apostles. As far as pork is concerned we promise that if we feel unable to consume it through habit, we shall consume everything cooked with it, without squeamishness or fear.[6]

And they furthermore pledged, by the Holy Trinity, to destroy with fire and by stoning, or to hand over to the authorities, any of their number discovered in violation of these obligations.

Repression was thus reducing the Jews to their lowest ebb in the century before the Muslim conquest of Spain, though on occasion a generous monarch would amend the laws of a predecessor; or a friendly bishop, torn by doubt, would protect the Jews of his diocese. Sometimes the regulations were openly ignored. None the less, the relief experienced by those seeking a haven in North Africa on encountering a religion strongly resembling their own can be imagined. Medina was forgiven. Not surprisingly, they provided valuable assistance, in the form of material aid and intelligence, to the Moors planning their assault upon Europe.

So far we have not been able to discuss the Jews of this period as a cultural force. Critical analysis of the Bible, such as had long been undertaken by Christian scholars, would have been deemed blasphemous to them. The Hebrew language, still with its imperfections perpetrated by early copyists, was in need of philological investigation, but it hung with its many obscurities unexplored. To be sure, Christian learning too was in a trough, awaiting the birth of national consciousness. Even so, monks of a more intellectual bent spent their time industriously among their books, preserving the past and studying the human condition in accordance with the Benedictine Rule. The rabbis were no match for

[6] Ibid., p. 517.

them. It seemed that, having produced the most sublime literature in the Bible, and then created an elaborate, substitute world in the Talmud, the Jews had, culturally speaking, burnt themselves out. It was a defensive condition, born of their fear of Christianity. Islam changed the situation. Its arrival in the West drew a response from the Jews which would have the effect of releasing them from a centuries-long stagnation of the spirit.

Islam recognised its origins in Judaism and Christianity. In his vision of the world newly reborn Muhammad believed the followers of both older religions would acknowledge his apostolate as fulfilling the promise of a Redeemer, and embrace the new creed. Neither Christians nor Jews were to be persecuted for their style of worship, though if they resisted *jihad*, the military progress of Islam towards control of the known world in the name of Allah, due retribution would be exacted.

The Jews had no temporal power or territory to protect against the advance of Islam, except perhaps some tribal lands in Ethiopia outside the Muslims' path. On the other hand Christianity had strong reasons to resist the thrust of what it recognised as a barbarian force. Not a quarter of a century had elapsed since the death of the Prophet in 632 and a vast empire was in the making; it had already embraced Arabia entire, all that could be described as Persia, and the crescent formed by Egypt, Palestine and Syria as far as the southern borderlands of the Caspian Sea.

The Arabs were builders, even as they destroyed. They learnt while they taught. As a civilisation unshackled by ancient feuds, Islam observed the historic conflict between Judaism and Christianity, which to them were the same religion and parent to their own, with incredulity. Cherishing the knowledge they gained in the course of their conquests, they preserved the science and philosophy of this other world. Aristotle has reached us through the avenue of Arabism. The Jews of the old Persian settlement clustered around Baghdad decided against enmity. They seized upon the role opened to them as a vehicle of communication between Christianity and Islam. No doubt also their subconscious rejoiced in the rise of a power strong enough to threaten the supremacy of their traditional persecutors. With the passage of time, some two hundred years after the Moors took their first

step on to the Iberian Peninsula in 711 – two centuries of incuba-
tion during which history is largely inarticulate on the collective
fate of the Jews – they would come into their own in Spain and
create a Judeo-Muslim symbiosis such as proved impossible
where Christendom reigned and theology had hardened into
attitudes of mutual hostility.

To the faithful of Islam, Jesus too was a prophet, born of the
Virgin Mary though not to be confused with God himself; nor
did he die on the Cross, for God saved him.[7] To the Jews, the
occupation of the ancestral homeland by the Muslims was less
offensive to their self-esteem than its occupation by the followers
of Christ, who regarded the destruction of the Jewish state as
divine retribution for the crime of deicide.

Once the Muslims perceived that neither Jews nor Christians
would surrender *en masse* to the Koran, they were allowed to live
as they chose, though at a price. They were forced into the
inferior status decreed for infidels. They were granted protection,
for which they were compelled to pay heavily in large tribute.
They were designated *dhimmis*, a privileged status in its way, and
could not be harmed: subject peoples to whom rights could be
awarded or withdrawn at the whim of their rulers. Only in
special cases could *dhimmis* merit the privilege and dignity of
bearing arms.

Such peoples could not simulate the ways of true believers. If
they rode horseback, for example, it was an act of particular
grace. They could not wear Arab attire, nor dress their hair in the
Muslim style, nor proselytise the faithful. Periodically, regulations were introduced ordering the wearing of a yellow badge on
the garments of Christians and Jews, or perhaps a distinguishing
hat or girdle. In regions conquered from the Byzantines the Jews'
latest masters continued the interdict against the erection of
additional synagogues, resulting in shabby improvisations. In
flight from Visigothic ire, the Jewish arrivals in North Africa
might have found these regulations irksome but by no means
insupportable.

Now, in 711, the Moors, seemingly all-conquering and
accompanied by a large detachment of Jews commanded by a

---

[7] Koran, Sura IV, p. 156.

soldier of their own faith, streamed across the Straits of Gibraltar. Cordova, Malaga, Granada, Seville and Toledo fell within a span of seven years. The Jews were triumphantly reinstated. It was a humiliation for Christianity such as it could never forget, as the Jews were later to learn to their infinite cost.

The Moors now felt ready to pick Gaul like a ripe apple from the sickly tree of Christendom. Over the Pyrenees they took possession of southern France with barely a show of resistance. Only in 732 at Poitiers, on the road to Tours, was the tide turned, at a battle in which the Franks found new courage under the leadership of Charles Martel, grandfather of the man whom history would know as Charlemagne, the saviour of Europe. At this point the Jews of Narbonne prudently changed sides. In the counter-offensive forcing the Moors into retreat, the Jews handed back the city to the Franks. Geography did the rest, and Islam was held south of the Pyrenees.

The Jewish reversal was an act of gratitude, for they had not fared as badly at the hands of the Frankish kings as they had with the later Visigoths in Spain. In Narbonne, despite the synods of militant Catholicism, their settlement survived in prosperity — illustration that any reconstruction of early medieval Europe must take into account Christian chivalry as well as Christian intolerance. Come Charlemagne, who was crowned Western Emperor in Rome on Christmas Day 800 by Pope Leo III, and they seem to have ascended to a rank hardly inferior to that now being achieved by the Jews in Moorish Spain. Charlemagne's domain embraced virtually the whole of civilised Europe: into Spain as far as Barcelona, much of Italy and beyond the Adriatic. Jewish advisers were a common sight at his court in Aix-la-Chapelle. The emperor employed one of them, known only as Isaac, for confidential missions, especially to the caliphate of Haroun el-Rashid in Baghdad. On one such embassy Isaac brought back an elephant for his master.

The bishops were not universally pleased with the favours granted by Charlemagne to the Jews. As early as 770 Leo's predecessor, Pope Stephen III, shocked that members of this evil people could rise to such heights in a Christian realm, sought by indirect means to inform Charlemagne of his displeasure; indirect because he dared not offend the man who was his protector.

Stephen protested in a celebrated document which has reached us through the Church records.

'We are distressed', he wrote in reply to a complaint from Archbishop Aribert of Narbonne,

> and aroused unto death when you inform us that the Jews, who always rebel against God and are hostile to our religion, possess free estates equal with Christians in Christian territory on the basis of privileges granted them long ago by the kings of the Franks. Christians till Jewish fields and vineyards; male and female Christians live under one roof with these traitors, who corrupt their souls through words of blasphemy. Day and night the unfortunate Christian servants must humble themselves before those dogs and carry out their whims. Justice demands that all the promises made to the unbelievers and their criminal fathers be abolished, because of the death of the crucified Redeemer. Is it possible for light to have communion with darkness, Christ with Belial, and the temple of God with idols?[8]

The protest was to no avail. Indeed, Charlemagne's son, Louis the Pious, enhanced the privileged position of the Jews. Their affairs came under the aegis of an administrator, the *Magister Judaeorum*, facilitating a large degree of communal autonomy and ensuring the non-violability of their status. They were still forbidden to own Christian slaves, but their pagan slaves could not be baptised without their approval. A clash between Church and emperor became inevitable. It was provoked by Agobard, Archbishop of Lyons. He published several epistles, among them *De Insolentia Judaeorum* and *De Judaicis Superstitionibus*, in which he asserted that this people of Antichrist, 'who sell Christian slaves to Muslim Spain', compelled their Christian servants to violate Church festivals and fast days. They sold wine and meat which they themselves regarded as ritually unclean. Agobard protested against permission being given the Jews to build new synagogues, and to change market days so as not to infringe their sabbath. Worse, Christians were known to attend

---

[8] Quoted in Dubnov, *History of the Jews*, Vol. II, p. 544.

Jewish houses of worship to hear sermons, and perhaps be deluded by them.

Agobard reiterated all the charges traditionally expressed in Manichaean terms. The Jews, he declared, were the sons of darkness, and it was unworthy for the sons of light to come into contact with them and fall under their shadow. He too was especially concerned lest Christian women in the Jews' employ be perverted by the Devil's children. Louis the Pious responded to the effect that although Apostolic teaching enjoined believers to do good according to the Christian faith, they were not forbidden also to render good to non-Christians. But Agobard dreaded the worst: mass conversion to Judaism. Louis's own confessor, Bodo, had converted in 839 and, adopting the name Eliezar, had settled in Saragossa with a Jewish wife. 'He lives among the Saracens and sits bearded in the synagogue of Satan', Agobard's successor Amulo lamented, 'and blasphemes against the church of Christ.'

Ah, Saragossa! A jewel of a city in the ninth century, among the most civilised of all Europe, the Jews enjoying a full life within a tapestry of races and creeds, each in its separate quarter of the city. Bodo maintained a lively correspondence with his former brothers in Christianity, impressing upon them the harmony of Muslims with Jews, Christians with both, and mosque, church and synagogue situated in gracious Romanesque propinquity. Saragossa was cosmopolitan, enterprising and relaxed. Though Muslim power had failed to penetrate the north-west of Spain – it never would – here in the north-east, fast by Carolingian-held Catalonia, stood a proud outpost of Islamic splendour, an intellectual focus and entrepôt of commerce.

To what extent did the Jews of Spain succumb? Inevitably many of them must have found Islam irresistible. Already in the East, Islam had made inroads against their Talmudic fortress, with the noble old office of Exilarch declining into a functionless honorific. Rabbinic Judaism demanded genuflexion to a narrowly authoritarian way of life; therefore it could barely hold out against this dynamic new force and patron of the secular disciplines – medicine, astronomy, philosophy. So it transpired also in Spain. Jews eagerly crossed into those hitherto forbidden areas of science.

While they generally hesitated from travelling the road entire, to the point of conversion, they nevertheless became charged with an urge to reappraise the tenets of their own self-centred belief. Signs had reached them from the other side of the Mediterranean of a new soul-searching in Judaism. There, Islam had catalysed into existence a radical Jewish heresy. It had emanated from Baghdad, the centre to which they would, by tradition, turn for doctrinal guidance. The heresy went by the name of Karaism, a word originating in the Hebrew verb meaning 'to read', and threatened to destroy the foundations of the faith.

Karaism took root about the year 800. Its adherents began by rejecting the Talmudic regulations as spurious – meaningless accretions fixed upon the oral law through seven hundred years of exile, with habit assuming the force of dogma. The totality of Judaism, claimed the Karaites, was embodied solely in the Scriptures. In their view Mosaic Law had been reinterpreted and distorted beyond recognition by teachers incapable of comprehending the true meaning of the Bible text. In consequence the Karaites introduced new restrictions to Jewish conduct as swiftly as they abandoned others. They returned to an ancient asceticism similar to that practised by the Essenes, though their constant revision of the minutiae in the dietary and other rules might well have left the average Jew in perplexity as to what was actually changed.

More significantly, the Karaites undertook a critical re-examination of the scriptural vocabulary (a blasphemy in itself) and reasserted the primacy of the Holy Land in religious thought. This reminded a people psychologically adjusted to Diaspora of the divine injunction to return to their homeland; not to create a state there – the political form was irrelevant – but to live out their lives in its sacred atmosphere. And in its strongly puritanical sectarianism Karaism willy-nilly leaned closer towards Islam as the exemplar of a pious existence.

Although always a minority, its following grew rapidly with the continued advance of Islam, not to decline again until the radiance out of Arabia faded hundreds of years later. By that time Karaism had exerted a profound influence upon Judaism. It cleared a path for the purification of the Hebrew language, which in the hands of traditional scribes and copyists was as remote from the clarity of the original as was pidgin-Latin from Virgil when spoken by itinerant medieval friars. For this, Jewish scholars had as their model the ordered syntax of Arabic. On reaching Spain, the Karaite turbulence reacted upon the Jews there with similar force. Their sages ventured into the philosophic realms of other peoples while producing a new literature of their own. This had not happened since the impact of Hellenism in the early Christian era. The awakening coincided with the ascension in the West of a Muslim empire independent of Baghdad and centred on a rival caliphate at Cordova.

Europe as a whole was yet to emerge from the obscurantist pall that had ensued from the collapse of Roman power in the fifth century, a pall closing over the creative springs of Graeco-Roman civilisation and sending the Jews scurrying from Christian hostility into a sort of protective hibernation. Although distant England could, in its relative Anglo-Saxon tranquillity, give birth to a truly epic poem, *Beowulf*, the continental lands had still to discover an identity before creating a climate ripe for a Thomas Aquinas or Nibelunglied. Nor was it yet time for the Troubadours, or Dante. For signs that Europe was capable of such a flowering one took the road to Cordova, Granada and Seville.

Early indication of a stirring within the soul of the more orthodox mass of Jewry was afforded in the writings of Saadia, a religious leader and savant born in Egypt in 882. He translated the Bible into Arabic, and his version remains to this day the standard in that language. Strongly influenced by the old Greek masters, he produced monumental works in Arabic to reformulate Hebrew theology, carrying Talmudic Judaism into fields occupied hitherto only by such thinkers as Philo and the Alexandrian school of ancient days. As a metaphysician Saadia repudiated the Karaite contention that the rabbis neglected the Bible or were ignorant of its real meaning. His system of thought is recognisable in the philosophy of Maimonides, his lyricism in the poetry of 'singers of Zion' about to arise in Muslim Spain.

This is not the place to describe that golden age in all its brilliance, except to remind ourselves how, in an atmosphere of toleration, a culture could develop not only for the Jews' own enrichment but to adorn the larger civilisation in which they were located. As leading light during the caliphate of Sultan

Abd-ar-Rahman of Cordova around the year 950 there stood the scientist-statesman Hasdai ben Isaac ibn Shaprut (Abu Yusuf to Arab historians). He brought to European notice detailed information on the existence in south Russia of the sovereign Jewish kingdom of the Khazars, which occupied a huge area between the Dnieper and the Urals with a capital near present-day Astrakhan. Hasdai Shaprut, in the hope of these people of Turkic origin being the Lost Ten Tribes of Israel, exchanged letters – until today the primal source of our knowledge of this nation – with its Khan. The Khazar rulers had embraced a form of Judaism some two centuries previously. Implementation of the Khan's laws reposed in a House of Judges chosen from all his subjects, Muslim, Christian, Jewish and pagan, whom it claimed to represent without discrimination. Soon after contact was established with the Jewish kingdom, however, it was extinguished by war and absorbed in Kievan Russia.[9]

Hasdai Shaprut won distinction also as a physician, while under his patronage a school of poetry flourished in Andalusia. Despite the stresses shortly to overtake the Cordovan caliphate he assumed the helm in a community which proudly proclaimed that Spain and the West had now wrested supremacy in the Jewish world from Baghdad and the East. Samuel ibn Nagrela, called by the Jews Hanagid ('the prince'), glittered in this firmament. He rose to be appointed vizier of the king of Granada and commander of troops, spending his leisure in producing a critical study of the Koran. The work was received with a deference not unmixed with displeasure by those for whom Samuel was, beneath the skin, merely a *dhimmi*.

Many such figures, Renaissance men *avant la lettre*, endowed the eleventh and twelfth centuries with a unique, romantic splendour. They came to eminence in a period marked by sudden political change, social fluidity and the interaction across a stark landscape of the various races that were to give character, despite the frequent blood-lettings and expulsions in store, to the hybrid Spanish personality as we know it today. Judah Halevi was the epoch's poet of protest, the lyricist who gave expression to the

---

[9] Some historians support the theory that East European ('Ashkenazi') Jewry is largely descended from the Khazars, not from the Semites of Palestine. See, e.g., Arthur Koestler's *The Thirteenth Tribe*, London, 1976.

yearning after Zion: 'My heart is in the East, while I am in the West.' Born about 1086 in Toledo, he lived for adventure, and his end is lost in a mist of legend during a journey to Palestine after its occupation by the Crusaders. Halevi bequeathed, in his immortal *Kuzari*, a work of powerful imagination in the style of Plato's *Dialogues* that included his personal reconstruction of the Khazars' discovery of Judaism. Out of Saragossa came Solomon ibn Gabirol, the Avicebron of Christian tradition and familiar to the Muslims as Sulaiman ibn Yahya. We have his philosophic system, blending ideas from Greece and Arabia, only in its Latin version, *Fons Vitae*.

But another Europe now lurched into control of history, the Europe of militant religiosity, its recharged confidence voiced in a clamour to drown all others. And so the seed-bed of this intellectual harvest was to be reploughed. A fresh wave of invaders, of a revanchist Islamic fervour, arrived from North Africa to replace the old Andalusian benevolence. Jews and Christians trapped in its fire had to choose between conversion and expulsion; for Jews it was a familiar dilemma. And further north the reconquest of the peninsula for Catholicism was now under way.

Against so formidable a collision of national and religious might the Jews could only be the victims, and for them the outcome proved a cataclysm: in social terms as momentous as the deprivation of their nationality in political terms had been at the hands of Rome. Their spirit must now seek survival behind an invisible curtain drawn across the continent, amidst dreams of redemption, hugging their past and re-enacting their classic role as the despised intermediaries of lowly commerce.

Their race had once expressed itself in God's own language, the tongue their tradition ascribed to Adam and Eve, and to the Unseen in addressing Moses on Sinai. But in their veneration of Hebrew the Jews had neglected it, adopting Aramaic, the speech of Jesus and Josephus, and with it Greek. Then, through the medium of Arabic, they were granted a brilliant, creative moment once again. Now they found themselves within the heart of European civilisation. On the upsurge of Christianity in Spain a proportion would avail themselves of Castilian, retaining its usage under the name of Ladino. The majority marked their segregation, and degradation, in cultivating a new language evolving in Northern Europe for themselves alone. This was Yiddish. By the twelfth century it had come to stay, its Germanic base mingled with Hebrew words and, in time, much else. Yiddish detached the Jewish mass from the current of European progress. Spoken by no other people, it would mark their flight to a shelter in mysticism, to be pierced only rarely by an outside light.

We cannot reflect upon the spread of medieval Judeo-Arabic lustre without noting that the period was distinguished also by the figure of Moses Maimonides, born 1135 in Cordova, died 1204 in enforced exile in Cairo. In a category all his own, he was a physician of renown acquainted with both the great Saladin and Richard Coeur de Lion. He approached Judaism as a Talmudist with an astonishingly independent mind, and perhaps a psychological detachment deliberately incurred. Maimonides stands as the most significant Jewish intellect and teacher from the time of the Prophets until Spinoza. By a process of natural selection (which can be applied historically no less than biologically), both the Arabs and the Spanish now claim him as one of their own.

Inspired by Aristotle, Maimonides researched into the sciences of mathematics and astronomy. His philosophy widened the frontiers of Jewish theology, for he accepted the truths to be discerned from other great religions. He was thus able to endow his system of thought with qualities that would one day react upon his people's rigid orthodoxy as a liberating manifesto: see, as an example, his *Guide to the Perplexed*, scrutinising the revelation at Sinai through the lens of reason. It was a work which generated violent controversy among other Jewish scholars, and branded Maimonides as a heretic. Some rabbis, returning to the Holy Land in response to the call of the Karaites, ceremoniously denounced him in Acre and disfigured the inscription on his tomb at Tiberias. Others burned his works in Paris and Montpelier. Conflicts surrounding faith and reason would linger for centuries. Maimonides terminates an epoch, for Spain was two-thirds recaptured for Catholicism by the time of his death. Eventually his Thirteen Articles of belief would be incorporated in the creed of Judaism, though not before his people emerged from the long night of darkness now awaiting them.

3

Homelands
in the Wilderness

Jules Michelet, radical historian and master of the elegant innuendo, often cast the Jew in the shape of a spectre stalking the passage of time. A son of the mid-nineteenth century though he might be, when the French and their Jews were fast interacting in an embrace at once fructifying and tragic, Michelet could not shake free from the portentous heritage that defined France as the eldest daughter of the Church. He summarised the role of the Jews during the period of our present concerns in these words: 'Whatever we might have thought of Hebrew letters and philosophy, we should not have forgotten the enormous claim to universal gratitude which the Jews merited during the Middle Ages. They maintained a permanent contact of commerce and light between the two worlds, Christianity and Islam, during the impious divorce of humanity, thus frustrating those two fanaticisms.'

But the condition could not endure. Not long into the Middle Ages, with the wreckage of a continent bereft of the Pax Romana only imperfectly rearranged to form identifiable provinces, and the two fanaticisms collided. War – national, religious and civil – took possession of four centuries. Where did the Jews stand in this? Deprived of control over their own destiny, they recurred as victims in the margin of other peoples' history. Span the period from the First Crusade of 1096 until their expulsion from Spain in 1492, and we find the Jews in a limbo, ubiquitous yet insubstantial, irreplaceable yet rejected. To the outer world they possessed capacities but lacked a soul.

Those four centuries saw the retreat of Arab Islam back to the desert whence it sprang, and the advance of Turkish Islam deep into the citadels of the Christian West. The Black Death mocked the passing triumphs of vainglorious kings by felling a third (some say a half) of Europe's population. Man in his progress chose a personality for the Jews and affixed it to them, perhaps with the Jews' own assistance, even eagerness. Persecution has at least one attribute in common with love: it invests the recipient with whatever characteristics are ascribed to him. The role allocated by medieval society to the Jews, if mostly humiliating, could also be turned to their advantage. For better or worse, they were to be imprisoned within that role until modern times.

Eras overlap. The Muslim–Judaic symbiosis still basked in its Andalusian brilliance as the Turks, Seljuk migrants from Eastern Asia, captured Jerusalem in 1073, and William the Conqueror brought over his personal Jews from Rouen after 1066.[1] (Their task: to impose an orderly fiscal structure upon those sullen rustics, the Saxons, by rendering land into its tax equivalents.) Alfonso VI of Castile restored Toledo to Christianity in 1085, though the struggle for Spain was far from over.

However, the First Crusade separated these events from the high Middle Ages, for it was the most striking landmark of the times. Christendom knew warfare in many guises but had not seen its like. To begin with, a rabble of an army fell into rough organisation. Blessed by Pope Urban II and led by a fantasist, Peter the Hermit, it gathered force as if by its own momentum. Rogues, beggars and devout Christians of all nations, often accompanied by their wives and children, took off across Europe in the general direction of the Holy Land. God would provide whatever they lacked, which meant they could plunder at will. A few knights – professional soldiers really – captained this force only with the greatest difficulty. 'Deus vult!' they cried as they burned villages and descended like locusts upon farms and storehouses for their provender. Unable to communicate with each other through the medley of languages (the Scots speaking Gaelic, the Pyreneans Basque; even the Franks found each other incomprehensible), the sacred mission which united these crusaders included, for no good reason, the sacking of Belgrade. They had set off in the spring of 1096 at the invitation of Byzantium, which was employed elsewhere against the Seljuks, and now Constantinople awaited them in trepidation. Many fell away or died *en route*, or were captured and sold into slavery by

[1] Joseph Jacobs, *The Jews of Angevin England*, London, 1893, p. ix, citing William of Malmesbury, *Gesta Rerum Anglorum*.

Magyars and Turks both; not the knights, however, whose friends at home ransomed them, often with money extracted from 'their' Jews. Amazingly, this band, through the deficiencies of the enemy rather than their own martial prowess, conquered Antioch, then Jerusalem.

The crusade became implanted in the matrix of Jewish–Christian hostility not because of the substitution of one gentile master in Jerusalem by another – a matter of no historic consequence for the exiled nation – but as the first recorded mass persecution of the Jews by an uncontrollable mob. For the soldiers of Christ left a trail of slaughter along their journey eastward. In the main, the feudal barons ostensibly in command of the polyglot horde were themselves guiltless, on many occasions curbing excesses and punishing the guilty. The Jewish communities were made to pay for this protection along the route from Flanders and the Rhineland in silver and gold.

But the Jew was 'the infidel among us', no less an agent of the godless than the infidel in possession of the Holy Land. He was rich, he was hated. And his wealth was identifiable, accessible and portable. The temptation to murder and despoil proved beyond control.

In the evolution of Europe towards a feudal economy the Jews were steadily losing ground as a trading community. New classes of merchants were taking their place; so, apart from their learned men, such as physicians and clergy, and the poor catering to a congregation's need for scribes, artisans, servants and the like, they found little occupation except the one expressly forbidden to Christians. They were driven more and more into credit finance and money-lending. Excluded from the lord–vassal relationship, Jews lacked an agricultural base, and although they held vast estates these lands were theirs in pawn against loans.

As financiers they were utilised by kings and granted privileges by kings, for a generous proportion of their usurious earnings went to fill the royal coffers. Therefore the conversion of a Jew to Christianity was not wholly good news, since it resulted in a loss to the exchequer. Not uncommonly, a medieval ruler reckoned his Jews as part of his personal fortune, to sell or barter in transactions involving the exchange of capital for territory. One feature the Jew shared with mankind in general: with money he could usually protect himself, flee from a tyrant, suborn princes and bishops; without it he could be outraged, victimised by malice and murdered in the street to die unlamented and unknown. Chroniclers tend to forget the Jews living in poverty. Even Jesus got it wrong: it is the rich who are always with us.

The crusading hysteria, however, swept across Europe with the elemental force of a natural catastrophe. It spared neither rich nor poor. Gathering confidence from the broad cross sewn on their ragged garments, the rabble proffered the Jews baptism; refusal meant torture and death. Castles and great houses were besieged to hunt them down when the Jews found refuge among Christians of a different stamp. French Jews living beyond the tornado's reach warned their German brethren that safety lay only in flight. It was to no avail, for in the Rhineland they deluded themselves that their settled state as a respected community within the Holy Roman Empire gave them security enough. They refused to budge, and the Rhineland shuddered.

So, the Lord presumably gazing down from heaven in satisfaction at the spectacle below of his Crucifixion avenged, the blood flowed. It happened first in Speyer, where a crazed band from Count Emicho de Leinigen's force, ignoring all remonstrance from their leader, broke into the locked synagogue and killed a dozen terrified Jews before an order to leave the wretched people unmolested reached them from the local bishop. They surged northward towards Cologne, mustering-place of the armies, their frenzy increasing with every wasted day. Now the slaughter knew no bounds. Some eight hundred died in Worms; another thousand in Mainz, where many Jews, after a fast of atonement in the hope of God's intercession, put up a fierce resistance and then turned their knives upon themselves. Cologne, Neuss and Xanten followed, though the entire community of Trier, led by its rabbi, are believed to have accepted conversion in return for their lives. Those of Regensburg were forcibly baptised in the Danube.[2] Prague was the scene of the final massacre, in July 1096, the passion at last spent.

---

[2] The validity of baptism under coercion was to be long debated by the Church. Some rulers allowed them to return to Judaism, to the displeasure of many ecclesiastics. Such Jews were likened by their detractors to 'dogs returning to their own vomit'.

To many of the Jews such a martyrisation could be explained only in the language of apocalypse. It had to be a sign from God, for wasn't it written that the redemption of Israel would be preceded by a holocaust? And sanctification of the Holy Name, by carrying the test of Abraham, in the near-sacrifice of his son Isaac, to the ultimate, assuredly gave them blessedness divine! Thus wives and children died at the hand of their menfolk, and brothers fulfilled a pact of suicide, rather than embrace the faith of their persecutors.

Some four to five thousand perished altogether by one means or another. The figure is of course dwarfed by subsequent catastrophes, but Europe's Jews were then few, and later carnage was better organised. We have the dates, and the numbers, from both Christian and Jewish sources. Earlier pogroms were recorded only in the vaguest of detail, sometimes exaggerated, sometimes diminished, and never exactly fixed in the calendar, as though violent death among the Jews fell within the natural order of existence. But the events of 1096 had to be enshrined, the Jews felt, in the eternal memory of man. The Christian Peter Abelard, immortalised doubly for his tragic romance with Héloïse and his fearless theological enquiry, spoke for them when he contemplated the First Crusade after a gap of some thirty years. The account is found in J. P. Migne's *Patrologia Latina*, that massive compendium of life and thought during the early centuries of our millennium.

'One would be accusing God of cruelty if one thought that the Jews' steadfast bearing of suffering could remain unrewarded', Abelard wrote, and:

> No other people has borne so much for God's sake. Dispersed among strangers, without king or prince, the Jews are oppressed with the heaviest taxes, as if each day they had to buy anew the right to live. The maltreatment of the Jews is thought to please God. For the servitude of the Jews can only be interpreted by Christians as a sign that they are hated by God. The lives of the Jews lie in the hands of their deadliest enemies. If they wish to travel they must pay large sums to gain the protection of Christian princes, who in actual fact desire their death so that they can seize their possessions. Jews cannot own fields

or vineyards, because they have no one to guarantee their ownership. So the only profession open to them is that of usury, which only increases the Christian hatred of them.

The scourge of the First Crusade receded, though not before the irregulars under Godfrey de Bouillon marked the recovery of Jerusalem for Christianity by slaughtering all the Muslims and Jews there daring to offer resistance. Painfully, the Jews of Europe rebuilt their lives. The Rhinelanders set about recopying the holy scrolls of the Torah as though guided by the hand of Moses himself. Scholars heatedly debated the multifarious facets of sin, to reach the conclusion, through a system of mystical exegesis, that rationalist challenge of the literal truth as revealed in Mosaic Law had roused the Unseen's wrath. The words of the Torah, their actual alphabetical structure, their juxtaposition and frequency of repetition, concealed measureless truths. Intensive speculation on the oracles made of Judaism a sort of theological algebra. This had the effect of detaching the Jews ever further from the cultural path of European society, recalling them, in fact, to their origins in the East.

Time healed, fear diminished, communities were reborn. In northern France and England the affluent among them built their houses of stone in the baronial style, rather than of timber like the commoners. Their places of worship could attract Christian envy, so powerfully did their adornments advertise splendour and confidence. When Bernard of Clairvaux railed in the twelfth century against the tendency in France to erect ornate churches, he compared them to synagogues: 'The immense height of the churches, their superfluous breath, their costly marble and strange designs, hinder the devotion of the worshipper and remind one of Jewish ritual.'[3] St Bernard, who was personally sympathetic to the Jews, and begged England to treat them kindly,[4] termed Christian usurers 'apostate Hebrews'. Over in Germany, under the protection of the Holy Roman Emperor, they were less prosperous though better educated. Also, it would

[3] J. C. Morrison, *Life and Times of St Bernard of Clairvaux*, London, 1863.
[4] See his letter of intercession on their behalf in Jacobs, *Jews of Angevin England*, pp. 22–3.

transpire, more secure. Roughly, they could be classed there as Christendom's *dhimmis*.

Notwithstanding the rabbis' efforts at regimenting their flocks' behaviour, often by the imposition of barbaric penalties (slicing off a woman's nose being a Jewish as well as a Christian punishment),[5] Jewry revealed its contrasts. These no doubt reflected the varying degrees of religious discipline obtaining in Western Europe as a whole. Spain and Italy permitted them to practise polygamy in medieval times long after the rabbinical interdict dating from the eleventh century. In southern France, always a problem for Church authoritarians, the Jews were similarly somewhat relaxed in their observances; their Christian and Moorish slaves enabled them to retain substantial holdings for agriculture and enjoy country pursuits unknown to the town-enclosed congregations of the Gothic north.

Life in the north could be austere, not to say arid. Society ensured the confinement of the Jews to whatever pleasures they might derive within their own closed world. In financial ingenuity they faced little competition. The Second Lateran Council of 1139 reinforced the Jewish position in money-lending —it was mainly to royal exchequers, the barons and the Church— by virtue of its decree denying the sacraments to any Christian discovered in the practice of usury. (Evidently many of them were at it, for the law required reiteration in 1179 by the Third Lateran Council.) Thus it happened that Aaron of Lincoln, who furnished credit to kings and financed the building of cathedrals, was widely regarded as the wealthiest man in England at the time of his death in 1186. The bulk of his fixed property then escheated to the Crown, so rendering the Plantagenets the ultimate usurers of England. To this day only those stone-built houses dating from Jewish ownership before the expulsion survive in Lincoln.

Outwardly, they worked at friendship with their Christian neighbours, though forgiving and forgetting were hardly distinguishing Jewish traits. A theological debate at a bishop's palace might be welcomed as an honourable exercise in inter-faith relations, but more often it resulted from a command to argue

[5] Yitzhak Baer, *A History of the Jews in Christian Spain*, Vol. I, Philadelphia, 1966, p. 323.

their defence against the charge of deicide, or to show why the 'Kingdom of God' had not been inaugurated with the First Coming. Despite their status as people without a nationality Jews hastened to send deputations professing their loyalty to a monarch on his succession. If they ventilated their hostility towards Christianity, it was usually reserved for converts in holy orders from their own ranks. Onward from the Middle Ages cases of such were numerous.

These apostates frequently took it upon themselves to inspire the very persecutions from which they themselves had previously suffered, in the way that no fanaticism can equal the fanaticism of the renegade. The shame of the earliest recorded charge of ritual murder against the Jews in European history belongs to a baptised Jew, the monk Theobald of Cambridge. The *Anglo-Saxon Chronicle* of 1137 tells of the discovery of a child's body in a Norwich wood, just before the festival of Passover. Theobald put it about that the Jews customarily used Christian blood as an ingredient in their unleavened Passover bread. The obvious deduction was made.

No Jew was convicted of the crime. Still, the belief refused to die (it became the subject of a popular English ballad down to the nineteenth century). Chaucer immortalised the case of Little St Hugh of Lincoln in his *Prioress's Tale*. Hugh disappeared in 1255, and a charge of ritual execution was fastened upon the local community; eighteen Jews refused to plead and were subsequently hanged. Chaucer made of the tale a miracle performed by the Virgin Mary: the child, a chorister, continued to sing her praises after his death.

How to explain the association of ritual murder with the festival of Passover? It could only be in the conviction, stubbornly held, that the Jews secretly re-enacted a Satanic version of the Eucharist. The power of the symbolism, the martyrdom of the Saviour constantly made material in the offering of bread and wine, the absolution thus rendered to the communicant, all these required their antithesis. Where virtue reigned, there also lurked evil. Little wonder that throughout the ages Jews have dreaded Good Friday above all other Christian holy days, particularly in Eastern Europe, where primitive religiosity spawned a ritual murder trial as recently as 1913.

Accounts of the profanation of the Host gave infinite, gruesome variety to the accusation. Sometimes the Jews were miraculously frustrated in the moment of their loathsome blasphemy. The Host was said to spurt blood, or it would turn into human form, or terrify the infidel Jew by preserving itself.

It would be superfluous to produce here a lamentable gazeteer of Europe by listing complete the places where Jews were compelled to answer to the allegation of ritual murder. Suffice to name Würzburg, Cologne, Gloucester, Bury St Edmunds, Bristol, Blois and Bray-sur-Seine in the twelfth century, resulting on occasion in Jews dying at the stake; Röttingen in the thirteenth century, culminating in the slaughter of all its Jews; and the notorious Brussels example (depicted in stained glass at St Gudule's Cathedral) that led in the fourteenth century to the death of twenty Jews. In Trent (Tyrol) torture produced a confession by nine of the murder in 1475 of the child Simon, later beatified. Another fifteenth-century incident, in Endigen, inspired a local *Judenspiel* to amuse the populace for decades.

The absence of a corpse was no hindrance to the legend. A chapel in the cathedral of Saragossa honours the patron saint of choirboys, Domingo del Val. He never existed, but was supposedly crucified by Jews in the thirteenth century. Some twenty miles from Toledo a village still celebrates the festival of Niño de La Guardia. A dozen Jews were brought before the Inquisition in 1488 charged with the *niño*'s murder – he too had not existed. Macabre statuary in a church near Innsbruck commemorated till recently the Blessed Andreas in the act of being tortured; following the Second Vatican Council of 1962–5 it was removed, though a ceiling painting remains. An adjacent plaque now advises the visitor of the story's fabrication.

Popular feeling, then as now, demanded a scapegoat to assuage the hardships and interrupt the tedium of the daily struggle for existence. The Jews, alien, mysterious, rich yet vulnerable, suited the need to perfection. The German Emperor Frederick II was appalled at his subjects' gullibility. In vain did Pope Innocent IV brand the entire idea of ritual murder and desecration of the Host as a wicked invention, a libel born of prejudice and twisted logic. His papal bull of 1247 stated, *inter alia*:

Although the Holy Scriptures enjoin the Jews 'Thou shalt not kill' and forbid them to touch any dead body on the Passover, they are falsely accused of partaking of the heart of a murdered child at the Passover, with the charge that this is prescribed by their laws. The truth is completely the opposite. Whenever a corpse is found somewhere it is to the Jews that the murder is wickedly imputed. They are persecuted on the pretext of such fables or others quite similar. And contrary to the privileges granted them by the Apostolic Holy See, they are deprived of trial and proper judgement. In mockery of all justice they are stripped of their belongings, starved, imprisoned and tortured, so that their fate is perhaps worse than that of their fathers in Egypt.[6]

Meanwhile the Second Crusade had come and gone, barely leaving its imprint upon history except in revelations of discord and treachery on the part of its leaders. The endeavour neither won glory in famous victories over the Turks nor, thanks to the intercession of Bernard of Clairvaux, incurred shame for infamous conduct against the Jews. The mythology of valour, however, revived in the Third Crusade of 1189. Four monarchs headed a cast of grand characters, and shocking slaughter was camouflaged as deeds of derring-do. The expedition eventuated in humiliation and misery for the fragmented soldiery of Christ nevertheless.

Saladin the Great had declared *jihad*. His Muslim counter-crusade soon placed an inglorious *finis* to the Latin kingdom of Jerusalem, arousing indignation in the West and injecting anew the necessary spurt of enthusiasm into what was now widely recognised as a tawdry cause. And, lest the impression arise of the Jews holding a monopoly in suffering during those times, it should be noted that Richard Coeur de Lion marked the capture of Acre by massacring 3,000 Muslims, Saladin's offer to ransom them notwithstanding. What a contrast to Saladin's treatment of Christian captives, for whom Christian charity could find no ransom, during his sweep through Palestine!

---

[6] *Les Registres d'Innocent IV*, Paris, 1884, p. 403, quoted in Léon Poliakov, *The History of Antisemitism*, Vol. I, London, 1974, p. 6.

Everything known about the Third Crusade prompts comment from the ironist. Failing in their reconquest of Jerusalem from the infidel, the warriors bravely captured Christian Constantinople instead. Booty was no longer abundant in Holy Land campaigns, but riches could be earned by Genovese and Venetian brokers from the crusaders themselves, in the exorbitant payments extorted for chartering their ships. Although fearing the worst, loss of life and worldly goods, continental Jews too profited vastly by the loans generated in the raising and provisioning of the Christian troops. But in far-away England a massacre did in fact occur on a scale to warrant inclusion in their martyrology.

Prior to his departure on the crusade Richard Plantagenet was anointed amidst heraldic panoply in Westminster Abbey. To join the throng of his devoted subjects a deputation of Jewish representatives arrived, bearing their gifts. Among them were men well known in court circles ever ready to demonstrate allegiance to a new king. However, they were forbidden entrance to the abbey (as were all women, for like the Jews they were susceptible to witchcraft). Two Jews nevertheless crossed the portals; one of them, the aged Benedict of York, ranked as leader of the English community. Such a presumption started a riot, soon to spread in disorders across the country. Benedict was taken and forcibly baptised, which marked as a somewhat benign punishment, for hundreds of other Jews lost their lives. Frenzied mobs, erroneously convinced the king had ordered death to all Hebrews to mark both his coronation and his departure on the crusade, besieged them in Norwich, Stamford, Lynn and Bury St Edmunds. They expired in their burning houses. Now it was the turn of York. The crowd set fire to the Jews' houses there, including Benedict's, a virtual palace – he had died on the journey home, to be buried in a common grave, since the Christians refused the body, while the Jews declined to inter a renegade. The terrified congregation of York took refuge within the city's well-fortified castle.

But the hysteria would not be stayed. Attempts were made to storm the castle. The Jews held their position within its ramparts. Days passed, the county militia took up stations under the command of the sheriff, while an Augustinian monk paced the walls uttering blessings over the siege. He became the first casualty, killed by a shower of stones hurled down against the attackers. When at length the rioters gained entry and penetrated the keep, known as Clifford's Tower, a scene of horror met their eyes. It was yet another Massada – collective suicide by 150, rather than submission to baptism, ordered by their French rabbi, Yomtob of Joigny – and it occurred on the Friday evening preceding the Passover of 1190. A few chose life, surrendering themselves to Christianity.

These events are described in all their detail by a contemporary, the historian and prior William of Newburgh.[7] In the absence of the king, his regent, William de Longchamp, marched north and punished fifty-two of York's citizens, some with banishment. Among them were noblemen bearing such names as Malbis, Percy and Faulconbridge. Richard Coeur de Lion himself, whose crusading career had terminated in Austrian captivity, returned home in 1194, thanks to a ransom of 150,000 marks paid in part by English Jews. Dismayed at what had transpired in his absence, he ordered an enquiry into the events at York. This revealed that the mob had proceeded from the castle to York Minster, where records of debts to the Jews had been placed for safe keeping, and made a bonfire of them.

Walter Scott's *Ivanhoe* (1819) recalls the period in that author's characteristically vivid colours. Knowledgeable on the Jewish situation, Scott gives central place in the novel to the Jewess, Rebecca of York. True to an established convention of fiction, she compensates for her odious father the usurer by her infinite endowments of beauty, intelligence, courage and purity of soul. Knights duel for her, offer her marriage, even a throne. She knows it cannot be, because of her race and theirs. Strangely, Scott makes no mention of Clifford's Tower; perhaps it was not remote from his thoughts when he causes Rebecca to entreat her father Isaac to escape the Christian kingdom: 'Less cruel are the cruelties of the Moors unto the race of Jacob', she reminds him, 'than the cruelties of the Nazarenes of England.'

Thus did the twelfth century reach its sombre conclusion:

---

[7] R. Howlett (ed.), *William of Newburgh*, Vol. I, p. 294, quoted in Jacobs, *Jews of Angevin England*, p. 99.

Europe's Jews in a condition of ostentatious splendour yet perpetual fear, the Christians responding with a combination of jealousy, exasperation and savagery, the Holy Land once more controlled by neither of them. Could the thirteenth century augur further ill-fortune for the soi-disant Chosen People?

It could. The scene shifts to the papal palace on Lateran Hill in Rome. In 1215 a council of 1,500 prelates debated yet again the troublous question of these strangers within their midst: their increasing wealth, the perils to which Christians became exposed by associating with them. The bishops cast envious glances upon the devices employed by Catholic princes to enrich themselves through Jewish usury. Surely some portion of those ill-gotten gains belonged to the Church? The council therefore ruled that tithes on land possessed by Jews in repayment of loans should flow directly into the ecclesiastical treasury, bypassing any royal intermediary. Also, annual tribute was to be exacted from every Jewish household in commemoration of Easter, that festival abominated by the Jews. More, rulers must dismiss their Jewish court officials, whom the council found far too numerous for the people's well-being.

And now the Jews' arrogance. Their womenfolk disported themselves in excessive finery. The men infringed a sacred taboo by frequently indulging in sexual intercourse with Christian women – no doubt while the best of manhood spent long periods 'Outremer' on the holy crusade. So, following the Islamic example, Jews were ordered to wear an identifying mark on their clothing. In France and Germany this was usually a wheel, or *rouelle*, of the brightest hue. In England it took the shape of two tablets, as if representing the Ten Commandments. Other sartorial distinctions included special headgear, often pointed like a dunce's hat. Laws debarred the Jews henceforth from any office granting them authority over Christians (a prohibition intended to include physicians and surgeons), they were not to show themselves in public at Easter, while volunteers for future crusades were automatically released from any debts outstanding to the race.

Truth to tell, the Church lacked instruments for the strict enforcement of the regulations, which indicate that despite their tribulations the Jews did not maintain what in today's vocabulary might be termed a 'low profile'. Church and state in fact pursued different policies in this regard: the Church was bent upon the Jews' disappearance through baptism, while the state wished to preserve them for what they were, so as to keep its coffers filled. And who could equal the Jewish physician in skill?

The Lateran Council nevertheless achieved its object to a considerable extent. The Jews were forced into a segregation bordering on pariahdom, to be allowed within the community of peoples only for their uses. Rulers might well adopt lukewarm attitudes to such intentions, but the birth of national literatures gave the Church an enthusiastic ally in the early mystery plays. Troubadours and clerics served up identical potions to condition the popular mind towards an instinctive antisemitism. Thus the Abbé Gautier de Coincy (1177–1236), from whom Chaucer borrowed his *Prioress's Tale*: 'They are more animal than the animals themselves. They are blind, unable to recognise a miracle, nor any prophecy.'[8] Pope Innocent III, in a judgement later endorsed by St Thomas Aquinas, described the Jews as being destined to perpetual slavery.

And what poetry did for the literate, architecture conveyed to the mass. On the southern portal of Strasbourg Cathedral two female figures confront each other as Church and Synagogue, the one proudly erect, the other bent, blindfold and shown with the Tablets of the Law slipping from her grasp. The confrontation is similarly expressed at the Church of St Severin in Bordeaux and on the façade of Bamberg Cathedral, while the blindfold Synagogue stands alone in Rochester Cathedral. Perhaps the Synagogue is one day intended to open her eyes to the true faith, but meanwhile we are reminded of those supreme opposites, Virgin and Whore.

Preoccupied though it might be with Judaism as the eternal insidious presence, Catholic religiosity reserved some venom also, with consequent cruelties, for other heretics. Crusading was a euphemism for mass murder elsewhere than in the Holy Land. Fear of an Islamic conquest of Europe, never remote from the medieval mind, prompted repressive ordinances against

---

[8] From *Les Miracles de la Sainte Vierge*, quoted in Charles Lehrmann, *The Jewish Element in French Literature*, Cranbury, NJ, 1971, p. 47.

Muslims still living under Christian rule. Moreover, no one was safe wherever the cult of Christianity took a wayward course. Innocent III, prior to the Lateran Council of 1215, inspired the most savage of religious enterprises against the Waldensians and Albigensians of southern France: the former denounced all private property as contrary to Gospel teaching, while the latter rejected the Resurrection as a phantasm, and made of Jehovah the source of evil as well as good. The pope now had a new army to perform his works – the Dominican Order of Friars. Under its guidance the sunny region of Languedoc, centre of the French heresies, turned into a scene of suffering and bloodshed enduring for decades. It desolated and depopulated the land, to leave the Midi to this day with a heritage of bitterness. Little wonder that Dante's *Inferno* describes a hell amply peopled by popes and monarchs, yet without a single Jew.

Not that the rabbis were themselves totally innocent of heresy hunting; the fever was contagious. Their most rigorous Talmudists undertook a meticulous search through the texts of Jewish teachers. Writing deemed offensive to the faith went ceremoniously on to a pyre, as in the case of Maimonide's works. Intolerance choosing the strangest bedfellows, these rabbis enlisted the expert assistance of the Dominican Order in reducing much of Jewish learning to ashes.

The rabbis had cause to regret their action. Not only did it initiate a process of theological conflict among themselves, and reciprocal excommunications without end, it also opened the door to repeated attacks upon the Talmud itself – by apostate Jews, needless to say. One of them, the Dominican Nicholas Donin of La Rochelle, was moved personally to denounce the entire literature to Pope Gregory IX for its slanders against Christianity. A hunt for copies was immediately under way. The pope charged the kings of England, France, Castile and Aragon with a thorough investigation of its contents.

Saint Louis of France alone responded, this being a seminal period for Bible studies under his patronage – the great translation by the University of Paris (1226–50) was already advanced. Conscious of his role as the acknowledged leader among Christian monarchs, King Louis ordered four rabbis to a public disputation with the Chancellor of the Sorbonne, who chose the eager Friar Donin as his expert witness. The event was staged with appropriate pomp in the presence of the Queen Mother of France. Of course, the rabbis understood that whatever their arguments they could never be pronounced the victors, but they also laboured under the additional disadvantage of lacking familiarity with Latin, a language detested by Jews. The result was as predicted. Twenty-five cartloads of the Talmud and other Hebrew manuscripts were brought into Paris to be consumed in flames. This happening, devastating in its consequences for Hebrew scholarship, was to be lyricised by a Würzburg minnesinger: 'Woe to the cowardly Jews, deaf and wicked; the Talmud has corrupted them and left them without honour.'

If Christendom intended the complete degradation of the perfidious race it had succeeded. But the logic demanded one further step: expulsion. And as in the case of the ritual murder allegation, the first example occurred in England. During the thirteenth century that country fermented in a state of almost perpetual discontent, what with the revolt of the barons, disastrous essays at regaining territory lost to the French across the Channel and more futile crusading at papal command. All this had to be paid for. Jewish wealth, exactly known to the state through a system of official book-keeping in Hebrew with Latin translation and called the Exchequer of the Jews, was available for plunder to finance both the king's business and the baronial rebellion in the areas outside royal control.

King John, deprived of funds following his loss of Normandy in 1206, had been excommunicated by Innocent III and therefore felt free to squeeze the Jews (and the Church) at will. To rescue his bankrupt treasury he levied a huge tax of 66,000 silver marks upon the Jews. Reluctance to pay up could be painful. Abraham of Bristol claimed inability to find his contribution of 10,000 marks. The king ordered the extraction of one of his teeth on each day of his refusal. Abraham discovered he had the money after losing seven of them.[9]

Between Simon de Montfort and Henry III, brothers-in-law without love lost, the Jews fell as booty in every clash, no matter

[9] See Michael Adler, *Jews of Medieval England*, London, 1939, p. 201, quoting from a contemporary annalist, Roger of Wendover, *Flores Historiarum*, ed. Coxe, Vol. III, p. 231.

the victor. What with blood libels and executions intervening, they decided, as had Scott's fictitious Rebecca in the previous century, that any place in Europe could offer them safer sanctuary than England. So, with the greater part of their estates and portable wealth declared confiscate, they sought permission to emigrate. Instead, King Henry sold them collectively to his brother Richard of Cornwallis, who was deemed more capable of handling them, for the bargain price of 5,000 pounds. They were now to pass through a succession of owners: first back to the king, next to his son Prince Edward of Wales and then to Italian money-lenders known as 'the Pope's usurers'. Evidently English Jewry, despite its pleas of poverty and apparent skill in the nefarious medieval art of 'coin-clipping', represented a worthwhile investment.

Succeeding to the throne as Edward I, the erstwhile Prince of Wales imprisoned all the leaders of the community against a ransom of 12,000 pounds, duly paid in 1287. But in 1290 he decided he needed everything the Jews possessed, that year being fixed for, among other commitments, the nuptials of his three daughters. And so he banished them, on All Saints' Day, to derive a percentage of all the debts owed to Jews by clergy, noblemen and commoners alike. Holinshed, in his *Historie of England* of 1577, gives the figure of 15,000 expelled in all, though a few escaped the edict by apostasy. These were sent for confinement to the Domus Conversorum in Chancery Lane, Holborn, an establishment that for decades had admitted such converts, to be schooled in Christian civilisation and to protect them, no doubt, from outrage at the hands of more stubborn fellow-tribesmen. According to Holinshed, writing some three hundred years after the event but with the benefit of records denied to later historians, the departing Jews were frequently robbed of their permitted residue of wealth by rascally ship captains, while one shipload drowned in the Thames beneath London Bridge. At all events, Jews were not officially allowed back in England until the seventeenth century.

Where did the exiles go? France seemed the obvious destination, and probably the majority found new homes there, others in Spain and Germany. This has never been exactly established: no Jewish records were preserved, if indeed they were ever made.

Again, we encounter the Jews' reluctance to chronicle their history while God chose to leave them suspended in the wilderness.

Those selecting France for shelter would have been speedily deceived had they anticipated a future in tranquillity. There the Jews were being shuttled back and forth across frontiers, blown by every change in royal fortune. Out they had to go in 1306 by order of Philip the Fair, to be recalled, at a price, by his son Louis X in 1315. These were unhappy years for the French peasantry in particular. A great famine in the north of the country was bringing thousands to starvation, or to acts of cannibal savagery. In the rising tide of social disorder, which sent the nobility scurrying to their strongholds, an army of shepherds (the *Pastoureaux*) decided grotesquely to embark on a crusade. It was their licence to kill whoever awakened their sense of injustice, and to destroy whatever institution might correspond in their imagination to the forces of oppression. Thus their trail southward was marked by the slaughter of Jews together with colonies of people regarded with like abhorrence, in the leper reservations. It was a repetition on smaller scale of the First Crusade – one encounter being even worse, at Verdun-sur-Garonne, where, after stout resistance in a fortress, five hundred Jews died. Their surviving children were taken into baptism.

The bizarre expedition of the shepherds collapsed in total disarray, though not before Pope John XXII had passed sentence of excommunication upon all its participants and anyone assisting them. The clamour it had raised against the Jews could not however be stilled. They were banished yet again, until they might be required once more. Such an eventuality occurred in 1361. The stalemated Hundred Years War had erupted in a battle that found Jean II a captive of the English. Money was needed for his ransom, and so another invitation of dubious hospitality was extended to the Jews. Yes, their taxes would be slight (only seven florins annually per adult, one florin for each child), they could practise medicine, acquire property in land and charge interest at 87 per cent on loans. Their communal affairs would not be subject to jurisdiction by the common courts. All this evidences some pretty shrewd bargaining on the part of the Jews, but the French needed three million *écus* in gold to buy Jean back. Even then the Jews were granted a residential charter for only twenty years, later extended to thirty-six. Finally, in 1394, Charles VI expelled them from the regions of his allegiance 'for ever'. The king's writ did not of course extend throughout the area of present-day France, for the country would long be a mosaic of independent principalities. Jews were to remain in the Comtat Venaissin and in Alsace. They reappeared at different times in other regions, while on the outbreak of the French Revolution in 1789 some emerged proudly to claim a continuous settlement of ancestors from before the expulsion.

While France and England engaged in their protracted struggle for territorial prizes, and the peasantry slaved for their masters, and the Church preached its message of salvation, and the Jews wandered from place to place as they wept for Zion, an eastern pestilence struck medieval society with an impartiality calamitous for them all.

The plague seized Europe in its pitiless embrace in 1347, and for three years the entire populace lingered on the edge of lifelessness. Pope Clement VI saw it as God's wrath for the wickedness of humankind in general. Astrologers at the University of Paris, consulting the heavens, discovered that a conjunction of Saturn, Jupiter and Mars in the fortieth degree of Aquarius had released an irresistible toxic vapour upon the world. That might have been the Devil's work. Masses of people had no doubt. The Jews, probably in alliance with other subhuman species, were acting out his sinister commands. Wild rumour accompanied the pestilence in its relentless sweep through town and country. Witnesses swore they had observed Jews congregating at the leper colonies; others spoke of secret Jewish visits to Granada, where the infidel Moor still ruled.

A cry went out: 'They are poisoning the wells!' A sorcerer's potion made of a mixture of human blood, secret herbs and the powder of the consecrated Host, all soaked in urine and flung into the pure water, was causing deaths by the thousand.[10] The Jews were bent on lordship over the entire world! Evidently they had made a promising beginning, for early victims of the plague included King Alfonso XI of Castile, Queen Leonora of Aragon,

---

[10] Bouquet, in *Recueil des historiens des Gaules et de la France*, Vol. 20, p. 704, quoted in Poliakov, *History of Antisemitism*, Vol. I, p. 105.

the Queen of Navarre, the wife of the Dauphin, the son of the Byzantine ruler, a daughter of Edward III of England, the mistress of Boccaccio and three Archbishops of Canterbury – all in the space of a year.

The pope, in his bull *Quamvis perfidiam*, 1348, made a brave but pointless attempt to destroy the myth of a Jewish conspiracy. He emphasised that the plague was spreading through countries uninhabited by Jews, and they themselves numbered among its victims. But nothing availed the cause of reason. Given that the Black Death was planted into the human race by Satan, it occurred to no doctors to trace his agent to the fleas borne by rats in the ships arriving from the East. As the epidemic travelled northwards into the heart of Europe, some Jews in Chillon, by Lake Geneva, were broken on the rack and actually confessed to infesting the wells. Against the fearful odour of bodies lying unburied in the streets or polluting the rivers, and amidst an almost universal fatalism at the hopelessness of human defiance against such a visitation, another slaughter of Jews was under way. Even those ostensibly under the protection of the Holy Roman Emperor were carried along its gory trail. The number burnt at the stake was calculated in thousands: four hundred in Basle; 2,000 in a huge St Valentine's Day pyre outside Strasbourg's city walls on the site of today's Prefectural Garden; 6,000 in Mainz, unlucky Mainz, following a Jewish armed resistance as in the case of the First Crusade. Occurrences on a lesser scale were recorded in hundreds of German towns – the flames leaping from synagogues and homes to consume gentile and Jewish dwellings alike.

Those escaping execution took flight, and again some drifted back on promises of restitution. In Strasbourg they were forbidden to sleep within the city walls, but could enter daily to do business. Royal protection failed to prevent their expulsion in 1370, fully twenty years after the plague's recession, yet shortly afterwards Jews were to be seen in the city once again. However, masses of them at last took the hint that Western Europe's hospitality was not to be relied upon. The Black Death and its consequences inaugurated a general movement eastward, mainly into Poland which somehow eluded the full effects of the horror.

We have yet to emerge from the era when 'the boast of

heraldry, the pomp of power' summoned crusaders to war against the infidel. While efforts to recapture the Holy Land for Christianity suffered recurring frustrations, the Teutonic Knights carried the banner of Christ away from the Mediterranean to the Baltic, where the pagan tribes of Old Prussians and Lithuanians constituted easier quarry than the Muslims. Simultaneously, the Spanish rulers, their Visigothic instincts reviving, proceeded step by step in the dislodgement of the Moor from the Iberian Peninsula. Little should have slowed their pace: the Arabs' descent down the martial scale had proved swift, to be equalled only by the decline of their culture and economy. Furthermore, disastrous internal rivalries, in which mutually hostile Muslims did not disdain intrigue with the Christians up north, might have rendered the Reconquista painless. It was not so. Although Alfonso VI of León and Castile, fortified with intelligence supplied by the Jews (they knew Arabic), had taken Toledo as early as 1085, the rest was a story of ups and downs. Still, it was a question only of time. One by one the petty kingdoms of al-Andaluz succumbed, despite the sacrifices of tenacious Negro slave-soldiers, till we reach the time when Granada alone, with its near environs, remained for Islam. Granada would fall at last in 1492, the year which signposted a turning-point for the Jews, for Spain and for civilisation as a whole.

While Spanish Jewry was spared atrocities during the Black Death on the scale suffered in other parts of Europe, the air rang with complaints against the tribe's immense political influence. The court of Pedro the Cruel, King of Castile, attracted suspicion for its domination by a Jewish counsellor, Samuel Halevi Abulafia, who maintained a style in Toledo almost as regal as his master's. He found the resources and provided the soldiers for Pedro's resistance in the civil war (1355–69) launched by the king's bastard half-brother, Henry of Trastamara. But it was Henry who won in the end, and the Jews paid heavily for making common cause with the wrong side. One of the usurper's most telling propaganda points was Pedro's obscure (and therefore Jewish) origin. Samuel Abulafia died under torture in 1360 – at Pedro's, not Henry's, order. He left a palace, several chests filled with gold and eighty Moorish slaves.

The long civil war brought a strongly clericalist party into power, with the result that thousands of Jews abdicated from Judaism in a vain effort to elude the religious storm about to break over their heads. Likewise, many Muslims forsook Islam. Spain had to be a purely Christian country, so fully one-third of its Jewish population ultimately obliged, to be granted not the absolute security they craved but existence on a precipice as 'New Christians'. Did they truly believe? The question anguished their rulers, as it anguished themselves: fathers in dispute with sons, Jewish observance covertly practised, heresy-hunting savagely conducted and some fanatical New Christians betraying old friends, spying on the synagogues and generally setting the pace. From the year 1391, anxiety was never far away.

Paradoxically, Jews remaining faithful to their Torah suffered less than the New Christians suspected of insincere conversion. These latter received the designation Marranos, a term that had its origin in some scabrous insult. They lived conspicuously in the cities but consorted secretly with traditional Jews. Converted Moors, known as Moriscos, attracted much less attention, for they generally were a peasant class tucked away in remote villages. Regarded as relatively innocuous, neither possessing friends at court nor enjoying a crucial economic role, the Moriscos were nevertheless an uncomfortable reminder that elsewhere, and not too far away, Islam still existed in statehood. On the other hand, Judaism was stateless. Moriscos could appeal for protection to the North African emirates, and of course to Granada. Remove the goodwill of fickle Christian rulers and the Marranos became vulnerable on all sides.

Against the background of a sorely disunited Spain, the paramount concern of its rulers was to achieve political cohesion through a drive towards Christian orthodoxy. The atmosphere of the rugged peninsula had always produced a Jew *sui generis*. With mass defection to Christianity his situation grew even more complicated, and in the century between the persecution that commenced in 1391 and the expulsion of 1492 Jewish fortunes rose and fell with the ocean tide. Signs of God's protection clashed against omens of doom for domination of the Hebrew mind like the cabbalistic conundrums in which their religion was then immersed.

In the year 1391 the tide rose against all heretics, Moorish and

Jewish, throughout Castile and its dependencies, stimulated in particular by the crusading eloquence of Ferrand Martinez, confessor to the queen. This Dominican friar roused envy and resentment against the Jews by citing the contrast between their aristocratic style and the general population's wretchedness. Little wonder, then, that the Juderias, or Jewish quarters, were penetrated and pillaged in a hundred towns. Martinez himself is said to have been shocked at the carnage wrought by the fury he had unleashed. Synagogues were seized and transformed into churches. The community of Barcelona faced total extermination, or baptism, or flight. Some died, some converted, some fled. The city was *judenrein*.

As to the Moriscos, they were given time, by the nature of their dispersed settlements, to organise armed defiance in the hills against their oppressors, demonstrating albeit briefly the fire that had made their ancestors superb warriors. It would never have dawned upon the Jews, so completely Spanish, to rise against this land, for it fulfilled all their aspirations for a surrogate Jerusalem. In fact the persecuting zeal of the Church was arguably all that stood in the way of their ultimate disappearance by total absorption. In those days as now it would require three generations in tranquillity to eliminate Jewish identity – 'the grandfather believes, the son doubts, the grandson denies'. But assimilation can work both ways, rendering indistinguishable the swallowers from the swallowed. Spain, in the eyes of foreign visitors, was pretty much a Jewish nation already by the beginning of the fifteenth century. The dread of it was never far from Christian thoughts.

The opening of the century saw Bishop Pablo de Santa Maria of Burgos, who had once occupied a synagogue pulpit but now acted as guardian to the boy king John II of Castile, much concerned at the dogged survival of Judaism as a faith and way of life. In particular, he could not abide the attachment demonstrated by so many New Christians towards their former brethren, whom by his lights they should have abhorred. In 1412 the bishop inspired newly repressive measures (the Laws of Valladolid) by which the Juderias were made into forced ghettos under close supervision. Jewish physicians could no longer treat Christian patients. Commercial relations with Christians were to be restricted, and Christian servants forbidden to them. All these prohibitions, a medieval familiar, revived ordinances long fallen in abeyance in Castile. The bishop decided that the Jew henceforth advertise his presence when venturing abroad, so he was forbidden to carry arms, to cut his beard or to use the title of Don.

To achieve the purification of the country Bishop Pablo chose collaborators in regular supply: Dominicans, Franciscans, apostate Jews. On his instructions Friar Vicente Ferrer took the anti-Jewish campaign to Aragon, where he received the blessing of Benedict XIII, the anti-pope from Avignon then without a home, to stage another of those grand disputations against the falsehoods of Judaism. Benedict agreed to preside in person. He chose as leading Christian disputant his own physician Geronimo de Santa Fé, a one-time Talmudist and exponent of Cabbala who bore the name Joshua of Lorca until seduced from Judaism by Bishop Pablo.

The debate was elevated into a happening of great pomp before an audience of the élite, at which they doubtless believed that Satan himself would be unable to resist attendance, in some subhuman form. The scene was set in the Curia at Tortosa, the proceedings continuing intermittently for twenty-two months, with the most learned rabbis conscripted to represent the opposition. One of the Jewish spokesmen described the opening scene, on 7 February 1413, as follows:

> We found ourselves in a huge court adorned with multi-coloured textiles. This was the site of the disputation, with seventy chairs for cardinals, bishops and archbishops dressed in garments of gold. There were about a thousand other Catholic notables, dignitaries and townsmen. We were seized with fear ... Then the pope spoke: 'You, Jewish sages, should know that I have come myself and summoned you not for the purpose of conducting a controversy as to which of the two faiths is the genuine one. I don't doubt in the least that my faith is the true one and that your Torah was at one time true but was later abolished. We shall at first discuss only the arguments of Geronimo, who will prove according to the Talmud of your ancient sages – men more learned than you – that the Messiah has already arrived. And you will reply only

to that question.' Whereupon Geronimo began his exposition with the words of Isaiah the Prophet, 'Come now and let us reason together ... If ye be willing and obedient, ye shall eat the good of the land; but if ye refuse and rebel, ye shall be devoured by the sword.' In his reply, delivered in Latin, Vidal Benveniste expressed astonishment that one of the parties set out with threats even before the disputation had begun. And the pope replied sarcastically, 'You are right. But this bad habit should not surprise you. After all, he [Geronimo] is one of your own.'[11]

The further proceedings need not detain us. Christianity triumphed yet again, and still thousands more Jews submitted to the waters of baptism. In fact, it was only with difficulty that the rabbis could now retain hold over their congregation. A fierce intolerance entered Jewish life itself, tyrannical discipline was imposed by the communal leaders, theological quarrels waxed furious, the study of Hebrew, long neglected, was made compulsory, and all Karaites discovered in Spain received short shrift. In their desperation to keep their people faithful to Judaism the rabbis resorted to mystical incantations, thus hoping to speed the arrival of the Messiah. Surely Jewish salvation could not be long delayed, they said in 1453, harking back to earlier omens, now that Constantinople, vainglorious Byzantium itself, had fallen to the Turks? Having made a good beginning with the defeat of hated Christianity in the East, God must soon signal the long-awaited reunion of heaven and earth, with all life divinely restored to a perpetual sabbath.

Not yet. First the mourning Israelites were to suffer the tribulations of the Inquisition, and then another exodus. When the Dominican Tomás de Torquemada was appointed Grand Inquisitor by the Holy Office in 1483, the institution had already existed for two years in Seville. The pattern had been established long before, in the thirteenth century, against the Albigensians of Provence: extravagant ceremonial prepared to the last detail and combining religious solemnity, gruesome torture and burning at the stake.

[11] Baer, *Jews in Christian Spain*, Vol. II, pp. 174 ff.

Under the jurisdiction of Torquemada, the name most reviled in Jewish memory until the advent of Adolf Hitler, the Inquisition conveyed the awe of a Last Judgement dispensed at the summit of Catholic power on earth. A commission sat on an elevated platform. Dignitaries of Church and state, surrounded by ghoulish instruments for inflicting agonies, took evidence of the heretic's guilt. Professing Jews were for the most part immune, by virtue of their station beyond redemption, unless suspected of leading Marranos into the clandestine practice of their rites, or of attempting to abduct other Christians from the true path. Old Christians (the term employed by Cervantes's Sancho Panza in describing himself) charged with protecting Marranos did not escape. They were brought before the tribunal, then under torture made to confess. If spared from the burning they would be sent for long terms of imprisonment. Applying the torch to ignite the pyre ranked as a high privilege and was frequently accorded to royalty.

Execution could take place by degrees, preceded perhaps by the chopping off of hands. Sometimes the simple act of burning was deemed insufficient, so a culprit would be quartered first, and the divided body then consigned portion by portion to the flames. The Holy Office produced a list of signs by which New Christians could be recognised as Marranos, *inter alia*:

> If they celebrate the Sabbath on Saturday, wear a clean
> shirt or better garments, spread a clean tablecloth, light
> no fire, eat the food which has been cooked overnight, or
> perform no work on that day; if they eat meat during
> Lent; if they take neither meat nor drink on the Day of
> Atonement, go barefoot or ask forgiveness of another on
> that day; if they celebrate the Passover with unleavened
> bread, or eat bitter herbs; if on the Feast of Tabernacles
> they use green branches or send fruit as gifts to friends; if
> they marry according to Jewish customs or take Jewish
> names; if they circumcise their boys or observe the *hadas*,
> that is, celebrate the seventh night after the birth of a
> child by filling a vessel with water, throwing in gold,
> silver, pearls and grain, and then bathe the child while
> certain prayers are recited; if they throw a piece of dough
> in the stove before baking; if they wash their hands before

praying, bless a cup of wine before meals and pass it round among the people at table; if they pronounce prayers while slaughtering poultry, cover the blood with earth, separate the veins from meat, soak the flesh in water before cooking and cleanse it of blood; if they eat no pork, hare, rabbit or eel; if soon after baptising a child they wash with water the spot touched by the oil; give Old Testament names to their children or bless the children by the laying on of hands; if the women do not attend Church within 40 days after confinement; if the dying turn towards the wall; if they wash a corpse with warm water; if they recite the Psalms without adding at the end: Glory be to the Father, the Son and the Holy Spirit.[12]

Powerful Catholic voices were at times raised in protest against the ruthlessness of the Inquisition. Pope Sixtus IV at first attempted to restrain Queen Isabella from permitting such institutionalised barbarism, charging that avarice, not piety, was the motive, since the victims lost their wealth with their lives. Then he gave it his blessing. The pope's successor, Innocent VIII, ordered all Christian rulers to send back to Spain any suspected heretics seeking refuge abroad. Those who could not be traced were to be burnt in effigy.

How many died or spent their lives in prison has never been exactly established, though it has been calculated that during the fifteen years of Torquemada's office as Grand Inquisitor from four to eight thousand secret Jews and suspects were burnt alive, besides a few Moriscos and other presumed heretics. ('Bloody' Mary, Queen of England, consigned a mere three hundred doomed souls to the flames.) Among those taken to the dungeons for life were several relatives of the Marrano Archbishop of Granada, a former confessor to Queen Isabella. The archbishop himself was made to walk bareheaded and barefoot in procession through the streets of Granada. It is not recorded whether, as a penitent, he was compelled to wear the *sambenito*, a scapular or rough smock over long striped trousers, and emblazoned with a St Andrew's cross. Those going to their death had the *sambenito*

[12] From Juan A. Llorente, *The History of the Inquisition of Spain*, London, 1826.

decorated with their likeness resting on a pyre surrounded by demons.

The Inquisition established itself in all territories under the Spanish crown, in due course travelling across the Atlantic to follow Christopher Columbus to the New World. The ruthless national melodrama could not have flourished in the name of religion alone: rather was it a response to the call for *limpieza de sangre*, purity of blood, an aspiration due to end forlorn, even after the immolation of 100,000 heretics and the final abolition of the Inquisition in 1834. Spain will ever be haunted by its criminal history even though, in the matter of the incineration of human beings, it has in our twentieth century found its master.

We have reached the final act, the one with which the victorious entry of the Catholic monarchs into Granada, and the voyage of Columbus, will eternally be intertwined: the banishment of the Jews from unified Spain, and from its provinces of Sardinia and Sicily, in the fateful year 1492. 'Baptise and remain!' the Jews were urged to the end. Yet many could not. Amazingly, though they suffered under a regime guilty of savageries then without parallel in Europe, the Jews made pathetic efforts to have the sentence, pronounced by king and queen in the newly won palace of the Alhambra, revoked. They offered a huge bribe. Torquemada is said to have taunted Abraham Senior, messenger of the Jews, as being a second Judas bringing another 30 pieces of silver. Senior, their principal rabbi and confidant of Isabella, then gave himself to Christ in apostasy – to save his own skin, or in a vain attempt to reprieve his people? No one knows.

Now, joined by thousands of Marranos openly declaring their Judaism while many hitherto true to the faith abandoned it, and amid scenes of anguished parting between parents and children, brothers and sisters, with tearful farewells to friendly Christians (both Old and New), the Jews uprooted themselves from the soil to which they had clung through every vicissitude. They were about 150,000 altogether, every one with a Spanish name and an allegiance to some portion of Iberia he would never forget. Beyond Spain there could be only one homeland, so they departed in the conviction of ultimate transplantation, after another symbolic forty years of wandering through some symbolic Sinai, to a resting place in the Promised Land.

Meanwhile they would find asylum wherever Providence allowed. The majority crossed the frontier to Portugal, others settled in the Low Countries or eastward through welcoming gates into the Ottoman Empire. They departed on 31 March. Three months later the 100 ton *Santa Maria* took Columbus out of Palos, near Cadiz, his interpreter, Luis de Torres, taking baptism on the eve of embarkation. Would that endeavour have reached consummation if, during the great navigator's period of frustrations and disappointments, he had not won the support among others of the Marrano Luis de Santangel, Comptroller of the Household, or of Isaac Abrabanel, scion of a New Christian family that later recanted? The latter had financed Ferdinand and Isabella's campaign against the last Moorish kingdom in Spain and then led his people into exile. Of such ironies is Jewish history written. As to the Moriscos, they were permitted to remain in their rural homesteads for a century more. Then, between 1609 and 1614, they too were expelled, mostly to join their kin in North Africa.

The Genovese historian Senarega described the wanderers' arrival in his city:

> No one could behold the sufferings of the Jewish exiles unmoved. A great many perished of hunger, especially those of tender years. Mothers, with scarcely strength to support themselves, carried their famished infants in their arms and died with them. Many fell victim to the cold, others to intense thirst, while the unaccustomed distresses, incident to a sea voyage, aggravated their maladies. I will not enlarge upon the cruelty and the avarice which they frequently experienced from the masters of the ships which transported them from Spain. Some were murdered to gratify their cupidity; others were forced to sell their children for the expenses of the passage. They arrived in Genoa in crowds, but were not suffered to tarry there long, by reason of the ancient law which interdicted the Jewish traveller from a longer residence than three days. They were allowed, however, to refit their vessels and to recruit themselves for some days from the fatigue of their voyage. One might have taken

them for spectres, so emaciated were they, so cadaverous in their aspect with eyes so sunken. They differed in nothing from the dead except in the power of motion, which indeed they scarcely retained. Many fainted and expired on the mole, which, being completely surrounded by the sea, was the only quarter vouchsafed to the wretched emigrants. The infection bred by such a swarm of dead and dying persons was not at once perceived; but when the winter broke up, ulcers began to make their appearance; and the malady, which lurked for a long time in the city, broke out into plague in the following year.[13]

Admitted with a reluctance that was only too apparent in Portugal – a price of eight crusados on every head – the Jews sat nervously perched on the ledge of Europe in the hope of the eight months of grace of residence accorded them being extended. After long delays King John II provided ships and ordered their departure. But many stayed behind, for reasons that are unclear, and the king began selling them off in slavery. This might have completed the operation of evacuation were it not interrupted by the king's death. John's successor Manuel I reprieved them. However, he later gave an undertaking to Ferdinand and Isabella, as a condition of his betrothal to their daughter, that he would Christianise Portugal. Thus there ensued the enforced baptism of all the Jews, in circumstances of the utmost coercion: another wickedness perpetrated in the name of the Holy Saviour.

The last vestige of stubborn Judaism was eliminated from Portugal through the institution of the Inquisition in 1536. For the most part they became totally absorbed in the national bloodstream. Nevertheless congregations of former Portuguese Jews sprang up in various corners of Europe during the sixteenth century, in accordance with the mysterious laws of this people's survival. They planted roots in the Indies, West and East, and on the American continent, following the Portuguese flag as though by some instinctive migratory compulsion: again that fierce Iberian-Jewish pride, emerging despite every humiliation.

[13] From his *Apud Mercatori*, quoted in C. R. N. Routh, *They Saw it Happen in Europe*, Oxford, 1965, pp. 144–5.

From our remote vantage-point, with passions cooled, it is difficult to comprehend the underlying causes of the Jews' banishment from Spain in that watershed year 1492. We may perhaps return for enlightenment to the historic Judeo-Christian tension dating from the Crucifixion, and its heritage of mutual contempt. Alternatively, we may advance to a secular age, for the circumstances leading to the expulsion bear characteristics strikingly similar to those existing in the Germany of 1933: two peoples growing ever closer, with the Jews gradually forfeiting their specific identity in the process. Yet such exercises in historical analysis are in the end fruitless. Spain developed into a nation, if indeed it ever became one, along a path that was neither totally Christian nor totally European. The question 'What is a Spaniard?' was as perplexing in 1492 as today the question 'What is a Jew?'[14]

The Jews had dwelt in the peninsula for a thousand years at least, and continuously. They themselves claimed the dignity of even more ancient settlement, a lineage pre-dating the Christian era. Hence the assertion of an antique alibi for Golgotha: their forebears, they declared, had left Palestine before the time of Herod. Family pride selects its own ancestors. The Bishop of Burgos, quondam Rabbi Solomon Halevi and now a royal counsellor, adopted on his baptism in 1391 the name Pablo de Santa Maria (and founded a dynasty of bishops) because, as a Levite, he proclaimed descent from the family of the Holy Virgin! He was in part responsible for the Laws of Valladolid in 1412.

If acculturation was a virtue, Spanish Jewry was rapidly attaining a state of grace: among the Muslims they were almost indistinguishable from the Moors, some of them actually professing Islam; amid the Christians they could be as Spanish as the grandees, whether they followed Christ or honoured Moses. Baptised or no, they tilled their own fields, crafted domestic articles in wood and copper, healed the sick, married into the

---

[14] Fernand Braudel, in his masterly work *The Mediterranean and the Mediterranean World in the Age of Philip II*, 2 vols., London, 1972–3, makes the point that the expulsion of the foreigner from the Iberian Peninsula was a necessary step if ever that land-mass, precariously exposed on the south-western extremity of the Continent, was to merge with European civilisation. Vol. II, pp. 825–6.

nobility, taught theology, translated the Bible into Spanish seated alongside Dominican and Franciscan scholars, and went to war. Of course, they had to fulfil their classic role also as banker to kings, money-lender to the mass; the dictionary still has the word *judiada* defined as 'usurious profit'. Exiled because they were Jews, they were recognised long afterwards in their dispersal as Spaniards – their Hebrew designation, Sephardim, proclaimed with fierce hidalgo pride.

Certainly, contradictions abound. A contributory factor in the tension leading to their catastrophe was the phenomenon of Jewish self-hatred. This was not an unfamiliar trait among Jews elsewhere – rarely in fact has it been entirely absent from their psychology. Ex-Jews, marginal Jews and 'New Christians', resentful of their drops of Judaic blood, numbered, as we have noted above, among the people's worst persecutors. First in rank stood Ferdinand of Aragon, descended from the Jewess Paloma of Toledo. His marriage to Isabella of Castile, which sealed the fate of the Jews, was largely arranged by Abraham Senior, Segovian rabbi and Isabella's principal tax-farmer. The La Caballeria family of Saragossa boasted among its descendants more than one bishop, the vice-principal of a university, the vice-chancellor of the kingdom of Aragon, the High Treasurer of the kingdom of Navarre, a leader of the Cortes, a comptroller-general and a notorious antisemitic writer.[15]

Thus the tragedy of Spain, like the tragedy of Germany in 1933, had its roots in the thoroughness of the Jews' accommodation to their environment. Even after the wholesale conversions which followed the great persecution of 1391, when many thousands died at the stake, it was virtually impossible to distinguish the baptised from the Mosaic faithful. Orthodox Jews hungered after the relaxed delights of Christianity, the *conversos* after the ancient Hebrew traditions which ambition, convenience or fear of martyrdom caused them to betray.

The pessimism filtering through the Jewish personality receives a poetic touch in the descendants of the medieval Iberian settlements. Spain was graciousness, Spain was honour, Spain was sorrow. Apply it to a man who died in 1985: Salvador Espriu,

[15] Cecil Roth, *A Short History of the Jewish People*, London, 1959, p. 242.

acclaimed poet of Catalonian life and language, candidate for the Nobel prize, yet one of the great Jewish voices of the century besides. Jewish? Proudly so, with a lifetime of creativity nurtured in his beloved Barcelona, the city where, in 1391, persecution was presumed to remove all trace of his despised people.[16]

[16] See obituary in *The Times*, London, 25 February 1985.

4

Outcasts of Europe

If we dared to isolate one epoch in history since the birth of Christianity when the Jews might conceivably have disappeared completely among the peoples with whom they dwelt, it would have been the two centuries following their exodus from Spain. Here, with the Renaissance risen to high tide, far-away continents brought within the colonisation process, Catholic centralism under siege from the Reformation and Turkish Islam on the march, the world was being shaped anew. Expulsion, persecution and pestilence had contributed to religious conversion and natural decline in depleting Jewish numbers. In the sixteenth century they comprised a bare million in Europe – the figure is conjecture, as was all demographic arithmetic in those days – and still fewer in the Muslim world.

Scattered among a general population of some fifty millions west of Russia, the Jews had repeatedly to liquidate and re-form their fragile congregations. Gloomy Prague within the Holy Roman Empire extended sanctuary to an important concentration, for it contained the oldest continuous settlement, though still less than 10,000 in size. Yet we are told of seven millions or so inhabiting the domains of the early pagan Caesars, one million residing in Egypt alone.

Now, decimated as a consequence of other peoples' wars, exhausted in disputes closer to their own concerns, sold into slavery or defecting from a faith that reaped universal abhorrence and contempt, they were reduced to a residue. Christendom might have begun their passive extinction as an identifiable people in the sixteenth century through a greater toleration, and the opening rather than the closure of gates. Christendom, aided to be sure by the obstinate streak in the tribe itself, decided otherwise. For it could neither live with the Jews nor live without them. As we have seen, the converse also held.

It was the old story, with a fundamental difference. Usury (call it by any other name, credit finance, tax-farming, they added up to the same) was condemned as unchristian. Let the Jews practise it. The difference lay in the enormous expansion of international trade. Feudalism was giving way to capitalism. The new economics required loans on a huge scale to mercantile princes as well as to princes of the blood. An international people was strategically placed to satisfy the demand. Wars ceased to be contests played out with bows and arrows, but took the form of campaigns involving great armies equipped with expensive weapons wreaking destruction upon entire communities; money again, to provision and pay the troops. So the Jew's growth in importance gave him a new stature, even though it kept him glued to his religion and his account books.

Everyone borrowed – popes, rulers, bishops, landowners, merchant adventurers. High interest rates were no obstacle: wealth beyond calculation, in silver and gold from the New Iberia across the Atlantic, and in spices, coral and diamonds from the East, flowed back to greedy Europe and percolated into the pockets of the rising middle classes. The traffic in slaves excited the lust of Christian and Jew alike. The argosies of Shakespeare's Venetian aristocrat, it will be recalled, plied the trade of Tripoli, the Indies, Mexico, England, yet Antonio momentarily lacked three thousand ducats for his life. The Jew could produce them.

Who could draw a safety net between usury and acceptable money-lending? It was a moot point. The Jews faced considerable Christian competition, and were in general rivalled by the more speculative Italians, for until the rise of the oceanic trade routes Florence and Genoa held pre-eminence in the banking transactions of Europe. Italian financiers practised usury whenever Church discipline relaxed; otherwise Jews were imported for the purpose. In England, France and Spain, countries that had sent virtually all their Jews packing, money-lending survived as a recognised occupation. The question exercised public attention throughout the sixteenth century in England, where dealing was finally legalised by Parliament in 1571.[1]

Culturally, the Jews passed through the sixteenth century with

[1] R. H. Tawney, *Religion and the Rise of Capitalism*, London, 1938, p. 183.

their eyes closed against the artistic and scientific flowering of the era. The newly invented printing press was important to them for the wider dissemination of their sacred writings, but beyond this they acknowledged no literary dimension. The Renaissance could not apply to a civilisation without a base in classical Greece and Rome. Therefore it conveyed nothing. Printing gave to Christendom tremendous impetus in biblical criticism, whence came the enrichment of language, thus lifting literature over the religious frontier to secular life. This offered the Jews an opportunity to enter into the dominant cultures of the day. They were not inspired. Montaigne, who combined all the ideas of the Renaissance in one mighty intellectual force, was of Marrano Jewish descent but he gave direction to Gallic, not Hebraic, thought. The Jews felt bound by the religious proscription against representing man or beast in print or stone: God forbade graven images.

Search for a Jew to rank with Botticelli, Michelangelo and Leonardo in the visual arts, with Rabelais or Ariosto or Shakespeare or Cervantes in literature, and you search in vain. They had no scientist to challenge religious obscurantism in the way that Copernicus and Galileo revealed new horizons to mankind, no Erasmus, no Giordano Bruno. These registered the dawn of modernity, but the Jews remained outside such a time-scale.

What were they, then, these Jews who centuries back had bequeathed poetry and philosophy to Spain's golden age? We cannot name many, for the records speak of the rich alone, and a few ecclesiastics. From Germany only one sixteenth-century name has come down to us, apart from the tempestuous apostates who hounded the Jews and obtained the emperor's sanction to burn the Talmud as the blasphemous literature of the Antichrist. He was the Alsatian money-lender Joselmann of Rosheim. A fortune made, and he spent his life as ambassador of his people throughout the Holy Roman Empire. He succeeded in protecting them from persecution whenever charges of ritual murder or desecration of the Host were raised against them, and in sixteenth-century Germany these were frequent. He warned off the pseudo-messiahs who periodically sent tantalising ripples of impending salvation among the gullible masses, and he gave the Jews a code of financial ethics. Joselmann then wrote his memoirs. By the time of his death in 1554 he had saved his people from the worst of all worlds as conflict between Protestant and Catholic erupted, and disaffected peasants, armed with cudgels, descended upon the towns of the Black Forest. Joselmann always received a courteous hearing from that powerful emperor Charles V, but he could make no headway with Martin Luther.

To the Jews every landscape was hostile, every gentile an enemy. They looked after their own, exposing themselves to public view in that obligatory yellow hat only when compelled by circumstance. Venice of course had the Jewish quarter which gave birth to the term 'ghetto', though such ghettos had already existed for centuries in Europe, sometimes, though not invariably, locked at night.

The ghetto defined in physical terms the gulf separating Jew from gentile, while their mutual religious repulsion defined their cultural separation. Memory of the ghetto evokes a resonance of discrimination and oppression, but it was by no means a barbarous institution. Prudence dictated that the Jews live together, for they were, for the most part, poor. As such their infamy was compounded – why suffer the detested deicide when he performed no valid economic function? The ghetto therefore secluded the less endowed. It concealed the poorhouses, the insane asylums, the crippled, just as it sheltered the artisans and old clothes dealers who ventured forth mainly on market days. The opulent few had a duty to sustain the numerous unfortunates, and their charity maintained schools and synagogues. A single bribe could purchase royal protection for thousands, while riches amassed through trading African slaves in the New World could be expended in liberating Jewish slaves from pirates and bandits in the Old. The practice of protecting their own, laid down in holy writ, ensured that Jews did not become a charge on the public exchequer. This had the doleful result, not unknown to this day, that the Jew frequently fostered resentment by revealing himself to the Christian only as a rich man, his wife an expensively caparisoned matron.

Time slumbered for them. But the sixteenth century cast up three factors to initiate a revival of Christian preoccupation with the Jews' history and fate. The first of these arose with the translation of the Bible into the profane tongues of Europe.

Hitherto the sacred text lay concealed in a linguistic prison made of Hebrew, Greek and Latin, with access denied to all except the educated élite. The second factor was the general availability of these Scriptures wrought through the miracle of print. And lastly, this was the century of the Augustinian friar who took a nun for his wife – Martin Luther.

Luther's was a noble character, but his agonising endowed him with a fire-eating tongue and a vitriolic pen. He employed these first against the corruption of the Church. The pope sentenced him to death for heresy, but he lived on to ascribe to the pontiff, bloated with worldly goods, all the vices of the Devil. History would never be the same again. Luther gave the Jews an opening to join the community of peoples. Like Paul and Muhammad in their day, he wished them to take their place behind the banner of his reformed faith. In 1523 he published his manifesto *Jesus Christ Was Born a Jew*. It clamoured as it pleaded:

> Fools, papists, bishops, sophists, monks, the rude asinine heads, have behaved towards the Jews in such a way as to turn good Christians away . . . They have been treated as though they are dogs. Yet Jews are our kinsmen and brethren of our Lord. God granted the Holy Scriptures to them . . . How can they improve when they are excluded from human society and driven to usury? We should apply the laws of love to them, they should be enabled to work and earn a livelihood together with us. That would convince them of the teaching and the good life of Christians.

Luther's words fell upon deaf Jewish ears. They spurned him and so forfeited his forgiveness. As a political conservative he could not forgive the Christian peasantry either, it will be recalled, for its revolt against the established social order. The apostle of the Reformation could also be its worst enemy. That tongue and that pen raised so much heat as to lead inexorably to the sword.

Twenty years passed, and in 1543 Luther circulated a diatribe against the Jews that would have done credit to Hitlerism. It was his pamphlet *On the Jews and Their Lies*, which advocated their elimination from all Christendom. Failing this, they were to be made slave labourers, with their homes, schools and synagogues destroyed, their holy books proscribed. Thus the era he inaugurated equipped the Christian alternative to Catholicism with a racial antisemitism to supplement its doctrinal arguments. Julius Streicher, editor of the Nazi *Der Stuermer*, named Luther as his justification (the word evokes heated theological argument, 'justification' implying forgiveness through faith) at his Nuremberg trial.

Protestantism fissured early enough to preclude any notion of a Lutheran doctrinal absolutism. It generated a multitude of different sects that exhausted each other in mutual animosities. They also addressed themselves to the Jewish problem, but otherwise than to resort to murder. Calvin, who may reasonably be described as pope of the new middle classes (though he ruled from a city, Geneva, that had expelled its Jews in 1491 and would not allow them back for three hundred years) interpreted the Old Testament in his commentaries without the offensive references to the blindness of Israel customary in Christian exegesis. All in all, this was a hopeful sign, and other reformers built towers upon it. Some extreme expositors of Puritanism soon to emerge out of the English mists offered their countrymen salvation through a Talmudic Christianity: the sabbath returned to Saturday; agitation to convert Parliament into a Sanhedrin of seventy elders; strict regulation of every detail of personal behaviour.[2] In Germany the first Hebrew grammar to be written by a Christian made its appearance.

Catholicism quickly reacted to the spread of heresies, which split Europe between north and south and threatened to engulf Rome itself. Hence the Counter-Reformation, set in train with the creation of the Jesuit Order in 1540 and the summoning of the Council of Trent five years later. Their presumed task, as the Church militant applied itself to regaining territories lost to the schismatics, was to clean up corrupt practices and call a halt to vulgarising conflict. Discipline needed to be restored on all fronts. Most ominously, the Holy Office of the Inquisition was established beside the papal seat in the centre of Catholic

---

[2] J. R. Tanner, *English Constitutional Conflicts of the Seventeenth Century*, Cambridge, 1962, p. 168.

authority. Though not directed against confessing Jews (for, as we have seen, in the judgement of the Spanish prototype institution such people were by their very nature beyond redemption), the Roman Inquisition scoured Europe for 'New Christians' suspected of secret Judaisation. But orthodox Jews could not be totally ignored, since the art of printing was bringing too many editions of the Talmud into circulation for the general good. Thousands of volumes were now consigned to the flames throughout Italy. A papal bull of 1554 reapplied in Italy the worst of the anti-Jewish laws of the Middle Ages, such as exclusion from all occupations except money-lending and second-hand clothes dealing, and stamping out the practice – not too successfully, it transpired – of Jewish physicians attending the Christian sick.

The most oppressive of these rules enjoyed only a brief life, for as always the Jews found defenders among the Christians just as they faced persecutors drawn from their own traitors. Nevertheless the climate of Central Europe, with those fierce cross-winds of religious controversy, augured no respite for them. Those without the material resources to protect themselves took their weary feet to the road, but then the ever-recurring question: whither? The road led them into Poland, that haven discovered by ancestors who had survived earlier travails. A large community of Jews assembled in the sparse regions beyond the Vistula which were then being opened up by German traders. It was a fillip for the burgeoning Yiddish language, the European Jews' specific dialect derived from *Mittelhochdeutsch* and replete with Hebrew-Aramaic assimilants together with Slavic neologisms. Thus did the strictly orthodox Hebrew traditions, forged on the anvil of medieval Rhineland homiletics, travel east. And here the tribe was destined to multiply, struggling amidst Poland's poverty, living and dying amidst Poland's conflicts. Yiddish to speak, and a near-virgin soil in which to dig roots, they coagulated into as close an identifiable nation as ever they would in Europe. Conceivably, Poland saved Jewry from extinction.

Along with Austria, Poland abutted Turkey-in-Europe and similarly felt the pressure of expansionist Islam. Poland was a geographical expression, uncharted, not yet consolidated in national terms and preserved from Protestantism by the zeal of the Jesuits. A land divided between nobility (the *Szlachta*) and feudal peasantry, it as yet lacked both an artisanate and a substantial merchant class. In this place the Jewish newcomer, still unsure of himself and therefore modest in aspiration, could meet the Poles' simple needs, live side by side with them in fact (no ghettos here), as craftsman, as itinerant pedlar, as cattle trader. At least, so it would be for a hundred years, till he jumped a few rungs, as foreigners would, and enlarged his role between absentee landlord and exploited peasant. The *Szlachta* commissioned the Jew to do its tax collecting, an occupation rendering him highly unpopular, particularly in the regions menaced by rampaging Ukrainian Cossacks.

Land-locked within that portion of the continent vainly engaged in the process of settling its frontiers (as if that problem would ever be solved!) the Jews of Poland, together with their kin remaining in the European heartland, constituted the Ashkenazi branch of the people. The name intimated their German provenance. They developed practically into a different people from those banished from the Iberian Peninsula in the previous century. Those, the Sephardim, made a promising new life for themselves under Ottoman rule, but they also spread into the Low Countries. Jealously conserving their Castilian names and dialect, they shared little except religion with the Ashkenazim, although some still insisted upon describing themselves as 'New Christians'. Perhaps they told themselves this was good for business. However, the gentile world referred to the Sephardim without distinction as 'Portuguese'.

While the Ashkenazi poor peddled their humble wares from village to townlet, and performed other functions too menial for their *Szlachta* protectors to undertake themselves, the Sephardim, living close by the sea, became captivated by wider horizons. They plied the new sea routes, set themselves up in the New World and made Antwerp, the centre of the new mercantilism, a sort of headquarters. They introduced printing machines and the destructive magic of gunpowder to Constantinople. Turkey suited them because there it was the Christians who were without privileges or pride. Marranism was a mysterious Sephardi attribute. It cloaked the distinction between devout

'New Christians' and closet Jews. This enabled them to sojourn as desired even in Portugal, where they established enterprises linked with kinsmen in Brazil and the West Indies, not to mention Bristol and London and Bordeaux and Venice – all achieved, no doubt, with the occasional switching of faiths.[3]

The Sephardim felt no restraints in shedding the external marks of Judaism. They shaved their chins and dressed like all other Europeans. By their standards intermarriage with the Ashkenazim, whose kinship they barely acknowledged, was tantamount to miscegenation.

They formed a minority within a minority, these resilient Sephardim, and an ever decreasing one relative to their Ashkenazi co-religionists. During their sixteenth- and seventeenth-century heyday, however, they were the true cosmopolitans of Europe, moving without hindrance in the freemasonry of commerce, a familiar sight wherever deals were struck and cargoes reached harbour. The Mendes and Da Costa families approached in power and influence the likes of the Fugger dynasty, Catholics who had loaned Charles V the funds to buy the crown of the Holy Roman Empire. Through their international connections they learned secrets of preparations for war: some energetic Sephardim appeared also in the role of intelligencer, to be wooed by monarchs. Elizabeth of England, as we shall see, took as her personal physician the Marrano Roderigo Lopez, whose interests strayed far from the fields of medicine.

But the Jews remained incapable of developing into a single organism. The trauma of expulsion from Spain and Portugal had left its mark upon them all, Ashkenazim as well as Sephardim. Religion continued to satisfy their every spiritual craving. Judaism could be rendered in such mystical terms as to offer the people kingdoms to conquer beyond the reach of earthly foes. Hence the appearance of exotic figures like the prophetess Inez of Herrera and the peripatetic preacher Solomon Molcho, who captivated thousands with visions of Israel reborn in power and glory – ideas which belied their New Christian protestations and led them ultimately to the stake. Thoughts of the impending

---

[3] For this interchange, see Brian Pullen, *The Jews of Europe and the Inquisition of Venice 1550–1670*, Oxford, 1985.

Messiah filled Jewish heads. Isaac Luria (died 1572) made Safed in Palestine the centre of a propaganda that inaugurated a general search for omens. The auguries, after all, were all too clear: God had endowed the Turk with particular strength to capture Constantinople from the Jews' traditional Christian enemies, and now the latter were evidently bent upon destroying each other. Weren't the Huguenots, the 'Jews' of France as it were with their prominence in the trading classes, being massacred by the thousand? Every battle, won by no matter whom, could only be a stepping-stone towards the inevitable triumph of God's chosen people.

Indeed, the persecution of Christian by Christian exceeded anything the Jews suffered in the sixteenth century. *Autos-da-fé*, roastings alive, Anabaptists drowned in groups – with such fanaticism, rivalling the Catholic Inquisition, did Protestants pursue dissenters within their own dissenting ranks. Jews might be mulcted of their wealth, or dispatched out of sight by ordinary society, but Christians were driving other Christians from their villages and abandoning them to starvation in remote caves.

Dogma makes fanatics of us all. The principal grievance against the Jews in Renaissance times, however, was political, not theological. Their ease in Islam made them suspect as the Turks' secret ally in Europe, a 'fifth column' undermining the struggle of the Austrian Habsburgs to keep Christendom safe from the Crescent. To the architects of the new literature that had begun to flower as entertainment rather than spiritual guidance, politics was safer than religion as a subject for comedy or satire. They could treat the Jew as an object of fun, a monstrous clown.

Christopher Marlowe, dramatist and English Renaissance figure extraordinary, placed the sinister Jew in a Turkish framework for his *Jew of Malta*, a play that enjoyed great popularity on the English stage in the closing years of the sixteenth century. Barabas, introduced by the spirit of Machiavelli, emerges with red wig and bottle nose, as if out of a puff of smoke. He is about as evil a creature as any representation of the Jew in the Middle Ages – poisoning wells, murdering his own daughter (not totally virtuous but wondrously beautiful), intriguing against Christian and Turk alike. Barabas the usurer is so grotesque one may well ask where Marlowe found his prototype.

Barabas was a caricature based upon Joseph Nasi, Duke of Naxos and counsellor to the sultan following the Ottoman seizure of a large segment of Hungary. This ambitious Marrano, son of a Portuguese royal physician, scion of the Mendes family, came to Constantinople in the course of a career in banking centred on Antwerp with ramifications in London, Lyon and Venice. On returning to Judaism he was circumcised as a grown man. Barabas in the *Jew of Malta* cunningly effects the transfer of Malta to Ottoman rule; Nasi had achieved such a stroke, which contributed to the mercantile decline of Venice, in the 1570 conquest of Cyprus. Barabas trusts no one, and is feared by kings. The incarnation of sin, he extracts devastating revenge for his grievances, real and imagined. Belonging nowhere, he dies unloved. This is Nasi again. When the property of the sultan's counsellor was confiscated in France by Charles IX, he responded by impounding French cargoes on their way to Egypt. He also got even with Pope Paul IV for persecuting the Jews of Ancona by effecting an embargo against that seaport's trade, thus terminating its role in Mediterranean commerce. Nasi won a reputation throughout Europe as a relentless adversary with a finger in every diplomatic and commercial pie. He sought a minor kingship for himself in Palestine (Barabas makes himself Governor of Malta), hoping to build his statelet over the ruins of Tiberias. But by this time he had lost influence over his ruler and so disappeared from history. Barabas is this man drawn to a ridiculous extreme, but Nasi is there, bestriding his world while all the time being rejected by it.

No doubt Shakespeare passed agreeable hours with Marlowe in discussing their respective Jewish villains. Characters and dialogue in *The Merchant of Venice* echo from *The Jew of Malta*, to illustrate, as in other works, the literary interbreeding occurring in such Elizabethan haunts as the Mermaid Tavern. Shylock laments his daughter Jessica's escape from the close Jewish hearth in the same breath with which he mourns his loss of money: 'Oh my ducats, oh my daughter!' Now Barabas: 'Oh girle, oh gold, oh beauty, oh my bliss!' *The Jew of Malta* has the Moorish slave Ithamore to manipulate the boos and jeers of the audience against his diabolical master. In *The Merchant* Shylock's clowning servant Launcelot Gobbo performs the function.

Shakespeare of course borrowed his plots without discrimination of source. In the earliest known version of the Faust legend, the *Faustbuch* published anonymously in Germany in 1587, Faust saws off one of his legs as pledge for a loan from a Jew. The money is repaid, the limb is redeemed, but unhappily it cannot be restored. The pound of flesh theme goes back much further, to an eastern folk-tale of the twelfth century unconnected with a Jew.

Some contend that Shakespeare could never have encountered a Jew in the life, for they were not to be readmitted to England until the Cromwell Protectorate. Nevertheless Shylock is a Jewish character devised out of acute understanding of the people. This is no Barabas. He embraces the normal human complexities, speaks in sublime poetic images and deservedly ranks among the greatest creations of literature. As to Shakespeare's ignorance of the Jews in reality, they were in fact in evidence in England, under their guise of convenience as 'Portuguese'. One of them had achieved national fame, or rather notoriety. The Marrano Roderigo Lopez, besides serving Queen Elizabeth as her physician, engaged actively in commerce, holding the monopoly of certain imports into England. Lopez joined with the Earl of Essex, soldier of fortune and the queen's favourite, in an attempt to put a pretender on the throne of Portugal. A kinsman of Joseph Nasi, he arranged the posting of one of their relatives to Constantinople. As secret agent of the English, he was to promote Elizabeth's scheme for a Protestant–Islamic alliance against Spain and the Holy See.[4]

Lopez evidently cast his net far and wide. Another of his Marrano secret agents was stationed in the Azores to watch out for the Armada on behalf of Sir Francis Drake. Did Lopez overreach himself? The facts are not satisfactorily established, but he became implicated in a plot to poison Elizabeth and was arrested by Essex, the two men now being enemies. Lopez protested his innocence, then confessed under torture and went to the gallows. From the scaffold he is said to have proclaimed his love for the queen and Jesus Christ, though during his trial, which seized public attention, his judges spoke of him as 'that vile Jew'.

[4] Lucien Wolf, 'The Jew in Diplomacy', in Cecil Roth (ed.), *Essays in Jewish History*, London, 1934, p. 395.

From Lopez's notoriety Shakespeare extracted the racial detail that germinated as Shylock, the archetypal usurer, dealer in blood-money, hater of all things Christian. As such, the play to this day touches the average Jew on the raw. He fears the profundities are lost in the stage production. Indeed, the irony, the suggestive eroticism and the pathos are best appreciated on the printed page: the austere Jew without nationality posed against those shallow, confident citizens of a mighty dukedom enjoying music and nature, and ever in quest of diversions as they live beyond their means. Each time the play is staged Jews protest that little except Shylock's lust for blood and ducats will remain impressed upon the audience's mind. Truly, apart from Portia no other character in the play merits recollection. Might not *The Merchant of Venice* contribute then to the fostering of antisemitism?[5]

Shylock has the best lines, reducing all other speeches except Portia's to feckless chatter:

> Sufferance is the badge of all our tribe.
> You call me misbeliever, cut-throat dog,
> And spit upon my Jewish gaberdine . . .
> It now appears you need my help . . .
> Should I not say,
> 'Hath a dog money? Is it possible
> A cur can lend three thousand ducats?'

And, ever recalled:

> Hath not a Jew eyes? Hath not a Jew hands, organs, dimensions, senses, affections, passions? fed with the same food, hurt with the same weapons, subject to the same diseases, healed by the same means, warmed and cooled by the same winter and summer, as a Christian? . . . If you poison us, do we not die? and if you wrong us, shall we not revenge? If we are like you in the rest, we will resemble you in that.

Portia recognises the validity of the equation in one of her

---

[5] For attempts to ban both *The Merchant of Venice* and Dickens's *Oliver Twist* from the New York public school system on grounds of antisemitism, see the *New York Times*, 7 May and 4 June 1949.

many pregnant asides. Confronting the repellent Shylock and the attractive Antonio, she asks: 'Which is the merchant here, and which the Jew?' Not an innocent question. Yet, on the final curtain, what impact? It must be of a creature belonging to a tribe deserving of every condemnation, a tribe that will assuredly meet its retribution, if not in this world then the next.

The Jews' reaction until the present to Shylock reflects their fractured, ambiguous relationship with society as a whole, demonstrated by their anxieties whenever 'black sheep' among their people are specifically identified. After all, Shakespeare's works are replete with evil men (Iago, Richard III) and women (Lady Macbeth, Goneril, Regan). Shylock was one among many, as the Jews are a few among many. So to what degree did *The Merchant of Venice* reinforce prejudices already existing against the Jews? In England, certainly, it had no effect at all. From Stuart times Jews good and bad began making an appearance in English literature, in about equal proportion.

Half a century after the first production of *The Merchant of Venice*[6] the Jews were formally readmitted into England, the country which had led Europe with their expulsion in 1290. Not by official decree, for Oliver Cromwell encountered considerable resistance to the step – wild allegations circulating, for example, that he planned to sell St Paul's Cathedral for a synagogue. The Protector had been negotiating the Jews' return with the 'Portuguese' rabbi of Amsterdam, Manasseh ben Israel. The latter based his plea on apocalyptic arguments relating to the 'discovery' of the Lost Ten Tribes in the natives of the New World (which he had visited). England featured as the completing element necessary for the advent of the Messiah, with Cromwell perhaps God's elected instrument in the final redemption of Israel. More prosaically, the Puritan statesman had English interests in mind, and the commercial and political rivalries of the day. The Dutch Republic especially worried him.

Throwing off their allegiance to Spain in 1581, the Dutch thereupon showed their versatile mettle and brought the lucrative trade of Antwerp, together with its Marranos, to Amsterdam. Cromwell's practical sense told him these descendants of

[6] First recorded performance, in the presence of King James I, was in 1605.

southern Jewish grandees could do the same for London. They had commercial intelligence to offer, skills to impart and connections with Spain of no small import to the conduct of his wars.

England was losing out in the expanding transatlantic traffic because Dutch ships plied every route. While the English were pinned down in the peatlands of Ireland, unable to provision their army, Cromwell searched in vain for an English contractor to undertake its bread supply. The business went to the Amsterdam Jew Abraham Pereira, who controlled a superb merchant marine. England had already reaped advantage from continental immigration in the thousands of Huguenots crossing the Channel to escape French persecution. So why not the Jews? Excellent religious reasons could be presented for a strict Protestant nation to welcome them. The reasons were by no means universally endorsed, but the Jews came nevertheless, to inaugurate their first synagogue in Creechurch Lane, implicit token of their formal resettlement, in 1656.

Despite Marlowe, Shakespeare and other popular though lesser writers, antisemitism (we apply the modern term *faute de mieux*) was henceforth conspicuous by its absence in England. Perhaps this was due to the paucity of Jewish numbers, and the toleration that is rewarded for voluntary extinction: in successive waves they came, they saw, they were conquered. Zealous research has of course rarely failed to uncover examples of prejudice against them: an anti-Jewish tract, a minor riot, frequent ridicule and occasional fear. England tarried in granting the Jews full legal rights. But their disabilities were of a piece with the injustices meted out to Roman Catholics. Anti-popery could be truly described as an English disease (contaminating their colonies and dependencies), while antisemitism proper had to await the twentieth century and its attendant complexities.

In France, however, the scarcity of Jews proved no obstacle to the continuance of a deep hatred for this people. The catechism ensured every child's familiarity with the New Testament version of Christ's sacrifice and the consequential eternal punishment of his murderers, as pronounced by St Augustine. The Church which had endeavoured to exterminate Cathars and Protestants could hardly be expected to call a truce in its crusade against Judaism.

Racine alone managed to forgive, recognising in those tender couplets of his biblical dramas the unbroken connection between the travails of Ancient Israel and its subsequent nostalgia for Zion. *Athalie*, Racine's masterpiece, was misunderstood and condemned. Bossuet breathed a different air, and soon there would come Voltaire, whose vitriol spattered church and synagogue alike.

Thus Bossuet, one of Louis XIV's favourite preachers, 'the last of the Church Fathers':

> They are a monstrous people, having neither hearth nor home, without a country and of all countries; once the most fortunate people of all, now the evil spirit and the detestation of the world. Wretched, universally scorned, they have been cursed to become the mockery of even the most moderate. We see before our eyes the remains of their shipwreck.[7]

The Jewish phenomenon of survival long continued to perplex the French moralists. To Pascal this could be explained only in terms of the traditional Christian view of divinely ordained punishment: 'Despite hundreds of attempts by powerful kings to destroy them', he exclaimed, 'they stretch from the first days to the last, their history embracing all our histories!' Montesquieu saw little point in the persistence of a people which had lost its *raison d'être*, 'without a single rabbi coming within even a minor order of genius'.[8]

Measured against the breadth of his own scepticism, Montesquieu was undoubtedly justified in his contemptuous dismissal of Jewish scholarship, particularly during his own period, the early eighteenth century. But the comparison is pointless. Here was a denationalised people whose every right of existence evoked intense debate. The French had no intention of admitting more Jews to add to the few they inherited by territorial acquisition. Luther had advised their enslavement. During the

---

[7] From a sermon delivered in Metz, published in Jacques Bénigne Bossuet, *Oeuvres Complètes*, Paris, 1863, Vol. II, p. 443.

[8] From Blaise Pascal, *Penseés*, ed. Léon Brunschvig, Paris, 1925, p. 620; Julien Weill on Charles Louis Montesquieu in *Revue des études juives*, XLIX, pp. 150–3.

Thirty Years War, Protestants regarded them as the power behind Catholicism, which in turn marked them as secret allies of the Reformation. Little wonder the Jews supported whichever side happened to be sheltering them, purchasing tranquillity wherever it could be found.

While Europe as a whole engaged in remaking itself during those painful thirty years, it dropped the Jews out of any calculations for its future. Poland chose otherwise, for their numbers there alone compelled recognition that Jewry constituted an element likely to persist. As we have already noted, Poland saved the tribe from possible disappearance. It granted the Jews considerable self-rule. This left the regulation of their internal affairs to their own leaders, clerical and lay, organised in a 'Council of the Four Lands'. A separate but associated council existed for Lithuania. It was a logical development in a country of changing frontiers incorporating diverse national groups. Jews could enter almost every branch of the nascent economy, which was based on the village, the salt mine and the pine forest. Frequently a Jew rented the local inn, for he was licensed to distil and market liquor, though only rarely consuming it himself. We must recall Poland in those days as a country of immense size, with a significant voice in the affairs of Europe as a whole.

The great landowners had good cause to value their Jews, for they constituted a buffer separating the nobility from the exploited peasantry. Still, they were alien intruders, unwelcome competitors of Polish craftsmen and petty merchants. More, religious fanaticism, ready to subside in the west, pervaded Eastern Europe as always, and rarely a year passed without that old scare of sacrilegious Jewish practices. Jesuit country interspersed with islands of Greek Orthodoxy hardly created an environment for novel ideas to flourish. But there reigned a tranquillity of sorts. Poland in 1648 emerged relatively unbruised from the Thirty Years War. Then the country exploded. For the Cossacks were in revolt.

They crossed the Dnieper led by a 'hetman' and ruler Bogdan Chmielnicki, whose similarity to his contemporary Oliver Cromwell has not passed unremarked by historians. During their respective careers of violence, both believed they had the Bible on their side. Here was a fearless cavalry leader fired by a Christian zeal (the Orthodox variety) whose successful campaigns left a trail of death on a huge scale. Cromwell had descended upon the Irish with a brutality he termed 'the righteous judgement of God'; Chmielnicki's victims were the Poles first, then with added ferocity the Jews. His enemies were more detestable to him than were the Irish to the Englishman, his fanaticism stronger, so the dead were many times greater. Chmielnicki's triumph brought the Ukraine into the arms of Russia, though his star would not remain long in the ascendant.

While victorious, he demanded the expulsion of Jesuits and Jews from Poland. In the case of the Jews he received a promise from the king, the erstwhile cardinal and Jesuit John Casimir. Many thousands of them had been slaughtered, women and children included, in battles which gave Chmielnicki brief control of Poland, reminiscent of the barbarian carnage of old. However, the promise of expulsion was not fulfilled. The Jews had fought side by side with the Poles at Nemirov and Lemberg in a struggle of desperation against the invader, when baptism of captured Jews offered the sole reprieve from death or transportation. Estimates of the martyred varied wildly, though the figure may well have exceeded 100,000.[9] Others left Poland in manacles, merchandise for the eastern slave trade. Chmielnicki was defeated in the end, but is revered still as the father of Ukrainian nationalism, while the antisemitism embodied in his mission would burst forth again among the Ukrainians on another day.

Could the Jews of Poland envision a future for themselves after this ordeal? Civil war continued to engulf the country until John Sobieski, its greatest leader, ascended the throne in 1673. The social turbulence sent a trickle of Jews westward again, to those parts of Europe that would have them; or to the sanctuary of their co-religionists who now prospered under Turkish rule. Some followed a career of vagabondage and turned up as beggars in the streets of Amsterdam; these are believed to have served as models for Rembrandt's Old Testament subjects. The Sephardim received their bearded Ashkenazi brethren with a cool welcome, barely concealed, both in Holland and elsewhere.

[9] For a description of the horrors, see Dubnov, *History of the Jews*, Vol. IV, pp. 29–37.

For those remaining in Poland, the vast majority, the weeping revived the memory of the destruction of Jerusalem, Jeremiah's Lamentations being prescribed reading in the synagogue: *From the daughter of Zion all her beauty is departed; her princes are become like deer that find no pasture and are gone without strength*. Redemption, they sensed, could come only through the utmost piety. The Council of the Four Lands imposed penance upon all, commanding austerity of conduct and modesty of attire. Thus Poland was rendered fertile territory for the coming of a new type of pietist, the Hassidim, who, wrote the historian Simon Dubnov, by warming the heart obscured the intellect. We have been here before.

The Chmielnicki massacre inaugurated another period of Ashkenazi stagnation, with only the unexpected to be anticipated. By contrast, the Sephardim adopted a global view of their affairs, for they lived as it were in a fluid situation. Furthermore, their dreams rested on a secure base of wealth and influence. They considered themselves to be controllers, not victims, of their fate. They had expelled from their community the philosopher Benedict de Spinoza, who dared to take God out of his specifically Jewish heaven and locate him pantheistically within a natural process of creation.

We have seen how another of those Sephardim, Manasseh ben Israel of Amsterdam, led the Jews along a new path by initiating their resettlement in England. His was only one manifestation of the messianic temper of the age, which permeated Christian and Jewish hopes alike. In the Orient a plausible messenger of God materialised with a charisma that was to deceive many thousands into accepting his claim. This one differed from his spurious predecessors in setting all Jewry agog with news of his mission, bringing unending repercussions in its wake. In that respect he may count as the true messiah.

Born in 1626 in Smyrna, Sabbetai Zevi could not have been less prepossessing a personality. He was the son of a merchant of modest estate whose business, much to do with exporting to England, had expanded phenomenally as Venice struggled against the Sublime Porte and the trade routes detoured away from Constantinople to this minor destination on the Turkish mainland. Smyrna grew in importance, and self-importance.

Sabbetai Zevi, a young rabbi and student of Cabbala, questioned the Holy Law and saw visions. He could not consummate his marriage. He committed a blasphemy (articulating the forbidden name of God) in the synagogue. Excommunicated, he wandered over the East, sojourned for a while in the Holy Land, attracted followers and, in 1665, returned to an ecstatic reception in Smyrna. There he prophesied the impending defeat and abdication of the sultan. The Jews would usurp his empire, re-establishing the Lord's rule in Jerusalem, when peace would reign eternally over the earth and he, Sabbetai Zevi, would be the King of Kings.

The endeavour embraced too many coincidental circumstances for it to have been schemed only from the brain of a crazed impostor. A solitary figure, he was given to depressions. While he must have spoken well, he wrote little except some brief messages and love-letters to a woman mysteriously saved, apparently, from the Cossacks in Poland who found her way from Amsterdam to Leghorn. He married her as his third wife in Cairo.

Sabbetai Zevi won adherents in high position and of great substance. Religious authorities accepted him at all the nodal points of his messianic compass. The tarnished old slogans of past pseudo-prophets at once assumed new majesty, captivating both Sephardi and Ashkenazi branches of the people. Thus the mystique crystallised into a movement. It was taken in hand by, among others, the 'prince' of the Jews of Egypt and head of that country's treasury, Raphael Joseph Chelebi. Level-headed merchants in Amsterdam and Hamburg, one of them Cromwell's bread contractor Abraham Pereira, declared their allegiance. Salonica, in seventeenth-century terms as Jewish a city as New York in the twentieth, became the brain and arsenal of Sabbetai's organisation, dispatching agents with secret instructions throughout the Diaspora. His own St Paul, alone, was missing; such a self-elected apostle, Nathan Levi of Gaza, arose to expound Sabbetaian theology for the instruction of the masses.

Here stood a new messiah who normally would have outraged Jewish susceptibilities through his defiance of religious ritual, his tolerant references to Jesus Christ as one deserving redemption along with all other past figures responsible for Jewry's tribulations, and his interpretation of passages in the Cabbala as woman's fiat of sexual liberation. Yet he induced otherwise rational men to surrender to his call. While awaiting his sign they halted the activities of their daily lives and prepared for their sublimation to an existence of heavenly eternity in the Holy Land. Pereira moved with his household to Leghorn, a location of key importance to the sect. Typical of the hysteria is the description offered by Glückel of Hameln, a widow of the genteel Ashkenazi bourgeoisie. Connected by family ties to Jews in the service of German royalty, Glückel wrote an autobiography in Yiddish, much of it tittle-tattle, that remains nevertheless as a rich source of authentic detail on contemporary Jewish life and mores.

When in 1665 news of Sabbetai reached Germany, she says, the excitement knew no bounds:

> Most of the letters were received by the Portuguese. They took them to their synagogue and read them aloud there. The Germans [Ashkenazim], young and old, went to the Portuguese synagogue to hear them. The young Portuguese on these occasions all wore their best clothes and each tied a broad green silk ribbon round his waist – Sabbetai Zevi's colour ... Many people sold home, hearth and everything they possessed awaiting redemption.
>
> My father-in-law, peace unto him, who lived in Hameln, moved from there, leaving things standing in the house just as they were, and went to Hildersheim. He sent to us here, in Hamburg, two large barrels of linen and all kinds of foods that would keep without going bad. The good man thought they would be leaving from Hamburg for the Holy Land. These barrels were more than a year in my house. At last, fearing that the meat and other things would spoil, he wrote that we should open the barrels and take out the food and so keep the linen unharmed underneath. They remained here for three more years, my father-in-law always expecting to need them for his journey at a moment's notice.[10]

[10] *The Life of Glückel of Hameln*, tr. and ed. Beth-Zion Abrahams, London, 1962, pp. 45–6.

Close interest was maintained in the Sabbetaian movement by the governments of France, England and Holland, all competitors for the valuable Turkish trade. The English Consul in Smyrna, Paul Rycaut, observed its progress from its beginnings. He sent home reports, corroborated by writers in other languages, that were subsequently embodied in an account that forms a primary source on the movement.[11]

That London was astir is attested in the diaries of Samuel Pepys and John Evelyn. Even the excommunicated Spinoza, the antithesis of Sabbetai Zevi in denying the mystical elements in Judaism, admitted to being impressed. The Secretary of the Royal Society in England, Henry Oldenburg, wrote to Spinoza requesting his views on a subject in which he, Oldenburg, expressed continued interest. The only reply extant is indirect, and appears in Spinoza's *Tractatus Theologico-Politicus*:

> The symbol of circumcision . . . is, I believe, so potent that I am convinced it alone will keep this nation alive for ever. I would go so far as to believe that, if the foundations of their religion have not enfeebled their minds, they may, if the occasion presents itself amid the changes to which human affairs are liable, even raise their empire anew, and God may elect them a second time.[12]

Evidently, there had grown around the personality of Sabbetai Zevi ideas to challenge the traditional definition of the Jews as a contemptible race of political impotents; a sentiment for the retesting of the Jewish belief in their destiny as the People of the Book. It was revolutionary, it was cohesive and it threatened the authority of gentile dynasts. It also threatened to divert Judaism into behavioural patterns radically different from those ordained by the Talmud, through which the Jews perennially charted their survival.

But was a yearning after a boundless horizon the total explanation of Sabbetaianism? The present writer, in a fictional work,[13]

---

[11] *History of the Turkish Empire from 1623–1677*, London, 1690.

[12] See, e.g., Franz Kobler (ed.), *Letters of Jews Through the Ages*, Vol. II, New York, 1978, pp. 535–6.

[13] Barnet Litvinoff, *Another Time, Another Voice*, London, 1971.

has interpreted the movement rather as a painstakingly woven conspiracy conducted with the utmost sophistication to embrace a terrestrial dimension. Too many important Jews, widely separated by geography and character, were united in their interpretation of unmistakable portents: the successful settlement of their tribe in the New World, the revival of a Jewish centre in England, the mutually consuming hatreds within the edifice of Christianity, the holocaust of lives resulting from the Polish wars. The occasion beckoned action. Proof is lacking, allowing fiction its rein. The novel depicts these men forging letters and inventing miracles because they firmly believed they were empowered to seize the day. Sabbetai Zevi, a drifting soul, met the specifications of a passive instrument of their scheme.

They could well have been setting the fuse to a political earthquake. Has there been a plot of grand destiny that did not enlist the help of the Supreme Accomplice? We know that before his final assault upon Constantinople, which took the form in 1666 of a caique loaded with a brotherhood of rabbis and scholars sailing towards the Bosporus, Sabbetai divided up the globe. He appointed his two brothers and other near associates kings and princes to reign as viceroys over each of his dominions. He then left the rest to God.

An anticlimax of the most crushing proportions ensued. We are now back in recorded history. The sultan refused to succumb to his expected fate. Instead, the messiah was seized and imprisoned. To save his skin he converted to Islam. What initially was feared by the Porte as a determined insurrection on the part of the Jews became exposed as a colossal fraud. And so, improbably donning the turban of the faithful, the great challenger received an appointment as a minor official of the seraglio. It was not the end of the dream. Some of his disciples followed him to Islam, and the mission of Sabbetai Zevi endured as an Islamic–Judaistic heresy. Retaining its centre in Salonica, it produced conspirators of a different kind some two centuries later, leaders in the Young Turk movement that broke the sultan's power in 1908. One day Sabbetaianism would re-emerge in yet another form, also with realistic objectives, and travel by the name of Zionism.

Meanwhile the sense of betrayal in the ignominious collapse of the venture demoralised a great part of the Sephardi world. Its seventeenth-century eminence suffered a calamitous decline together with the mighty Ottoman Empire in which it was nurtured. This branch of the Jewish people would now surrender primacy to the Ashkenazim, in scholarship, in national pride and ultimately also in commerce.

These Ashkenazim had likewise to pay heavily for their gullibility. They returned to familiar pastures, reconciled to an exclusively economic role in the state, both in Eastern Europe, where it was a modest one, and in the West, which permitted their ascent to the financial peaks. They feared change. And while they produced illuminati to expound copiously on man's relationship to God, no son of Israel emerged to question the Jew's relationship to man. But Sabbetai Zevi and Spinoza had each cast a stone into a pool of still waters that could not revert to their former stagnation.

Discussion within a wider stream was beginning to focus at last upon the Jews as a sociological anachronism. Must they forever remain outside society? We have referred above to Montesquieu's low estimation of their culture. But he also made a powerful plea for religious toleration: Judaism was not an excrescence, it was the trunk out of which both Christianity and Islam grew. Given the opportunity, why shouldn't the Jews live like all other civilised peoples?

This refreshing mood spread outward from France, Catholic *malgré soi* and also innovator of the eighteenth-century European 'Enlightenment'. It could bring emancipation to the Jews. Unhappily, it was contested by the most strident voice of the age, Voltaire's voice.

As an unremitting enemy of the Catholic Church and fervent admirer of the English deists, Voltaire made freedom of thought his passion. Yet he could not allow such freedom to the Jews, whom he regarded only as 'a miserable little nation whose obscure existence as a nomadic tribe in an isolated corner of the Orient occupies such a small place in the annals of the civilised world'. In order to strike at Christianity through its 'trunk', he revived every ancient instrument of disparagement directed against Judaism by the early Hellenistic disputants: that the Jews were descended from a leper tribe whose book, the Bible, evolved by compounding the legends and hagiographa of earlier civilisations; and that their term for God, *Adonai*, derived from the Phoenician *adonis*, and from the same source came their account of the creation of the world in six stages. Old Testament stories were largely Arabian, said Voltaire, angels and demons Chaldean plagiarised during the Babylonian exile.

So, Samson was Hercules with a Jewish nose, and the great religions of the world, in Voltaire's construction, drew as much from divine revelation as did a municipal by-law. We do not propose to argue its validity. What is relevant here is the weight of malice loaded by the acknowledged tribune of the Enlightenment against any idea of accepting the Jews as equals. Voltaire was the cosmopolitan spirit whose works sparkled with the irony and iconoclasm that all Europe's intelligentsia recognised as necessary to eliminate society's imperfections, its bigotry and political wilfulness. The Inquisition still operated in Spain, Portugal and their colonies, sending 'New Christians' suspected of lapsing into Judaism to the stake. Twelve of them were burnt alive in Lisbon in 1737, when Voltaire was forty-three.

This French arch-cynic also had an affection for money. He aspired to be rich, very rich, and in pursuit of wealth he had dealings with Jewish financiers in Holland, England and Prussia. Voltaire quarrelled with them all, hurling accusations of treachery at them because his progress to the status of grand seigneur was suffering frustrations. He is the glory and the embarrassment of France, as is Luther to the Germans. Voltaire's Judeophobia, a paranoia, wearied some of his contemporaries, not least his sworn enemy Rousseau. Still, his genius and eminence transformed him into an institution ranking in authority with every god he ridiculed.

Voltaire even found apologists among Sephardi Jews ('emancipated Portuguese' of Bordeaux) who took his calumnies as applying to the 'primitive' Ashkenazim, and of course many Christians endorsed his attacks upon the frailties of the Church. Nevertheless, in seeking a primary source for the antisemitism of modern times, we must point to this pupil of the Jesuits. His *Dictionnaire Philosophique* says of the Jews: 'An ignorant and barbarous people who for a long time have combined the most sordid greed with the most detestable superstition and the most invincible hatred for all the peoples who tolerate them and enrich them.' The quotation comes from the 1769 edition of the *Dictionnaire*, but was omitted in the version published in 1936, which was edited in part by the Jewish Communist philosopher Julien Benda.[14] With the German occupation of France in 1940, Nazi teachers triumphantly resuscitated these calumnies, compiling a volume[15] that enjoyed a shameless vogue in the circles of Vichy.

Voltaire understood well that Christendom had fashioned Jewry to a shape suited to its own purpose, with dolorous results for both. Speaking as a Christian, he tells the race: '*We* have placed *you* between the devil and the deep blue sea for centuries; *we* have torn out *your* teeth to force you to give us your money; *we* have driven *you* out at times through greed, and *we* have recalled *you* through greed and stupidity.'

He was a persecutor in the monkish, medieval mould, this champion of liberty, wishing the Jews away to some distant, perpetual exile. But Voltaire stopped short of consigning them to the gallows or pyre. He was, after all, patron saint of the authors of the Declaration of the Rights of Man. Jean-Jacques Rousseau cherished human dignity more convincingly. His novel *Émile* spoke of a Jewish right of reply: 'I won't believe', says one of his characters in the course of a discussion on faith, 'that I have heard the full explanations of the Jews until they have a free state, schools, universities, where they can speak and argue without risk. Only then shall we be able to know what they have to say.' And again: 'These unhappy people feel they are in our power. The tyranny they have suffered makes them timid.'

Hardly a lover of the Jews himself, Rousseau nevertheless marvelled at the greatness of Moses the Lawgiver, whose teaching preserved this people when so many other civilisations sank to oblivion:

> The laws of Numa, Lycurgus, Solon are dead; the very much older laws of Moses are still alive. Athens, Sparta, Rome have perished and no longer have children left on earth, while Zion, destroyed, has not lost its children.

---

[14] See Poliakov, *History of Antisemitism*, Vol. III, 1975, p. 492.
[15] Henri Labroue, *Voltaire antijuif*, Paris, 1942. Voltaire on the lowly origins of the Jews in his article 'Dieu', *Collected Works*, Vol. XXVIII.

> They mingle with all the nations and never merge with
> them; they no longer have leaders and are still a nation.
> They no longer possess a homeland and are always citi-
> zens of it.[16]

No doubt about it, conditions were ripening for the impending
emancipation of the Jews. The absolutism of monarchs, the
obscurantism of religion, the injustices of inherited privilege, all
these were on the wane. England had begun the trend a hundred
years earlier, albeit driving to extremes: an army politicised,
cathedrals vandalised, a king executed. The English preferred
pastoral managers to conduct their worship rather than priests
half-way up the pedestal to sainthood. To be sure, they swung the
pendulum too far, reducing the adherents of another religion –
not Judaism but Catholicism – to the status of *déclassés* in their
realm. Still, Englishmen spoke of government by consent in a
way that would have received short shrift among their neighbours across the Channel while the cardinals ruled there.

The myths surrounding Judaism, and its disqualification from
participation in normal society, had rarely been questioned until
the arrival of John Toland, the early English Deist. He published
a pamphlet in 1714 advocating the naturalisation of Jews, native
and foreign-born. He thought of transforming the wretched
multitudes in Poland into productive Englishmen. In Holland the
Protestant pastor Jacob Basnage had by this time completed
many years of research to produce his comprehensive record of
Jewish history and civilisation. It was the first of any significance
since Josephus, filling a gap of sixteen centuries. Now the thrust
assumed an inexorable momentum. Basnage accorded recognition to a people who, like any other, had their tragedies, conflicts
and triumphs, their achievement under stress, their failings and
the scars inflicted by their anomalous situation over the ages. The
work was eagerly absorbed by friends of the Jews, now growing
in number, who argued for their emancipation.

Such harbingers were still in advance of their times. Europe
hesitated. Make the Jews citizens like all others, with their

---

[16] But Rousseau could not abide the angry, vengeful God of the Old Testament.
Thus, in *Émile*: 'Your God is not ours. He who begins by selecting a Chosen
People, and proscribing the rest of mankind, is not our common father.'

avarice, devil-worship, denial of the Christian sabbath and that primordial crime against God? Why, the Jews were taught to hate the Christians! Some rulers still thought to expel the reprobates, such as the Austrian Empress Maria Theresa who in 1744 wanted them out of Bohemia on the pretext that they spied for Prussia. And yet Maria Theresa's son, that enlightened monarch Joseph II, who abolished serfdom, edged forward. He did away with the poll-tax and the Jews' badge of identification. In 1782 he removed obstacles to their working in agriculture. He opened the schools to their children, and sanctioned Jewish entry into the craft guilds. And finally, Joseph granted them the privilege of serving in his imperial army. They had already proved themselves in Poland's war against Chmielnicki, alongside the Dutch against the British and most recently in the American Revolutionary War.

How did they themselves react to these auguries of change? Where they resided in great numbers, that is, in Eastern Europe, they generally regarded with profound suspicion any move to release them from their Talmudic cocoon. Science and mathematics did not strike them as appropriate subjects for their children's education. They clung to the caftan, their special attire. To the rabbis, emancipation was another word for temptation. Their holy books contained all the culture they possessed, or needed, to be kept pristine so that they might be in fit condition to welcome the Messiah (the true one this time, not like the charlatans of the past). And he could arrive at any moment, perhaps this very day. Citizenship, secular knowledge, military service — these implied temptation, association with immodest women, assimilation and horrors unimaginable. Let the 'goy' keep them. The rabbis felt the subject settled for another millennium.

But in the meantime a Jew imbued with the spirit of the Enlightenment had arisen in Germany. Traditional ideas would fight on, but this man took large numbers of his people kicking and screaming into the modern age. In October 1743 a note of livestock permitted to enter the city of Berlin appeared in the daily journal of the guard at the Rosenthaler Gate as follows: 'There passed through the gate today six oxen, seven pigs, one Jew.' The last item related to a young student of Talmud named Moses Mendelssohn. He hoped, through a chain of recommendations, to have his residence regularised as a *Schutz-jude* ('protected Jew') of the King of Prussia. On his death in 1786 he was mourned by Goethe as 'our immortal'. Germany was bidding farewell to its Plato.

As always, Germany was a special case. It retained harassing restrictions against the Jews while simultaneously granting those with resources and initiative opportunities for advancement to an indispensable financial role in its conglomeration of principalities. Moses Mendelssohn was born in Dessau, Duchy of Anhalt, in 1729, the son of a humble Hebrew scribe. The Jews of Dessau, a hundred families all told, enjoyed the status of *Schutzjuden* by courtesy of the duke, but the privilege was not transferable to other German states. The only commerce sanctioned to them sent them on the road dealing in silver jewellery. Somewhere in the background hovered a more important co-religionist to watch over the little community's rights and ensure it fulfilled its obligations of special taxation. He was of the station known as *Hofjude*, 'Court Jew'.

Mendelssohn's era saw the Court Jew at his zenith. A specifically Central European type (though Joseph the Israelite, in the service of his Pharaoh, might justly be termed the earliest Court Jew), such men had risen to prominence as army contractors, hardly a pauperising occupation, during the Thirty Years War. They subsequently performed essential functions on behalf of impoverished rulers throughout the Holy Roman Empire, still so-called. Their extensive connections across continental Europe enabled them to negotiate loans for their princes and generally to organise their exchequers. Glückel of Hameln tells in her memoirs of kinship to such men in the higher banking reaches of Lorraine and Hanover.

The most celebrated Court Jew at the time of Mendelssohn's birth was Joseph Süss Oppenheimer – the Jew Süss of Feuchtwanger's novel. He controlled the finances of the Duchy of Würtemberg. As keeper of the privy purse Oppenheimer also enjoyed the monopoly of minting coin. This by no means absorbed the whole of his energies, for he engaged in lucrative commercial sidelines apart from acting as spokesman of the Jews at the royal palace in Stuttgart, which was hardly grander than his own.

The ubiquity of Oppenheimer's operations inevitably inspired envy. Resentment of his power on the part of both nobility and peasant farmers endangered the situation of all other Jews, rich and poor. This became especially acute as he was not immune from contamination by the political intrigues of the day. And, like others before him, he overreached himself. With the accession of another duke 'who knew not Joseph', Oppenheimer died by public execution in Stuttgart, in 1738, apparently with the Hebrew prayer *Hear, O Israel* on his lips.

Mendelssohn's coming to Berlin thus coincided with an inauspicious period for his people in Germany. His poverty was the least of his disadvantages: he was hunchbacked, and afflicted with a stammer. Frederick II of Prussia, having made the unwelcome discovery that the Silesia he had torn from Maria Theresa of Austria contained an inordinate number of Jews, took precautions against their moving to his capital. He permitted residence to only one child per family in Berlin, lest they multiplied to unacceptable proportions. They paid heavily in special Jewish taxation, the alternative being to leave Berlin. Prussia set the pattern for the rest of Germany. In the Free City of Hamburg, where twelve Dutch Jews had in 1619 created the first money exchange and banking system, they could not qualify for even the most menial government employment, nor could they maintain an open shop. Pedlars hawking their second-hand clothes and cheap household goods from door to door stereotyped the Jew. In Prussia Frederick forbade them from shaving off their beards, but when ordered in Hungary to go bare-chinned they petitioned the emperor, unsuccessfully, to retain them.

What to do with such a people? They baffled their rulers. Too many Jews were an offence, too few and the revenue dwindled. In Frankfurt they could not, in the eighteenth century, marry before the age of twenty-five, or leave the ghetto on Sundays and religious holidays. In walking out they were ordered to the open country so as to acquaint themselves with the farmer's life.[17] Court Jews were privileged to adopt the manners and dress of civilised citizenship only to be caricatured by the satirists for their pretensions to emancipation. Mendelssohn, a fervently orthodox

[17] Ludwig Boerne, spokesman of German political liberty, writes of his upbringing in the Frankfurt ghetto in his *Gesammelte Schriften*, Vol. II.

Jew devoted to the ancestral culture, accepted his lot; but he also peeped over the wall to the greener pastures beyond. He perfected himself in Latin and studied the secular philosophers, Locke particularly. He also mastered the German language and pored over its literature. According to the rabbis, he had taken a path strewn with roses and therefore leading to perdition.

Mendelssohn secured permission to sojourn in Berlin through the influence of his employer, a silk manufacturer. (Frederick the Great relaxed certain anti-Jewish restrictions in his capital if they encouraged industrialisation by starting factories.) He began working on essays in metaphysics, and won the friendship of Gotthold Ephraim Lessing who, at the age of twenty in 1749, had written a one-act play, *Die Juden*, containing the first generous treatment of a Jew in German drama. In 1763 a philosophical work by Mendelssohn gained first prize in a competition organised by the Prussian Academy of Sciences, with no less a thinker than Immanuel Kant receiving merely an honourable mention. The work earned Mendelssohn national recognition, a place among the literary élite and the legalisation of his residence in Berlin. He was now the most liberated Jew in Europe, and mentor to all his co-religionists with aspirations to emancipation.

The association of Lessing with Mendelssohn powerfully reinforced the movement of humanism in Germany. The one was not the greatest of poets, the other hardly the most original of philosophers. Yet together with Kant they rescued German thought from its provincialism and marked out a trail for the classical masters Goethe and Schiller. In his *Laocoon* Lessing spoke for the spirit of aesthetics, while Mendelssohn elaborated his anti-rationalist ideas on the immortality of the soul with his *Phaedo*. The two collaborated in various periodicals, and at length Lessing translated their friendship into a public monument by adopting Mendelssohn as model for his final work, *Nathan the Wise*. It is a poetic drama based on the story of the three rings made popular by Boccaccio. The rings represent the three religions, Christianity, Judaism and Islam, and in weighing their respective merits the play makes a plea for the introduction of light into the darkness of theological bigotry. Lessing accorded to Nathan the role of apostle of tolerance.

Was their new Moses leading his people to a latter-day Euro-

pean Promised Land breathing political and spiritual freedom?
Mendelssohn wished for nothing more than to bring the Jews
into the mainstream. The man whose major oeuvre, *Phaedo*,
was now available in a dozen European tongues, believed passionately that the time had arrived for the Jews to abandon their
Yiddish for speech of richer tradition and broader culture:
Hebrew for a start, neglected by the majority of Jews except in
the clockwork repetition of their prayers; and German, which
Mendelssohn himself wrote with supreme elegance. He united
the two languages with a new translation of the Pentateuch into
German supplemented by a critical commentary on the text in
Hebrew, and he bequeathed the synthesis of ancient and modern
with his heart. Together with his disciples he published a
magazine in Hebrew devoted not to religion but to *belles-lettres*.

To diehard conservative clerics he had tampered with words
which to them must remain inviolate. Furthermore, the old Ashkenazi teachers, especially those entrenched in Eastern Europe,
detested his propagation of pure German in the place of Yiddish
as treason towards a language specific to themselves. The
Sephardim of course remained detached from the controversy,
Yiddish being as alien to them as Mandarin Chinese. The German Jews, nearest to the fresh winds blowing from France,
succumbed willingly and speedily to the Mendelssohn reforms;
in Austria too. But the storm would rage deep into the nineteenth
century. Jewry as a whole would not radically change unless
change could be wrought in their condition in Poland. There, in
the dying eighteenth century, they were two million strong. Most
would soon be located within the narrows of Catherine the
Great's despotic Holy Russia.[18]

By strict orthodox calculation, Jewish tradition nurtured a
culture more precious than any secular substitute. It was eternal.
What ensued in Germany and its near neighbours abundantly
proved the argument. As we shall see, in breaking free from the
clerical stranglehold and in ascending the social and cultural

[18] Most of the Austrian Empire's half-million Jews were at this time located in
its Slavic possessions and in Hungary. Official figures were less, due to concealment of Jews out of fear of recruitment. Those regions of Poland and Belorussia
absorbed into Russia by 1795 accounted for three times this figure. See Dubnov,
History of the Jews, Vol. IV, pp. 656–57, 684.

scale, many Jews, four of Mendelssohn's own children included, shuffled off the onerous coils of Judaism. He had opened the flood-gates to complete assimilation.

Mendelssohn was the principal internal agent of Jewry's change. The external world demanded it of them also, and ever more pressingly. Mendelssohn died in 1786, three years before the French launched a revolution to wash the last traces of European medievalism out of existence. The revolution could not but carry the Jews along in its tide. Did the liberalisation of society spell the end of their troubles? It did not spell the end of anybody's troubles. The politics of religion would make way for the politics of class. The Jews put their faith in that struggle too; but then, alas, would come the politics of race.

5

Steps towards
the Racial Divide

While the storming of the Bastille on 14 July 1789 counted for little more than the demolition of a cenotaph, a gesture of farewell to an already declining Bourbon absolutism, the rationalist philosophies spreading from Paris shook all European society to its foundations.

In the old order, Europe was controlled through an informal league of interconnected monarchies which in their turn were sustained by a vast cosmopolitan aristocracy. Louis XVI hired a German legion for his Parisian garrison; his consort Marie Antoinette was the sister of the Holy Roman Emperor, Joseph II of Austria, and related to half the reigning families of the time. Religion divided up the continent more effectively than frontiers. The word 'nation' covered a vague concept and had little meaning except as a term of convenience. Now, at last, conditions had ripened sufficiently to accelerate human progress both in the direction of justice and to segment Europe into a diversity of separated peoples. This latter development portended benefits and perils for all.

Nationality as applied to these groupings was until the French Revolution devoid of any ingredient of racial egotism. For this reason if no other, the Jews, by virtue of their segregation, their exclusive traditions, their collective memory and sense of historic grievance, had constituted a nation of sorts, albeit despised and dispersed, among the rest.

Now no longer. The principle of nationality, newly emerging, became invested with concrete attributes, co-ordinated by language and culture and strictly related to soil. As the revolution took hold, and the French faced hostile armies intent upon restoring the *ancien régime*, France crystallised as a *patrie*. Its enemies were composed of equally identifiable entities. Europe moved away from the age-old internationalism that entitled rulers to rearrange frontiers at a whim. But the Jews? They faced the dilemma of where to belong, and whether to belong. Manifestly, they could not be a nation in the new sense for they possessed neither a territorial base nor a pyramid of responsibility leading from the masses to a symbol at the apex. Their culture corresponded to nothing in modernity. They had inherited laws from their ancients to regulate personal behaviour, but for the rest they remained an ethnic cipher, as regards both identification and relationships.

Had they been like the gypsies, few in number, itinerant by choice and as poor, this would not have mattered. But even in Western Europe they were a conspicuous quantity (4,000 in France, for example, and five per cent of Berlin's population), and although most of them shared the humility of the poor, some were rich, very rich. These few earned a reputation as a negative factor on the surface of society because they largely made their money by trading in money – holding kings, landed aristocracy and merchants in their debt. Mayer Amschel Rothschild, born in the *Judengasse*, the Jew Street of Frankfurt, in 1743, stood low down in the scale of affluence as compared to some of his neighbours, but with the Napoleonic Wars his time would come. Wealth was not equally shared among all Jews, only the resentment attaching to it.

Moses Mendelssohn, who died three years before the storming of the Bastille, had by his example as philosopher and honoured man of letters in Berlin inspired a certain reappraisal of the Jews' status throughout Western Europe. His association with other beacons of the Enlightenment, French as well as German, had alerted them to the injustice of the Jews' disabilities, their restriction to residence in prescribed areas, denial of entry into many trades and professions and exclusion from the public service. Frequently, as for example in Frankfurt and Hamburg and throughout Alsace,[1] the law forbade them from marriage without permission. Mendelssohn had aroused the Christian conscience while simultaneously disturbing the leaden stillness

[1] Alsace, with a large part of Lorraine, was a French possession but lay within the German language sphere and acknowledged a quasi-spiritual allegiance to the Holy Roman Empire.

of rabbinical orthodoxy, according to which any kind of change was invariably suspected as a threat.

Mendelssohn alone could not have affected a transformation. The climate of the times was proving propitious for greater tolerance. England continued its restrictions upon the Jews, but as regards its overseas empire they were accorded complete freedom in 1740. More directly, the English colonies in America, having won independence, glowed from across the ocean as a paradigm: religious rules ceased to narrow citizenship down in many of the states within the new confederation. The Age of Reason spread its light, and, as we have seen, Rome was losing a great part of its authority, and its mythology, under the scrutiny of the sceptics. Perhaps the Jews had indeed committed a crime against God, but was it right for man to make the cosmological dimension as revealed by the Resurrection an instrument of daily oppression? Was it not precisely the discrimination they suffered which debased the Jews, fortifying their hostility and driving them into avenues guided solely by self-interest at the expense of others? The medieval mind had relegated them to a species akin to the animal world, but could they not in fact be brought within the family of man? John Toland had so contended decades earlier, and the message was heard at last.

But it owed much to the spirit of Mendelssohn that the message reached the direct attention of an influential public. During his latter years his eminence in Germany made of Mendelssohn the unofficial spokesman for his people throughout Europe. And he proved a more effective champion in that role than the Court Jews, for he addressed the conscience of men, whereas they purchased favours from rulers through bribery. He was besieged with pleas from Jewish communities everywhere to intercede with their governments and secure amelioration of their lot. Among these was a request from their leading figure in Alsace, the army contractor Herz Cerf-Berr, who begged Mendelssohn to produce a memorandum on his community's civil disabilities and its burden of extortionate taxation. Though Cerf-Berr was himself no minor personality – in fact he had received French citizenship by royal dispensation and had waged a successful battle against the city fathers for his right of residence in Strasbourg – it was an astute move to introduce a campaign for Jewish emancipation as a moral issue. Cerf-Berr, who did not give the same thought to neighbouring Lorraine, a more recent French acquisition, would ensure the memorandum's submission to the king's advisers.

Mendelssohn decided this would best come from the pen of a gentile. He enlisted for the task his friend and admirer, Christian Wilhelm von Dohm, a Prussian official and historian, in whose hands the memorandum came to life as a two-volume work receiving wide circulation.[2] This was fully eight years before the Declaration of the Rights of Man was born in Paris.

Writing with German conditions principally in mind, Dohm accepted that the Jews were circumscribed by a religious faith which all righteous men must detest. But to persecute them on that score was unchristian, and furthermore harmful to the state. Grant the Jews equality and they could be seduced from their usurious occupations and play a valuable part as useful, productive citizens. For as individuals they were honest and law-abiding, virtuous in family life and learned in their culture. They should be allowed freedom of residence anywhere in the state and granted admission to the trade guilds. Their taxes should be no more excessive than those levied upon other citizens; they were entitled to enter the liberal professions and perform military service. All schools, and even the universities, should be open to their children.

Dohm hastened to assure his readers that he was not blind to the Jews' deficiencies. He conceded the bigotry of their teachers, who offended the Lord by preaching contempt for Christianity. But intolerance of other faiths was surely a characteristic of dogmatists in every creed. He had no doubt that their concentration in trade gave the Jews a tendency to cunning, though no more so than other folk similarly engaged. They should be required however to make their ledgers and records available for inspection by keeping them in the language of the country of their residence, not in Hebrew or Yiddish as was their custom. Most Ashkenazi Jews could not sign their names in Latin characters.

Cerf-Berr did not agree with all of Dohm's conclusions (neither did Mendelssohn, who particularly condemned his

---

[2] *Über die Bürgerliche Verbesserung der Juden*, Berlin, 1781.

recommendation that the jurisdiction of the rabbinical courts in civil as well as religious matters, with power of excommunication, be retained) but Cerf-Berr nevertheless had the work translated so as to give it the widest circulation in France. It led Mirabeau, shortly to become a powerful influence in the French constitutional debates, to write his own work on the Jews advancing a similar thesis.

Publication of Dohm's report coincided with the Edict of Toleration promulgated by Joseph II in Austria as related in the preceding chapter, and prompted further moves in France for discussion of the Jewish question. Louis XVI took a personal interest in the subject. He entrusted an investigation, which also embraced consideration of the remaining Protestant disabilities, to Charles de Malesherbes, a disciple of Diderot and minister of the royal household. Dutifully, Malesherbes plunged into the subject with a will. He undertook a thorough enquiry, went to the roots of Jewish belief with a study of the people's early history and took the precaution of consulting Cerf-Berr for the Ashkenazim and another Jewish spokesman, Abraham Furtado, for the Sephardim. Sharp differences were known to exist between the two branches of the tribe.

The French Sephardim, almost wholly concentrated in the Bordeaux region of the south-west, and already partially assimilated to French life, had emerged from a long period of Marrano hibernation. As a consequence they were less disciplined in their religious observance. In particular, they resented being joined in unpopularity with the Ashkenazim of Alsace, who were reputed to be the agents of the peasantry's impoverishment. The Bordeaux 'Portuguese' lived by a more acceptable commerce and eschewed such obnoxious practices as money-lending. They made no secret of their contempt for the 'alien' Alsatians and rejected suggestions that they were in any way linked, except in religion. The nuance, so important to them, failed to impress the Christians of France.

Malesherbes's researches, during which he struggled with such questions as Judaic doctrine and the fear expressed by French commercial interests of new competition, assumed the nature of a public enquiry open to any interested citizen. In 1785 the Royal Academy of Arts and Sciences of Metz announced a literary competition on the subject 'How to Make the Jews Happier and More Useful in France'. Nine essays were submitted, only two of which opposed all ideas of emancipation. One of these proposed the transportation of the Jews to the remoteness of Guiana (Devil's Island for Dreyfus a century hence), while the other likewise reminded the academy that the case was forlorn: nothing could be done for a people condemned to exist in perpetuity under sentence of God's punishment.

The most noteworthy contribution, however, and one of three essays to receive special commendation, came from the pen of a minor cleric on his way to advancement as a bishop, Abbé Grégoire. He proposed complete and unqualified emancipation for the Jews. He could not, he wrote, accord the same privilege to the Protestants: their heresies placed them rather than the Jews beyond redemption.

A reformer capable in the late eighteenth century of so mean a distinction between the two religions dissenting from Catholicism must surely have been nurtured on the sermons of Bossuet rather than the literature of Rousseau. Grégoire, to be sure, had difficulty in exonerating the children of Israel from all guilt. On the contrary, he assigned to them every depravity, declaring that it would be easier to regenerate them if they were savages. Their conduct was rigorously ordered by their Talmud, which he described as 'a vast reservoir in which all the frenzies of the human mind are accumulated'. Evidently the lower the abbé pitched his estimation of their current way of life, the greater would be the measure of Christendom's achievement in bringing the Jews up to standard. But his principal argument, and Grégoire would make it with great force on his subsequent election to Louis XVI's Estates General, placed the blame for their deficiencies firmly at the door of Christianity for never accepting the Jews as a normal people. He cited Mendelssohn as indicator of their potentiality for improvement, and looked forward to the day when they would happily and thankfully allow themselves to be received in the bosom of the Church. Coming from one who visualised no salvation for the Protestants, and who could not abide their presence in this most Christian of countries, it promised reward indeed!

Malesherbes was now ready with his own recommendations.

In 1788, despite the misgivings of the likes of Grégoire, he proposed full equality for the French Protestants. By this time King Louis had other issues more pressing than the Jews to engage the attentions of his advisers: in brief, a depleted exchequer, a flagging regime and a rebellious populace. The storm broke. France snatched power from the king and handed it to the people, not without some hesitation requiring the strong voice of the Comte de Mirabeau to silence the protests of the doubters. He was a renegade patrician with a tract on the emancipation of the Jews in his pocket. And so there was inaugurated the France of the Tricolour, aristocratic privileges abolished at a stroke, all oppressions removed and every inhabitant a free citizen. On paper at least.

During the early delirious months of that dawn 'when bliss was it to be alive', with the monarchy isolated and many aristos in flight, the National Assembly swiftly did its duty by Rousseau and got down to its Declaration of the Rights of Man. Then it attacked the prodigious task of repairing the deficiencies of French society, leaving in its wake a mountain of legislation, a great babel of oratory, a maze of factionalism and the shadow of bankruptcy. The Jews might easily have been overlooked had not the peasants of Alsace, guided by the universal fever, violently reminded Paris of their long-borne grievances. They demonstrated against the aliens in their midst, flung the charge of 'usurer' at any and every Jew and, armed with pitchforks and staves, chased hundreds of the tribe out of the villages, through the towns and even across the border to Switzerland.

Only then could Abbé Grégoire concentrate the minds of the legislators on the question with which he was now obsessed. Many deputies had considered the subject already settled in the Declaration of the Rights of Man, wherein it was stated that no one should be molested because of his religious views.

This was hardly the answer to the Jews' situation. They deserved all the freedoms, said Grégoire, in a condition of absolute and unambiguous equality. Now resistance emerged, mainly from the bloc of Alsatian deputies. They refused to recognise their Jewish neighbours as an integral part of the French people. In any case, they claimed, only a small minority of Jews evinced any desire to become citizens.

The charge was not devoid of truth. Many of them feared the erosion of their cherished culture and the disappearance of their internal autonomy. Their own courts dispensing Mosaic law were empowered to judge civil disputes, punish infringements of their separate sabbath and enforce the rules of marriage. Take away this privilege and they trembled for their civilisation's survival. The deputy Comte de Clermont-Tonnerre perceived how the old concept of a nation now conflicted with the new spirit of nationality. It was indeed the cardinal issue. In a ringing formula that has guided Jewish attitudes in France ever since, he declared: 'To the Jews as individuals we offer everything; to the Jews as a nation nothing!'

It was touch and go, bringing an intervention by Robespierre with an eloquent restatement of the Jewish case: 'You have heard tales about the Jews which are either gross exaggerations or the reverse of the historical truth. Jewish vices are rooted in the lowly status to which you have reduced them ... We must atone for our own misdeeds by restoring their inalienable human rights, of which no human power may deprive them.'

In the end the assembly refused to commit itself. It decided to postpone the issue – the debate took place on Christmas Eve 1789, the session marked by cancellation of all remaining Protestant disabilities. The following month, however, the 'Portuguese' of Bordeaux, who had been secretly pressing their specific claim, stole a march on their 'German' co-religionists of north-eastern France. Arguing for the Sephardim alone, they showed how successive kings had virtually granted them equality by letters patent. Their situation merely awaited formalisation by the revolutionary regime. And so, almost imperceptibly, some ten per cent of the Jews of France, clutching for certificate of purity their notional descent from Babylonian exiles of the Iron Age, gained admission to the halls of freedom. One of them became mayor of a small town near Bordeaux.

Now the others, the Ashkenazim, humiliated at so flagrant a discrimination, channelled their dismay into renewed agitation. Led in the main by Cerf-Berr, they encountered opposition at every turn. Abbé Grégoire and other of their supporters were suspected of being in their pay – perhaps were secret Jews! It took an uphill struggle of almost two dramatic years – years which saw the flight abroad of the king and queen frustrated by the vigilance of the local postmaster at Varennes – before the royal seal was affixed to the law granting them unqualified citizenship. The signal flashed across Europe. France was at it again, blowing its nose so that all Europe had to catch a cold.

The Revolution was however imperilled by a hostile coalition in the making, organised by an Austrian emperor fearful for the safety of his Bourbon kin. France, ruled by the most extreme of the Jacobins, now assumed the nature of a religion for itself, its cult the worship of Reason, its communion the Reign of Terror, its God a demystified Supreme Being. Churches and synagogues became the property of the state, which meant they were available for conversion into warehouses.

With the reformation of the calendar (the inauguration of the Republic in 1792 and execution of the king early in 1793 being bracketed as Year One), a ten-day week was instituted. The sabbath, be it on Saturday or Sunday, fell awkwardly at variable points, and Jews who wished to honour theirs in the traditional form did so secretly, for discovery was rewarded with imprisonment. It was a brave father indeed who took his newly born son to an illicit circumcision. But many French Jews demonstrated powers of adaptation hitherto untried, and eagerly accommodated to the new order. They endorsed the Revolution wholeheartedly by applying for military service, joining rival political factions and defiantly taking non-Jewish wives. There were no Jews now, they proclaimed, and no Christians. They spoke too soon.

What, then, prevented Judaism from complete dissolution in this delirium of liberty, equality, fraternity? Mostly, the sudden exhaustion of revolutionary passion throughout the country. The battles forced upon the French by the European coalition turned swiftly from a desperate, costly struggle to protect the endangered *patrie* into a war of aggrandisement waged on foreign soil. Handsome acquisitions of territory were brought under the control of Paris. The Reign of Terror died in the Thermidorian reaction, Robespierre himself, 'the incorruptible', following Danton, 'the great patriot', to the guillotine. True, much change had been telescoped into the five years since the fall of the Bastille, but five years are but a moment in the evolution of society, shorter still in a Jewish society. To the resentment particularly of the citizenry of Alsace and Lorraine, the Jews appeared to hang back from the total disbandment of their community. Their rich remained rich, their poor peddled their wares as before. Each congregation managed to retain hold over its own affairs, as indeed did the Church over its flocks, landlords over their possessions and generals over their troops. Whatever else Judaism proved to be, at its core there burned a fierce emotion, rendering the law impotent against it.

Defectors abandoned the faith amidst the turmoil, perhaps in their thousands, but the slide towards a collective hara-kiri halted. France looked upon its Jews and found they were much as they had always been: free citizens, to be sure, but clinging to their old exclusiveness, deferential towards their religious symbols, addicted to their traditional commercial habits. The country as a whole lapsed into its basic, obstinate pattern: weak at the centre and unruly in the provinces. It retained all it had won abroad and remade these regions into images of itself—liberty for all, equality if possible, fraternity in theory. The Jews had no cause for complaint there, for wherever France triumphed the ghettos became a shame of the past. Added to this, a fresh awareness swept across the continent, affecting individuals and nations alike. Prussia dislodged Austria from hegemony in their part of Europe, but Germany as a whole stayed faithful to its own history as an arena where achievement never quite caught up with promise.

In exporting its political and philosophical adventurism France had done well, brushing cobwebs from every last nook and cranny of medievalism. Yet the volatile population at home craved for a strong hand, and after a confusing succession of constitutional experiments the country found a master. Napoleon Bonaparte had carried all before him as a soldier. In 1799 he conquered Egypt and almost frightened the Turks out of Syria. He then returned home to clean up the streets and rule an empire. In the words of Citizen Sieyès, that proverbial survivor, 'il sait tout, il peut tout, il veut tout'.

Bonaparte's expedition to the Near East had started tremors of apocalyptic excitement among the Jews of Egypt and Palestine when he appeared in their neighbourhood in 1798. His ambitions had led him into a campaign whose objectives were by no means clear. Certainly a back door could be opened through Turkey to threaten Russia, but the venture was far more likely undertaken as a cover for his reluctance to gamble on a frontal attack against the English across the Channel. He would instead cripple their economy by severing their commercial sinews and lines of communication to their wealth in India. So talk of an early appearance of the Messiah was idle. In no fashion did Bonaparte reciprocate the interest in him demonstrated by the Jews of the Orient – and nowhere else, except perhaps in Italy, where they lauded Bonaparte as a protector; among other benefits, he had released them from the spies of the papal Inquisition.

It suited the nature of Jewish thought in the Orient, primitive by any standards and wholly in keeping with the mystical propensities never remote from this cultural backwater, to apply omens to the arrival of the legendary captain, now the most powerful man in Europe. He could be the instrument of the Providential intervention they anticipated to restore their national grandeur in Jerusalem. Such stuff had no basis in the Corsican's plans. He virtually ignored the Jews. They constituted a negligible, pathetic quantity in Egypt, and still more so in Palestine.[3]

Bonaparte handsomely defeated the Mamluk Turks outside Cairo, only to lose his supply base in the destruction of his fleet at the hands of Admiral Nelson in Aboukir Bay. He now needed more time, and therefore had no alternative but to advance northward. A crusade perhaps, to complete that unfinished Christian business of the Middle Ages? More disappointment. After a half-hearted attempt to reduce the fortress of Acre he decided to cut his losses and extricate himself, without so much as a backward glance at the Turkish forces ranged to resist him outside Jerusalem, or the multi-religious population within.

At home, Bonaparte was brought up with a start against his

[3] Mystery shrouds the appearance of an item in the *Moniteur Universel* of Paris, dated 3 prairial of Year VII (22 May 1799), referring to a proclamation by Bonaparte inviting 'all the Jews of Asia and Africa' to rally to his banner for the re-establishment of Jerusalem. The proclamation has never been traced, and was most probably fathered in the imagination of a proto-Zionist Christian dreamer. See Simon Schwartzfuchs, *Napoleon, the Jews and the Sanhedrin*, London, 1979, pp. 24–5.

country's festering social and economic problems. Ominously for the Jews, he restored to the Catholic Church a large measure of its old authority through his dramatic concordat with the pope, and thus reintroduced the religious education which never forbore to mark the Jews with the stigma of their historic infamy. Then there was the hardship inflicted upon the masses by the steep inflation accompanying the circulation of paper money. Land, that sacred commodity, was heavily mortgaged, to pay off the debts of lean years. The peasants suffered everywhere throughout the country, but the loudest complaints arrived from Alsace.

Many Jewish army contractors were in fact domiciled in that province. Their wealth was as conspicuous as the peasants' poverty. Jewish money-lenders trooped regularly to the Strasbourg courts in efforts to recover their unpaid loans. By the summer of 1806, following the triumphs that translated the First Consul into Emperor, over 3 million francs were owed to Alsatian Jews. This calculation was made at a time when the aggregated land tax for the entire region totalled less than two million francs annually. François Kellerman, the rough-talking Alsatian general, sent a bitter report to Napoleon, who had visited Strasbourg the previous January. The Jews, Kellerman said, had more or less taken the province completely in their grasp. They should be compelled to forsake their iniquitous money-lending and adopt productive trades; otherwise he recommends their expulsion.[4]

Napoleon concluded that the Jewish question was no nearer solution than it had been before the decree granting this people equality in 1791. Clearly, the Talmudic laws they honoured took precedence over the laws of France. They indeed remained a nation within a nation. But why? What was it about the ways of Christendom that turned a Jew inward, preventing his assimilation, or at least his adaptation? On their part they vociferously denied the allegations made against them as a whole and asserted that they were being accorded no opportunity to defend themselves. They admitted to the existence of a few black sheep, but angrily rejected the general charges against them as a people.

[4] Schwartzfuchs, *Napoleon*, p. 30, citing official documents in *Archives nationales*. The subject is also dealt with authoritatively in Robert Anchel, *Napoléon et les Juifs*, Paris, 1928.

Christian freedom of worship and assembly had been restored in the case of both Protestants and Catholics. Muslims suffered no hindrance in their mosques. Yet the Jews still awaited official recognition for their cult, and their rabbis could not minister to their congregations in open synagogues without restraint.

The emperor lost his patience. He raised the subject of the Jews with his Council of State, heard out his advisers and then abruptly cut discussion short with his directives. France should verify from the Jews themselves, by their own submissions, where they stood. He ordered the convening of an assembly of Jewish representatives in Paris which would produce specific answers to the questions troubling the country and offer suggestions as to the regulation of Jewish life. In the meantime, and for one year, all contracts relating to Jewish loans would be suspended.

Now that Napoleon offered the Jews what they demanded, an opportunity to rebut the accusations heaped upon them from every side, they felt apprehensive as to the outcome. It was putting Jewry as it were on trial, and could be a trap, to expose their weakness before the nation. They were convening by edict, not of their own volition. They were not to elect their own delegates, who would be nominated according to substance and authority by the departmental prefects. The Ashkenazim wondered how they would fare in harness with the more sophisticated Sephardim. Jews they all were, but by what common denominator? They had no vernacular speech common to them all, while their religious convictions ranged from the strictly ritualist to the downright agnostic. Without an excess of enthusiasm therefore, though with fulsome declarations of loyalty and gratitude to the emperor, eighty-six nominees gathered in Paris in July 1806 and established themselves as an Assembly of Notables in a discreet building behind the Hôtel de Ville. Fifteen were rabbis, one of them, David Sinzheim of Strasbourg, being the brother-in-law of Cerf-Berr, now dead. In fact several members of Cerf-Berr's family had been nominated to the assembly, including three of his sons. Four delegates arrived tardily from conquered Italy.

A government commission of three, led by a man who had lately drafted a memorandum inimical to the Jews, was appointed to oversee the notables' deliberations. Recognising the delicacy of their situation, they managed to steer a path between excessive subservience to this commission's authority and unseemly controversy among themselves. The first session was commanded for a Saturday, and some delegates were stung by the sight of their colleagues arriving by coach, and not as behoved the sabbath, on foot. They nominated Abraham Furtado of Bordeaux, more a disciple of Voltaire than a student of Talmud, as chairman, and settled down to work.

No problem concerning the agenda, for there it was, prepared from above, in the form of twelve questions to which they were enjoined to give unanimous, unequivocal answers. Perhaps the government commissioners anticipated that some or all the questions would confuse the Jews into revealing their ambivalence as Frenchmen. If so, the commissioners were disappointed. Even the rabbis, they found, Sinzheim particularly, acquitted themselves as men of the world, determined to safeguard their religious heritage but nevertheless prepared to acknowledge that the passage of time necessitated interpretations consonant with modernity. Furtado would have willingly discarded Mosaic law in its entirety, but he held back in deference to the majority.

Some questions gave little trouble and no cause for painful debate. Was polygamy permitted in Jewish law? In the Orient it still existed, they replied, but it had been abolished by a synod of European rabbis in the eleventh century. Regarding divorce, was it valid even if not pronounced in a French court of justice? This could well ensnare them in undesirable dialectics, since Jewish law entitled a husband to divorce his wife, though not the reverse. They eschewed the problem after lengthy argument without stating a position on civil divorces unsupported by religious sanction. Intermarriage with a Christian, was that permissible? A fierce debate ensued; many notables, sensible of the grievance regularly laid against the Jews on this score, were prepared to cross the Deuteronomic divide and affirm that conditions had so altered as to render mixed marriages acceptable. The rabbis however held their ground: they deemed the practice an abomination. Formulation of a reply involved reconciliation of the opposing views through a subcommittee. By a compromise, they responded that Jewish law neither prohibited nor encouraged such alliances. The law forbade marriage only with idolators, which Christians manifestly were not. However, a mixed marriage could not receive rabbinical authority (nor, Napoleon's commissioners were reminded with a tart *tu quoque*, the blessing of the Catholic Church). It would remain a civil marriage only.

So far so good, but the questionnaire engaged them in other matters not so readily disposable. Were Frenchmen, in the eyes of the Jews, considered to be brethren or foreigners? What did the law prescribe in relations with the French people? Did those Jews who were born in France acknowledge loyalty to this country, obey its laws, defend it to death? Yes, yes, Jews loved all Frenchmen as brothers, but such fraternity had to be mutual. No differentiation existed in relations between gentiles and Jews, for they considered themselves French absolutely, prepared to fight the enemies of France even if Jewish. To the commissioners, this enthusiasm lacked the ring of sincerity and failed to give an unequivocal assurance that the Jews were not a separate nation. The commissioners subsequently expressed their dissatisfaction on this score in their report to the Minister of the Interior.

Several days of discussion had now elapsed, but the thorniest questions were still to come. The notables experienced difficulty in explaining the status and functions of the rabbis, how they were appointed, the legal validity of their judgements. As it happened, the rabbinate was organised differently in all parts of the world, and markedly so in Ashkenazi as contrasted with Sephardi custom. But all this the commissioners found reasonable. What concerned them most, and Napoleon too, was the matter of usury. Did the law forbid the Jews to take usury from their co-religionists? And what of usurious loans to gentiles?

It was the nub of the enquiry, as the assembly fully realised. They began their explanation by pointing out how the Talmud demanded of a father the teaching of a trade to his son as a foremost obligation. But they kept silent on the complications entailed for such a worker in a Christian society: the dietary laws, for example, and the sanctity of the sabbath. As to usury, they declared that loans carrying even the lowest interest were expressly forbidden in the case of one Jew to another, for loans to meet a pressing need involved an act of friendship, and brotherhood. A loan for business purposes, even to a fellow-Jew, fell into another category, since it embraced the element of risk. Here no discrimination between Jew and Christian should arise. Such loans could bear interest, at a moderate rate.

Mosaic law, the notables emphasised, had been conveyed to the Jews prior to their dispersal among the nations, which was an eventuality which Moses had not foreseen and thus did not cover in his legislation regarding loans to foreigners. Admittedly, some Jews made this a pretext for usurious practice, but they were few, so why should the rest be calumniated as a consequence?

The commissioners understood that this was skating round the problem. It was no explanation for the enrichment of numerous Jews to the point of national scandal. In fact, in considering the reply, Minister of the Interior Jean Champagny sensed here a means of making usury punishable in civil law. He went further, suggesting to the emperor measures by which all the characteristics which kept the Jews a separate nation of sorts could be induced to disappear: a law against usury properly defined, the rabbis to be confirmed in office by the state and become part of the civil structure with government salaries, the swearing of an act of loyalty as a condition of French citizenship, compulsory attendance at the public schools – once the haphazard education system was put in order – and if possible the forcing into apprenticeship of Jewish boys. Finally, an edict should abolish the appellation *Juif*, because of its unsavoury connotations. Frenchmen of that faith should henceforth dignify themselves as *hébreu*.[5] The religion itself could stay, having been rendered innocuous.

Taken as a whole, the Assembly of Notables found with no little relief that it had in large measure satisfied the government as to the Jews' patriotism. Except in its minutiae their way of life was not so different, they had established, as to disqualify them from the title of Frenchmen. Their religion did not absolve them from fulfilling their obligations for military service, and some had already won awards for valour on the fields of battle. The usurers among them undoubtedly reflected badly on the rest, but they did not exceed two hundred in a community of some 40,000, and could be adequately dealt with by the civil courts. Christian

---

[5] The word has no feminine form, and was substituted by *israélite*.

usurers, particularly in Lorraine, laid an equally pernicious weight upon the peasantry yet they did not stain the reputation of Christendom as a whole. As to other deficiencies of the Jews, real or imagined, these were rooted in their history of persecution, forcing them into antisocial occupations. All this would now cease, promised the notables, with the reforms to be instituted under the benevolent guidance of their wise emperor.

The Napoleonic imagination had not been idle during the sessions of the notables. Their discussions had frequently referred to the great Sanhedrin of ancient times as the last authority the Jews could cite in interpretation of the laws of Moses. Talmudic sources described the structure and enactments of this Sanhedrin. Since France was now renovating society for all men the Jews would wish to be included, in every sense. But their religious rules, made in the days of Rome's imperial glory, refused to cohere with the general rules of society. Napoleon would therefore revive the Sanhedrin in his own, hardly inferior, modern empire, inviting Jewish dignitaries to Paris from all Europe; the sages would then give his new regulations a like authority.

A fantasy perhaps, yet Napoleon could make it a reality. Such a Sanhedrin, embracing seventy-one elders attired in ceremonial uniform and puffed with decorum, convened in February 1807. A medal was struck to honour the occasion. The majority of seats, two-thirds, were accorded to the rabbis, Sinzheim presiding. Despite the call to all Europe, representatives arrived only from Amsterdam and Frankfurt in addition to Italy.

Furtado was allocated the role of driving force. He embodied the Gallic concept of ideal Jew, so who better to act as rapporteur and liaison with government figures? Yet he must have experienced misgivings: that formidable array of rabbis, mainly Ashkenazi of course, was a prospect he did not relish. Moreover, surely the very concept of a Sanhedrin would frighten the Jews' enemies, confirming all their superstitions about this people? Already Napoleon, having defeated Russia and Austria combined at Austerlitz, and subdued Prussia at Jena, was spoken of as the Antichrist preparing the final struggle between good and evil for domination of the globe: the alleged Jewish conspiracy, in fact.

Indeed, the Holy Synod in St Petersburg instructed the priesthood to publicise Napoleon's Sanhedrin in terms of the direst foreboding. Recalling his foray into Palestine, the synod circulated rumours of the French emperor's intention to declare himself the Jews' Messiah. He was about to defy the anger of God and restore the rabbis to that infamous tribunal which had dared to commit the Saviour to the Cross.[6] Terrified, the Jews of Russia, grovelling under the whiplash of tsarist oppression, hastened to assure their own government of their utter contentment; they wanted no truck with such emancipation as France offered.

In Paris, the Sanhedrin, during eight uneventful sessions, endorsed the conclusions of the Assembly of Notables practically without demur, thus conferring upon it the authority of a court of religious law. It was then summarily dissolved by order of the emperor. Napoleon decreed that the Assembly of Notables itself should continue in existence, however, and he charged it with reconstituting French Jewry into one central and seven regional consistories, similar to the system in operation for Protestantism. In this way official surveillance over the Jews would be maintained, with their internal affairs under the supreme jurisdiction of a single nation-wide body carrying responsibility for implementation of all regulations pertaining to the Jews, throughout the country and wherever French dominion prevailed. And those who had not already adopted surnames were to do so forthwith, abandoning the confusing biblical style of identification by patronymic (Isaac the son of Abraham, etc.).

That capacious intellect, the Napoleonic mind, was in 1807 preoccupied with the rearrangement of Europe entire, contemplating an invasion of Portugal and bent upon a treaty of mutual interest with Russia. His campaigns took him far from Paris, yet he continued to concern himself with his Jewish subjects back home. He announced a series of measures that could have the effect only of accentuating rather than diminishing their feeling of discrimination. These measures, provisionally for ten years, included the continued suspension, with certain exceptions, of the debts owing to Jews. They were forbidden to move domicile except for the purpose of engaging in agriculture. Should they

6 Dubnov, History of the Jews, Vol. IV, pp. 728–9.

wish to enter commerce they had first to obtain a certificate of good conduct from the consistory, together with a city council licence attesting that the business contemplated had no connection with usury. Jews must provide recruits for military service in accordance with their numerical proportion in the general population, and should one of them have good reason to supply a substitute, a privilege granted to all Frenchmen, he had to be a co-religionist.

So they were not after all to be regarded as Frenchmen in every sense, but to be shackled with restrictions imposed purely because they were Jews, and placed on a probationary period, as it were, of ten years' good behaviour! They felt they had been duped. Wasn't the practice of usury already being contained by the general laws of the land, which also regulated military conscription and trade? Why should Christian clerics receive their salaries out of general taxation, which applied to all, but not the rabbis? It shocked the Jews to discover that despite all that had gone before, and the emperor's protestations of goodwill, they were to be administered by a body of law not applicable to the rest of the population. Furtado was particularly incensed, to the point of undertaking a journey to Tilsit, where the emperor was encamped in readiness for his forthcoming meeting with Tsar Alexander and the pledge of peaceful coexistence for all eternity between Russia and France.

In all likelihood Furtado failed to achieve an interview, for no record of one has survived.[7] But the intention and the journey itself to military headquarters on the eastern extremity of Poland speak eloquently of a new confidence among the Jews of France. And although the new regulations were not extraordinarily onerous, merely a blow to *amour propre*, France being a bureaucrat's paradise, they loudly protested. In the event, the Bourbons who followed the dissolution of the empire in 1815 buried the Napoleonic decrees while leaving the consistorial system intact. The state paid the rabbis' salaries from 1831.

Truly, a new era had dawned with the birth of the nineteenth century. It was impossible for Jews anywhere in Europe not to be affected by the principles of individual liberty established

7 Schwartzfuchs, *Napoleon*, p. 120.

through the French Revolution, even to the point of creating ripples within the measureless expanse of feudal Russia itself. Reaction would set in, religion would again be enlisted by despotic rulers to smother dissent, intolerance would continue to bar the Jews (as in some countries Catholics, in others Protestants) from certain professions. But what France had begun no one had the power to halt.

If some aspects of the Jews' disabilities required government edict before they could be removed, there existed also disabilities in the realm of the spirit, over which every man could be his own master. Rabbinical authority, certainly a positive force in keeping Judaism alive, induced upon the Jewish mind a sort of paralysis. Mendelssohn had, by his own exertions, broken out of his cultural ghetto into the free world of the intellect and, as we have seen, created a storm in Jewish society. Berlin inspired the Jews as Paris inspired the world. Berlin set the pace for Prussia, which one day would grow into Germany. By a striking time-warp, in that city of Berlin history skipped an epoch for the Jews. A woman there could already be her own mistress.

The course of Germanisation charted by Mendelssohn among the Jews of Central Europe increased in momentum with every new turn in the French Revolution. This was only logical and inevitable, for, since the era of the Sun King, Germany had led Europe in studied imitation of French brilliance. France had, in the Age of Reason, taken the spirit of the times captive. Out of this climate arose the political-cultural salons of Berlin (and Vienna), where to speak the language and read the books issuing from Paris became slavishly *de rigueur*. These salons were most usually presided over by Jewish women of a particular breed. They were generally self-educated, it being rare for them to receive formal schooling, and their lives imitated art in the adjustment of their Jewish personalities to the claims of a broader, more enticing civilisation.

Willingly, these women rejected their past, sometimes with a ferocity that could only be equated with the Jewish self-hatred practised by the converts who have chastised their fellow-Jews throughout the ages. The ambience generated by their accomplishments and liberated conduct entranced the intelligentsia of every hue – poets of the German Romantic school, politicians and their literary hacks, foreign diplomats, even a prince, the brilliantly endowed Louis Ferdinand. When French arms made short shrift of the old European alliances, to wreak humiliating defeats upon Prussia and Austria, these Jewesses, like Aspasia of old, gathered around themselves the strands of the German cultural resurrection. They numbered Jews, Catholics and Protestants among their friends without discrimination, even though some (Jews included) spoke and wrote in tones often employed by modern antisemitism. This was no impediment in the salon society established by the Jewesses of Berlin. Their leading spirit for a time, Rahel Levin, imposed only one qualification for entry into her celebrated attic in the Jägerstrasse: unquestioned reverence for the works of Goethe. In the early years of her prominence he still awaited national recognition.

She was the daughter of a Berlin jeweller, and for the major part of her life railed against the misfortune of her Jewish birth. Thinking about it made Rahel ill. She could escape from herself only in the patriotic fervour with which she promoted those works of German literature she deemed humanist and universal, and this signified her rejection of certain writers of the Romantic school, whose subjective nationalism and predilection for Charlemagne and the Middle Ages she could not abide. Born in 1771, her first words were in Yiddish, her earliest writing in Hebrew script. Rahel's destiny seemed prescribed: a conventional marriage dedicated to the rearing of children, a secluded existence decreed by the subservience of Jewish women to the demands of their menfolk. From this fate Rahel was redeemed by her originality. Without a husband until the age of forty-three (not for want of trying – three heart-rending affairs with Christian lovers before rescue by a junior diplomat and minor littérateur thirteen years younger than herself), she fought her way to great influence by her friendships. Among Jews Rahel ranks with Mendelssohn, among women with the formidable Madame de Staël, among Germans with the brothers Schlegel. She wrote no books; all she had to say appears in her letters and diaries, or in conversations recorded in the works of others.

Prussian Jews pointed to the French example and were clamouring for citizenship. They received it in 1812, with the reforms Prince von Hardenberg could at last introduce to shake the remaining vestiges of feudalism out of the state structure. Even then Jews could not enter government service, not professing Jews at any rate, despite the protests of the ex-soldiers among them. The struggle for emancipation did not interest Rahel. In a role that fell into no established category she fulfilled herself in guiding the careers of others and rejoicing in their achievements. Georg Brandes, the Danish critic, described her as 'the first great and modern woman in German culture'.[8] Rahel Levin finally exorcised her Jewish demon when she baptised on marriage, to become Frau Legationsrätin Varnhagen von Ense.

Wars accord dazzling opportunities to a privileged few just as they distribute tragedy among the many. While the Napoleonic era left the majority of European Jews in their traditional condition of social ostracism and economic hardship, so that they died in oblivion faithful to Judaism to the end, the recurring clashes of arms multiplied the fortunes of a group of bankers with Mayer Amschel Rothschild of Frankfurt-on-Main at their head. He flourished in his way while Rahel gained celebrity in hers.

Rothschild had the foresight to station one of his sons, Nathan, in England, the power which financed resistance against the French. From the rise of Napoleon until his defeat in 1815 the number of private banks in London swelled from 230 to 940, all booming through the expansion of industry for war purposes and the payment of subsidies to governments overseas. Few of these were Jewish, but Nathan had the major part of the business in his hands. Rothschild credits left London by various secret routes bound for Frankfurt and Vienna and St Petersburg, to end up as gold in Rothschild strongrooms. It was in the manner of the operations of the 'Court Jews' during the Thirty Years War. Goethe knew the ghetto of Frankfurt from his younger days in that city, and he spoke of old Mayer Amschel, who died in 1812, as 'omnipotent'. Only slightly less affluent was Heinrich Heine's uncle Salomon in Hamburg, whose money stretched back to ancestors related to Glückel of Hameln; for all his astuteness he could never understand his capricious nephew's addiction to poetry.

Goethe spoke of Rahel's personality and intellect with undi-

[8] In *Young Germany*, Vol. VI of *Main Currents of Nineteenth Century German Literature*, London, 1896.

luted admiration, but he could find little to commend in the Jews when he wrote in *Wilhelm Meister's Wanderjahre* that 'the Israelitish people never was good for much, as its own leaders, judges, rulers, prophets have a thousand times reproachfully declared. It possesses few virtues, and most of the faults of other nations. But in cohesion, steadfastness, valour, and when all this would not serve, in obstinate toughness, it has no match.'[9] The followers of Judaism must now be classed as heathens, disqualified therefore from entry into Goethe's ideal society.

It was the Olympian view, hardly corresponding to German realities. The Berlin to which Mendelssohn had arrived in boyhood as an alien in 1743 had by the turn of the century become the fulcrum of a German-Jewish symbiosis that could find its parallel only in that golden Jewish age during the Moorish ascendancy in Spain. Wealth played its part, as always, to force an entry into general society. But Rahel was not so fortunately endowed. She lived austerely, as did some other Jewesses rivalling her in fame. Henriette Herz achieved the status almost of goddess among writers of the Romantic school. She was their 'tragic Muse'. Henriette had a notorious relationship, long a topic of ribald though unjustified gossip, with the Protestant preacher and mystic Friedrich Schleiermacher, in whom respect for Jewish virtues competed with contempt for Jewish theology. Henriette's husband, the physician Marcus Herz, led his wife through the intricacies of Kantian philosophy. She sat at his 'tutorials' on the subject, among other students who included members of the Prussian royal house.

Henriette Herz received Mirabeau in her salon, which was attracting the intelligentsia while Rahel was still in her teens. The awakening of the French statesman's interest in Jewish emancipation stands to the credit of both Henriette and Mendelssohn. On her husband's death she supported her family by teaching languages, Wilhelm von Humboldt being her pupil in the elements of Hebrew grammar. To the good fortune of the Jews, politics sent Humboldt into the Prussian Ministry of Religions, so Prince Hardenberg found a willing collaborator to oversee his decrees abolishing the anti-Jewish laws.

[9] Carlyle's translation, 1904 edition, Ch. XI, p. 225.

Once the Jewish élite secured its place beside the German intellectual élite, there could be no arresting the flight to full assimilation. Jews in the past had gone to the stake or committed suicide rather than accept the Cross; now changing their religion involved no more anguish than changing their underwear. Henriette Herz cast her spell over Friedrich Schlegel, who with his brother August Wilhelm gave the German Romantic movement its philosophical base. Together Henriette and Friedrich hatched out a *Tugenbund*, or League of Virtue, in her salon, promising sex equality and vengeance against the French conqueror in the same breath. Friedrich took as his mistress Henriette's friend Dorothea, eldest daughter of Moses Mendelssohn. It was a passionate affair, related to the last intimate detail by Schlegel in his novel *Lucinda*. Beginning as the conformist Jewish wife of yet another banker, Dorothea embraced Protestantism, then deserted her husband and quickly moved over with Schlegel to the Church of Rome. Thereupon their joint careers distorted freedom into a caricature: she anti-Jewish, anti-Protestant, ultra-conservative and absent-minded, he a self-indulgent, epicurean civil servant in the suspicious Austria of that arch-reactionary Chancellor Metternich.

In due course it became rare among such Jewesses, and their menfolk, not to convert. Henriette Herz took the step on her mother's death, while most of the progeny of Moses Mendelssohn capitulated. His composer grandson Felix, baptised shortly after his birth in 1809, began as a youth to entrance the nobility, including Goethe at Weimar, with his piano pieces, creating his *Midsummer Night's Dream* at the age of eighteen. Jewishness expired except in traces of sentimentality in the family begotten by Judaism's great reformer. All within a generation. The rabbis no doubt gloated as they sighed. It was as they had warned.

This acculturation, and the religious abdication it could not resist, had no parallel in Eastern Europe. That abundant reservoir of Jewry held firm; from its seepage westward the people recharged their religious capacities and so survived. Of course there could be no turning the clock back, neither in France nor in Germany; nor in Austria, despite the authoritarian reaction, with the so-called Holy Alliance struggling to suppress the libertarian mood. Humiliating restrictions upon their right to enter the professions continued against the Jews in German-speaking Europe, affronting any true definition of equality. But relaxation was on the way. The conservative statesmen at the Congress of Vienna, some with Jewish wives or mistresses, celebrated the defeat of Napoleon at the lavish balls given by Fanny von Arnstein, whose father had been head of the Jewish community of Berlin. A select band of Jewish financiers took up station in Vienna, collecting on their promissory notes, arranging flotations for the post-war recovery and pressing the cause of Jewish citizenship in countries where it was still withheld. Fanny's banker relatives, along with various Rothschilds, haunted the *couloirs* – a reminder to the assembly that money could perform where conviction failed.

Fanny von Arnstein entertained Rahel and the Schlegels and Wilhelm von Humboldt along with Talleyrand and Hardenberg, not to mention the Duke of Wellington and Tsar Alexander himself. Men were besotted with Fanny. Prince Karl von Lichtenstein fought a duel for her, and was killed. No study of antisemitism can fail to comment on the artistic irony of the situation: the Jewess Fanny von Arnstein as the damsel for whose favours knights were prepared to die evokes the lurid fiction of *Ivanhoe*.

Vienna boded well to consummate Western Jewry's impregnation of privileged society at its apogee. Metternich had all five Rothschild brothers elevated to the European nobility (a dignity somewhat devalued by that time) in recognition of their crucial function as doctor to many ailing exchequers. But to judge by the portents, the relationship between Judaism and Christianity rested on the same fragile base as before. These early nineteenth-century Jews convinced themselves of their complete emergence into the sunlight. In fact they were precariously balanced between the forces of attraction and rejection: not sunlight, rather a chiaroscuro. In Vienna journalists and political hangers-on whispered against the Jews while feeding upon their generosity. One of these, Friedrich von Gentz, a particular favourite of Rahel's and her close friend of twenty years, prepared Metternich's briefs demanding a truly Christian Europe. He wrote in a private letter: 'All the misfortunes of the modern world, when traced to their furthest roots, come manifestly from the Jews.

They alone made Bonaparte emperor.' This did not preclude him from simultaneously drawing a Rothschild salary for flattering the family in the press.[10]

Jewish participation in the German cultural rebirth aroused consternation among *echt* German patriots, those like Johann Fichte, who, in his *Addresses to the German Nation*, emphasised purity as the basis of their nationalism. The Jews, said this rector of the newly established Berlin University, bound themselves to a duality of standard, because of the primitive conception of their relationship to God; it would be best for mankind if they were sent back to Palestine. Napoleon had all but conquered the Holy Land (at the behest of the Jews no doubt) and he had revived the Sanhedrin. Fichte, with his brother-in-spirit Ernst Moritz Arndt, could not divorce Jewish emancipation from the revolution which had started the landslide in Europe and engaged in excesses within France to bequeath untold misery everywhere. Wars yet to be fought between Germany and France were to keep the recollection alive well into the twentieth century. Arndt, the poet-philosopher, would have Heinrich Heine among his students when he delivered his lectures at Bonn on the *Germania* of Tacitus. Perhaps this was the seed of Heine's love-hatred for the country of his birth.

If Jewish converts to Christianity who wrote poetry, fought wars and gave their children in marriage to unblemished Protestant and Catholic spouses could not be considered fully as Europeans, which Jews could? Certainly not those in the East still attired in their traditional caftans, lisping their vulgar dialect, absorbed in their incoherent literature. We have arrived at that fateful development where the racial factor entered into questions surrounding the position of the Jews. They might attend church or frequent the synagogue, eat pork or regulate their lives by the Talmud, control great banking houses or scratch a living with packs on their backs: they did not, any of them, qualify as equals before God. For they carried in their veins another, genetically inferior strain.

Paradoxically, the closer they came to full identification with

[10] On Gentz, see *inter alia*, Friedrich Heer, *God's First Love*, London, 1970, pp. 180–2; Adolf Kober, 'The French Revolution and the Jews of Germany', *Jewish Social Studies*, October 1945.

European culture the more they encountered a neurotic hatred. Advocates of judgement by racial categorisation arose in Germany and Central Europe while the Napoleonic Wars still raged, to swamp the bookshops with their pseudo-scientific effusions. Perhaps Voltaire was the father of them all: early in his career he contended that Europeans 'seem to me superior to Negroes as Negroes are to monkeys and monkeys to oysters'.[11] Painful to relate, such ideas, ostensibly so out of key with nineteenth-century rationalism, persisted in a hydra of relentless expositors.

The Jews were accustomed to charges against their business methods, their insularity and arrogance. Given the opportunity to do so, they changed their occupation and their ways. But once their critics decided they sprang from an inferior breed of Asiatics they were condemned from birth; or rather, before birth – to their antecedence reaching back to whatever moment might be selected as the beginning of time.

We take the case of Karl Wilhelm Grattenauer. His pamphlet *Wider die Juden* ('Against the Jews') made its appearance in Berlin in 1803, to sell 13,000 copies within the year. Grattenauer, a friend of Gentz and the Romantic poets regularly patronising the Jewish salons, asserted that the descendants of Israel, as an alien transplant from the Orient, possessed characteristics intrinsic to their physiology so pernicious that they could not be harboured within the boundaries of Europe. It was the 'leper theory' of the Graeco-Egyptian historian Manetho eagerly appropriated by latter-day anthropologists to support their 'Aryanism'. Grattenauer wanted a bust of Voltaire to replace the one in Berlin commemorating Mendelssohn. He revived the ancient myth of a specific odour, the *faetor judaicus*. He it was who raised anew that old spectre of a Jewish conspiracy of world domination that was soon to find its spurious evidence in Napoleon's invention of a modern Sanhedrin. One of his imitators produced a solution to the problem that was nothing if not radical: castration of all male Jewish children at birth, though out of some obscure mercy he excepted the first-born.

The Jews of Prussia observed this rash of pamphleteering, which prompted some colourful counter-volleys from indignant

---

11 Poliakov, *History of Antisemitism*, Vol. III, p. 129, quoting Voltaire's *Traité de metaphysique*.

liberals, Christian and Jewish, with increasing dismay. They petitioned the government and obtained suppression of all argument, of their champions as well as their opponents, in the public prints. Government edict, however, cannot destroy a disease carried down through the centuries. Other Grattenauers were ever biding their time in the hostile wings, in liberal countries equally with autocratic ones, among atheists and pietists, in the New World as well as the Old.

The Grattenauer ethnology doubtless belonged in those days to a lunatic, if resourceful, school of no measurable status. Nevertheless it caused the Jews to tremble, because their history inevitably endowed them with insecurity as a sixth sense. Their intellectuals, haunted by the shadow of catastrophe no less than the common mass, hugged a perennial fear of even the most hollow fragment of Judeophobic literature. In their eyes any sheet of scurrilous paper could gain sufficient endorsement to create a trend, influence regimes and unleash a whirlwind. At no stage did they take their acceptance for granted, for they recognised a glimmer of truth in the antisemite's charge. They *were* different – and if no more accurate definition of the difference presented itself, racially so.

Rahel Varnhagen strove all her life to be only a German. Then, in a final confession to her husband (or was it to her God?) written four days before her death, she said:

> My story is of a refugee from Egypt and Palestine, who came here to find help, love and care from you. God guided me to you, dear August, and led you to me! And in solemn transport I think of this origin of mine, and of the interconnection of destinies through which the oldest recollections of the human race link up, across time and space, with the newest. What for so long a period of my life appeared to me the greatest ignominy, the bitterest suffering and misfortune – to be born a Jewess – I would not now renounce at any price.[12]

As for those fears, they were to be tragically justified. Jews had

---

[12] See B. Litvinoff, 'Rahel Levin: The Apex of a Triangle', in *German Life and Letters*, Vol. 1, Oxford, July 1948.

the effrontery to arrive as students at Würzberg University in 1819, and when welcomed by their professors received as greeting from fellow-students a howl of 'Hep! Hep!' The cry, signifying *Hierosylma est perdita*, travelled to Frankfurt, the Rothschild headquarters, during a riot, as well as to Hamburg and Karlsruhe. The brothers Grimm entered the term in their dictionary, ascribing it to another source, but now it would ever be associated with calls to violence against the Jews.

If Rahel could at last speak with gratitude to her Maker at being born into the despised people it was from a sense of fatalism, not pride. She had in her lifetime witnessed (indeed nurtured) the rise of Heine as the German poet posterity would, with qualifications, set beside Goethe. Felix Mendelssohn already filled the void left by Beethoven, and Jews started winning, or as it were stealing, eminence in science and painting, as empire-builders, soldiers, journalists and politicians. Nothing seemed beyond their aspiration, provided they paid the price: elimination of every Jewish instinct. If hatred of the Jew was a neurosis, so was abdication from Judaism by the Jew. This rendered the psychology of the proselyte a cliché. Hard though it might be to remain a Jew, becoming a non-Jew proved equally difficult, for it saddled the persona with that depressing baggage, a guilty secret.

For some time it seemed easily carried. But Heinrich Heine was kept glued to his origins by close family ties and his association with the younger German-Jewish intelligentsia. The conversion of that friend of his youthful days, Edouard Gans, in order to secure a philosophy chair, took him by surprise and filled him with scorn. Heine's allowance came from an uncle engaged in banking, the Jewish trade he treated with contempt. This did not prevent him from lunching in London and Paris with the Rothschilds. However, his education was begun in Düsseldorf by the Jesuits, to give him a relaxed perception, undistorted by Jewish introspection, of his roots in ancient Judea. Heine's love-hatred for Germany found its antidote nevertheless in love-hatred for his Jewishness; as to his own baptism in 1825, he termed it his 'ticket of admission to European culture' and then promptly proclaimed his regrets.

Prodigiously endowed, Heine spread his talents wide and thin.

Rahel would chide him, show him that writing was a craft, not a way of life. He wanted a mother-figure, but she was a critic, and when he left her salon one day she cried: 'Open the windows!' A cycle of poems in his *Buch der Lieder* is dedicated to Rahel.

Bitter towards the land of his birth at not granting him the official academic post which, he admitted, was the sole reason for his conversion, the author of *Die Lorelei* regarded the French Revolution as the best thing that had so far happened to mankind. Napoleon had taken Germany by the scruff of its stiff neck, and Heine made no secret of his ardour for another revolution to complete Prussia's democratic transformation. As a result he was forced into exile in Paris, where Metternich put his agents to spy on him. 'Germany doesn't deserve Heine', said Alexandre Dumas, and the French gave him a pension. As for the Jews, they were in his eyes cowardly, snobbish and obsequious, imitating all that was bad among the gentiles, to the degree that Heine declared he preferred the Polish Jews 'with their dirty fur caps, teeming beards and smell of garlic' to those of his own country in their top hats. Certainly, like his fellow-Jewish revolutionary, fellow-convert and fellow-Francophile Ludwig Boerne (as beholden to Henriette Herz as Heine was to Rahel) he was a malicious satirist in the Voltairean mould, choosing to praise whatever could be regarded as the opposite to himself.

Boerne's origin followed him around too, like a faithful but smelly old dog that he hadn't the heart to put down. 'Some reproach me for being a Jew', he wrote in 1832, 'some praise me for it, some pardon me for it. But no one allows me to forget it.'[13]

These two, Heine and Boerne, numbered among the principal founders of 'Young Germany', the movement that infused culture with an independent political role and agitated to disperse the long oppressive hangover consequent upon the French occupation of their country. Their writings inspired the 1848 revolution in Prussia. Their lives also exemplified that mutation within Jewry which embraced its own corollary: an assertion of the right to participate in national politics everywhere, as free citizens. The dawn of the millennium, or the beginnings of tensions anew?

[13] From his *Briefe aus Paris*, quoted in Hannah Arendt, *The Origins of Totalitarianism*, New York, 1973, p. 64.

6

Perils of Emancipation

The Jews in the West fought every step of the way to win their emancipation. By the middle of the nineteenth century only the removal of some degrading barriers, usually associated with the swearing of a Christian oath of allegiance, remained to grant them absolute equality. In some countries such an oath excluded confessing Jews from parliaments, military service and the professions. In others residential prohibitions were enforced against them. One by one, these restrictions would be swept away, or fall into disuse.

In Eastern Europe as we have seen this was not the case. There, the Jews dragged their feet most reluctantly towards change. The majority evinced little desire for emancipation. They had no wish for secular education and no aspirations to citizenship – neither the privileges these could grant, nor any of the obligations. They had survived as a compact ethnic, religious and cultural mass, in some towns and villages the majority of the population – perhaps 900,000 at the birth of the nineteenth century out of about ten million people altogether within the compass of traditional Poland alone – and were immediately recognisable as such, by virtue of their distinctive dress, specific language and unsettled economic pursuits. Poland itself had ceased to exist as a political entity through the successive plunderings of Russia, Prussia and Austria. The Jews there formed only one of several minority groups, all of which defied assimilation to the Polish majority and lacked a Polish national spirit. Another million Jews, sharing their outlook, inhabited adjacent lands to the east.

Exceptions immediately spring to mind, of course, to qualify so categoric a description. In the desperate insurrection led by Poland's national hero Thaddeus Kosciuszko, the Jew Berek Joselowitz raised a cavalry force from among his people to defend beleaguered Warsaw against a combined assault by Russia and Prussia. The year was 1794, and Joselowitz's appeal, 'To earn our freedom we must show we deserve it!' received pride of place in the official government gazette.[1] They fell, most of them, in the city's Jewish quarter, and Warsaw went under with what remained of struggling Poland in the Third Partition of 1795. Joselowitz himself survived to join Napoleon's army and fight another, more successful battle another day.

However, neither the revolutionary fervour emanating from France nor the cultural renaissance bringing pride to Germany found significant response among the Jews concentrated within Slavonic Europe. The mass of them, cheated of every opportunity for economic advancement, denied entry into the higher occupations and many trades, suffered doubly, for they were simultaneously at the mercy of their own archaic communal apparatus. This combination of forces kept them immobile at the lowest level of society. Their fortunes had sunk with the decline of the old landed aristocracy, the *Szlachta* whom they had serviced, while their ignorance was intensified by the iron discipline commanded by their rabbis, among them bogus miracle-workers and mystics of a power no external authority could equal, or indeed challenge. Generally, the Poles supported Napoleon and the freedom from Russia portended by his victories. The Jews, however, fearing the consequences of emancipation, cleaved to Russia as the lesser evil.

Mystics and miracle-workers? One might have supposed their time to have passed, now that entrenched religious superstition was being superseded by the new rationalism. Not in retarded Eastern Europe as a whole, and less so for the Jews multiplying fast in the lands between the Baltic and the Black Sea. The Sabbetaian heresy of the seventeenth century, when the young rabbi of Smyrna assumed the role of messiah, had in its death-agonies begotten in this region of long winters and impenetrable forests new extravagances and more impostors. Sabbetai Zevi received reincarnation in the bizarre career of a ruthless adventurer, Jacob Frank, who gathered around his person a brotherhood indulging in secret rites and perverted sexual practices

[1] Dubnov, *History of the Jews*, Vol. IV, pp. 697 ff.

which he justified by a most individual interpretation of the Cabbala. His religion, if that is the word, shared with the Karaites their rejection of the Talmud, which Frank replaced with generous appropriations from the theology of Islam and a Trinitarian admixture imported from Catholicism. Denounced by the Jewish authorities as a devil, imprisoned by the state for propagating a sacrilegious Christianity, Frank flourished in adversity and ultimately established a splendid court of his own at Offenbach, near Frankfurt. He assumed a title of rank and proceeded to enrich himself with contributions from his thousands of adherents. On his death in 1791 Jacob Frank's mantle passed to a man who died alongside Danton on the guillotine. Then his daughter Eva inherited his magic and re-enacted his apotheosis as the 'Holy Mistress', almost Mary the Virgin resurrected. The Frankists disappeared in the course of the nineteenth century by full conversion to the Church of Rome, taking their exit clouded in another Polish paradox, for many of them ascended the social and economic scale and furnished recruits to swell the ranks of the already inflated Polish nobility.

Together with Frankism, though much more persuasive, and pervasive, a second dissident Judaism took root, entrancing the spirit and blunting the perceptions in this seedbed of obscurantism. Hassidism (literally, 'Piety') began with a vision experienced by a simple manual labourer described as 'Master of the Good Name' in mid-eighteenth-century Ukraine. It grew into a sect and exploded in a thousand sparks to capture the Jewish masses and undermine the very existence of Jewish orthodoxy. The followers of Hassidism turned their backs on the traditional learning disciplines of Judaism. They substituted a doctrine of anti-scholastic emotion. The Jew could attain sanctification by inducing within himself a religious ecstasy through total absorption in the Torah (the Pentateuch) and the repetition of sung devotions under the hypnotic influence of a wonder-working guide in whom all knowledge reposed. Soon a host of such leaders emerged, often in conflict with each other, each claiming to receive his powers through divine selection and patronage. Orthodox rabbis, sensing here a primal force against which no logical argument could prevail, were appalled. They had kept the Jews within the fold by a regimen of Talmudic analysis and the rigid application of the Mosaic law deferentially interpreted. But here was risen a movement directly opposed to all intellectual endeavour, and substituting a psychosis of grace for the elimination of human pain and daily preoccupations.

Latterly Judaism has come to legitimise Hassidism, which though much diminished still exists to this day, as a positive development in the people's history. Certainly its excrescences disappeared over the years, to heal in part the divisions it wrought in Jewry. Martin Buber, the modern philosopher and theologian, wrote of Hassidism as the necessary mystical ingredient in a personalised religion that fortified the Jewish character in the face of man-made adversities. Immunisation against lust, vanity and envy purified the spirit and rendered the individual eligible for direct communion with his Maker. And the Nobel prize-winning author, Samuel Agnon, Galician-born, has revived Hassidic lore in Hebrew folk-tales of inspiring beauty.

Be that as it may, Hassidism at its nineteenth-century zenith absolved many Jews from the need to meet the challenges of the time. It held them to a childlike optimism and secluded them from social and intellectual intercourse with the outside world. The controversies between adherents and opponents struck deep into Jewish society, crippling the people's capacity to regulate their congregations, administer their laws, finance their welfare and improve their schools.

Neither Russia nor Austria, which between them had annexed the greater part of Poland, could ignore these conflicts: they were conducted in public, and sometimes led to violence. Each camp appealed to the secular forces of law to redress its grievances against the other. The Jews constituted a problem to the state authorities as well as to themselves, and thus there existed a rational basis for antisemitism.

Additionally, this indigestible Jewish mass increased rapidly in size. Infant mortality was no longer exacting its dreadful toll in the region, thanks to improved hygiene and the elimination of the more common hazards associated with childbirth. The Jews raised larger families than their neighbours, since parents habitually arranged marriages for their children on reaching the age of thirteen. Eastern Europe was lagging roughly a hundred years behind the West in cultural and economic development, and the Jews fended as best they could in the cracks opened by the hesitant transformation of crippled Poland from a feudal into a capitalist society. A large proportion of Jews subsisted on communal charity, or pursued mean livelihoods in congested townships as cobblers, tailors and woodworkers, or as push-cart pedlars and stall-holders.

Besides these extremes of poverty, other Jews numbered among the richest merchants, prominent in the great cities of Warsaw, Cracow and Lvov (Lemberg). Only rarely did such men follow the Hassidic style of life, which was the refuge of the poor. They conducted business at all the leading European trade fairs, acquiring their wares wholesale and transporting them into Russia's vast interior for distribution. The Zbitkover and Kronenberg families possessed fortunes as great as any in Poland, while there existed also a developing intelligentsia speaking the language of the state and leaning in the direction of German cultural influences.

Contrast the Jews with the peasantry and one gauges the accuracy of the charge that these people remained a nation within a nation. A natural selection of roles fated them to be intermediaries between town and country. They acted as agents for absentee landowners and bought grain and livestock from the peasant farmer, bringing manufactured articles in return. Or they lived permanently in Christian villages, as tavern-keepers, a traditional Jewish occupation of ill repute, for drunkenness kept the peasants passive and impoverished. A perceptible element among the Jews, equally ignorant, survived in total pauperdom, to wander from place to place and haunt the doorways of synagogues in public display of their piety as though it were the tools of a trade.

Russia was determined to modernise. It will be recalled that ever since the reign of Catherine the Great skilled workers and entrepreneurs had been enticed to settle the interior on undeveloped expanses of virgin lands. The invitation specifically excluded Jews. With very few exceptions they were a people quarantined, sentenced to live out their lives within a clearly defined area on the western marches of Imperial Russia known as the Pale of Jewish Settlement. It contained other races not deemed authentically Russian. The region ran the length of

Russia's western provinces, already overcrowded in the early nineteenth century, indirectly administered by locally appointed magistrates, to a certain extent self-governing, a place where Jews and Christians eyed each other with the hostility invariably engendered among impecunious populations jostling in competition for a crust.

Successive rulers, both Russian and Austrian, sought to turn the Jewish subjects inherited with their rape of Poland into citizens. But the equation was circular. They tried conscription into military service, secular education, driving them off the countryside into the towns or, alternatively, forcing them into agriculture.[2] All to no avail. The Jews complained of double taxation (collectively to the state and individually to their own communal bodies), of economic ostracism, of denial of opportunity to join the professional classes. All will be open to you, the authorities promised, if only you abandon your self-excluding practices, your sidelocks and beard. Learn the language of the country, they were urged, teach your children in up-to-date schools, enrol in the army. The Jews replied that this concealed a trap, to make them forsake their religion for Christ and so destroy their cherished relationship with the God of their fathers. When persuasion failed, the Russians turned to compulsion.

In 1827 Tsar Nicholas I ordered Jews resident within the specifically Russian areas of the Pale of Settlement (i.e. not Poland or Bessarabia) to present ten young persons out of every thousand for 'cantonisation' in military schools, to be followed by army service of up to twenty-five years. Since the reign of Peter the Great, Russian serfs had been the largest source of military manpower through this policy, which followed the Turkish pattern for turning Greek and other 'infidel' children into janissaries faithful to Islam. Here the Jews of course were intended to become Christians. Recruitment was placed under the jurisdiction of communal elders, primarily the rabbinate, with results that can be readily imagined. Sons of the rich and influential escaped, while 'kidnappers' went in search of children, some no more than eight years old, from among the deprived to fill their

[2] See, e.g., *Encyclopaedia Judaica*, Vol. IV, col. 1539, for the 1789 pamphlet of Mateus Butrymowicz, 'A Way of Transforming the Jews into Useful Citizens of the Country'.

quotas. In contrast, four true Russians per seven thousand of population entered military service. The barbaric practice had the effect of coercing thousands into complete assimilation, until 1856 when the system was abandoned. Conscription for all was introduced in 1874, for periods up to fifteen years, one reason for the wholesale flight of Jews from the Pale, mostly across the Atlantic – a saga to be recounted in a later chapter.

To complete this doleful picture of a people whose residence in these parts went back almost a thousand years but in the nineteenth century were still regarded as strangers, we must return to the subject of their language; nothing identifies a people more, or contributes so much to their national pride. But the development of East European Jewish culture was likewise a casualty of the rabbinical wars, impeding the arrival of Yiddish into a fully structured, syntactically disciplined tongue. In general, Western languages have come of age through the exercise of translating the Bible. This process languished in the case of Yiddish. An unquestioning reverence for the literal Hebrew text persisted despite the example in Germany of Moses Mendelssohn and his disciples, so that the holy books were never properly available to the populace in its vernacular. As a consequence, unlike other minority tongues with a Teutonic base, for example Swedish and Afrikaans, the refining of Yiddish was retarded. It struggled painfully to achieve a secular literature worthy of the antecedents of the Jewish people, but in fact did not do so until the last third of the nineteenth century, by which time the attraction of other cultures began to spell its decline – to the degree that, except for some isolated devotees, Yiddish has degenerated today into a sort of clown-language, employed almost exclusively for the utterances of imprecations and the retailing of jokes.[3]

Truly, the Jews of Eastern Europe were made to pay dearly for their survival, given that at this time every conduit of social, political and economic advancement was opening up for their brethren in the West. Little wonder the more ambitious and motivated among them began travelling in that direction soon after the 1815 Congress of Vienna, through Pomerania and

---

[3] See Leo Rosten, *The Joys of Yiddish*, New York, 1968, which started a trend.

Silesia into Prussia, and through Galicia into other, more liberal provinces of the Austro-Hungarian Empire.

In the Western countries of Europe, notably England, France and Germany, the Jews believed their emancipated world protected them against identification with their kindred in the dark, intractable and measureless Jewish hinterland. Though not entirely. They searched for signs, hoping to find none, that they were the object of a similar distaste. The habit worked like a neurosis. They wished to be accepted for what they were, Englishmen, Frenchmen, Germans, rather than Jews; or at the most a relaxed and fortunate compound of the two. Yet they suspected, not always wrongly, that the Christian West saw in them bearers of particular attributes rendering them alien to the dominant civilisation, and therefore holding its established rules in a certain disregard.

Manifestly, man had progressed to a tolerance hitherto undreamed. Europe had its quotient of reactionary thinkers, to be sure, hoping for a return to the pre-Napoleonic state, with every man and woman, Jews included, back in their traditionally ordained place. The thought was foolish, and the hope futile. In England, Roman Catholics swept the greatest of their disabilities away in 1829 and shocked many Protestants by gaining admittance to Parliament, though professing Jews would still have some thirty years to wait. On the Continent the revolutions of 1830 and 1848 brought power to the bourgeosie, albeit in gentle doses. The spread of liberalism, the imperatives of industrial growth, the struggle for markets and the rivalries of politics were together rendering discrimination on the basis of religion a philistine vulgarity.

However, a stereotype of the Israelite (Shylock perhaps) had firmly implanted itself in the Christian mind. The highly cultivated Jews who drew their intellectual nourishment from Shakespeare and Bentham, Montesquieu and Rousseau, Herder and Goethe, endeavoured by their patriotic fervour, professional achievements and very deportment to show that the stereotype was an antisemitic fiction. To their chagrin the archetypal Jewish character, 'with teeming beard', as Heine had described him to taunt the top hats, really did exist, in Eastern Europe and now spilling over to the West. And could anyone fail to be aware of the financier with nations in his debt? Innumerable Rothschilds, offshoots of the stout Frankfurt tree, covered the stock exchanges; and neo-Rothschilds too, from other families of more recent affluence, but prepared when the occasion arose to supplant the originals.

Every Jew, baptised or not, felt the presence of his ancestral shadow. He sensed that his gentile neighbour, be he ever so friendly, was distrustfully conscious of it. The young Macaulay, in that famous parliamentary performance of 1830 – it was his maiden speech – advocating removal of Jewish disabilities in England, exposed the prejudices of his countrymen in these words:

> The English Jews, we are told, are not Englishmen. They are a separate people, living locally in this island, but living morally and politically in communion with their brethren who are scattered over the world. This want of patriotic feeling, it is said, renders a Jew unfit to exercise political functions . . . It is the logic which the wolf employs against the lamb . . . If the Jews felt a deadly hatred of England, if the weekly prayer of their synagogues were that all the curses denounced by Ezekiel on Tyre and Egypt might fall on London . . . still their hatred would not be more intense than that which sects of Christians have often borne to each other. But in fact the feeling of the Jews is not such. It is precisely what, in the situation in which they are placed, we should expect it to be . . . The statesman who treats them as aliens, and then abuses them for not entertaining all the feelings of natives, is as unreasonable as the tyrants who punished their forefathers for not making bricks without straw . . .
>
> Rulers must not be suffered thus to absolve themselves of their solemn responsibility. It does not lie in their mouths to say that a sect is not patriotic. It is their business to make it patriotic. The English Jews are, as far as we can see, precisely what our government has made them. If all the red-haired people in Europe had, during the centuries, been outraged and oppressed, banished

from this place, imprisoned in that, deprived of their money, deprived of their teeth, convicted of the most improbable crimes on the feeblest evidence, dragged at horses' tails, hanged, tortured, burned alive, if, when measures became milder, they had still been the subject of debasing restrictions and exposed to vulgar insults, locked up in particular streets in some countries, pelted and ducked by the rabble in others, excluded everywhere from magistracies and honours, what would be the patriotism of gentlemen with red hair?

... It is said the Scriptures declare that the Jews are to be restored to their own country; and the whole nation looks forward to that restoration. They are, therefore, not so deeply interested as others in the prosperity of England. It is not their home, but merely the place of their sojourn, the house of their bondage ... It was in this way that our ancestors reasoned, and that some people in our time still reason, about the Catholics ... The law which is inscribed on the walls of the synagogue prohibits covetousness. But if we were to say that a Jew mortgagee would not foreclose because God had commanded him not to covet his neighbour's house, everybody would think us out of our wits. Yet it passes for an argument to say that a Jew will take no interest in the prosperity of the country in which he lives, that he will not care how bad its laws and police may be, how often it may be conquered and given up to spoil, because God has promised that, by some unknown means and at some undetermined time, perhaps ten thousand years hence, the Jews shall migrate to Palestine ... The argument applies to Christians as strongly as to Jews. The Christian believes as well as the Jew that at some future period the present order will come to an end. Nay, many Christians believe that the Messiah will shortly establish a kingdom upon earth, and reign visibly over all its inhabitants.[4]

---

[4] Speech in House of Commons, reproduced in Lord Macaulay, *Critical and Historical Essays*, London, 1874, pp. 134–41, with the ensuing quotation in George Trevelyan, *Macaulay's Life and Letters*, London, 1901, p. 115.

Macaulay marshalled other absurdities of their situation, whereby, for example, the Jew denied a seat in the parliamentary chamber could, nevertheless, 'be the richest man in England. He may possess the means of raising this party and depressing that; of making East Indian directors; of making members of parliament. The influence of a Jew may be of the first consequence in a war which shakes Europe to the centre.'

Without doubt, to the English mind Jews walked in the spirit of Rothschild and Sabbetai Zevi combined. The motion under discussion was lost. As late as 1850 Lionel de Rothschild could not be seated in the parliament to which he had been elected,[5] and several times re-elected, because he refused to take the oath 'on the true faith of a Christian'. Another elected member, and sometime Lord Mayor of London, Sir David Salomons, forced his way in and voted without the formality of the oath (the outraged Commons fined him £500 for each vote). At last, in 1858, Lionel de Rothschild was accepted as, head covered, he swore loyalty to the crown 'and so help me, Jehovah'. A French israélite (the term Juif being wished out of existence in France) had been a deputy in his chamber since 1834, to be joined by two more in 1842 under the bourgeois monarchy of Louis Philippe. In 1848 Gabriel Riesser of Hamburg, the campaigner for full Jewish emancipation in Germany, won a seat to the Frankfurt National Assembly, Germany's Vorparlament, with election as a vice-president.

So they were at last taking their rightful place among men of goodwill in the legislatures of Western Europe, and confidently, as behoved the times. But that shadow, and that sixth sense which detects distrust, could lead some Jews to extremes of thought and action, extremes so mutually hostile as to question whether such men could have emerged from a common root. Two of these nineteenth-century figures, both baptised Christians, would leave their mark upon the age: a Sephardi, the Conservative British statesman Benjamin Disraeli, and the Ashkenazi prophet of revolutionary Socialism, Karl Marx. The first would speak of the people to whom he was paternally affiliated

---

[5] By the City of London, which Englishmen took to be the natural Jewish constituency as County Clare was O'Connell's.

with a ludicrous racial arrogance, the other in a dialectic of animosity worthy of Martin Luther.

Neither man arrived on the political scene as a meteor unannounced. Jewish emancipation had rendered less visible but could not entirely obliterate the Judeo-Christian tensions bred across the centuries. The common psychological denominator in Disraeli and Marx was prefigured in the quixotic appearance and precipitous eclipse of that strange movement known as Saint-Simonism, which arose in 1825 in France to contest a spasm of that country's recurring ultra-clericalism. Henri de Saint-Simon, who claimed descent from Charlemagne, condemned the post-Napoleonic era for its return to traditional religion with its stifling by-products. Narrow and formalistic as always, the Church failed to comprehend, still less to accept, the irreversibility of change. It ignored the consequences of industrialisation, it collaborated in the exploitation of man by man. Saint-Simon's solution was a neo-Christianity, or neo-Judaism, to effect the harmonisation of the spiritual and physical worlds. Such a doctrine, not remote from certain interpretations of the Cabbala, attracted Heine to Saint-Simonism – he described the French, in his *City of Lucca*, as the Chosen People – as well as Rahel Varnhagen in old age and a group of young Jews of position and substance, mainly from Sephardi families flourishing in Bordeaux. The founder's death in the year of the movement's birth injected a necessary mystical element into the creed.

Stripped of their picturesque externals – attire in a uniform (red beret, blue tabard) to reduce differences in the male and female appearance, an expedition to the Orient in search of a Jewish 'messiah mother' and a ceremonial procession to the synagogue on the Jewish New Year to affirm their fidelity to the Hebrew prophets – the Saint-Simonians had a refreshing approach to economics. They preached a Christian Socialism that would abolish wealth and leave the distribution of a nation's purse to a hierarchy of banker-industrialists, creative artists and savants. All would come under the guidance of two leaders, described as the Supreme Fathers. Prosperity would ensue from the religious principles upon which all commerce would be based.

Of the many Jews in the sect some were not strangers to the

arcane art of money-making. The brothers Eugène and Olinde Rodrigues belonged to a family of financiers, while their cousins Isaac and Emile Péreire were bankers engaged in railroad construction, a transatlantic shipping concern and the Crédit Mobilier, enterprises destined to collapse from relentless Rothschild competition in 1867. The Seligmann banking dynasty contributed Gustave d'Eichtal; he proposed the erection of a monument to Moses in the Place de la Concorde and campaigned simultaneously for Negro rights and the use of Greek as a universal language. A Rodrigues grandfather had created sign language for deaf-mutes. Léon Halévy was a professor of literature and brother of the opera composer Fromenthal Halévy.

This Saint-Simonian recipe for Utopia, despite its mixture of naïve idealism and plutocratic condescension, gained the support during its brief heyday of Catholic Frenchmen eminent in philosophy and the arts. It was denounced by other Catholics, equally eminent, as a sinister Jewish plot to conquer Christian civilisation. Undoubtedly it invested the era, particularly in France, with a lining of anxiety, even among liberals, to reinforce the suspicion that tolerance had released hitherto suppressed energies in the Jews of an awesome magnitude and potency.[6]

Such exceptional characters, be they proselytes, anticapitalists or Tory romantics, defined, with unintended irony, the new horizons proffered by Jewish emancipation. But the Jews of the West by and large kept to their mainstream. Citizenship of a free country they saw as a possession to be neither despised nor trifled with. It represented hard-won justice, not a fiat for complete detachment from fellow-Jews still oppressed in less advanced societies. They regarded that attitude as cowardice. In fact they saw their duty as moving to the offensive, so as to win for these others the equality they had gained for themselves. An early opportunity arrived with the Damascus Affair of February 1840.

A Capuchin friar, Father Thomas, superior of a Franciscan convent in Damascus, had disappeared along with his Muslim servant. As a consequence a storm erupted to disturb that city out

[6] For a fuller account of Saint-Simonism, see, e.g., J. L. Talmon, 'Social Prophetism in Nineteenth Century France', *Commentary* magazine, August 1958.

of its uneasy Oriental torpor, on the basis of a rumour that the two had been abducted and killed for the sake of their blood – by the Jews in preparation for their Passover. A formal charge, duly laid against eight prominent Damascene Jews, led to their torture and conviction. Of the eight, two died under interrogation, which was accompanied by such refinements as the gouging out of eyes and the crushing of genitals, and one saved himself by conversion to Islam. Confessions were extracted from the remaining five. Syria was at that time ruled from the pashalik of Egypt by Mehemet Ali, the dangerous enemy of his national overlord the sultan of Turkey. For a European protector and champion Mehemet Ali looked to France, the power with traditional capitulatory, extraterritorial rights over Roman Catholics in the Near East.

It had been a long time since the atrocious medieval allegation of ritual murder had been trumped up against the Jews. Now again honourable men languished in dungeons awaiting execution on grounds impermissible in any civilised court of law. One of them claimed Austrian protection, for he happened to be a subject of the Habsburgs. The honorary consul of Austria in Paris, it transpired, was Baron James de Rothschild. Superfluous to add, Turkey in those days was labelled the Sick Man of Europe. All the European powers took a close interest in his maladies, not so much to effect a cure as to be present at any contemplated post-mortem.

At this stage two noted Jewish philanthropists entered the scene: the advocate Adolphe Crémieux in Paris, vice-president of the central consistory established by Napoleonic decree, and Sir Moses Montefiore in London, stock exchange genius, a Rothschild brother-in-law and president of the Board of Deputies of British Jews (the body had come into existence as early as 1760, without official edict from above or fanfare *à la française*). These two, both of august Sephardi lineage, decided that the travesty of justice called for specific fraternal intervention. They started a press campaign, chivvied the Rothschilds into activity and initiated an international outcry with the object of securing restitution for the victimised Jews and repentance by their persecutors. Austria, supported by Russia, appealed to France. But the French were bent on retaining the goodwill of their man, Mehemet Ali. They supported the verdict that the crime had indeed occurred and the punishment was deserved. England's interest lay with Mehemet Ali's suzerain the sultan, and therefore wished disgrace upon the latter's ambitious enemy. Palmerston, the Foreign Secretary, took up an aggressive stance on the side of civilisation and justice. Thus did religious superstition combined with antisemitic prejudice create the climate for international rivalries to reach a state of crisis. Armed with hindsight, we observe here the birth of Britain's Zionist alliance with the Jews in containing French (and Russian) aspirations in that part of the world.

Fighting their corner, the French saw themselves isolated by a predatory coalition of Jewish and foreign governmental interests. They raised doubts as to whether Western, emancipated Jews really knew enough about their primitive Oriental brethren to rule out so absolutely the existence of ritual murder in the mysterious passageways of a Levantine community. Adolphe Crémieux was shocked. That his beloved *patrie* could fall into such a position! His allegiances under strain, he nevertheless travelled to Egypt with Montefiore in a British frigate and obtained a rescission of the verdict, with the release of those charged. He owned to a Jewish loyalty and a French loyalty; sadly, they could sometimes conflict, but no self-respecting Jew could live at peace with himself with the libel of ritual murder unrefuted. Together with Montefiore he completed his mission with a visit to the sultan in Constantinople, following which a *firman* was published banning court proceedings on the basis of blood accusations throughout the Turkish Empire.

Adolphe-Louis Thiers, who presided over the Paris government during its humiliation, and the rekindling of smouldering rivalries between France and England, lost his customary restraint in speaking of the role played by the Jews in the affair. He regarded their independent *démarche* as a usurpation of his authority; this, surely, was not what the great Revolution intended in bringing them out of the shadows. Angrily, he vented his bitterness on those people 'who are more powerful in the world than they pretend'.

Crémieux forfeited nothing in reputation for an ostensibly unpatriotic stand, and went on to a career of great honour in his country, leading to appointment as Minister of Justice in the provisional government of 1848 and later as a life-senator of France. He had demonstrated that a liberated Jew need not fear the consequences of remaining faithful to his heritage (his wife thought otherwise: she had their two sons secretly baptised). Crémieux joined others of like mind in forming the Alliance Israélite Universelle, established in 1860 to make the under-privileged of the race, no matter where they lived, its most important preoccupation.

Strangely, in one West European state, Prussia, the intellectual and cultural centre of enlightened Jewry, no protest at events in Damascus was heard. The Prussian Jews had travelled a long distance on the road to full emancipation in this very Christian country, but not so far as to make them available for common cause with an obscure, persecuted Jewish community in the Orient. They refrained from being a Jewish nuisance. Too proud, and still too insecure, they preferred silence. Gabriel Riesser was at that time strenuously protesting to his dubious government that a circumcised German was a German none the less; the status of Jews in more antiquated societies was irrelevant to him.

Post hoc, we remind ourselves, does not equate with *propter hoc*. However, an impassioned examination of the Jewish situation followed the Damascus Affair and undoubtedly ensued from that event. Socialist philosophers, their arguments reinforced by theologians and historians, now raised a familiar spirit from the vasty deep of historic tensions. They were to a significant degree inspired also by Friedrich Hegel's critical assessment of this people. The Jew, if not an enemy, was at least an anomaly. True, he could also be a noble creature as bearer of the universal message of one God over all, but he remained an anomaly still. One man now wrote in a publication that enjoyed only the briefest life with a minute readership: 'The social emancipation of the Jew will mean the emancipation of society from Judaism.' Another put his ideas into the mouth of a character in a widely read novel:

> At this moment, in spite of centuries, of tens of centuries
> of degradation, the Jewish mind exercises a vast influence
> on the affairs of Europe. I speak not of their laws, which
> you still obey; of their literature, with which your minds

are saturated; but of the living Hebrew intellect. You never observe a great intellectual movement in Europe in which the Jews do not greatly participate.

The first statement appeared in a contribution by Karl Marx to the *Deutsch-Französischen Jarhrbücher*.[7] The second in *Coningsby*, written by Benjamin Disraeli. They were published in the same year, 1844. Could both be right? They could certainly both be wrong. The significant point is the failure of these writers, and so many of their contemporaries, to refer to the Jews in an ordinary, human, neutral position. The mere insertion of the adjective 'Jewish' served to load a sentence with an absolute. Within the tribe itself the word was frequently regarded as an unfair, cruel epithet, though others of course took it as Disraeli intended, and wore it like a sharpened sword, proudly holding it aloft.

Karl Marx, baptised son of a baptised father, rarely if ever spoke of his origins, though study of his life and career forces a constant reminder of them. Both his grandfathers were rabbis, from a long line of German rabbis. And there was money too: a banker uncle, Lion Philips, gave his name to what would become the great Dutch electrical concern. Marx himself was entirely purged of all Jewish sentiment. A thinker of his remarkable intellectual discipline, dedicated to a life of arduous toil entailing suffering and abject poverty for his family, dared not admit to instinctive loyalties or influences. He was prompted to write about the Jews in response to an invective against their emancipation by the influential German philosopher Bruno Bauer, Marx's old professor at Bonn University. The latter had, in an extended essay *Die Judenfrage* ('The Jewish Question'), reworked the argument that Judaism, by its very nature, precluded its adherents from citizenship. It locked them into laws and customs peculiar to themselves and incompatible with statehood in the European sense. Judaism in fact flourished in slavery. And although no man was totally free, for Christianity too was an aspect of despotism, the Jews, by refusing to submerge their beliefs in the prevailing culture, stood outside the common strug-

[7] See Marx, *Early Writings*, tr. Rodney Livingstone and Gregor Benton, London, 1975, p. 241.

gle for freedom. Thus they disqualified themselves from a place in the sunlight. The argument caused a furore in Germany, among Christians and Jews alike.

Marx's review of Bauer's *Die Judenfrage*, which he subsequently repolished as an essay of his own, *The Holy Family*, was equally hostile. The Jews worshipped money, and lived by huckstering in the market-place, which was the basic characteristic of capitalist regimes. Christianity, he said, having sprung from Judaism, was now dissolved back into Judaism. In this world the Jew practised to the highest degree that egoism universal in all materialist societies. Marx identified the stock exchange with the synagogue, so while the Jew should be granted emancipation this should be for the purpose of destroying the force which made his existence possible – the pursuit of economic self-interest. Apparently this bourgeois champion of the proletariat was oblivious of the presence of the growing Jewish proletariat in his own country.

Having delivered himself of these thoughts on the Jewish question, in which he argued that capitalist economics and state religion were virtually one and the same, Marx ignored the subject for the remaining forty years of his life. His great treatise *Das Kapital* has virtually nothing by way of direct reference to the Jews. But when expressing impatience or scorn for the many Jews within his circle and on its periphery, he rarely omitted a jibe drawing attention to their race. In this respect Marx resembled Heine, whom he admired, and indeed the two expatriate Jews had much else in common: rich relatives, for example, to emphasise their own 'unJewish' penury, and a lack of charity towards old friends who deserted them in search of greener pastures.

Ironically, Marx became attached to every anti-Jewish polemic, as both the tar and the brush. Moses Hess, his early admirer who drifted from Socialism to Zionism and back again, was derided in their circle as the 'Communist rabbi'. He so bombarded Marx and Engels with his thoughts on the Jewish question that the latter wrote to his soul-mate: 'Shall we never escape from that imbecile!' Marx shared an ideology with Proudhon ('property is theft'), who reviled all Jews. He crossed swords with the antisemitic anarchist Bakunin, in whose eyes

Marx appeared as a traditional Hebrew in the mould of Moses. For a New York newspaper, the *Daily Tribune*, he actually forced himself to produce some inconsequential hack-work with the Jews of Jerusalem as its theme. Marx spent happy hours in mutual admiration – though one meeting was enough – with the pioneer of modern Jewish historiography Heinrich Graetz. He sponged upon the unbaptised Ferdinand Lassalle, in whom he diagnosed a 'Jewish whine', suspecting Negro blood. In choosing Jenny von Westphalen, Marx married into the Prussian (and part-Scottish) aristocracy, but Jewishness dogged his lifelong footsteps. His daughter Eleanor Aveling loved the society of Jewish Socialists and regarded herself as one of them.[8]

Manifestly, the ideology of the Left in those formative years had already sprung the antisemitic leak which would accompany its progress ever after. Broadly, either its apostles were Jewish themselves by birth or origin, or they detested the Jews as a principle. Marx found himself in both camps. His debate with Bruno Bauer revealed how two revolutionaries could argue from different premises, contemptuously dispose of each other's logic, yet wind up with roughly the same conclusion. Bauer knew infinitely more of Jewish history and theology than Marx. In fact the latter kept himself deliberately ignorant on the subject. Yet each in his way advocated the disappearance of the Jews as an individual people, not for their own sake but for the sake of mankind.

It makes a somewhat bleak picture, this gallery of intense Teutonic revolutionaries furiously scribbling away in complicated styles that confused meaning and almost defeated comprehension, while they ran from country to country in quest of cover beyond the attentions of the secret police. They were planting for a distant reaping, this they knew. But their efforts would be rewarded in the end, even in the case of the tiresome Moses Hess. His *Rome and Jerusalem*, published in 1862 but hardly noticed for a generation, posited the return of the Jews 'to the track of world history' by their restoration to Zionist independence in their ancestral homeland.

[8] See Julius Carlebach, *Karl Marx and the Radical Critique of Judaism*, London, 1978, quoting from a work in Yiddish by Morris Vinchevsky.

However, the times produced a man without their patience, not to say profundity, though endowed with a conception of the forces at work in society more appropriate to those days. The existing order suited Disraeli, the old legends intrigued him, and his Jewishness, far from showing like stigmata as in the case of Marx, blazoned defiantly about his person. Disraeli did not have to await the full political emancipation of the Jews in England to find his mark. As a church-going convert of the ancient race he abolished conflict between the two religions, to his own satisfaction at least. Some opponents of the Jews referred to Christianity as Judaism consummated, and thus perfected. For Disraeli, Christianity represented a return to its Jewish root. He turned his thoughts on the subject into fiction, and then acted out the fiction in his life. At first the English laughed, then they listened, then succumbed.

Disraeli's father, a man of letters of not inconsiderable reputation, utilised a tiff with his synagogue as a pretext for withdrawing his son from the fold.[9] This was in 1817, and Benjamin, at thirteen, was due for his formal induction as a congregant, his barmitzvah, for which he was being prepared by a private tutor. Obviously the father, Isaac D'Israeli, soaked in English culture, had little inclination for the irksome restraints of Judaism as contrasted with the relaxed company of writers and artists. Benjamin followed his footsteps into the world of letters. But he maintained an enduring if platonic affection for his tribe, a characteristic by no means uncommon among those who are a generation removed from it. Something of the Regency buck clung to him – a certain bohemianism, flamboyance and an easy eloquence. His first book, the political morality tale *Vivian Grey*, earned him acclaim at the age of twenty-two. He then travelled, to drink in the mysteries and splendours of the Orient, and to remind himself of the knightly heroics of the Crusades. On his return he perpetrated a 'Zionist' novel based upon the fortunes of a supposed messiah, David Alroy, who was believed by some to have intended the Hebrew conquest of Palestine in the twelfth century – the counterpart Jewish crusader of legend.[10]

---

[9] He refused to pay a £40 fine for declining the office of warden of the Bevis Marks Synagogue in London.
[10] *The Wondrous Tale of Alroy*, 1839.

Disraeli now turned his thoughts to a parliamentary career. He was captivated by the British aristocracy from which, as the grandson of an Italian-Jewish merchant, he was genetically excluded. He consequently invented an aristocracy of his own, absorbing into his family tree all the paladins of Israelite lore, from Solomon and David through to the Sephardi noblemen of al-Andaluz until Moses Mendelssohn, about whom his father had written an article.

Plunge this arrogant young man into the rowdy maelstrom of early Victorian politics and you have a measure of the absurdities and attractions of English public life. Cosmopolitan and too clever by half, without a landed estate, Disraeli must presume to tell the cream of the ruling families of Britain, thick with Scottish and Irish accents, how to run their country! At his first parliament, in 1837, Disraeli's maiden speech, with which he confronted no less an adversary than Daniel O'Connell on a matter of Irish electoral law, was laughed out of the debate. He eyed the mediocrities ranged on both Tory and Whig benches, and promised that 'one day, they *will* hear me'.

While awaiting his opportunity to shine as a Tory he took up the cause of the labouring classes – the Saint-Simonian reflex – and produced his most significant novels. These works enabled him to embellish his political philosophy with a quasi-religious hierarchy of virtue: at its summit the Crown, beneath which men of high rank and great heart defy the political placemen in order to bring justice to the underdog. He could not resist laying before his readers the superior nature of the Jewish people. In *Coningsby* they were exemplified by Sidonia, a ludicrously vain self-portrait to which was generously added the wealth of the Rothschilds. 'Dizzy' had by this time led a Tory revolt of his 'Young England' group against their chief, Sir Robert Peel. With income tax an arduous seven pence in the pound and declining, he was now married to a rich widow.

Disraeli was wont to allow his poetic imagination to run riot, but he must none the less be reckoned a racialist in today's pejorative meaning of the term. He needed to establish the Caucasian origin of all Semitic peoples, then boast that the Jews had bequeathed everything of value to civilisation. They appear in his writings as the indispensable element in the progress of science, in the advancement of humanity, in the achievement of nations. Sidonia, he raved,

> had exhausted all the sources of human knowledge; he was master of the learning of every nation, of all tongues dead and living, of every literature, Western and Oriental . . . One source of interest Sidonia found in his descent, and in the fortunes of his race. As firm in his adherence to the code of the great Legislator as if the trumpet still sounded on Sinai, he might have received in the conviction of divine favour an adequate compensation for human persecution . . . Sidonia was a great philosopher who took comprehensive views of human affairs, and surveyed every fact in its relative position to other facts, the only mode of obtaining the truth.

Virtues in abundance, yet the ultimate impression borders on the sinister.

What was the moral to the tale, however? Undoubtedly, that Disraeli alone could lead England to its rightful place as the world's dominant power. How fortunate for the country that his grandfather had selected England to rear a family! How happy for the Tories that the grandson had chosen them rather than the Whigs! And gratefully the Tories entrusted him, 'the crypto-Jew', as Gladstone called Dizzy, to do the job.

Yet he was as good as his promise. His Reform Act expanded the parliamentary electoral base twofold, his Employers' and Workmen's Act established trade union rights, and his Merchant Shipping Act removed Britain's floating slums from the high seas. These and other measures earned his party the reputation of Tory radicalism at home. Abroad, his imperialist policies gave Britain a half-share in the Suez Canal (acquired for a song with a Rothschild loan) and turned a Russo-Turkish war to British advantage when, for a small fee, he helped Turkey against the ambitions of its northern neighbour. The fee was the occupation of Cyprus, a nicely timed reinforcement for the route to India.

He could now retire to the House of Lords, having brought his country 'peace with honour' and a smug belief in its invincibility. Such heroes may no longer be *à la mode*, but by the time Disraeli died in 1881 as the Earl of Beaconsfield, the name served to inspire millions of Jews dreaming of self-fulfilment in Eastern Europe and elsewhere. More, it established in the Jewish mind an admiration for Britain not to diminish until the Anglo-Jewish confrontation in the twentieth century over their respective roles in the colonisation of Palestine.

What could Disraeli have in common with Marx? This depended, in the nineteenth century as today, on the position adopted by the observer. Isaiah Berlin, in a brilliant essay, nevertheless strains too hard for a basis to couple the two as dislocated souls in search of an identity to replace their lost Judaism.[11] But to the many who saw the Jew, at last freed of all discrimination, as 'one of us', what could be more natural than to find him in every social class, every political camp, every economic level? Yet to describe a man as a Jew – Disraeli to his pride, Marx to his discomfort – evoked an effect far different from describing him as a Catholic or a Frenchman or, as Macaulay said, a man with red hair. It was a denominator unrelated to nationality or religion, and for which the term 'race' could be only an unscientific approximation. To an enemy, the Jew reconciled Communist with capitalist in a hated internationalism, or cosmopolitanism, that contradicted the normal human instinct of love of country.

Shylock, wrote Victor Hugo in his study of Shakespeare, is the embodiment of Jewishness, 'that is to say his whole nation, the high as well as the low, faith as well as fraud'.[12] The same writer's *Marie Tudor* features a usurer who is named only as 'a Jew', other identification evidently being superfluous. The one depicted in that Gothic drama *Cromwell*, almost approaching grand guignol, performs the Devil's work as the repugnant agent of the regicidal Englishman. He is named as Manasseh ben Israel, none other than the Amsterdam rabbi who in reality negotiated with the Protector for the return of his people to England. Victor Hugo's Manasseh, a monster intriguer more in the dimension of Marlowe's Barabas than the Jew drawn by Shakespeare, though with the same hatred of Christianity, must have anguished many

[11] 'Benjamin Disraeli, Karl Marx and the Search for Identity', reproduced in *Against the Current*, London, 1979.
[12] *William Shakespeare*, tr. Melville B. Anderson, London, undated edition, p. 174.

a patriotic French *israélite*. Was this how their liberal country-men truly perceived them?

Perhaps the author had by this time realised he had gone too far, for Hugo redeemed his reputation as the greatest of all French Romantics with his portrait of Jewry suffering at the hands of Christendom when he wrote his *Torquemada*. And as the most eminent of littérateurs, he presided in old age over a committee to aid the persecuted Jews of Russia. But our old friend Shylock is back again in *The Mississippians* of George Sand. In that play her Samuel Bourset places the capitalist where Karl Marx left him, in the bosom of the synagogue, and trafficking with lives in his pursuit of wealth. Did George Sand learn from her lover Alfred de Musset, or the reverse? Doubtless both believed they were transcribing from life. Musset's rascally Jew features in *The Green Coat* (*L'Habit vert*) as Munius, old clo' dealer and petty thief who, because this is comedy, is finally tricked at his own game by a street girl of pure Gallic descent.

We need not restrict ourselves to France for examples of the evil Jew as nineteenth-century cliché. Thanks to Scott and Dickens, Isaac of York and Fagin (the organiser of child crime in *Oliver Twist*) live on vividly in the English imagination. Trollope's Augustus Melmotte (*The Way We Live Now*) is another Jew of the most horrendous intent, while George du Maurier contributed Svengali in his *Trilby*, though this character may be wryly accepted as the necessary antidote to Disraeli's more than perfect Sidonia. And although in the case of Germany the conception of the Jew was not fully realised in nineteenth-century fiction (as opposed to other literary forms), leading novelists there who reinforced the generally adverse picture included Gustav Freytag,[13] Wilhelm Raabe and Felix Dahn.

In France as elsewhere, the 'good' fictional Jew is liberally interspersed with the 'bad' Jew – though never to the degree of neutralising his impact. Fiction is by its nature an art concerned with the exceptional: violence, betrayal and adultery reign more strongly in the psyche than order, loyalty and virtue. We all know

[13] Freytag produced the classic Jewish villain in his novel *Soll und Haben*, 1854, but was himself the reverse of antisemitic, virulently condemning Wagner for his diatribe 'Judaism in Music'.

Fagin, but who recalls the noble Jew Riah in Dickens's *Our Mutual Friend*? Thus our subject compels a return to French literature for the influences leading to the wave of antisemitism, culminating in the Dreyfus case, that overshadowed that fair country's domestic scene as the century wore on. And if one author in particular might be said to have fostered the sentiment, it was unquestionably Honoré de Balzac.

Balzac is the giant of nineteenth-century French fiction, on account of both his monumental output and the audacity of his art. Born in 1799, Balzac succeeded before his death in 1850 in creating a universe: the cycle of novels collectively titled *The Human Comedy*, which documented the social dislocation of his country as it leapt from a despotic monarchical system into a regime controlled by the bourgeoisie. His works introduce the reader to an endless panorama of familiar, everyday people whom no one really knows. We are among the *nouveaux riches*, the shopkeepers, the prostitutes, the loners. For Balzac, the primary forces in society emerge from the dual instinct of greed and sex. And in establishing this theme, his eye perceived, with a pained fascination, the spread of the Jews into every avenue. Could these be the timid, obsequious Hebrews of yore? Active in politics, finance, industry, scholarship, the theatre; writers, parish priests, courtesans, criminals – the Jews had indeed arrived in France as nowhere else, in many cases abandoning their religion, certainly their inhibitions, but according to Balzac (and not to him alone) remaining what they always were, intruders in a Catholic country and already, it was plain to see, fast dominating it.

He did not invent. Balzac drew the characters of his *Human Comedy* from life. Pervading their atmosphere, like an enervating wind from some distant wilderness, breathes Nucingen the avaricious banker. He was patterned upon a man whose acquaintance the author enjoyed, James de Rothschild. (The Rothschilds, quite understandably, intrigued writers in many languages and they stalk in a variety of shapes through nineteenth-century fiction.) Nucingen is a despised Alsatian, which emphasises his intrusion. He is the 'Napoleon of finance', one of a dozen initiates into Cabbalistic secrets and thus mysteriously equipped to cast a web ensnaring all Europe. Balzac gives us other, lesser endowed Jews excelling in the menial Jewish accomplishments: usurers of course, but also spoilers of innocent minds and dealers in works of art sold as authentic though in fact forgeries.

A Jewish playwright is not simply a playwright in Balzac. The sniggering, social-climbing Nathan must be the son of a bankrupt second-hand furniture dealer labouring unsuccessfully to conceal his origins, though Nathan is easily recognisable as a distortion of the writer Léon Gozlan, whose father was a Marseilles shipowner. The celebrated tragedienne Rachel supplied inspiration for the courtesan Esther, for whom Nucingen develops an illicit passion, his only human feature. She, however, in the honoured tradition of writers unable to abide the Jewish male, is a beauty of transcending goodness who will accept baptism, submit to concealment in the shadows and eventually kill herself so that her great love, a gentleman, might marry into his own class. Balzac knew his Walter Scott.

He did not aspire to a reputation as a doctrinal antisemite; goodness knows, enough of those already existed among his contemporaries. The effect was the same none the less. He also disapproved of Protestants, but the Jew against morality is essential to the theme running through his works. Balzac the master story-teller led generations of readers to a critical perception of human frailties, such as to turn a questioning gaze upon their parents, their neighbours and themselves. No Frenchman could be unaware of Nucingen's prototype. James de Rothschild attracted the scrutiny of anyone, of the Right or Left, or innocent of all politics, in search of evidence that the destiny of France was in the power of a foreigner belonging to the despised race. James never honoured the country of his residence even by the small gesture of adopting French nationality. In this regard the Rothschilds, while at their nineteenth-century zenith, featured in Jewish calculation as both a blessing and a curse.

They had served the rulers allied against France during the Napoleonic Wars. They were identified with the repressions of the Holy Alliance following the Congress of Vienna in 1815. Now James, with an outlander's title and outlander's accent, domiciled in France but part of a widespread family operating in concert, stood at the gravitational centre where politics and economics wrought their best and worst. On the ascent to the throne of the bourgeois Louis Philippe in 1830 he received trust of the king's private fortune. He floated international loans, financed the industrialisation of France and put journalists on his payroll. Jew and gentile equally shared in his charity, which was munificent and largely anonymous. Wherever a cause had need of a benefactor its sponsors turned inevitably in the direction of the baron's bureau in the rue Lafitte, or his mansion, once the home of Talleyrand, in the rue Saint-Florentin. Those charged with the welfare of Jewish paupers, Jewish immigrants, Jewish hospitals, Jewish schools, were forever knocking on his door. With a Rothschild in Paris no other wealthy Jew need put his hand in his pocket to succour the less fortunate among their people.

Naturally, James de Rothschild could hardly be reckoned a popular figure in France. No shaft of anti-Jewish propaganda, released in whatever direction, failed to find a target about his person.[14] The dismissal of Thiers as chief minister by the king following the Damascus Affair of 1840 was at his instigation. This was common, inflammatory knowledge, but he claimed the cause was right – to prevent a war France could ill afford. No, charged the banker's enemies, he had engineered the humiliation of the *patrie* to serve his own selfish interests. There hung about the name of course the glamour of high society, affluence beyond computation, mysterious accomplishments. A Rothschild wedding brought royalty in throngs to the synagogue and assumed the grandeur of a coronation.

Every Jew in France, be he beggar in the streets, petty tradesman or eminent man of letters, found himself spattered with the Rothschild reputation. No co-religionist could be considered honestly poor, or authentically French, or really patriotic; how could he be, when behind him loomed the colossus of the rue Lafitte, with all the implications of omnipotence? This worried the Jews themselves. They despaired at any mention of Rothschild in the press. They desired neither his honey nor his sting.

To their shame, they recognised in this man the last of the

---

[14] See Jean Bouvier, *Les Rothschild*, Paris, 1970.

'Court Jews', a breed identified with their people's humiliating status in times past and in countries less advanced than their own. So what, after all, had the French Revolution signified? What had they achieved by emancipation?

Others saw the matter differently. The Jew had achieved nothing less than the ownership of France, declared Alphonse Toussenel in his book *Les Juifs rois de l'époque*, published in 1845. It was now time to snatch the country back from their grasp, as it had earlier to be snatched from the Church, and the military. France should return to the situation before 1791 and withdraw citizenship rights from this 'tribe of Satan'. Toussenel spoke from the standpoint of a Socialist, but his sentiments would re-echo in every political camp, and haunt every major crisis in French political life for the next hundred years.

7

Wagner, Dreyfus and the Liberal Paradox

Despite their long segregation in all the countries of Europe, be it from social, religious or jurisdictional causes, a bridge connecting the Jews with their Christian neighbours had existed for centuries through music. True, as a trading people the Jews also penetrated into the wider world through their commercial enterprise, their money-lending and their internationalism. But such avenues served only to reinforce their alienation, forming a barrier rather than a link. Music, on the other hand, scaled the language divide and surmounted mutual animosities. Culturally bypassed in the Renaissance, the Jews acknowledged the arts hardly at all, yet music flowed to them from Christendom and back again. Neither absolutely secular nor exclusively sacerdotal, music found its place in the synagogue as well as the church. Sounds of melody enjoyed a sublime neutrality in the wars of religion, not to mention the race for markets and the conflicts of nationality.

The Christian detested the Jew for his credal heresies, and forced a status upon him which froze him into an object eternally outside society. The Jew feared the Christian as whipping-master and despised him as corrupter of the word of God. Yet the one could be drawn to the other through this divine medium, in which speech, philosophy, doctrine, all dismissed themselves as superfluous. Jewish minstrels were a common sight even in laggard Eastern Europe from about the late seventeenth century, performing at gatherings of gentiles with whom intercourse in the total sense was neither expected nor desired. Within living memory we find a parallel in the United States of America. Negro jazz musicians delighted their white audiences, but not until the conclusion of the Second World War would they dare to an equal place in general society.

Jewish instrumentalists and composers appeared first on the wider musical scene during their era of Sephardi ascendancy, coinciding with the time of Monteverdi and inspired like him by the scintillating palace life of the Medici and Gonzaga courts. But to come into full creative bloom they had to await their intellectual emancipation in the liberalising climate of Northern Europe, particularly Germany. Felix Mendelssohn-Bartholdy (the hyphenated appendage was a baptismal present to himself by his father Abraham, son of the philosopher) won over the entire continent with his *Midsummer Night's Dream* overture, composed and first performed in his nineteenth year, 1827. His subsequent renown enabled him to offer encouragement and support to many younger musicians, among them Richard Wagner, and also to retrieve compositions of Johann Sebastian Bach from near oblivion.

Mendelssohn of course was now far removed from his Jewish origins. Not so Giacomo Meyerbeer, an illustrious figure in the mid-nineteenth century, who though born in Berlin went in search of recognition to Italy and found his spiritual homeland in France. There, Fromenthal Halévy, brother of the Saint-Simonian Léon Halévy, composed in the year 1835 the first grand opera, still performed, on a specifically Jewish theme, *La Juive*. As professor at the Paris Conservatoire, Halévy had among his students Gounod and the ever-devoted Bizet, who became his son-in-law. Another Jew, Jacques Offenbach, is inevitably grouped in musical history with Meyerbeer and Halévy, for some of their works are virtually interchangeable. Son of the cantor of a Cologne synagogue, Offenbach chose like Meyerbeer to make his home in France, where he earned his unique reputation as an innovator in the field of light opera and lent his name and fame to the artistic glitter of the Second Empire.

Seeking an explanation for the Jews' affinity to music, which during the last century aided their cultural leap into general society, has led some scholars to discover it in the need for a refuge by an unhappy, ever disturbed, people. We can safely leave such conjecture to the social psychologists. Certainly, they spread from composition into every area of musical expression, as singers, *Kapellmeisters*, instrumentalists, arrangers and critics. Pianists and tenors escaped by the hundred from a life sentence in the stuffy, poky concert halls of provincial Russia and Poland and descended upon Berlin, Paris and Vienna. Jewish conductors rested in the grandest spas and married into the gentry. But it was in Germany above all that they were welcomed, encouraged, cherished.

One man observed the development with a jaundiced eye. He consorted with Jewish musicians, employed their talents and sometimes borrowed their themes. In the whispering gallery of rumour his own origins were often discussed for a possible Jewish association. Richard Wagner, Socialist revolutionary and composer extraordinary, master of the complete music-drama, deliberately set out to disqualify the Jews from European culture. Less deliberately perhaps, he founded a school of antisemitism in Germany that attracted many eager pupils, and naturally received the adoration of Adolf Hitler. Thomas Mann suffered miseries over the contradictions in the composer he worshipped; his essay, 'The Sorrows and Grandeur of Richard Wagner', which was greeted with bitter condemnation in his native land, prompted the Nobel laureate's self-imposed exile from Nazi Germany.[1]

It is intriguing to ponder on the ambiguous parentage of Wagner; many have done so. He was born in 1813 in the Jewish quarter of Leipzig. *If* Ludwig Geyer, whom his mother married in 1814 shortly after the death of her first husband, was in reality his father, and *if* Jewish blood flowed in Geyer, and *if* Wagner knew all this, then we might perceive the great man's antisemitism as a classic example of Jewish self-hatred. Much of his work and thought could then be conveniently explained within that typology. But the likelihood is that none of those 'ifs' has any basis in fact. Strenuous attempts to inflict Judaism upon Wagner have not proved successful.

More to the point, we know of his early association with Jews, beginning with his youthful crush on Leah David, daughter of a banker. Later, as a left-wing rebel involved in the Dresden disorders of 1849, necessitating his flight to Switzerland, Wagner would have been in conspiracy with many of them. German-Jewish intellectuals by this time featured prominently in every

---

[1] See Thomas Mann, *Pro and Contra Wagner*, London, 1985.

revolutionary agitation. Wagner's native city drew thousands of Jews every year to its annual trade fair, which was one of the most important in Europe. The composer also found himself entangled with money-lenders from a young age, and presumably some of these at least would have been Jewish. But why his subsequent enmity towards this people, so unrelenting, so injurious to his own psyche? His biographers date its possible emergence to a sense of victimisation he suffered at the hands of Mendelssohn. This related to Wagner's hope for a performance of his Symphony in C Major in 1835. He had sent it as a gift to Mendelssohn while the latter had the Leipzig Gewandhaus Orchestra in his charge, but the score was neither acknowledged nor performed. The two must have remained friends, however, for Wagner subsequently paid court to the older man in his home, despite his gibe that under Mendelssohn's baton Leipzig wore the character of a 'Jewish metropolis of music'. An ambivalence of attitude came naturally to Wagner. He could praise a man and condemn him in the same breath.

He chose Jewish collaborators almost as a wilful gesture of eccentricity as he embarked upon his one-man crusade against the musical conventions of his century. To berate the Jews as a key factor in what he castigated as European decadence did not inhibit him from fulsome admission of their contribution to his achievement. *The Flying Dutchman* theme, Wagner tells us in an autobiographical sketch, appeared to him as a blend of Ulysses with the Wandering Jew. He owed its inspiration to Heinrich Heine's version of the legend: 'I obtained the consent of Heine himself to turn the legend into a subject for opera.' The myth concerned a certain Ahasuerus, condemned to perpetual vagabondage, the mark of Cain on his forehead, and never to find repose in death. The powerful tale, reinforcing a general conception of the tribe suspended in an eternal limbo for denying Christ, made frequent appearance in literature. Still, Wagner could himself identify with Ahasuerus. He had never known his true father, he was misunderstood, he travelled alone, his music was ignored, he was Siegfried – one can almost hear him cry, 'Nobody loves me!' as he leaps from the piano to dash off another angry tirade at his writing table.

Wagner came too close for comfort to some Jews who,

paradoxically, saw the world through a lens similar to his own. He felt himself to be at one with Young Germany, that cultural-political movement of which Heine and Boerne, outside the covenant of Abraham now and exiles into the bargain, were among the commanding figures. Besides *The Flying Dutchman* he adopted other subjects utilised by Heine – Tannhäuser, the Nibelungen, Siegfried and the Valkyries – and the two men were occasionally to be seen dining together in a favoured Paris restaurant. But Wagner owed to Meyerbeer most of all the sustenance necessary to maintain his creative purpose in periods of adversity. He readily informed the world of this debt. When Paris proved apathetic towards his completed *Fliegende Holländer* he feared for its rejection by Berlin. 'I sent it to Meyerbeer', he wrote 'with the petition that he would get it taken up for the theatre in that city. This was effected with tolerable rapidity.'[2] It was already 1843, and Meyerbeer was by now accustomed to such pressing demands. He had been helping Wagner for years: 'In Paris, entirely without any personal references, I could rely on no one but Meyerbeer. He seemed prepared, with the most signal attentiveness, to set in train whatever might further my aims.'[3] Seeking an avenue into the tight musical establishment of Paris without such patronage would otherwise have represented the doom of Sisyphus. But then, in 1850, there appeared Wagner's 'Das Judentum in der Musik', published pseudonymously in *Die Neue Zeitschrift für Musik*.

'Judaism in Music' reflected the hallucinations of a tortured soul. Wagner had long before vented some favourite hatreds: Catholicism, France and all Latinity, as well as journalism entire for appropriating popular art and transforming it into a corruption of culture. Now came the turn of the Jews. Taking his cue from Martin Luther, he observed in them a people of mongrel origins whose survival in Europe debased the human race. The Jews, Wagner wrote, had no part in the evolution of European civilisation and belonged in no sense to any European community. They spoke European tongues only approximately, as foreigners would. Still less, then, was a Jew capable of music, for

[2] *Wagner on Music and Drama*, prose works selected and arranged by Albert Goldman and Evert Sprinchorn, London, 1977, p. 252.
[3] Ibid., p. 248.

'song is merely talk aroused to the highest passion'. Baptism could not alter a situation so bereft; it could result only in the abandonment of the Jews' own folk culture without the possibility of transfer to another. True poetry existed beyond their reach, along with true music and true art.

What then of Heine, whose *Two Grenadiers* so entranced the composer that he sought the poet's assistance in transcribing the words to music? Heine in fact proved his thesis, declared Wagner. He was a 'poetising Jew' rather than a poet, himself recognising and attacking the falsity of those so-called artists of his own race. More, Heine's poetry was a form of self-deception, and so effective was his masquerade that Germany's authentic composers (Wagner referred here to Schubert and Schumann) did not refrain from setting his 'versified lies' to melody. Heine was the conscience of Judaism, just as Judaism was the evil conscience of modern civilisation.

Wagner intended to kill Mendelssohn's reputation with a single poisonous shaft – an objective momentarily achieved in his own country when his admirer Hitler expunged that composer from Germany's musical memory. He dismissed Mendelssohn as a copyist devoid of originality, whose appeal lay in the craving for amusement, not to 'the deep and stalwart feelings of the human heart'. Judaic works of music 'often produce in us the impression of a poem by Goethe being rendered into Yiddish'. Thus in fostering Bach, Mendelssohn mimicked the language of a genius without reproducing his spirit. It is as well to point out that this astonishing diatribe came into print three years after Mendelssohn's death.

'Judaism in Music' appeared over a pseudonym so transparent that the entire musical world spotted its authorship at once. Certainly this was Wagner's intention. That it should have issued from the pen of a man whose defiance of society's rules inclined towards anarchism, a man ever complaining of persecution by the politicians, a Saxon challenger to overbearing Prussia – all these pointed to a reaction against the essay not so much of disgust as bemusement. This was not yet the era when the term 'antisemitism' would gain general currency (it was rarely employed until much later in the nineteenth century), and to categorise the Jews as a menace, or social disease, did not evoke condemnation as a moral offence. Wagner's critics were aghast at the musical standpoint he adopted; it exposed a brittle intolerance that lumped him with the Jesuits he affected to despise.

The essay greatly disturbed his friend and future father-in-law Franz Liszt, who had just staged the first performance of *Lohengrin* at Weimar. In a letter to Liszt, Wagner explained:

> I nursed a long-suppressed grudge against these Jewish goings-on, and that grudge is as essential to my nature as bile to the blood. An opportunity presented itself when I was most annoyed at their accursed scribbling, and so I eventually let fly. It seems to have caused a tremendous stir, which suits me well, because all I really wanted was to give them a fright of that kind.[4]

These excuses, if such they could be called, were hollow. 'Das Judentum in der Musik' was not an aberration activated under impulse. Wagner expanded the piece and reproduced it, with his true signature, seventeen years later. He had first written it with Meyerbeer particularly in mind, and over the years his resentment against his old patron grew from a prejudice into an obsession. Innumerable references to the woeful influence of Meyerbeer on the development of music occur in Cosima Wagner's diaries, all inspired by her husband. He had nightmares about that infuriatingly successful composer, and delivered himself of a long and somewhat incoherent philippic on his cultural decadence which lavished pity on Augustin Scribe, the unfortunate librettist, for having to 'cobble together those bombastic, rococo texts' for Meyerbeer.[5] And during a bout of depression, which attacked him as he read catastrophe into the expansion of Prussia, he even likened his country to the Jews: the Germany of Bismarck, that Greater Germany that had humiliated Austria and crushed France, was less a unified nation now than a metaphysical condition, without an identity.

Detach the music from the man and what are we left with? A self-seeking, egotistical provincial who never had a friend but he must be betrayed, never looked at a handsome woman but he

---

[4] The translation by J. Maxwell Brownjohn, in Martin Gregor-Dellin, *Richard Wagner, His Life, His Work, His Century*, London, 1983, p. 207.
[5] Goldman and Sprinchorn (eds.), *Wagner on Music and Drama*, p. 116.

must possess her, a petulant who cringed before the eminent and sneered at them when their backs were turned. But the music *was* the man, and this one was a genius, leaving his imprint permanently on German history. He could live by his own rules alone, and if Germany elevated him as the high priest of its cult of nationalism it must answer for his faults as well as his virtues. Nations pay the price of hero-worship. Friedrich Nietzsche the philosopher came under Wagner's spell as a young man, but ultimately could not abide his arrogance, his paranoia and particularly his attitude to the Jews, so that in his final summing-up he saw the activity surrounding the Festspielhaus and the Wagnerian court at Bayreuth as a German tragedy.

Though many rail against the ban, in the independent state of Israel public performance of Wagner's works is forbidden. Yet Jews clung to him throughout his lifetime, serving him so faithfully as to become enshrined in his immortality: Hermann Levi, the chosen first conductor of *Parsifal*; Karl Taussig, his favourite pianist: Angelo Neumann, the baritone turned impresario who took *The Ring* to audiences throughout Europe; his impecunious friend the Greek scholar Samuel Lehrs, upon whose early death Wagner said: 'He formed one of my life's most beautiful friendships.' We can but wonder at the devotion of the pianist Joseph Rubinstein. He hated Schumann on account of the latter's dismissal of Wagner's music, and then committed suicide because there was no life for him after his master's end. And how would Bayreuth have survived without the constancy of those hundreds of moneyed Jewish patrons willingly covering its yawning deficits? They were discomforted less by Wagner's fulminations against the Jews than by his attacks upon their other hero, Bismarck.

Could it not have been the paganism that attracted them? Wagner may have venomously disposed of Judaism, but he was equally destructive of Christianity. He acknowledged the springs of European culture only in the ancient Greeks, whose glories had seeped through and survived the ignorance and cruelties of the Church. A religion of the aesthetic as offered by Wagner, replacing the Christian saints by the denizens of Valhalla, seemed tailored to resolve the dilemma of growing numbers of Germany's assimilating Jews. Since the age of Moses Mendelssohn they had been seeking, as an alternative to the Rubicon of apostasy, a revisionist Judaism more adjusted to modernity, purged of *ostjüdisch* associations and receiving the approval of the liberalised society of which they now formed a part. Wagner recycled the Teutonic myths to resuscitate the pristine virtues of the pure German lineage. They could faithfully subscribe to this 'New Testament', for it lent validity to their own symbol of continuity with a heroic Old Testament past. And if the accretions of medieval Christianity could be repudiated by Wagner, why could not the accretions of medieval Judaism be equally repudiated by themselves?

Indeed, many Jews were doing so, discovering in a neo-Judaism the formula for absolute fusion with German culture. Under the leadership of Abraham Geiger (1810–74), a rabbi steeped in secular learning, they introduced the German language to a place beside Hebrew in the liturgies of the synagogue. As for the Talmud, it could have only the slightest relevance to life in the industrial age, so they demoted its authority as the sole interpreter of holy writ. Above all, they substituted the Rhine for the Jordan, rejecting the concept of a Messianic return from exile to Zion. Berlin was their new Jerusalem, and if Jews in England, France or the United States substituted London or Paris or New York, they had like justification for doing so. *Ubi bene, ibi patria.*

Their cry for acceptance as Germans, though of the Mosaic persuasion, was destined to go unheeded. Animosities survived. Judaism disguised as a half-way house to a secularised Christianity remained Judaism none the less. Wagner's operas appealed to the German subconscious by their affirmation of the *Volk*: the ethos of a people made, as God made the world, out of primeval mists and natural force. The dangers to which Wagner so frequently adverted in his writings arose because Europe had been degraded not only by a Christianity hypocritical and corrupt, but from a panmixture of blood.

Ethnology as a path to the understanding of personality and national essence was in the air. The race factor in history developed automatically from the study of philosophy, anthropology and economics. It was by no means restricted to Germany and had its exponents among Jews and gentiles alike. In 1853–5 Comte Arthur de Gobineau produced a four-volume work, *Essai sur l'inégalité des races humaines*, which divided the human species into three basic groups: white, yellow and black. The white or Aryan race held primacy, and possessed the greatest potential for creativity and advancement. However, it was facing the prospect of degeneration through cross-breeding with other groups. This, Gobineau maintained, had already transpired in the case of the Latin and Semitic peoples. So far, the Germans retained their Aryan purity, but this happy condition could not endure in the perilous ferment of modern society.

The thesis has suffered all but total demolition in our own age, not least through the spectacular achievements demonstrated by the Japanese and other Oriental peoples in science, literature and the plastic arts. But at that time Gobineau's ideas, not intentionally directed against the Jews, were swallowed whole. He naturally found in Wagner a man after his own heart, for the composer had himself sent out the danger signals some years before the appearance of Gobineau's study. Ironically, the same racial argument had already been advanced on the Jewish side by Benjamin Disraeli, and would soon be adduced also by the 'Communist rabbi' Moses Hess, to justify the hope both men nursed for an eventual infusion of the dynamic Jewish character into the somnolent Holy Land.

Race could thus be enlisted as an all-purpose weapon in any political cause, though nowhere more eagerly than in Germany. Gobineau regularly made the rounds of Gobineau Society branches that sprang up in that country, and in old age spent weeks at a time at Bayreuth as Wagner's guest. In Germany the spectre of ultimate destruction, as the Wagnerian school was to see it, took the form of a polluted alliance between Catholicism and Judaism. That was a circumlocution implying France. From the other side of the Rhine the same fear was represented as the Protestant menace, for, as every good Catholic knew, Protestantism was Christianity suborned by Judaism.

The drift towards the conflagrations of 1914 and 1939 had started, with those ubiquitous Jews nominated as the scapegoats for catastrophe. In Eastern Europe antisemitism, though widespread, had not turned to theories of race for its assumptions. There, the economic argument prevailed. The Jews were now less a wretched mass isolated by their pauperdom and piety, more an identifiable rival in the market-place. Their long trading tradition in what still largely remained as agricultural regimes gave them advantages stemming from their resources of liquid capital. A bourgeoisie had emerged in the higher reaches of the Jewish economic pyramid, to be observed with hostility and to be marked for a coming retribution. The continent was preparing itself psychologically for a final reckoning with the Jews as a European problem.

We must remain for the present in the West, which set the pace and utilised the race principle to grind another axe: European expansion into the non-Christian world. In seeking a moral justification for his scramble after Africa, and his subjugation of the Islamic peoples, the white man's hypocrisy resorted to his claim of a cultural and technological superiority. This he vaunted as an obligation to carry the benefits of civilisation to peoples less advanced. Colonialism, with Bible and sword, expressed the cult of ethnology in geographical terms. We are speaking particularly of the late nineteenth century. Colonialism did not offend the rules of civilisation; it reinforced them. It opened a door for the exercise of a virtuous sentiment – European nationalism – in territories long regarded as spiritually featureless.

A spark from this self-justifying fire fell among the Jews. The wisdom of the day regarded them as emanating from the darker side of the globe. Were they not intruders in Europe, feared as a danger to its civilisation? Very well, they too could find a 'colonial' aspiration. Only their justification was less cynical, and the reverse of hypocritical. They had nurtured their aspiration before Europe was born, clung faithfully to it for almost two millennia, dreamed and prayed for its realisation by divine intercession. We shall hear, before the termination of the century, a still, small voice. It will announce the arrival of political, as opposed to metaphysical, Zionism. The founder of the movement, Theodor Herzl, was a law student in Vienna not yet roused to his mission when Wagner died in 1883. He resigned from his college fraternity on the day that a fellow-member, at a memorial meeting to honour the composer, spoke with enthusiasm on the theme of 'Wagnerian antisemitism'.

Manifestly, in any discussion of antisemitism much hinges on the definition of 'race', a term over which oceans of ink have been excitedly spilled. Whether the word could express anything but an approximation did not deter its common utilisation in the late nineteenth century. Some Jews proudly affirmed their membership of a specific race, while others vociferously denied it. Since the epoch of Adolf Hitler, and his adoption of a racial argument in his ambitions for Germany, the ear trembles at the categorisation of the Jews as a race. At the least, the term is conceived as a judgement loaded with irrational prejudice. Its extension to 'racialism' or 'racism' implies unfair discrimination against a person on the grounds of ethnic origin, and leads the imagination to the oppression of one people by another, and so to the ultimate horror, genocide. We know from very recent history, not associated with the Jews, how human nature possesses this monstrous capability.

The Breton historical philosopher Ernest Renan travelled the same road as the Comte de Gobineau with his classification of language into Indo-European (Aryan) and Semitic families. Renan failed to arrive at a consistent definition of race, but his researches into the history and culture of the Jews, unequalled in his time, led him to accord to them attributes, positive and negative, as if this people were the representative of Semitism in all its facets. In his *Life of Jesus* (1863) he made them both the part and the whole. Earlier he had written: 'I am the first to recognise that the Semitic race, as compared to the Indo-European race, essentially represents an inferior store of human nature.'[6] Scholars employed the term 'race' as applied to 'people', and vice versa.

According to Renan, the Jews, ever under the illusion of an exclusive relationship to their Maker, had exhausted their interest in secular development of our civilisation; by their own admission they were anticipating the renewed intervention of God in their history. For an element of truth in Renan's thesis one had but to observe the Hassidic communities in their East European redoubts (and surviving to this day on the fringes of Jewish society in the West). The propaganda of antisemitism thus gave birth to its own contradictions. The Jew was a Janus, with two faces. On the one hand he excluded himself; on the other he

[6] *Histoire générale et système comparé des langues sémitiques*, Paris, 1855, p. 4.

intruded to an intolerable degree. Better for these people to have remained beyond the pale. If only they would keep within their isolation, and cleave to their prayers! But they permeated every facet of modern society. Racial politics saw them as invaders.

Renan was not opposed by Jewish scholars, secular or orthodox, his Christian arguments notwithstanding. On the contrary, they admired his originality and supported his claim to the professorship of Hebrew at the Collège de France. He collaborated with other savants in Judaic studies and wrote articles for learned Jewish journals. Renan refrained from crediting the Jews with racial purity, a quality which in any case he would never have classed as a virtue. But in contributing to the myth of Aryan superiority he left a woeful legacy of fanatical disciples. The race myth had now become ethnological fact, to be taken a stage further by Houston Stewart Chamberlain, an English worshipper at the oracle of Bayreuth.

Chamberlain came to Wagner as a young man and remained in Bayreuth as ever-faithful acolyte. The son of a British admiral, he was born in Portsmouth, but ill-health sent him to the Continent to be educated, whereupon he relinquished all contact with his native land. He wrote in German, adopted German citizenship, became entranced by the Richard–Cosima Wagner partnership and eventually married their daughter Eva. Chamberlain, an ardent member of the Gobineau Society, suffered a succession of mental breakdowns which were usually followed by intensive literary labour. Works on the German classical writers, on Wagner, on Christianity and on race streamed from his pen. Unlike Renan and Wagner himself, he described the Jews, whom he examined in great detail in his *Foundations of the Nineteenth Century*,[7] as one of the pure races of mankind, and in measuring their attainments he ranked them equally with the Germans and vastly above the Latins. Jesus however was not a Jew; his Galilean background indicated membership of the Aryan race. So there was a starting-point for racial conflict in Herod's Jerusalem, and from it ensued the deservedly catastrophic history of the Jewish people.

Houston Chamberlain's book first appeared in German in

[7] English edition published 1910.

1899, and it subsequently found a place on the shelf of many an upper-class German home, feeding a national vanity supremely personalised by Kaiser Wilhelm II. Naturally, he became required reading for every Nazi sympathiser as Hitler agitated his way to power. Of the many nineteenth-century writers on race, he alone is mentioned in *Mein Kampf*.[8] Chamberlain provided the philosophical basis for an ideology already espoused, not by any means in Germany alone, by a host of ambitious European politicians. It was a case of the practitioners anticipating their own theoretician.

'The Jews are our misfortune', wrote Heinrich Treitschke in the course of producing his monumental history of Germany between 1879 and 1894. Eugen Dühring the economist agreed: they were not only parasites, they had Judaised the Christian religion. The sentiment was not a monopoly of the far Right. Socialists and liberals of moderate stance knew in their hearts that peasants, artisans and the shopkeeper class would not be averse to the imposition of curbs upon the Jews. Bismarck the conservative Iron Chancellor had unified Germany in 1870 with the aid of the liberals, and against the desires of landowners in the provincial states jealous of their regional rights. The Jews, as an urban population slipping automatically into the liberal camp, enjoyed the soundest economic base (bank balances, not farm-land) to help them adjust to the transition. The German pro-letariat, on the other hand, stood in the draught of growing unemployment. Then again, the Jews felt more at home in the Protestant north, an engine of rapid industrialisation, than in the Catholic south. They could forgive Martin Luther, but Rome still made them shiver.

Politicians of every hue knew that antisemitism, largely irrelevant as a programme while Germany was fragmented, could now bring easy dividends. The evidence of Jewish achievement was there for all to see. According to the authorita-tive Jewish statistician for the period, Jacob Lestschinsky,

> in the phenomenal growth of Germany's economic, polit-
> ical and even cultural power, the Jews had a major share,

[8] p. 245 of the English edition translated by Ralph Manheim, Boston, 1943, and London 1974.

both in quantity and quality. The class of big capitalists among them trebled. The middle classes also grew in number and acquired status and influence. A Jewish intelligentsia came into existence and achieved rank in German literature, art and science. Many people asserted that the Jews were now dominating the cultural life of the German people ... and they should voluntarily withdraw from the positions they occupied so as to avoid irritating the nationalistic ambitions of the 'genuine' Germans.[9]

Lestschinsky adds that contemporaneously a quarter of all the Jews residing in Prussia were pedlars eking out a bare existence, while another fifth were domestic servants and artisans. Such people made little noise and did not come within the focus of attention.

A favourable moment of alert to the Jewish danger arose with the Congress of Berlin in 1878. Convened by Bismarck to resolve questions of conflict between Russia and Turkey, the congress offered a commanding role centre stage for Disraeli. The British Prime Minister brought a solution all cut and dried to Berlin whereby Turkey, though much diminished, would retain a place in Europe – this despite the Porte's abhorrent atrocities perpetrated against Christians in the Balkans, which had aroused universal ire. Most important, the Russians would be kept out of Constantinople. As for Bismarck, all that he could show for acting as 'honest broker' was a defensive alliance, portending unpredictable commitments, with Austria-Hungary. Disraeli availed himself of the occasion to lecture the newly emerging countries in the mosaic of South-Eastern Europe, Romania particularly, on their behaviour towards their Jews.[10] Then, with Cyprus in his pocket, he departed in a trail of glory.

Germany alone of the concerned Powers had gained nothing. The point rankled. It obsessed Adolf Stoecker, the imperial court chaplain in Berlin. He haunted the corridors as the statesmen bargained and cajoled and intrigued. He had watched Disraeli's

[9] See his contribution to *The Jewish People, Past and Present*, New York, 1946, p. 366.
[10] Adolphe Crémieux of Paris had pleaded with Disraeli to intercede on behalf of the Jews in these countries. Seven articles of the Treaty of Berlin specified equality for the Jews, though Romania failed to honour its undertaking.

performance fascinated. He saw the power of Jewry casting its shadow over all Europe. Yes, it was time to call a halt.

Beginning in politics as a Socialist, Stoecker had first tested the water with the establishment of a Christian Social Workers' Party. The result disappointed him. But he made a speech in 1879 on the menace of Judaism, and this inspired the formation of an antisemitic students' organisation of considerable strength. All the universities sent delegates to a central body, which came out with a manifesto declaring the exclusion of Jews from membership. Unpleasant scenes occurred as Jewish lecturers confronted hostile faces in the *Hörsäle*. Stoecker felt he was on his way, but he carried only a minute following with him when he gained election to the Reichstag in 1881. His movement stumbled along with difficulty, splintering, regrouping, amending its policies, but always faithful to its anti-Jewish base. Nevertheless in Berlin it held firm, and soon an international alliance spread outwards, attracting supporters in Austria, Hungary, Russia, France and Serbia. They clamoured against the proliferation of Jews in the universities, in the press, in commerce. Stoecker was disappointed to discover that his views were received with such disgust in London as to bar him from speaking at a Luther festival there. This was 1883, and signalled the waning of his star.

One of Stoecker's admirers, Bernard Foerster, broke away, forming a movement of his own to strike still more virulently against the Jews by sending gangs of toughs to attack them in the streets. Foerster was Nietzsche's brother-in-law, and likewise a frequent visitor to Bayreuth. But Nietzsche, unable to abide antisemitism, refused to acknowledge Foerster and as a consequence became estranged from his sister Elizabeth. The philosopher believed antisemitism was beating at an open door: the Jews would ultimately disappear completely through intermarriage, now commonly practised in the larger cities. Foerster persisted none the less, and launched a petition against the Jews, calling for their exclusion from all public offices, including the teaching profession. Some two hundred thousand signatures were gathered, though notabilities were markedly absent, and Wagner himself refused to sign.

Given the weight of popular opinion behind this antisemitic campaign, which was fuelled by the influx of East European Jews whose arrival at Schlesischer Bahnhof in Berlin became a regular daily bustle, it is noteworthy that Germany remained to a great extent unmoved by Foerster's activities. He reached the high point of his career in 1893, when sixteen candidates, electioneering on an anti-Jewish ticket, won their way to the Reichstag. Significantly, not one of them was from Berlin. Before long the wave passed, leaving a dwindled band of faithfuls to join the incipient National Socialist (Nazi) labour front after the First World War.

Meanwhile, in the Catholic strongholds of Central Europe problems of industrialisation and workers' rights, pressing though these might be, were stirring the national awareness rather less than ancient controversies of faith. Almost a century since the innovations of Europe's great reformist monarch Joseph II, yet medievalism survived alive and well in the Habsburg polygon. Every murmur of religious prejudice found its echo in these parts, particularly the Hungarian portion. Eternal damnation rivalled the weather as a regular subject of conversation, to be either wished upon others or feared by oneself. For an indication we must return to the Italy of 1858, and the notorious Mortara case.

Superstitious embers burst into fierce life that year over the forcible abduction from his family of a six-year-old Jewish boy, Edgar Mortara. Four years earlier, without the consent or knowledge of his parents, the boy's nursemaid had taken him to her priest for baptism. This was in fact an expression of her love for the child; she wanted to spare him the Jewish doom of roasting in hell, and instead ensure his afterlife in the Christian paradise. Unfortunately she was unable to keep the secret. The boy was wrested from the parental home by Swiss guards on the order of the Holy Office of the Inquisition, all this having taken place in Bologna, at that time still part of the Papal States. Rome gave instructions for Edgar to be hidden away and preserved in the true faith.

Even Catholic leaders were horrified, and sentiment whipped up against Rome reached the pitch that Napoleon III of France himself protested. But in the main the Catholic masses stood by the Papal Office, and nowhere more so than in the Austrian Empire. The Mortara case became an affair that endured for decades, for the family refused to accept defeat and in consequence was reviled for a stubbornness considered so characteristic of the Jews. Anti-Jewish feeling was particularly strong in Austria-Hungary, to the degree that the community there, fearing reprisals, refrained from joining the campaign for the boy's restitution to his parents. He never returned to them, but entered the priesthood as an Augustinian friar and even preached before the Vatican Council of 1870. Father and mother, involuntary instruments of Catholic resentment against the Jews, took the pain of their bereavement to the grave.

The repercussions had not completely expired in Hungary when, in 1882, another case stirred the old instincts anew. This time the charge was ritual murder, that Passion Week ghost, in the small town of Tisza-Essler in north-eastern Hungary. Here the population, isolated within the *puszta*, still lived with the memory of the Black Death. The circumstances have a tiresome familiarity to those with even the barest acquaintance with Jewish history and hardly bear repetition. It was a young girl of fourteen who disappeared this time. Who could have wanted her blood but the Jews, when else than at the Passover! Accusing fingers pointed to the local synagogue as the scene of the crime, and a witness was enlisted under pressure to testify against his own father. Despite mounting protest led from his Milan exile by the patriot Louis Kossuth, and the shame of it, a prolonged trial was staged. Fifteen defendants, all of them elders of the congregation, were eventually cleared. But a wide gulf can separate the establishment of innocence and vindication of the accused. The Jews quaked as they walked the streets of Budapest during the excitement of the 1884 elections to the Hungarian Diet. The antisemitic party gained seventeen seats.

Sporadic explosions of primitive antisemitism could not impede the steady advance of the Jews into the mainstream throughout the Austro-Hungarian domain. Two centuries earlier they had been expelled from Vienna. A century back and they were still forbidden to erect a synagogue there. Now they had the vote, and the freedom of the professions, including the army. They could reside wherever they chose. The Jew Adolf Fischhof, Hungarian-born physician, had commanded the student legion in the abortive revolution of 1848 and enjoyed the status of distinguished elder statesman until his death in 1893. True, rabbinical Judaism still had its adherents determined to maintain their hold upon the Jewish soul. But despite substantial immigration from Galician Poland and Romania, the Jews of Vienna and Budapest plunged into secular studies, beat down the doors of the finest universities (a quarter of the entire student population of Vienna in 1900, though in numbers less than nine per cent of the city as a whole) and, needless to say, thronged the coffee houses. Austria had its own branch of the Rothschild dynasty at that time, so the poor did not want for charity.

All about them the subordinate peoples within the Dual Monarchy under its Austrian figurehead – Czechs, Slovaks, Italians, Poles, Serbs, even Ukrainians and Croats – were finding their national voice, and strident it was too. But manifestly the Jews could not be included in any aspirations to autonomy. Germanic culture alone interested the Jews; Vienna was their magnet. This placed them in a special dilemma. Their instincts led them to the pan-Germanic political parties, but they received no welcome in that quarter, for pan-Germanism sought its ideological base in a racial purity. The youth movements, with their open-air creed of physical fitness, camping and mountaineering, wanted no truck with the Jews. In the event, a polarisation of the young developed in such working-class Viennese districts as Leopoldstadt, inhabited by a solid Israelite mass.

Vienna resembled a European, land-locked version of New York, and was likewise in the process of demographic change. The city bore the brunt of newcomers swarming out of the suffocating atmosphere first of Galicia, then of Russia and Romania. In 1800 barely a thousand Jews resided there; within the space of a hundred years they numbered nearly 150,000, most of them with only one desire, to put the old Jewish way of life behind them and escape from the poverty and harassment to which tsarist law in the Russian Pale of Settlement condemned them. Vienna could count itself fortunate as the chosen catchment area of an industrious body of immigrants who adapted easily to the conglomerate character of Austria's imperial capital and revealed an immense variety of gifts.

Large numbers of Viennese, however, were distinctly unappreciative. As the century came to its close two politicians in particular exploited a general mood of working-class discontent. Georg von Schoenerer and Karl Lueger stand in direct line politically to Adolf Hitler – the first as a nationalist parliamentarian with a programme of 'sending the Jews back to where they came from', the second as a city boss in the American style with his roots in the proletariat. Schoenerer, diligent pupil of the historian Treitschke, gained support among all classes for his insistence that Austria and Germany must be purged of every Jewish influence. In his thinking that influence stretched as far as the imperial court at one extreme and to the executive of the street-sweepers' trade union at the other. Schoenerer enjoyed a martyr's renown by spending five years in prison for affray, only to return to parliament with twenty-one of his supporters in 1887 on a quasi-Socialist programme inside a Greater Germany.

He could have achieved more, but he lacked a true understanding of the electorate's psychology. Schoenerer struck a pose, cultivated in his newspaper the *Ostdeutsche Rundschau*, as a politician of European dimensions, but in truth he was a minor provincial aristocrat more of a nuisance than a threat. In a country of defined social divisions, and a parliamentary system not yet out of its apprenticeship, he flattered the workers while simultaneously offending upper-class Catholic susceptibilities. As a result his glory was short-lived. But Karl Lueger took over where Schoenerer left off, and wasted no energies in agitation for Austria's inclusion in the German confederation, in his eyes a futile issue. Active in municipal politics, Lueger's election as Bürgermeister of Vienna stirred contention regarding his propriety for the office, but he was endorsed in 1897 and wore the chain until his death thirteen years later. Workers' friend and upholder of Catholic order, he even numbered one or two Jewish trade unionists among his closest associates and received praise not only from Hitler in *Mein Kampf* – 'the greatest German mayor of all time'[11] – but also from the Jewish writer Stefan Zweig in his autobiographical *The World of Yesterday*. Yet Lueger squeezed Jews out of his city's administration, vilified them in demagogic speeches and used his authority to restrict their entry into the city's university.

[11] Tr. Manheim, p. 51.

What was Europe groping after? Politicians everywhere echoed the ancient prophets with their call for freedom, equality and justice; but the continent responded all too frequently with outbursts of hatred and intolerance. Revolution had succeeded revolution, new nations entered into existence, older ones found the ideological cement to give them unity. But what had become of those promises of a golden age? They dissolved into conflicts about class, and race, and religion, in which every argument had its spurious relevance. Ever since 1848, the year of radical protest, wars had followed each other with the regularity of the solstice, only to leave the bulk of Europe's fast-growing population discontented and deprived. The British, sanctimonious as only the uninvolved can be, chased the Irish out of their impoverished island to distant territories; Italy, now one country, placed itself upon a shelf and drew false consolation from its past grandeur; Germany assumed mastery over Europe, claiming superiority of intellect, the precedence of Hohenzollern over Habsburg and the right of might. A sprinkling of Jewish magnates, many with names current to this day – Speyer, Rothschild, Seligmann, Wertheimer, Oppenheimer, Poliakov, Günzberg, Hirsch – had long discarded the religious blinkers of their ancestors: authentic nineteenth-century men, they worshipped civilisation's newest deity, science. Their grandfathers could write only in Hebrew, and speak only in Yiddish, but these entrepreneurs stood in the vanguard of industrialisation. They mined the subsoil's riches and constructed railways across the length and breadth of Europe, rendering a journey from Paris to Vladivostok feasible within days. The masses, however, lived and died in their city poverty without ever catching a glimpse of the sea.

The Dual Monarchy, that 'despotism mellowed by indolence',[12] constituted a zoological garden of rivalling tribes hung upon the fragile Vienna–Budapest axis. Russia freed the serfs at last in 1861 but continued as a place of mystery and famine. Russia failed to digest the Jews, now numbering in millions, that it had swallowed in the reign of Catherine the Great. The European working classes acknowledged Karl Marx as the prophet of

---

[12] Thus described by Victor Adler, Jewish founder of Austria's Social Democratic Party, at an international conference in 1889.

their redemption, though very few had so much as seen a copy of *Das Kapital*.

Europe was not ready to explode – not yet at any rate. A safety-valve existed. This was emigration, principally to the young democracy across the Atlantic. It involved a hazardous nine weeks on the high seas to reach the other side, but evidently few new Americans regretted having chanced the voyage. From the time of American independence until 1830 new settlers were few, then in the next ten years 600,000 shook the European dust from their feet and journeyed west. In the following decade the number increased to some two millions, almost half of them from Ireland. The Irish were driven by hunger, the others, Central European radicals for the large part, had been thwarted in their hope of freedom with the débâcle of 1848. And there was the lure of Californian gold. The Americans spoke of their country's 'manifest destiny', so people poured in from the Old World to claim their share in it. During the ten years 1880–90 more than five million Europeans arrived in the United States, raising the population of the country to 63 millions. America then took a deep breath.

In general, those flocking to America in the latter period were the depressed classes, Irish, Italians, Jews and Serbs, from the stagnating fringes of the old continent. The New York Jewish poet Emma Lazarus saw them as 'the huddled masses yearning to breathe free'. Abundant employment awaited them, and they discovered a market for anything they could make with their own hands, at home, in the sweatshops, along the quays. Milan, Genoa and the prospering north of Italy sent hardly any of their children, but whole stretches of Sicily were depopulated. Jews took off from Bialystok, Odessa, Warsaw and Bucharest, as well as from a hundred smaller townships, though less frequently from Vienna, Berlin, Budapest or Prague (notable exceptions included Jacob Schiff, of a banking family once occupying the house next door to the Rothschilds in the Frankfurt ghetto).

To be sure, the Jews of Central Europe had little cause to yearn for distant horizons. They constituted a compact, optimistic group rapidly ascending, most of them, into the middle classes. To the gentile onlooker they appeared to monopolise the medical and legal professions, and were turning their shabby little clothing stores into splendid emporia of fashion within the twinkling of an Aryan eye. They owned newspapers, wrote novels, sat in parliaments. Suggestions that they be expelled *en masse*, frequently heard, were tempered by the warning of history in Spain and Portugal: great nations that had sent their Jews forth only to suffer catastrophic decline. Jew and gentile thus cohabited in Germany and the Dual Monarchy as a marriage of convenience, the Israelites frequently doing their hosts the honour of adopting the dominant religion, Protestant in one empire, Catholic in the other. Like others before them, they acted more out of resignation than conviction. Not having been particularly good Jews, they did not make particularly good Christians. As Paul Claudel, the French symbolist who agonised over the confrontation of the faiths, was later to write sardonically: 'It takes a lot of water to baptise a Jew.'[13]

Although the Jews eluded any satisfactory definition of their peoplehood – not a race, nor a nation, nor just a religion – Jewishness on the other hand yielded more precisely to a linguistic equivalent. Jewishness was a *condition*. Its essence came close to a psychological state, arising from their situation as a minority everywhere. This transcended their religious preferences, be this orthodox Judaism, baptised Christianity or atheism. They shared a collective memory descended from their national origin in biblical times. All Jews inherited a sense of outrage at being the object of hatred for a trumped-up charge of judicial murder ostensibly committed in the first century AD. That occurrence was recorded in a book they most likely had never read but which Christians only rarely put aside.

A minority will always be vulnerable. The Jews' vulnerability however was compounded by the ineradicable stigma of that deicide myth. As a result they had developed an exceptional communal solidarity. Although their environment had vastly changed with the progress of time, the tolerance of man and the loosening of bonds, Jewishness obstinately persisted as a psychological condition. Tolerance not being the most reliable of human characteristics, the Jews spared no effort at pleasing their host nations, and at justifying themselves (ingratiating

---

[13] In his drama *Le Père humilié*, 1917.

themselves?) in the eyes of the majority. Jews knew they were different from the mass; indeed some of them, the most traditional and rigidly pious, insisted upon emphasising that difference, by close adherence to earlier rules of dress and life-style. But mostly they preferred invisibility. Their antennae detected every incidence of hostility, and frequently suspected hostility where none existed.

Following their nineteenth-century legal emancipation, the Jewish yearning for acceptance could approach extremes, combining an element of servility with a drive to excel, be this in commerce or the professions or in the recognised virtues of society. They recoiled from registering in the minds of others as a burdensome minority. Thus they protected their poor from the cold benefits of government charity. The Jews, they seemed to proclaim, repaid the conferment of equality with interest. Surely their achievements made of them an asset, not to say an adornment, to the nations they joined! Naturally they had to suffer their deviants (who didn't?), but their mentality directed them by the end of the century to the disappearance of their peculiarities, except in the oppressive regimes of Imperial Russia and Romania where, as it happened, they were most numerous.

As for anti-Jewish prejudice, this was irrational, self-defeating and, in their view, degrading to Christendom. Deprive the Jew of legitimate human rights in a country and that country forfeited the rewards of Jewish talent freely given.

The condition of Jewishness begot its flaws. One of them was a pronounced naïvety, which restrained the Jews from a thorough and realistic examination of their own past. For example, they confused history with memory. Until the nineteenth century the writing of systematic Jewish history since Josephus had been a monopoly of Christian scholars. It seemed that having produced in the Bible the earliest, most extensive and inspired interpretation of history of any people, they themselves attached little interest in recording what followed: a most revealing failing, given that the Old Testament canon stands as the historian's model for strict adherence to the principles of continuity and precision in describing national development. Doubtless the Jews were inhibited by religious precept from writing up their past, for this would imply critical assessment of God's design in guiding his Chosen People. Further, being disrupted by periodic cataclysms, they feared the recorded exposure of their weaknesses to a hostile audience. Even in the nineteenth century, when German-Jewish scholars at last inaugurated more searching study of the people, their historiography assumed the nature of apologetics. These scholars gave the Jews a passive role within other people's history, ever the innocent victims of cruelty or fate. Their chronicles spanning eighteen hundred years largely comprised accounts of oppression, expulsion and martyrdom which broke into the narrative to disturb the stream of Jewish cultural-religious consciousness. Economic and sociological factors were little understood and for the most part ignored. How unlike the Bible story! No worship of the golden calf; no treachery; no hatred of other peoples; no angry prophets; no corruption through power. Interestingly, this did not inhibit Jews from producing significant histories of other peoples.[14]

Because of their tendency either to overlook their flaws or to explain them away, outbreaks of antisemitism invariably caught the Jews by surprise. They presumed that a gesture of generous charity, or an outstanding example of academic brilliance, or an act of bravery on the battlefield, should wipe from the record instances of disloyalty or venality. A single act of virtue brought credit to the whole people, they calculated, though an isolated sin should not drag them all into disrepute. Jewishness hardly comprehended that the endowment of a hospital or a school, say, paraded not only the benefactor's generosity but also his inordinate affluence. On the conclusion of the Franco-Prussian War in 1871, Baron Alphonse de Rothschild underwrote a loan of five billion francs to pay off the Prussian war indemnity well before its due, thus enabling the early removal of occupation troops from the sacred soil of France. *Voilà*, the Jews said, an exemplary act of patriotism! France however replied: 'That was *our* money, acquired by a ruthless, scheming family that had never suffered, only enriched itself, in war.'

[14] Jewish historiography began with Isaac M. Jost, whose nine-volume work was published 1820–9. A more profound history came from the pen of Heinrich Graetz in eleven volumes, 1853–76. The Saint Simonian Léon Halévy wrote a superficial history of the Jews in 1828; his grandson Élie ignored the Jews but devoted five volumes to his notable *History of the English People in the Nineteenth Century*, first published in French 1912–32.

To illustrate the point, and to judge by references in the press and to parliamentary debates, Alphonse de Rothschild, then head of the Paris branch, loomed probably as the most hated man in his country. This also prepares us for the Jewish situation in France at the century's twilight, and brings the generalisations expressed in the preceding paragraphs to specific application in the most antisemitic country of the Western world, the one in which the Jews excelled most, assimilated most and were distrusted most. We are in the foreground of the Dreyfus Affair, which divided France and sent its Jewish community reeling with incomprehension and dismay. For *l'Affaire* warned the Jews that their condition was perhaps incurable.

Allow the French the extenuation which is their entitlement. The Franco-Prussian War, a gamble on the part of Napoleon III to buttress his slipping edifice, humiliated the French so completely as to afflict them with doubts as to their capacity to create a workable system of government. Their emperor, together with 84,000 of his soldiers and thirty-nine generals, had surrendered on the field of battle. Alsace and Lorraine fell to a newly unified nation of frightening strength with a frontier pressing towards the Meuse. As the war ended in 1871 Paris stood beleaguered and near to starvation, while a ferocious civil war had to be fought out under the nose of the Prussian army of occupation. Grievous unemployment followed, political extremism, a disaffected military, Catholic reaction confronting atheistic schoolmasters—the mixture produced an *avant la lettre* Fascism going by the name of Boulangism. Could this be the country which the day before yesterday had inaugurated a social revolution to set the world by its ears, and had overrun most of Europe in a decade?

Now the word on everyone's lips was revenge, *la revanche*. The new Republic needed a saviour and a scapegoat. It found the first, approximately, in Léon Gambetta, and the second more obviously in the Jews. To the critics of republicanism, and they were many, a return to an old secular system, which had chained down the Church and insulted the pope, implied the triumph of Judaism. Gambetta was the key figure in re-creating the Republic. Some believed, wrongly, that he too must be a Jew. Perhaps they identified him with his close adviser Joseph Reinach, the celebrated journalist who served as *chef de cabinet* in Gambetta's administration of nine weeks in 1881–2. So many prominent Jews with German names! Manifestly the hated conqueror from across the Rhine had left his agents to poison this nation of pure Gallic stock.

Estimates of the number of Jews in metropolitan France varied. Some would reckon only those registered with the regional consistories established in the time of the first Napoleon, but gradual defection from their community, often without actual conversion, falsified the figures. Then, what of those who, following the amputation of Alsace and Lorraine, remained in the lost provinces? Only a proportion of their 30,000 opted, as was their right, to quit their old homes and move to the interior. It happened in the case of the families of Léon Blum, the future statesman, for example, and Alfred Dreyfus, and the writer André Maurois (originally Émile Herzog), as well as Marcel Proust's Jewish mother. Were the baptised to be included? Surely not, they themselves insisted; but public opinion saw them differently. Still more were half in, half out – not totally rejected, yet not accepted. These were the East European Jews arriving in quest of better opportunities. They came, bundles on their backs, from the early 1880s, to swell the numbers in the larger cities, by some accident halting here rather than in Britain or Germany, never to make the onward journey to New York.

No census in France after 1872 demanded particulars of religious affiliation, but it was generally agreed that by the end of the century the Jewish population had reached some 70,000, of which the majority, 45,000, were concentrated in the Paris region. Excluded from all calculations were another 45,000 or so resident in Algeria, enjoying full rights as citizens of the Republic but in no sense considered true Frenchmen by anyone, gentile or Jew, inside France.

The Jews thus comprised a negligible percentage of the country's 40 million citizens. But only in statistical terms. Solidly ensconced in Paris, handsomely represented in banking and the professions, they appeared on the public scene as energetic politicians, graduates of the élite schools and, as already noted, musicians of renown. Journalism particularly attracted them, as did the theatre. In this respect they shared the Jewish characteristics of London, Berlin and Vienna. There, however, similarity ceased. French Jewry took its nationality more earnestly than did any other. Patriotism had all but supplanted Judaism as a religion.

In their eyes the Tablets of the Law given to Moses on Mount Sinai had been duplicated by the French Revolution and the Declaration of the Rights of Man. Service in the armed forces counted as a *mitzvah*, a moral imperative as though belonging to the 613 sacred obligations enunciated by the ancients. Some five hundred Jews held commisions in the army, and in 1889 five of them were listed as generals.[15] The rabbis, since 1831 paid by the state and therefore quasi-civil servants, thundered out revanchiste sermons from their pulpits, while Joan of Arc won their devotion in no measure less than the heroines of the Old Testament. Subservience to national dogma reflected pathetic ironies, as on the occasion of the Franco-Russian Entente of 1891. Prayers offered in the synagogue at that time for the health of Tsar Alexander III coincided with demonstrations, led by distinguished Christian figures, against the same ruler's persecution of the Jews in the Russian Empire. In the words of a celebrated actor, Albin Valabrégue (related by marriage to the as yet unknown Captain Dreyfus), 'We are not the legitimate children of France but only her adopted children, and so we have the obligation to be twice as French as the others.'[16]

The ease with which the Jews of France could subsume the Hebraic element of their personality within the national *esprit* received striking illustration in the evolution of the Halévy family, which began with the arrival from Bavaria of a humble synagogue cantor in the late eighteenth century. Fromental Halévy the composer was one son; Léon the Saint-Simonian, a poet and dramatist, was the other. The latter's non-Jewish wife gave birth to Ludovic, librettist of Offenbach's *Orpheus in the Underworld* and operas by Bizet. Thereupon the family deserted Israel with a vengeance. Ludovic's elder son Élie, a Protestant, wrote his *History of the English People* noted above; while the younger, the Catholic Daniel, an intimate of Proust, was destined

[15] Michael R. Marrus, *The Politics of Assimilation: The French Jewish Community at the Time of the Dreyfus Affair*, Oxford, 1971, p. 41.
[16] In a letter published 14 September 1893 in *Le Matin* and other newspapers. Marrus. *Politics of Assimilation*, p. 156.

to rule as uncrowned king of the literary establishment. His salon on the Quai de l'Horloge beside the Seine attracted every important writer of the first half of the twentieth century, and Daniel himself came through the Second World War as a champion of Vichy France and apologist of its antisemitic ordinances.

The example of the Halévys, by no means unique, fulfilled to the letter Clermont-Tonnerre's famous 1789 compact with the Jews ('Give them everything as individuals, nothing as a nation'). The community stifled its Jewish voice, repudiated Jewish solidarity and left the preservation of its traditional culture to a few isolated scholars. It nursed a dream: to implant the glories of French civilisation in less fortunate Jewries overseas. Hence the Alliance Israélite Universelle, founded by Adolphe Crémieux in 1860, which strung a network of schools along the Mediterranean littoral. The Alliance schools constituted a rescue operation for the underprivileged Jewish children of North Africa, Egypt, Palestine, Turkey and the Balkan states. Judaism was taught in them, of course, but an equal purpose was to guarantee a Jewish child's maturity as a Francophone, Francophile being within what had rapidly become a French cultural preserve.

La patrie must be proud of us, the Jews told themselves. So it seemed, until the year 1881 when a law on press freedom allowed the most scurrilous attacks on whatever group any paranoid journalist, incensed by the demotion of his native land to fractious secondary status in Europe, chose to select. Freedom to publish exposed the sickly xenophobia at the heart of clericalist France.

The year 1881 had not yet ended before the first openly antisemitic newspaper, *L'Anti-Juif*, came off the presses. For a brief period it had this category of journalism to itself, yet failed to survive. Soon it was followed by *L'Antisémitique*, which likewise died after a few issues. Then a spate of books appeared: *La France juive*, by Édouard Drumont; *Les Rois de la République*, by the socialist writer Auguste Chirac; *Du Molochisme juif*, by a former left-wing publicist, Gustave Tridon. Judeophobic literature, never a rarity in France, was now co-ordinated in a barrage of vilification. Its message offered no scope for compromise: the country had been laid low by the Jews, in the immediate past through their conspiracy with Protestant Germany, and across the ages by their traditional negation of all virtues Catholic, of which la belle France was the paradigm.

As though descending like a benediction from on high to sanctify the mood, a Catholic bank, the Union Générale, crashed in 1882, bringing ruin to 40,000 small investors. Pope Leo XIII had blessed the endeavour on its foundation four years earlier, for it aimed to loosen the grip upon the French financial system of a camarilla of Jewish and Protestant houses, all of them with international family or co-religionist alliances. A consortium of conservative, monarchist financiers had entrusted the steward-ship of the Union Générale to a man of unimpeachable Catholic antecedents, Eugène Bontoux. He had learnt his trade as an official of Rothschild Frères. Apparently he took on his previous masters in their own territory. Bontoux stretched his resources by allying Union Générale with the Austrian Länderbank, a rival of the Rothschilds' Kreditanstalt in Vienna. Suddenly share values in Union Générale slumped. The result was inevitable: liquidation.

Convincing evidence of Rothschild implication in the crash is hard to come by, but they had done it before, not least in the case of the Crédit Mobilier, itself a Jewish institution (see page 161). Few people now doubted that Jewry's premier family had moved in not simply to destroy the competition but to deal a mortal blow at a laudable effort to wrest the fate of France from alien tentacles. Certainly this constituted Bontoux's defence of the management of his bank.[17] His version was accepted across the whole spectrum of political opinion, including the Socialists, and inspired Émile Zola to work the story into his plot for the novel *Money*, with Alphonse de Rothschild in the guise of the enigmatic Gundermann. This was just one of several works of fiction casting the family cabal of the rue Laffitte as villains of the piece.

Little wonder, then, that Drumont's *La France juive* proved an instant sensation on its appearance in 1886 — fourteen reprints within a twelvemonth. Its author, a petit-bourgeois on the Social-ist fringe, attired in faded redingote, had been sitting all but

---

[17] Jean Bouvier, *Le Krach de l'Union Générale*, Paris, 1960. For an excellent survey of the Parisian financial scene, see also Denis Brogan, *The Development of Modern France 1870–1939*, London, 1967, pp. 268–95.

anonymously at a sub-editor's desk in the bureau of *La Liberté* for ten years. The newspaper was owned by the Péreire brothers, of Saint-Simonian and Crédit Mobilier fame. Suddenly, all the bitterness storing up in that modest breast burst into impassioned exposure of the national neurosis. Drumont became a public hero at forty-two to lead a crusade for the expulsion of the Jews from France and ultimately win for himself a seat in the parliamentary chamber. And in antisemitism he also struck upon a lucrative cottage industry. He followed the 1200 pages of *La France juive* with two more books on the same theme, and founded the Antisemitic League in 1889. The next step was the establishment of his own daily newspaper. The first issue of *La Libre Parole* appeared in 1892 – its business manager a baptised Jew – and was launched with a dire warning against the multitude of Jewish officers in the army. The subject was a shade remote for the average reader. More to the point, because of its closeness to a large number of pockets and its appeal to the fierce anti-Republican temper in the country, came Drumont's exposure of the Panama scandal.

Here antisemitism required no mystifying of issues. The man was right. Ferdinand de Lesseps, hero of the Suez Canal, proposed repeating his triumph (at the age of eighty!) on the Isthmus of Panama. But a morass of engineering complications not encountered in Suez arose, and the ill-planned project crawled at snail's pace, crippled by a shortage of funds and without effective supervision. Lesseps was being advised by a group of Jewish financiers led by Baron de Reinach (uncle of a trio of distinguished brothers, Joseph, Salomon and Theodore, and father-in-law of the first) and Cornelius Herz. Note the names – all German.

Both Reinach and Herz figured prominently in political society. Friends of Clemenceau, welcome visitors at the Palais Bourbon, they were frequently in the news as patriotic gentlemen of the first rank. They counselled Lesseps to raise a lottery-loan from the public to the order of 700 million francs. This required the passage of an enabling act by the Chamber of Deputies; no problem there, but the loan failed miserably, only some 200 millions being subscribed. The canal scheme ended in disaster.

Drumont hunted for evidence of a Judeo-German plot. It was

presented to him on a silver salver. Politicians leaked some unsavoury details to him. The company had resorted to the wholesale bribery of journalists and parliamentarians to achieve the lottery-loan – how many no one could exactly say, but the figure of 150 was mooted as members of the Chamber in receipt of dirty money. Drumont contended that three million francs was disbursed this way.

What next? Reinach and Herz, sharing a secret now known to millions and suspected as the guilty men, fell out. Reinach went to Drumont and proposed a deal, which was accepted; he delivered a list of bribed politicians against the condition that his own role in the affair be suppressed. Drumont kept to the bargain and pin-pointed Herz. It was too late for Reinach. The scandal was being aggressively investigated not just by Drumont's *Libre Parole* but throughout the press. The baron, sensing the onrush of doom, committed suicide. Said the writer Maurice Barrès, a quiet antisemite until he emerged from the closet in later years: 'Like a patriarch of old, he sacrificed himself for his tribe.'[18]

Reverberations there had to be. Clemenceau protested his innocence, fought a duel,[19] but was not believed. For years afterwards every politician's public speech had to begin by exculpating himself or besmirching others. Its reputation tarnished, the Jewish community clung to the expectation that time would wash away the odour of Panama. After all, scandal was not unknown in Catholic quarters, antisemitism could not but be a passing phase in this most civilised of nations, and Drumont won as many enemies as he did friends. His guns misfired on one occasion, and he wound up in prison for libel. In the words of the eminent Grand Rabbi of France, Zadoc Kahn: 'Antisemitism is neither French, nor Christian, nor human.' True, capitalism was on trial, but life on the boulevards took its customary gay course, the crowds flocking to the daring eroticism evoked on the stage by the Jewish playwright Georges de Porto-Riche. The Jews

---

[18] Quoted in Rabi (W. Rabinovitch), *Anatomie du judaïsme français*, Paris, 1962, p. 65.
[19] Rather, did not fight it. The duel, against the Boulangist Paul Déroulède, was one of those mock affairs common at the time. The parties fired into the air three times. Then, honour satisfied, they went home.

confronted Drumont with what they fondly termed the silence of contempt. However, another ordeal was in gestation.

Late in September 1894 a memorandum was discovered by French intelligence indicating the sale of military secrets to Germany and Italy. The following month a court martial unanimously found Captain Alfred Dreyfus, of the General Staff, guilty of treason. The officer was deprived of his military rank and sent to Devil's Island for life. Hardly anyone took notice, though the Socialist leader Jean Jaurès availed himself of parliamentary privilege to declare in the Deputies that Jewish power had undoubtedly moved in to prevent the culprit's execution.

Naturally, the shame of it stunned the family of Dreyfus, wealthy merchants of Alsatian provenance – stunned them all into grieving speechlessness. Except for his brother Mathieu. Convinced of Alfred's innocence, Mathieu sought out every approachable man of influence – politicians, writers, Jewish notables – with a plea for the reopening of the case. Alfred's public degradation, performed with deliberate theatricality before a great crowd in the courtyard of the École Militaire, had been accompanied by cries of 'Death to the Jews, death to the traitor!' But nothing helped. Then Mathieu spoke of his belief of a miscarriage of justice to a young firebrand of the Left, the Jew Bernard-Lazare.[20]

Bernard-Lazare seems to have been a minor Paul the Apostle in reverse, though premature death at the age of thirty-eight denied fulfilment to his mission. Born the son of a wholesale clothier at Nîmes in 1865, he turned up in Paris twenty-one years later a dedicated anarchist, hoping for success as a writer. He betrayed little interest in the Jews, except to endorse the opinions of Karl Marx on the subject, and to wish for their total extinction by assimilation. Early in his career he made the acquaintance of Léon Blum, like himself a contributor to *La Revue Blanche*, favoured medium of the Symbolist followers of Stéphane Mallarmé. None of that group, even the acknowledged Jews among them, would burden himself with so tiresome an issue as the Jewish question. They held themselves for aesthetics. Problems no doubt existed, they conceded, imported from alien regions.

[20] Or Lazare Bernard, or Bernard Lazare. He switched his childhood name.

But authentic French Jews, long absorbed into their original environment, shared nothing with the recent wretched arrivals caricatured in the antisemitic press, whose interests would best be served by a return to their previous homelands.

However, Bernard-Lazare soon caught himself out with second thoughts. A metamorphosis began in earnest following a visit to the poor Jewish quarter of Amsterdam. There, he said, 'voices long since dead' beckoned to him. He dipped into Jewish history, and this brought him to the study of antisemitism, as though in the footsteps taken in this same Paris a generation earlier by that other revolutionary Moses Hess. Bernard-Lazare completed a book on the subject two years before the trial of Dreyfus.[21] This argued that the Jews had been hated in the past for keeping themselves separate, and were now abused for their enthusiastic adaptation to general society. The solution, he wrote, lay in the direction of a new Jewish nationalism, the cultivation of a positive Jewish identity rather than its suppression. Bernard-Lazare had not as yet met Theodor Herzl, the Austrian journalist in Paris who would witness the degradation of Dreyfus in January 1895 and go back to his rooms to initiate the Zionist enterprise with his pamphlet *The Jewish State*.

Édouard Drumont took up the Dreyfus case in *La Libre Parole* (its slogan: France for the French) when the trial was all but forgotten. Hadn't the disgraced officer vindicated his campaign, Drumont argued, against the traitorous Jewish penetration of the army? Surely Dreyfus was but the tip of an iceberg. The Jews were scheming to deliver France to her German foe, and the many true Frenchmen who consorted with Jews, pandering to their wealth, should be branded equally as enemies of the state. Other papers joined in, notably *La Croix*, which supported the military clique striving to keep Boulangism alive.[22] Throughout this period the Jews of France made no effort at a response. Their official policy, dictated from above, continued as the silence of contempt. They refused to stoop to Drumont's level, and went so far as to repudiate the insolent propagandising of Jewish

[21] See Nelly Wilson, *Bernard-Lazare*, Cambridge, 1978, pp. 90–109.
[22] General Georges Boulanger had founded the League of Patriots in readiness for his contemplated *coup d'état*, but lost his nerve, fled to Brussels and was condemned *in absentia* for treason. He committed suicide in 1891.

arguments in obscure periodicals circulating among the new immigrants – newspapers lacking the dignity expected of established Jewry.

Caring nothing for the official view, Bernard-Lazare wrote a pamphlet *The Truth about the Dreyfus Affair*, in which he placed the officer squarely in the role of sacrificial victim of French antisemitism. Mathieu Dreyfus, discomforted by so broad a generalisation, accepted advice that a publication by the wrong man at the wrong moment would harm his brother's cause. Moreover, the Jews were themselves divided as to the man's innocence. They rejected the connection with antisemitism. The pamphlet did not reach the printer's.

Not that Drumont was having everything his own way. He was impugning particularly the honour of Jews in the army, where disputes were customarily settled on the duelling ground in satisfaction for personal insult. Drumont himself accepted a challenge from a Jewish captain of dragoons, when both parties incurred slight injury. On an earlier occasion the young officer Armand Mayer, nephew of a rabbi, faced an antisemitic aristocrat, the Marquis de Morès, and died of his wounds. Grand Rabbi Zadoc Kahn, attired in his canonicals, led the cortège at Mayer's funeral, which brought into the streets the cream of Parisian Jewry to grasp at the opportunity of reminding France of the Jews' sense of honour, even to the point of death. Though the tragic, or heroic, encounter occurred in 1892, Mayer's death raised the stock of Jewish pride enough to sustain morale in the difficult Dreyfus years.

This is not the place for a complete exposé of the Dreyfus Affair, about which new volumes with fresh revelations continue to pour forth. Suffice to say that at every turn, from the moment of the innocent man's condemnation, ramifications came to light of an elaborate design to protect the army's reputation at all costs. German and Italian intelligence disclaimed any knowledge of Dreyfus. When an officer at the War Ministry, Major Georges Picquart, disinterred a hitherto undisclosed file containing doctored material secretly communicated to the court-martial judges during the trial of Dreyfus but denied to the defence, he was peremptorily posted abroad. The information escaped into the headlines of the newspaper *L'Éclair* notwithstanding. Suspicion, directed against a certain Major Ferdinand Esterhazy, now received confirmation through the interception of a message addressed to this officer by the German military attaché, Colonel von Schwartzkoppen. The net tightened around Esterhazy. The army closed ranks.

Bernard-Lazare meanwhile engaged Drumont in highly publicised controversy. This resulted in another duel for Drumont in which Bernard-Lazare, who had little patience for such stagy exhibitions, was his reluctant antagonist. Neither man was hurt. At this point Mathieu authorised publication of the pamphlet written by his brother's only constant champion. It began: 'Did I not say that Captain Dreyfus belonged to a class of pariahs? He is a soldier, but he is a Jew, and it is as a Jew above all that he was prosecuted.'[23] Thus the issue came alive at last in the national conscience. Le Matin published a facsimile of the original memorandum (the bordereau) which had convicted Dreyfus, and proved it to have been the crudest forgery. Matthieu thereupon made an open denunciation of Esterhazy, and doors opened to Bernard-Lazare which had formerly closed tight against him.

In January 1898 Esterhazy came to trial, and amidst international disbelief won his acquittal. Two days later Émile Zola's 'J'accuse!' filled the front page of L'Aurore, edited by Clemenceau, to tear at the most basic French assumptions and bitterly divide the nation between Dreyfusards and anti-Dreyfusards. A famous cartoon of the day depicted the captain as Christ crucified.

On a wider horizon it was France against the world, as at the time of the Damascus ritual murder case of 1840.[24] The affair might never have burst into the open had not Bernard-Lazare, anarchist and Jew, lit the torch. He converted Joseph Reinach, the once-powerful right hand of Gambetta though now shadowed by his father-in-law's lamentable role in the Panama scandal. He turned the doubting Zola, won over Clemenceau, Jaurèz and a host of celebrated academics. Anatole France, long

---

[23] Quoted in Wilson, Bernard-Lazare, p. 183.
[24] A significant exception to the general condemnation of France was the rabidly antisemitic August Strindberg, the Swedish playwright, who insisted upon Dreyfus's guilt to the end, labelling him 'Antichrist'. See, e.g., Michael Meyer, Strindberg, London, 1984.

silent on the matter, at last gave his support. The Jews as a whole, despite important exceptions, still tried to hold themselves aloof, but with such noted men speaking for Dreyfus they could safely come down on the side of the angels. By righting a cruel injustice, the Dreyfusards felt they would eliminate a cancerous growth on the national body politic, restore their country's reputation in the world and strike another blow, in the glorious tradition of their beloved motherland, on behalf of all humanity.

The opposition ranged against them fought for their kind of France, disciplined, homogeneous, Catholic: the General Staff knew best; Drumont had those eminences Maurice Barrès, Charles Maurras, Léon Daudet and the patriotic organisation L'Action Française behind him, and therefore could not be wrong. What the working-class mass believed it was impossible to tell, though in the streets of some large cities, in both metropolitan France and Algeria, gangs ranged undisturbed, beating up Jewish passers-by. Naturally, they encountered only proletarian Jews; the others rode in carriages. Reporting on the ferocity of the anti-Jewish riots in Algiers on 2 February 1898, *La Croix* declared: 'This day Algiers has declared itself for Christ.'

Zola faced a charge of criminal libel, and on his conviction could escape imprisonment only by fleeing to England. As to the forgery of War Ministry documents, a certain Colonel Henry confessed and then died, probably by his own hand, in mysterious circumstances. Drumont nominated him a martyr, and started a fund-raising campaign for his widow and young son. Sensational stories of *la patrie en danger*, of honourable men trapped by the falsehoods coming from their own mouths, of demoralisation in all walks of life, held the population in a collective trauma. Bernard-Lazare, over-zealous by Jewish standards and awkward as an ally, found he was no longer wanted; in 1898 he had himself elected as one of the very few French delegates to Theodor Herzl's second Zionist Congress in Basle.

It was now the turn of the handwriting experts. They scrutinised the mountain of documents harvested over the years, in an effort to separate real evidence from hearsay, truth from forgery. To admit error in the case of Dreyfus required as it were a herculean act of will on the part of the authorities, military and civil. Finally, in June 1899, the Court of Appeal referred the case for reinvestigation to the War Council at Rennes. Now white-haired, the gaunt ex-captain emerged from his colonial prison only to be convicted a second time, but with extenuating circumstances. The council reduced his sentence to ten years, with a recommendation for clemency. This gave him an immediate pardon. The affair, and its torrent of mutual recrimination, nevertheless refused to die.

Bernard-Lazare was already in his grave when Dreyfus, now able to fight his own battle, demanded absolute clearance of his name in 1903. On 12 July 1906 the Court of Appeal struck out the ten years verdict, absolved the officer from all guilt and returned him to service. The War Council promoted him to lieutenant-colonel; the government decorated him with the Legion of Honour. Joseph Reinach's history of the case required seven volumes.

Not just a man, but an entire nation had stood trial, and in that nation the Jewish community itself. With the exoneration of Dreyfus the disposition of power in the country underwent a change. The Republic triumphed over clericalism and royalism, and immediately set about the separation of church and state. The official Jewish consistories, which had regarded every manifestation of antisemitism as an aberration best ignored, drifted like vessels deprived of their bearings, never to regain the authority granted them in the Great Revolution. That proud body, the Alliance Israélite Universelle, refrained from sending Alfred Dreyfus an official letter of congratulation. Bernard-Lazare? The citizens of Nîmes honoured their distinguished son with a statue in 1910. Local ruffians bespattered it with mud.

8

Pogrom: the Jewish Response

Caught in the toils of its geographical dilemma between Europe and Asia, Russia yearned during the nineteenth century for recognition as a part of modern civilisation. But its autocratic rulers hampered national advancement through their unrelenting grip upon the country's diverse racial elements.

The Romanov Empire embraced most of troublesome Poland in Europe and assiduously pursued a dominating role for itself in the Manchurian Far East, coveted by Japan. Too much land, with too many people located in the wrong places: were it not for the support of entrenched religious authority, and the zeal of a ubiquitous secret police, the over-extended bureaucracy would have collapsed beneath the load of its administrative tasks. Goodwill existed in abundance among those in the twin capitals of Moscow and St Petersburg wrestling with Russia's problems. The plight of the masses lay heavily on many an official's heart. But ideas of reform, in travelling to their points of application, usually gave way to hurried improvisation or indefinite postponement.

As a result, Russia zigzagged like an injured tortoise towards the goals that now marked the exertions of liberal statesmen and thinkers elsewhere. It was as though the sunlight directed its beams upon one half of Europe only, leaving the rest in a perennial night. The disabilities suffered by the Jews in this multiracial empire were shared in large part by the population as a whole; it could not be otherwise in a society of peoples stretched across an immeasurable space. Until 1861 the condition of the serfs, chattels of the landed aristocracy, paralleled Negro slavery in the New World. Tribal enmities among a population divided by language, culture, development and aspiration contributed to the general malaise.

Imperial Russia was not however to be written off as a place condemned to eternal stagnation. It revealed a propensity for sudden movement, bringing great industries and profound social reforms into life and heralding indications of a long-delayed dawn. Then the corporate inertia would set in to defeat promise of change. For decades at a time the different peoples would exist side by side in relative tranquillity, but with the slightest provocation they could hurl themselves against each other in violent strife. Enlightened aristocrats, educated in Paris, risked their lives to secure justice for the peasantry. Manifestos of revolution broke through the web of censorship while the rhythm of St Petersburg and Moscow inspired intellectual and artistic endeavour. Within the bourgeoisie a ferment of discontent lay uneasily suppressed; it harboured elements which would not hesitate at the assassination of a monarch to alter entrenched constitutional ways.

What role did the Jews occupy in all this? Antisemitism was a disease endemic to the system. It crossed class and racial divisions, though many Jews loved Russia dearly (or, where applicable, Poland). They would not dream of settling in another country. Their emancipation, they said, was bound up with the destinies of this nation as a whole. Others among them formed a static *Lumpenproletariat*, never to move except with the herd. The Jewish bourgeoisie stood in some measure apart. Its youth was impatient, volatile; so the secret police, aided by its Jewish spies, kept open files and a close watch.

The vast majority of Jews remained locked within the Pale of Settlement, but they could spill across its frontiers by submitting to baptism, or consenting to resettlement in agriculture, or through the privileges of wealth. Jewish farmers tilled the soil in the Ukraine, and their engineers and capitalist entrepreneurs were among the first to develop the mineral riches of Siberia and the Caucasus. No one impeded the Jews' economic advancement any more than the system denied this to the people as a whole. But it had to be within rigorously enforced limits of enterprise. Holy Russia feared for its sacred integrity as the second Byzantium if the Jews spread from the areas in which they had for so long been quarantined. Hence their escape westward: a trickle at first, then a flood. All other Russians – intellectuals, aristocrats, peasants and artisans, along with the Poles — applauded their departure.

An alien people, and totally so? Indeed, and thus so different from their fraternals in other parts of Europe who divested themselves of their Judaism (at any rate its outward signs) at the earliest opportunity. Sheer numbers had turned them into a nation of sorts. Honed by centuries of discrimination, cleaving fast to their own folkways, rooted in an isolationist culture by virtue of their adherence to that stringent old religion, they had given themselves, or rather discovered, an identity all their own. It was the Mendelssohnian doctrine of assimilation totally reversed. This would cost them dear, in time to come, but in nineteenth-century terms they constituted the sole reservoir for Jewry's collective survival. Thousands couldn't have done it; the process required a concentration of millions. Out of Eastern Europe there would gestate a specifically Jewish literature, all but contemporaneous with the birth of the Russian literature that began with Pushkin. Five and a half millions strong in 1880, some three-quarters of the entire tribe, they had generated cultural loyalties and the elements of a co-ordinated will. Every year thousands of young men reluctantly departed for service in the lowest ranks of the tsar's army, returning as strangers to the families they had left behind in tears.

Only a small minority among them could, in this period, read or write in the Russian or Polish language. Yiddish fulfilled every daily purpose, and though the Jews could hardly be described as an educated people by and large, their literacy nevertheless exceeded their neighbours', be these Polish, Ukrainian or authentically Russian. What the Jewish mass had of education centred on scriptural history with a touch of Talmud, despite the intense efforts of German-Jewish pedagogues imported by successive governments to lure them to secular studies. This at least gave them a familiarity with Hebrew. It was as if an English boy had been reared exclusively on a syllabus of New Testament Greek. Girls received no schooling at all.[1] Change, however, was on the way.

---

[1] As to the rabbinical hold upon education, Dubnov (*History of the Jews*, Vol. V, p. 199) writes: 'The slightest digression from ritual and tradition, and the least "heresy" — that is, wearing a short-cut coat or a trimmed beard — was

Dostoievsky, then languishing in Siberia, had not yet properly embarked on his literary career, and Tolstoy was still deliberating over the course his life should take, when the first modern Jewish work of fiction, by Abraham Mapu of Kovno (now Kaunas), burst upon the anachronistic scene. Scorning Yiddish as a medium too debased for literature, Mapu wrote his *Love of Zion*, on a biblical theme, in Hebrew. Only the truly educated Jew could read it, but the idea of a novel written by one of their own (this was in 1853) delivered a powerful blow for Jewish morale in Eastern Europe. The work was eventually translated into Yiddish, to gain a larger readership, and then into other languages. Mapu lighted the way towards a minor Augustan age in Jewish letters. A poet, perhaps the most creative force in Jewish Russia, quickly followed: Judah Leib Gordon. Inspired by Lermontov and schooled in the European classics, he too wrote in an elegant, lyrical Hebrew, addressing the social problems of his people, the subordinate role to which their women were condemned, the injustices of the tsarist regime. A journalist and educator too, Gordon sought to rally the Jews out of their inferiority complex, though he himself succumbed on occasion to a pessimistic view of their fate.

Neither Mapu nor Gordon was a writer for the populace, which of course could only be served by Yiddish. Newspapers in that language, issuing from Warsaw, Odessa and St Petersburg, began to circulate in large editions throughout the Pale, rearing a generation of Yiddish authors in the making. Other periodicals, in Hebrew, Polish and Russian, catered for the élite. At last East European Jewry could boast a literature to rival the quality and output of 'normal' peoples of similar size. Mendele Mocher Seforim (a pseudonym meaning 'Mendel the Bookseller') of Odessa was strongly influenced by Turgenev's realism. He switched early from Hebrew to the common vernacular, as did Isaac Peretz, born in Austrian Galicia. The latter abandoned a career in law, open to Jews under the Habsburgs, and changed to

---

severely punished. Reading a book of the Jewish literature of enlightenment, and particularly a book in an alien tongue, was penalised . . . The entire system of education rendered men ne'er-do-wells. Women would be the breadwinners while their husbands went wool-gathering in the house of study or the Hassidic synagogue.'

authorship so as to mine Hassidic folkways and reveal the inner life of the mystics. He frequently returned to Hebrew, wrote for the stage and went to jail for preaching Socialism at illicit meetings.

These writers emerged from the ranks of the middle-class Jewish intelligentsia, in itself a thin segment with multilingual cultural interests. They could pass for Poles, or Russians, and were in fact tempted to follow the Western pattern of assimilation. It would have been easy for them. Still, they shrank from what in their own eyes represented spiritual betrayal. East European Jewry retained their loyalty but earned their fury: by its philistinism, its torpor, its resigned acceptance of pariahdom almost amounting to willing confirmation of the antisemitic stereotype.

Living by obligation among the masses and writing for them, such men strove to convey their ideas of Jewishness as a way of life stalwart in adversity and rich in expectation, and containing within itself a capacity for cultural renewal alongside all Europe. Yiddish may have suffered from its mongrel beginnings, but they now proclaimed it as a language come of age. They could not foresee, as we have already noted, how Yiddish would be unable to withstand the transplantation of the Jews to other climes, nor how the Nazi machine would kill the language along with the people. The most expressive and popular of these authors, the Ukrainian Shalom Rabinowitz, adopted as his pseudonym 'Sholem Aleichem', the universally employed greeting (literally 'Peace unto you') between Jews. With his quixotic turn of humour, he is the classic witness to the East European Jewish condition in the twilight of the last century, as vivid a story-teller as Dickens. Sholem Aleichem, through his ironic approach to the working classes, filtered the pathos, the frustrated hopes and the limited horizon of a people indestructible within the tsarist empire, on to the Yiddish page. Unlike his fellow-literati, whose works were doomed almost to oblivion with the decline of Yiddish in the twentieth century, Aleichem lived on. Such characters as Tevye the dairyman became familiar to a world audience and inspired the art of Chagall. Tevye translated successfully to stage and screen. *Fiddler on the Roof*, based upon Aleichem's tales of the ghetto, was one of the most widely seen films of its day.

But Russia refused to accept the Jews on their own terms. The Orthodox Church insisted upon extracting from them the penalties of which the Gospels speak. They must expiate to the last degree their alleged crime in first-century Jerusalem, re-enacted, it was claimed to this day, in the desecration of the Host at the Jews' secret enclaves. More, here the Manichaean concept of struggle between God and Satan held firm; the Jews, with their Talmud, their refusal to accept Christ, their obdurate faith in eventual repossession of the Holy Land, could not be other than the Devil's children on earth.

This is not to say that the tsar himself, or his bureaucrats, automatically accepted such primitive theological extremes. A confessing Jew, however, was disqualified by his nature from recognition as a truly patriotic citizen. Not only did he resist every endeavour to acculturate and place his children in the Russian schools, he tried to evade military service on the grounds that this would seduce him away from Judaism. Employment in agriculture offered exemption from recruitment and relief from heavy taxation, so why didn't more of them go on to the land? Russia decided that the Jews were not to be trusted. Even in the Pale of Settlement they were for a long time debarred from living within thirty-six miles of its western frontier, bordering on Prussia and Austria, for fear of their engaging in espionage or contraband.

Suspicion directed against the Jews had no need for substantiation in fact. Yet Russia's rulers knew that a minority of such size could not be held for ever in a sort of legislative bondage without inviting social upheaval. Every Draconian attempt to Russify the Poles had failed; certainly none would succeed in the case of the Jews. The disasters of the Crimean War of 1854–6 had shaken the regime into a realisation of the weakness derived from its own iniquities. Hence the emancipation of the serfs, main source of Crimean cannon-fodder, in 1861; equally, slight relaxation of the rules containing Jews within the Pale. As early as 1859 Jewish merchants paying over 500 roubles a year in taxation could reside anywhere in Russia. The privilege was extended to those with university degrees and now eligible for government employment, in 1861; certain artisans too, in 1865; and finally in 1867, soldiers and their descendants who had served their gruelling term in the army of Nicholas I. These were goodwill measures by Alexander II 'the Liberator', only half-intended. The tsar was rewarded by the rise of a new kind of Russian Jew, as already indicated. Tantalised by the prize of full equality, he now seized at every opportunity for education in the widest sense, similar to his Western co-religionists. Moreover, he regarded his newly discovered love of his Russian homeland as authorisation to join any dissident force working to democratise the regime. To paraphrase Alexander Pope, a little freedom is a dangerous thing, intoxicating the brain. It was now the turn of the Jewish revolutionary, usually from a middle-class, conventional home but remote indeed from the characters depicted in Sholem Aleichem's sketches of struggling townlet Jews and their private arguments with God.

Not enough of such people, mostly young, broke away from tradition to ring a profound change of outlook among their own, but they rose in sufficient number to attract the interest of the secret police. The Crimean War (and its successor, against Turkey in 1877) had given rise to a nationalistic Slav pugnacity, among Poles, Russians and Ukrainians alike. This sentiment seized hold of artisan and peasant and priest, and inevitably expressed itself in hostility towards the stranger impinging dangerously upon the Christian foundations of their society. We must recall also the absence of cohesion in a political sense among the Jews themselves. They could not define a path for their progress because the communal leadership, if such it could be termed, was itself bitterly divided. Those promoting self-emancipation, through modernised education linked to the industrialising process then in train, faced conservative adherents of an immutable way of life, Hassidim prominent among them, for whom every advance had to be obstructed as a stage towards the ultimate disgrace of conversion. A form of limited autonomy through localised organisations known as the *kahal*, originating in Poland, had been abolished long before, in 1844, much to the relief of the Jewish masses. These councils were dominated by the well-to-do acting through the clergy. The *kahals* were remembered as government instruments supervising the special Jewish taxation and conducting the heinous recruitment system discussed in Chapter 6. The average Jew believed he could receive better protection from the general town councils, where Jews were allowed minority representation. The more progressive sector likewise welcomed the dissolution of the *kahals*, doubtless because of their character as sterile debating societies which held up all business while they split hairs over the subtleties of Judaic law.[2]

It thus transpired that the Jews possessed no cohesive organisation outside the synagogue, and were compelled to rely, as in the rest of Europe during times past, on the influence of opulent but unofficial intermediaries of their faith to lodge grievances and demands with the government. This role was eminently filled by the Günzbergs in St Petersburg, an erudite family of bankers close to the court, and by the Poliakovs, railroad magnates of legendary wealth, in Moscow.

The patient reader will no doubt be wondering at what point the modern history of Russian Jewry may be said to begin. The year 1881, when a bomb thrown in St Petersburg terminated the life of Tsar Alexander II, initiated an epoch of change for this people in Eastern Europe, and consequently in the Jewish world as a whole, as dramatically as 1066 for the English and 1789 for the French. They regarded 'the Liberator' as a well-wisher, and lamented his assassination equally with all of Russia, which became enveloped in a state of shock, suspecting treason at every corner. One immediate effect was to place the Jewish question into the centre of national concerns. Hitherto the Jews constituted little more than an administrative conundrum in a land burdened by a surfeit of problems, rarely encountered except in the course of trade, and so low in the hierarchy of peoples in this region as to arouse no emotion in others greater than indifference.

A search through the pages of the Russian classics yields only slight preoccupation with the Jews as literary material. Balzac has no equivalent here. Naturally Benjamin Disraeli, who barred Russia's way to Constantinople, was recalled as a Jew rather than an Englishman, for none but a Jew would dare to protect infidel Turkey against the new Byzantium. Dostoievsky could not forgive the Jews for Disraeli, though never to the point

2 For this, see Salo Baron, *Russian Jews under Tsars and Soviets*, New York, 1964.

of obsession. However, he did suspect them of seeking to control the world, and in *The Brothers Karamazov* he throws out, through the mouth of Liza, the suggestion that they indeed occupied themselves with such practices as ritual murder. Tolstoy confessed to being impressed by the judgement of Houston Chamberlain regarding their corrupting influence on the Aryan peoples, but they feature as only minor, derisory figures in his novels. Similarly, they emerge undefined earlier in the century in the works of Turgenev and Gogol. The exception was Lermontov, who at the age of sixteen appears to have been so touched by the Jewish fate as the scapegoat of history as to produce a drama, *The Spaniards*, on the theme of the Inquisition.

Only following that 1881 watershed did Russia's major writers awaken to a frontal awareness of the Jews and their desperate predicament in their country. Vladimir Korolenko and Maxim Gorky principally, as well as lesser authors, now applied themselves to depicting the people in fuller characterisation. By this time the long-simmering, subcutaneous unease between Jew and gentile in the empire was reaching its point of eruption.[3]

The tsar had died at the hands of nihilists of the Narodnoya Volya (People's Will Party), a growing force numbering young Jews among its members. A call went out for retribution – against whom it was impossible to say, though the strictly controlled press, led by the once liberal organ *Novoye Vremya* ('New Times'), lent a consistently antisemitic coloration to the news. A chilling wind swept through the ghettos of every south Russian town. What would happen now? Fearfully they recollected the Crusades, the Black Death, the massacres by the Ukrainian nationalist Chmielnicki in 1648. For many, this was all the Jewish history they knew, apart from the Bible.

As if by a signal, an armed rabble intent upon punishing the Jews took to the streets, to loot, to destroy, to kill. The police stood by (some said helplessly, others insisted deliberately) while houses burned and women and children were assaulted. As the months passed new outrages occurred almost daily, to be tardily suppressed only by the intervention of the military. Russian had a

[3] For the image of the Jew as conveyed to the Russian reader at this time, see Joshua Kunitz, *Russian Literature and the Jew*, New York, 1929.

word for it – pogrom – and it destroyed the illusions of millions
that they would ever be allowed to dwell unmolested in this land.

The pogroms assumed the proportions of an epidemic.
Though contained in the main within the Ukraine and White
Russia the contagion reached into Warsaw – surprisingly, for
Polish sentiment for the fallen tsar hardly attained to any degree
of affection. This was the solitary example of anti-Jewish violence in Poland. The storm's epicentre remained in the south, to
rage in some 160 towns and villages, localities where not infrequently the Jews formed the majority of the population. Horace
de Günzberg led a deputation of Jewish notables to the new tsar
and was informed of the government's intention to control the
mood. Popular anger, Alexander III claimed, indicated no special
animosity against the Jews, but rather a general disorder
fomented by the revolutionaries to destroy the monarchy. In fact
the pogroms continued far into 1882, despite condemnation by
many Russians and protest demonstrations in all the capitals of
the Western world, of which the most impressive was that convened by the lord mayor of London. By the sorrowful standards
of the present day the death count was not great, perhaps a
hundred in all, but the wounded could be numbered in their
thousands, and whole streets were reduced to rubble as if by an
earthquake. The most effective method of encouraging a police
chief to keep the *pogromchiks* at bay was for the Jews to resort to
bribery, Russia's traditional lubricating oil.[4]

Russia's infamy became a byword. One particularly discredit-
able outcome fastened culpability on the Jews for their own
disasters. In May 1882 the authorities enacted 'temporary laws'
(they were never repealed) with the object, they said, 'of improv-
ing relations between the Jews and the native population in the
Pale of Settlement, to protect the former from the hostility of the
latter, manifested in outbursts against the person and property of
the Jews, and to lessen the economic dependence of the native
population upon them'.[5] By virtue of this legalised antisemitism
rural Jews were at a stroke deprived of their rights of residence in

[4] Charles Low, *Alexander III of Russia*, London, 1895. The pogroms were fully
reported by a correspondent of the London *Times*, whose articles were repub-
lished as *The Persecutions of the Jews in Russia*, London, 1882.

[5] *Jewish Encyclopaedia*, Vol. VIII, pp. 384–6.

the villages, where they had long been employed as traders, storekeepers and innkeepers – by implication activities which exploited the peasantry. Not a word about the real cause of impoverishment in the countryside: the absentee landowners to whom the peasants, often liberated serfs, were indentured for the bulk of their crops. But the landlords remained at their ease in their distant palaces, or in the fashionable spas of Europe, while the evicted Jews, their livelihoods destroyed, swamped the proletariat in the teeming townships. Little work existed to support so many newcomers, unwelcome as strangers and feared as competitors. The result was to compound the humiliation with a catastrophic decade of penury.

A vast enterprise of charity, initiated among the Jews of London, New York, Paris and Berlin, sprang to their assistance. This was succour, not a solution. Hope for Russian Jewry pointed in only one direction: emigration. Precisely, said Russia, thus spared the evil term 'expulsion' with which history had cursed Spain since 1492. Let those that could, depart. The rest should enter the family of true Russian citizenship by conversion; otherwise let them starve.[6] 'The western border is open to them', declared the Minister of the Interior, Nicholas Ignatiev. 'They have already made use of this opportunity and no one has put obstacles in their way.'[7]

So began another exodus, partly with the help of voluntary agencies in the West led by the Alliance Israélite Universelle and the Anglo-Jewish Association, partly uncontrolled, partly stimulated by competing shipping companies offering passage at bargain rates in the hulks of their ocean-going liners. Financing the task required the intervention of a Croesus, and one such appeared, Baron Maurice de Hirsch of Paris. Originating in Bavaria from a line of court bankers, the man might have stepped out of legend. Hirsch enjoyed one of Europe's largest fortunes, gained from constructing the so-called BBB, the railway connecting Berlin, Byzance (Constantinople) and Baghdad. Racehorse owner and bon viveur, he hunted with the Prince of Wales and

---

[6] Such was the formula attributed to Constantin Pobedonestsov, Chief Procurator of the Holy Synod, who at one time tutored Alexander III in his religious responsibilities and was now a principal adviser to the tsar.

[7] Mark Wischnitzer, *To Dwell in Safety*, Philadelphia, 1948, pp. 38–9.

amassed wealth enough to allow him an occasional snort of contempt for the House of Rothschild. In 1891 he allocated forty million dollars through his Jewish Colonisation Association for the evacuation of his less fortunate brethren from Eastern Europe and their resettlement in America, North and South, and elsewhere. The tsarist government provided passports free of charge to emigrants under this aegis and freed them from obligation to military service.

Moving the refugees onward assumed the character of an art, for no Jewish community, large or small, relished the prospect of being stuck permanently with them: an institutional bed for the night, a hot meal, a small subsidy if required, and then the next train, and the next, till they boarded ship at Hamburg or Antwerp. The miseries the emigrants left behind now extended to the miseries of a voyage in the most unsanitary, crowded conditions undertaken by large families for whom every stage of the journey was a plunge into bewilderment. In the ten years to 1892, 650,000 Jews, almost all from Eastern Europe, reached the United States of America. These are the official statistics from the US Bureau of Immigration, and to them must be added, principally, 70,000 or so who came to Britain, where exact figures were not recorded. Older established (and therefore 'nicely' established) Jewish communities in both countries stoically took the strain, though not without misgiving. Accusations flew across the Atlantic and the English Channel charging their continental co-religionists with sweeping their unwanted, unskilled, other-worldly brothers on to their doorsteps. Apart from the British colonies and Argentina – underpopulated lands which opened their gates to a few thousands – America and Britain deserve recognition as the only countries not to place serious obstacles against immigration in those arduous early years.

Flight from the tsarist empire, with its ancillary stream from Austrian Galicia, would ere long transfer the gravitational centre of Jewry to a different continent, almost another planet. It had its parallel, arising from like circumstances of deprivation, in a similar exodus from Romania. That country, finally extricated in 1878 by the Congress of Berlin from its vassalage to Turkey, assumed full independence with an exalted sense of its Latin roots – ironic comment on the atavistic compensations available even to the most depressed of societies. Romania fixed its Jews in a category of aliens with a trebly reinforced strait-jacket: according to law, to race and to religion. Traditionally, the Jews drew their solitary guarantee of protection here from the intercession of foreign governments, or by prominent Western Jews bearing the authority of their governments. Both Moses Montefiore of London and Adolphe Crémieux of Paris, arriving at Bucharest to protest at the persecutions suffered by their hapless co-religionists, were received by the country's rulers (doubtless terrified of forfeiting substantial foreign credits) with elaborate displays of repentance and humility.

Promises counted for little. Despite assurances given to Disraeli and written into the Treaty of Berlin (see page 191) the Danubian kingdom continued to treat its Jews with feudal disdain. They shifted for a livelihood in the drifts of an economic backwater, enabling the few to attain riches while the mass subsisted wretchedly at the bottom of the social pile. Religious superstition on the part of both gentile and Jew made hostility mutual. We shall not rake over the details; the story is edifying to neither side.

Xenophobia, congenital to the Balkans, stirred by ethnic rivalries and exacerbated by the valid grievances of the poor, led to periodic outbursts of antisemitic frenzy in the name of the Cross. Altogether 45,000 Jews resided ghettoised in Bucharest. Not that they could be easily classified as a group. Ashkenazim confronted Sephardim as strangers. Some claimed a questionable superiority based on their Russian origin; others wore the vestigial characteristics of a more favourable status derived from Ottoman rule; still more clung obstinately to a Hassidic nirvana here on earth. Citizenship reluctantly conferred on a chosen few, and therefore inordinately prized, produced a core of emancipated, middle-class Jews detached from the rest. The word 'solidarity' was entirely absent from the Jewish lexicon in Romania.

Paradoxically, it was the emigration from Romania which first inspired their northern brothers to follow a like road westward. During the 1870s they began, some of them, to walk, bundles on their backs and guided by instinct, from Bucharest to Hamburg, where providence in the guise of Jewish charity granted them a passage out of Europe. Faith drew a small number to dare a journey across Turkey, through Syria, to a resting-place in northern Palestine. How could Romanian Jews, scarce in resource let alone initiative, have been selected to lead the way?

It happened through the somewhat bizarre appointment of Benjamin Franklin Peixotto, a Jewish philanthropist from Cleveland, Ohio, as US Consul in Bucharest. President Grant gave him the diplomatic post, the first American mission in this remote corner, at the behest of wealthy sponsors in America, France and England. They covered the expenses of Peixotto's office on the tacit understanding that his real assignment was to pressure the Romanian government into dissolving all restrictions upon the Jews. Here was a Joseph indeed come to Pharaoh's court. In fact he transpired to be a Moses in disguise. Observing little hope for his people in this Latin fortress set within a vast Slavonic sea, he preached instead their departure on a grand scale, to his own hospitable land. Only in America could they shed their bonds, seize the opportunities awaiting all who reached its shores and make good. Naturally, Romania proved amenable, though not so much the Jews of the West; they had not reckoned on so drastic (and costly) a solution to their co-religionists' woes. Peixotto sowed better than he knew. Soon the Jews were on their way. One-fifth of the total Romanian Jewish population, some 50,000 people, crossed the Atlantic by 1900. The era of Ellis Island had begun in 1892. Newcomers of all nationalities, processed there by harassed, distrustful officials only too ready to exclude paupers, illiterates and those suspected of contagious disease, reached at times a peak of five thousand a day.

We must return to Eastern Europe to rectify the picture obtaining in the West of a totally helpless underclass reduced by antisemitism to passive acceptance of a fate from which it could be rescued only by the efforts of fellow-Jews in the democratic world. The generalisation, as the reader will have observed, fell short of the truth. It betrayed an ignorance of the organic development so great a concentration of the people could accomplish. Simultaneous with the urge to resettle in another region within their Diaspora, a neo-national ideology, still awaiting the description political Zionism, was germinating among East European Jewry; indeed, at this stage it was less political than cultural, even spiritual. Its advocates took their cue from gentile romantics besides earlier Jewish thinkers. We have already encountered Moses Hess. Other Jews saw the revival of Hebrew letters in the nineteenth century as a regenerative instrument, restoring long-severed links with the Holy Land. The subject also inspired poets, philanthropists and divines, liberal statesmen such as the social reformer Lord Shaftesbury, a host of Christian mystics, even antisemites desirous of ridding Europe of the accursed race – the philosopher Fichte leaps immediately to mind.

The Russo-Jewish intelligentsia had not been deaf to the 'Zionist' message in the works of that most distinguished if wayward son, Disraeli. More, George Eliot's impressive novel of the Return, *Daniel Deronda*, published in 1875, reached it with the impact of a thunderclap. And of course for a textbook nonpareil they had the Bible. The realisation now dawned on a small, minute rather, group in Russia and Romania that shifting people around the globe failed to touch the Jewish problem at its root: homelessness. Only Palestine could do that. It had long been their dream. Couldn't it be turned into a reality?

An organisation, Hovevei Zion ('Lovers of Zion'), was born in Odessa as the first truly radical movement in modern Jewish history. It sent out a signal to the people that now, at last, the threnody of consistent hostility, sporadic violence and permanent alienation in the Diaspora could be ended by their restitution to their own cherished land. An ancient community already inhabited Palestine, to be sure, but Hovevei Zion was an invitation to normalise their situation with a creative existence in husbandry on the soil, to give that soil, which the Jews had neglected for countless centuries, its promised renewal. The Odessa headquarters released publications, dispatched the first pioneers to Palestine and encouraged similar groups in other countries. At first they had no great ambitions, or expectations. They stumbled. Colonies of hopeful families established on desert land would have foundered had not a desperate appeal to Edmond de Rothschild in Paris been handsomely answered.[8] But consider the audacity of these pioneers, innocent of political

---

[8] His benefactions extended over fifty years and were continued, as an inherited responsibility, by later generations of the Rothschild dynasty.

issues, apprentices in agriculture, to confront Turk and Arab and Christian, all of whom despised the Jew, in staking a claim in this tiny land anew. They were not the first to try, for Jews had been returning to Palestine from some indefinable commitment since the Dispersion, to plant a tree, build a house, raise a family, point a moral and end their days. These of the late nineteenth century, however insignificant in number compared to those turning westward, were the first to succeed.

Draining off East European Jewry's surplus population should have enormously reduced the remainder. It didn't. Statistics are unreliable, but we know that their natural increase, since the sharp decline in infant mortality, worked like a multiplication table. Furthermore, loss to the Jewish mass through conversion and intermarriage, already making deep inroads among the smaller communities in the West, was a much rarer phenomenon in this region.[9] Those departing were quickly replaced via the conjugal bed.

The Russian authorities, anticipating a grand thinning out, were disappointed. Manifestly, life under Romanov rule was still too comfortable for enough Jews to abjure its benefits. The government tightened the screw, annulling some reforms introduced in the reign of Alexander II. Jews were beginning to avail themselves of the privilege of high school and university entrance to an unexpected degree. So the barriers went up. The authorities introduced a quota system – not more than six per cent of students in any institution, though Jews numbered half the total population of Vilna, one-third in Odessa. This edict stunted the creation of an adequate Jewish intelligentsia, especially as the wealthier element now sent their children of both sexes to throng the liberal universities abroad, and not infrequently to stay away for ever. Then, in 1891, a direct expulsion order drove some 15,000 Jews from Moscow and other towns situated outside the Pale. They were for the most part skilled artisans, and the order

---

[9] As examples of the contrast, we may cite the German, Italian and French experience, where attrition through assimilation had begun a century earlier. Germany's Jewish population, reinforced by an eastern trickle, remained stable. In Italy and France they failed to keep pace with the general population growth. But in the USA and Britain replenishment through immigration compensated vastly for the wastage. See Harry L. Shapiro, *The Jewish People, a Biological History*, Paris, 1960.

gave strong impetus to the emigration, so that 140,000 left the country in the year 1892 alone.

Describing the eviction order from Moscow, *The Times* correspondent reported:

> About a hundred Jewish artisans who have served their time as soldiers with the colours have sent a petition to the Tsar to the effect that, after having passed through the ranks of the Russian army and being now settled down in Moscow, they are to be sent away from their homes like felons. They are ready, as they say, to sacrifice themselves when necessary on the altar of the Fatherland, and are proud of having been Russian soldiers; but if they are thus covered with shame and contumely how can they again serve his Majesty in case at any time they should again be called into active service? It is very doubtful whether this petition will ever get near its destination. When the emperor came here recently the police ordered that no Jews were to appear in any of the principal streets, under pain of arrest and imprisonment.[10]

Stultification, pogrom, exile. The young rebels of the community refused to contemplate the fate in passivity. They concealed arms beneath the floorboards of their homes, and even their synagogues. Their determination strengthened with a recrudescence of violence in the 1890s, when the antisemitic bands to their consternation encountered resistance; the despised tribe was actually shooting back! That was one outlet for Jewish frustration. Another was for hundreds, then thousands, of young men and women to abandon home and hearth, Lev Bronstein (Trotsky) among them, and give themselves wholly to revolutionary activity. Thus were the Jews marked out as prime suspects by an officialdom acutely disturbed by the turmoil that lay beneath the surface tensions of the empire. It became as common a feature at the annual Passover table to lament for a son or daughter banished to Siberia as to pray for next year in Jerusalem. In 1903 Theodor Herzl, absolute commander of the Zionist Organisation he had founded six years earlier (though

[10] *The Times*, London, 13 June 1891.

not totally in harmony with the men of Odessa who had been preaching the cause since 1881), was received in St Petersburg by Count Sergei Witte, the Minister of Finance, to be informed: 'There are only seven million Jews [an exaggeration] among our total population of 136 millions, but their share in the membership of the revolutionary parties is about fifty per cent.'[11]

This could even have been an underestimate. Chaim Weizmann, himself to lead the Zionist Organisation in later years and to become the first President of the State of Israel, was at his Russian home in Pinsk about this time. He subsequently reported as follows to Herzl:

> Hundreds of thousands of very young boys and girls are held in Russian prisons, or are being spiritually and physically destroyed in Siberia. More than 5,000 are now under police surveillance, which means the deprivation of their freedom. Almost all of those now being victimised in the Social Democratic movement are Jews, and their number grows every day. They are not necessarily young people of proletarian origin; they also come from well-to-do families, and incidentally not infrequently from Zionist families. Almost all students belong to the revolutionary camp . . . which has already captured masses of young people who can only be described as children.[12]

One revolution, in psychology, was already achieved. Hitherto every advance by Russian Jewry had required Western initiative. Now it assumed responsibility for its own, and by extension affected the people's situation everywhere. It was a transformation, irreversible. They had planted a root in Palestine, they were on the march at home, they appeared to be taking American Jewry by storm. No longer could they be categorised as an indigestible lump, a retarded society encased within a petrified religion. Russia, pursuing a course of administrative antisemitism, had forced them into it. With their plunge into agitation for

[11] Raphael Patai (ed.), *The Complete Diaries of Theodor Herzl*, New York, 1960, p. 1530.
[12] Letter to Theodor Herzl, 6 May 1903, in Chaim Weizmann, *Letters and Papers*, Vol. II, Oxford, 1971, p. 307.

political and social equality the Jews gave a lead to the Russian population as a whole. And by taking up armed resistance against the *pogromchiks* they wiped away the image that had shamed them for centuries.

Equality could be attained here, many of them said, but only in a Socialist society. Translating the thought into a programme of action, a secret enclave met in 1897 in Vilna, the Lithuanian city which had never suffered a pogrom, and established Russia's first non-terrorist revolutionary party, the Bund.[13] Its objective was the recognition of the Jews as a national group with cultural autonomy in a multiracial Socialist state. The group adopted a policy for the here and now: education of the proletariat, co-operation with non-Jewish workers, trade unionism, strikes. Its leader, Julius Martov, stemmed from a middle-class family prominent in the revival of Hebrew, but realism dictated that the Bund reject all such connotations of élitism and bring its message to the masses in Yiddish. Repudiating Mosaic law and trust in the divine, Bundists drew their inspiration instead from Karl Marx and Leo Tolstoy.

Thirteen conspirators started the Bund officially in September 1897. One month earlier Herzl, the noted journalist with an instinct for publicity, had founded the Zionist Organisation at a congress attended by hundreds, and in the presence of the world's press. Yet the Bund immediately attracted thousands to its illegal banner while Zionism remained for years a movement of the bourgeoisie, narrowly based: two diverging paths, each a response to antisemitism and marking the Jews' tardy entry into the arena of European nationalist politics.

A man possessed, Herzl travelled alone. He wanted the Powers, who could so easily bend Constantinople to their will, to help him forge a gentlemen's agreement with Turkey – he called it a Charter – for large-scale Jewish colonisation in Palestine. Until starting out on his quest he had no knowledge of his movement's prefiguration among 'Lovers of Zion' in Odessa, or the isolated farming communities already scratching at the soil in the Holy Land. He believed that the organisation of his creation,

---

[13] Literally, 'Union'. Its full name was General Jewish Workers' Union of Lithuania, Poland and Russia.

based in civilised Vienna, had arrived to rescue inarticulate, demoralised, persecuted East European Jewry not only from tsarism, but also from itself. The Russian 'Lovers of Zion' joined with him, albeit reluctantly. They were appalled by Herzl's low estimation of themselves, and by his supercilious ignorance of Hebrew culture as a historic bond with Palestine. He would learn.

The Bund on the other hand brought to public attention the existence of a substantial Jewish proletariat, exploited as were all workers, in every town and city of the Pale. Hitherto Russia saw the Jew as a parasite, rarely manually employed, belonging to a tribe with abhorrent social and religious laws, the enemy of all righteousness. But here they came, already seasoned political agitators when the Russian Social Democratic Labour Party was formed in 1898, bringing three delegates on to its nine-man committee and eager to affiliate their Bund to the new Marxist front. The Bundists infused much-needed new blood into the revolutionary movement, most gratifying to its progenitors Lenin and Plekhanov. It would be a true marriage, Lenin felt, for he was free of racial prejudice, and in any case Socialism would dissolve such reactionary sentiments as nationalism in the tide of man's economic emancipation.

Not so fast, however. The combined movement soon revealed its inherent contradictions. The Jews obstinately clung to their separatist culture, fostered by the Bund equally with their agitation to improve the worker's lot. The Bund dared not leave the message of Jewish creativity to its arch-rival, the Zionist Organisation. And so divisions within the Marxist ranks were at first simply bewildering, then troublesome, and finally they resulted in fierce enmity between the partners. Plekhanov scoffed at the Bund as 'Zionists scared by the thought of a sea voyage'. He managed to convince some leaders of the Bund, seducing Martov himself, and thousands of the rank and file. The Jewish organisation bowed to the inevitable. It split off from the Social Democratic Labour Party in 1903: both a loss and a gain. The Bund became an object of derision to those Jews who now concentrated with Lenin and Martov on creating a unified structure. But we are in schismatic territory. Lenin and Martov had profound differences too, and the latter went into an ideological no-man's-land with his Menshevik wing of the party. The Bund, stripped of some illusions, henceforth shied away from embarrassing alliances.

Meanwhile, events in Russia were spinning out of control. Assaults upon the Jews, repression of industrial workers by an undisciplined gendarmerie, inter-racial strife, they followed each other in a cycle of tragic regularity. Three days of pogrom in Nikolayev during the Passover of 1899 had the peasants trundling their wagons back to the countryside loaded with plundered Jewish property before the police stepped in. A barricade manned by young Zionists at Ekaterinoslav in 1901 prevented ugly incidents from turning violent. But then events in Kishinev in Bessarabia stood out in savagery. The self-defence units there had been forewarned of an anti-Jewish demonstration planned for Easter 1903. The police disarmed the Jews nevertheless, on a false promise of protection. In the event forty-three Jews were killed and hundreds injured, the sorry picture being completed in the glow of food shops and housing aflame. No one could be in doubt regarding the guilt of Kishinev. Only one newspaper was licensed there, published by a virulent local antisemite, Pavel Kruschevan (a Jew later attempted to assassinate him, and received five years in Siberia). Tolstoy, joined by Maxim Gorky – the latter an eyewitness to a pogrom at Nijni-Novgorod in 1894 – raised his voice to charge the Church with complicity in the succession of outrages.

Kishinev would register in the minds of the Jews as a particular humiliation, parading their impotence. They could have fought back, had they not been duped. It was Kishinev that brought Herzl to Russia for interviews with Witte and the Interior Minister, Vyacheslav von Plehve, to discuss a *mariage de convenance* between antisemitism and Zionism. If Russia wished its Jews away, why did it not help persuade Turkey to adopt an open immigration policy? His mission did not bring Herzl many new friends among the Jews of the Pale. Plehve was the criminal ultimately responsible for Kishinev; they declared that Herzl disgraced his people by talking to him.

Russian despotism might with difficulty suppress the general mood of disaffection at home, despite regular warning signals. It failed however to perceive the degree to which it was exporting resentment abroad. In fact the Achilles' heel of tsarism was located on the banks of the Hudson, in New York City, where the majority of America's recent immigrants by this time resided: close to a million people with hearts still beating in Yiddish, and in unison with brother-exiles domiciled in Britain and elsewhere. They kept agitation against Russia alive when gentile campaigners against antisemitism flagged. Tsarism reaped a harvest of hatred, coinciding with the retribution of that extraordinary venture into *Machtpolitik*, war against the Rising Sun.

Russia saw the hope of a solution to its economic problems (and who knows? perhaps a salve for its social maladies too) through expansion eastward – hence the Trans-Siberian railway and ambitions for spoils out of the Manchu Empire crumbling in China. Japan, assured of Britain's connivance at its challenge to the tsar in these parts, prepared for a clash, and in February 1904 attacked Port Arthur. The world's press lyricised in admiration for the 'plucky little Japs'. But Japan's resources proved too slender for a long war against the Slav Goliath, and emissaries hastened to the City of London in search of funds – with little success. Fortuitously, Jacob Schiff, once of Frankfurt, now of New York, happened then to be in London. He was in his financial prime, nearly as powerful on Wall Street as John Pierpont Morgan.

Schiff headed the banking house of Kuhn, Loeb, whose victories included stock flotations for the industrialisation of the American West and productive enterprises wherever the earth's riches required the pollination of finance. As a transatlantic version of the Rothschilds, Schiff's family retained its affiliation to Judaism. He felt a strong obligation towards the well-being and adjustment of the Jews descending in waves upon his country from Eastern Europe, even though the sight of them somewhat offended his German-American sensitivities. Naturally, he harboured a deep loathing for Russia, parent of their misfortunes, and while in London he lent a ready ear to the problems of the Japanese in paying for their war. The result we know: Schiff returned home to fulfil a promise to raise 200 million dollars for Tokyo. He enlisted Morgan, then Rockefeller, and the money was as good as there. Japan went on to demolish the tsar's war machine on land and sea. Schiff was showered with honours during a visit to Tokyo – the first white commoner to lunch at the Mikado's palace, no less.[14] But in Russia his fellow-Jews could be stigmatised anew, as traitors. Jewish power was ever a double-edged sword.

Filling the battle-lines in the Far East left Russia dangerously under-garrisoned at home, where the troops habitually served as a regional militia. Reports of alarming casualties advertised the misdirection of a war originally conceived by the government as a walk-over. Inevitably, discontents multiplied. Minister Plehve fell to an assassin's bullet in July 1904, while down in the Baku oilfields Tartar and Armenian labourers, who might reasonably have united to register their legitimate grievances as workers, vented long-nurtured fury against each other instead, in the name of religion. Mutual slaughter ensued in the Caucasus, on a scale unheard of in the anti-Jewish excesses. This brought intervention by the gendarmerie most feared by the populace, the semi-official Black Hundreds. They were a brutal force of ardent patriots who, in the name of Slav purity and the Christian faith, also rushed to the protection of the mob during the pogroms, and themselves spread terror among the Jews.

Add to its other troubles the vacillations of a weak-willed tsar surrounded by corrupt officials, and the full measure of Russia's inability to cool the atmosphere can be gauged. Strike followed strike in the factories, demonstrations in the streets, a naval mutiny at sea. Panic seized the royal guard one Sunday in January 1905, when a huge procession of workers, accompanied by their families and led by a priest, made for the Winter Palace in St Petersburg with a petition for Tsar Nicholas II. They had come as much in homage to a monarch they venerated as to register their grievances. The palace guard, for no obvious reason, fired into the crowd. Some reports spoke of at least a thousand men, women and children dead, all in their Sunday best, though Alexander Kerensky, who witnessed the scene, put the figure at between 200 and 300.[15] However calculated, Black Sunday rang the empire's knell. To the social revolutionaries there could be

[14] See Cyrus Adler (ed.), *Jacob H. Schiff, His Life and Letters*, Vol. I, New York, 1928.
[15] Alexander Kerensky, *Russia and History's Turning Point*, New York, 1965, p. 48.

only one explanation for the massacre, and they decided that the priest, Father Gapon, was in fact a police agent deliberately provoking the people. He had to die. They chose from their number a Jew, Pinchas Rutenberg, to discharge the errand. This man, later a pioneer Zionist industrialist in Palestine, tracked the priest to Finland and shot him at point-blank range. Soon afterwards the Governor of Moscow, the tsar's uncle Grand Duke Sergei, met his death by a terrorist's hand as his carriage approached the Kremlin walls. War against Japan still raged; the strikes continued, as did the bitterest of the pogroms.

At last, fearing a Russian Bastille, the tsar consented to listen to the people. He issued a proclamation in October 1905 announcing free elections for a parliament, the Duma. Why this should not have been greeted with more approbation remains a mystery. Of course it did not go far enough to satisfy the revolutionaries; in some localities they boycotted the elections. The Bund, branding the royal proclamation a hoax and the Duma a capitalist joke in the worst possible taste, likewise ignored the poll. Millions of loyal Russians detected a Jewish plot against their beloved tsar, and expressed themselves accordingly.

We move to Odessa, on the Black Sea, the cosmopolitan city where between them Jews and Greeks, never the warmest of friends, controlled the vital export trade in grain. Here the Jews acclaimed the tsar's October manifesto as a great victory in their struggle for civil equality. Workers of all races marched through the streets, their red flags aloft, with no thoughts of drawing blood. Yet the situation deteriorated; lawless bands took over and made a rush for the poorer Jewish quarters. The Jews, aided by Christian students and other sympathisers, held their ground. The dead reached a total of 300 in exchanges of fire before an uneasy peace was restored. It was the highest casualty figure in this phase of the disorders. Further violence broke out in Kiev, Gomel, Zhitomir and Bialystok, to name the principal centres of antisemitic outrage. Thus 1905, which held portents of Jewish emancipation in Russia, terminated as the most costly year for them since the time of Chmielnicki in the seventeenth century. Some 800 Jews perished that year. They might have resisted more effectively, for they were prepared. Unhappily they failed to co-ordinate their response or even, in some instances, to assist each other. Defence squads composed of Zionists refused to make common cause with Bundists. A Soviet Jewish historian, Nathan Buchbinder, who would have shown more sympathy for the latter, charged the Bundists with going so far as to turn upon the Zionists during the pogroms, so incidents occurred when Jew found himself battling against Jew.[16]

With Russia almost at the edge of an abyss, the Imperial Duma, embracing representation from all races, convened in St Petersburg in April 1906. Twelve Jews had been elected – that is, twelve self-acknowledged Jews, others being Christian converts – all of the liberal Constitutional Democratic ('Cadet') Party, or the Trudoviki, more to the Left. One of them, Shmarya Levin (representing Vilna), took his seat, as he remarked in his first speech, despite having no legal rights of sojourn in the capital.[17] The Cadets chose another Jew, the lawyer Maxim Vinaver, as their deputy leader. It was a token of the emergence of this people from their long segregation in a political vacuum.

What to discuss first? Agrarian reform, so that the peasants might eat, or the pogroms, so that the Jews might live? With benches crowded with Poles, Ukrainians, Muslims and Armenians all clamouring for national autonomy, the agenda stretched to an endless list. Since most of the members were of the dominant race of Russians properly called, they finally agreed to commence business with a demand for the immediate replacement of tsar's ministers by men better acquainted with the volcanic situation threatening to destroy the regime.

Those twelve Jews seemed an augury: evidence that their people no longer constituted a voiceless mass of despised aliens condemned to grovel for recognition on the fringes of society. Parliamentarians equal to all others, they presented themselves with their colleagues inside the Winter Palace to hear the speech from the throne. And as if that were not wonderment enough, Baron Horace de Günzberg himself saluted them at his residence (a more modest winter palace), recognising here twelve Jews of another ilk, and products of a strange mechanism, the ballot box. The occasion marked the baron's redundancy. Wealth had

---

[16] In his *History of the Labour Movement in Russia*, in Yiddish, Vilna, 1931.
[17] Shmarya Levin, *Forward from Exile* (autobiography), tr. and ed. Maurice Samuel, Philadelphia, 1967, p. 409.

brought him privileges and immunities beyond the imagination of the ordinary man in the street in this most complex of societies. His nod and a wink could save Jews from Siberia, open the doors of a university, sometimes prevent a pogrom. That eminence had been their shame. But now the reign of the 'court Jew' was over, even in Russia.

Maxim Vinaver, the Mirabeau of the 1905 revolution, personified the new spirit of defiance. He spoke for the oppressed of all races and nationalities within the empire. A democratic Russia under a constitutional monarch; what a prospect of greatness could he create with his impassioned words! What Russia received in response was a slap in the face. The first Duma was peremptorily dissolved before a single reform could reach the statute book. The revolution failed virtually as it began. Vinaver joined with others in a call for civil disobedience, thereupon to be sentenced to three months' imprisonment and deprivation of his voting rights. Absolutism restored its initiative.

The nationality question had sunk the experiment, for the government justified its action on the grounds of safeguarding the Orthodox, Slavonic state from the non-Russian minorities – Poles, Armenians and Jews above all – who plotted the overthrow of the Romanov dynasty. It was a pretext, of course, to deprive them of their specific representation. Peter Stolypin, head of an openly antisemitic movement, the Union of Russian People, was placed in control of national security, which made him a policeman of unassailable power. Later sessions of the now emasculated Duma served until 1917, but solely as an ultra-conservative rubber stamp. Jews sat there, but in much diminished number, unidentified and totally bereft of influence. disillusionment bit deep into the Zionist soul. A thousand or two took themselves off, with a Socialist-Zionist dream, to Palestine. But those departing for America between 1905 and 1908 numbered 540,000, incidentally rendering New York into a thriving centre of Bundist philosophy.

To evoke the sense of despair among those left behind we must recall one more episode, unbelievable, unspeakable, yet perhaps inevitable: the trial in Kiev of Mendel Beilis in 1913. Jewish history in Imperial Russia thus concluded with a throw-back to medievalism in a charge of ritual murder. For many external observers of the East European crisis, President Woodrow Wilson being among the most vocal, this represented the nadir of ignominy. In the war that burst upon Europe the following year few neutrals could find a word of sympathy for Russia in its conflict with the Central Powers.

Just as the Dreyfus Affair had less to do with alleged treason by one man than a spreading cancer within an entire society, so did the Beilis case expose the symptoms of self-destruction wished upon itself by Russia. To its credit, the Orthodox Church hierarchy rejected absolutely the charge that this working man Beilis, foreman of a brick kiln, had enticed away the boy discovered dead in a cave on the outskirts of Kiev. Testimony against Beilis could be volunteered only by a Roman Catholic priest. Still, Black Hundred members, prominent in the city, distributed leaflets at the boy's funeral declaring him the victim of a Hebrew sacrament.[18] In fact a gang of thieves had perpetrated the crime, and the police knew it, but the Minister of Justice, Ivan Shcheglovitov, compelled them to press charges against Beilis. Amidst a wave of public indignation the trial, by a jury of peasants, dragged on for months. Before its termination a plenary meeting of the St Petersburg Bar Association adopted a resolution describing the proceedings as a mockery of justice and a 'slanderous attack on the Jewish people condemned by all civilised society, imposing upon the court the propagation of racial hatred and national hostility. This outrage disgraces Russia before the world.' Twenty-three lawyers, including the future liberal Prime Minister Alexander Kerensky, were in consequence convicted of disseminating a slander against the state and sent to prison.[19] It took almost a year for the jury finally to acquit Beilis, and so yet another Jew, unable to endure his native land, packed his bags and left.

In summary, two million Jews, enough to make a nation in themselves – indeed they were as homogeneous as this people would ever be – escaped the oppressive climate of Eastern Europe between 1880 and 1914. The Atlantic crossing could now be made in under two weeks. New York City absorbed them with

[18] For the best account, see Maurice Samuel, *Blood Accusation: The Strange History of the Beilis Case*, London, 1966.
[19] Kerensky, *Turning Point*, p. 86.

their language and religion intact. No need for apprehension here regarding the sensitivities of a hostile indigenous population, for what did indigenous signify in this unformed civilisation? They brought their ghetto mythology along with their rabbis and agnostics, to open synagogues, publish Yiddish books and spread the Socialist doctrines born of the pogroms in the Pale. Their mental baggage included aptitude at the sewing machine and an irrepressible instinct for buying and selling.

Infected by the universal optimism in America, they struck root as nowhere else. It was a discovery of no little significance to find millions of other Europeans who, like themselves, had been driven from the tired old continent by hunger and oppression. The Jews numbered some eleven per cent of all newcomers to the United States in those years. Disgorged into three or four square miles on either side of the bend in the East River where Manhattan divides from Brooklyn, they crowded against Poles, Magyars, Italians, Slovaks, Croats, equally bemused by the intricacies of the English language. It was as though each tenement harboured its portion of the detritus of centuries. New York became not only the new Jerusalem but the new Rome, with more Italians than in the Eternal City. But many Italians tended to return home, or shift forward and back; for the great majority of Jews, like the Irish before them, there could be no return journey.

Anxieties there had to be. Who was without a relative in the old country for whom the passage money had to be saved, a room found, a job bespoken? Not for a moment would their ears be deaf to news coming out of Europe, its wars and revolutions and famine – it was always the disasters that reached them from across the sea, never the good times. Sweatshops in America were somehow different, the market stalls displayed better bargains, and the Jews saw, as they stood with those others in the dripping shadows of the elevated railroads or meekly waited in line at the tenement water-tap, that a 'goy' in New York could be no more at home than themselves. Yet how quickly one learned to adapt, and divide one's waking hours between the workbench, the trade union meeting and the night-school! A great institution opened its hospitable doors to them. They needed no second bidding. In 1903, of the 2,100 students enrolled at the College of the City of

New York, no less than 1,900 were Jews, mainly of recent East European provenance.[20] Where were the Italians, the Irish, the Slovaks, the Croats?

No one would have dreamed of asking: 'Where are the Negroes?' The most significant discovery those Jewish pariahs, the *Urvolk* of Europe, made in this other world was the existence of another *Urvolk*, more of an underclass than they had ever been. Harlem was still a *gemütlich* white suburb at the turn of the century. Nearly 60,000 blacks none the less inhabited Manhattan, mostly in the notorious 'Tenderloin', a mid-town block of miserable streets on the West Side. These too were recent immigrants, though from another part of the United States, not from across the ocean. The Tenderloin harboured the most abject poverty in the English-speaking world, where child-mothers gave birth to stillborn babies in doorways. Vice and squalor reigned; rats infested the tenements whose occupants were classed in this most humane of societies as less then human.[21] Their Yiddish-speaking neighbours over on the East Side might have few possessions and likewise exist in slum apartments. They too had to work themselves sick for every dollar. But their skins were white. Soon naturalisation would grant them citizens' privileges – the vote, and a path to the professions. Munificently endowed Jewish charitable organisations would help them along the way, so Americanisation could proceed apace. The blacks on the other hand had not even the illusion of equality. Excluded from 'respectable' neighbourhoods, good only for the meanest of occupations, objects of derision and worse, they subsisted on the leftovers from the plenty being enjoyed all around them. The comparison needs to be stressed, for Jew and Negro in America would be juxtaposed minorities for decades to come, moving upwards in the social and political scale together, though at different velocities, and striking a relationship that would sway from co-operation in friendship to polarisation in enmity.

As to the Lower East Side, it had its smaller counterparts in London, Paris, Chicago and Toronto: alien Jews similarly con-

---

[20] Article 'Universities', in *Jewish Encyclopaedia*, Vol. XII, p. 379.
[21] See, e.g., Gilbert Osofsky, *Harlem, the Making of a Ghetto: Negro New York 1890–1930*, New York, 1966.

tending for survival in a strange environment, except that here in loosely stratified New York the only true aliens were those whose forefathers had arrived as slaves, two centuries before the first *pogromchik* punished his first Jew for drinking Christian blood in Elizavetgrad, province of Kherson. So, given motivation and initiative, it was relatively easy for the Jew to prosper in the transatlantic capitalist paradise. Many failed or fell victim to the struggle, such as the 143 seamstresses who died in that Washington Square fire-trap of the Triangle Shirtwaist Company in 1911. Strikes and lock-outs occurred every day, but thanks to David Dubinsky, with his past in the Bundist climate of Brest-Litovsk, unionisation of the garment trade workers spread to other crafts across America, and labour conditions soon left older industrial countries far behind.

The population transfer from East to West released Jewish creative energy in every direction, not least in the glamorous arena of mass entertainment, to bring a profound and enduring cultural influence upon America as a whole, and hence upon the world. Adolf Zukor, Samuel Goldwyn, Jesse Lasky, Marcus Loewe, the Cohn brothers and the Warner brothers were just a few of the Jewish pioneers who put the film industry among America's greatest wealth producers. Not to universal approbation: to quote Scott Fitzgerald, some Americans saw Hollywood *kitsch* as a Jewish holiday but a gentile tragedy. Al Jolson starred in the very first talking picture, an event of historic dimension, and naturally its theme, so beloved of the time, was of a Jewish boy's conscience stretched between the duty to remain faithful to his religion and the call to theatrical fame. This being America, he could have both, so cinema-goers across the globe were treated to a climax in pure Sholem Aleichem style: Jolson rushing from his Broadway audience to chant the *Kol Nidrei* prayer in his dying father's East Side synagogue. Paul Muni, Eddie Cantor, Danny Kaye, Irving Berlin and George Gershwin likewise had their origins in the Pale of Settlement, along with George Burns, the schmaltzy Sophie Tucker, Jack Benny and the rest. The lift from the depths of despair into a world of laughter and make-believe, with its ingredient of self-mockery, proved a tribal catharsis.

Classical musicians emerged from that setting too, Arnold Schoenberg (of Galician ancestry), Aaron Copland and Fritz

Kreisler, for example, and such artists as Max Weber, Jacob Epstein, Mark Rothko and Ben Shahn. Jews began early to build commercial empires, or to write, and all of them proclaimed: 'We too are America!' And though Hollywood, being a redoubt of so much Jewish enterprise, graphically recorded the activities of Italian gangsters and their dull-witted Irish associates, it depicted the chosen ones pure as the driven snow. In fact the Mafia had its Jewish substructure, and big-time Jewish hoodlums in plenty carved fiefdoms out of prostitution and gambling rackets.[22] No one whose American education came from the movies would have known it – that is, not until the 1960s, when television and independent film producers led the art into a less self-conscious, deliberately iconoclastic era, with third-generation Jewish Americans released from every ancestral inhibition.

More crucial for the destiny of this people, mass settlement in the New World transformed the Diaspora, hitherto considered a source of Jewish vulnerability, into a force in international affairs. This would give rise to new categories of antisemitism, but on the other hand it armed the Jews with a capacity to confront their enemies to a degree never before achieved.

[22] For Jewish criminality in America, both before and after the First World War, and the careers of such tsars of the underworld as Arnold Rothstein, 'Dutch Schultz' Flegenheimer, Moses Annenberg and Meyer Lansky, see, e.g., Charles E. Silberman, *A Certain People*, New York, 1985, pp. 127–30; Jenna Joselit, *Our Gang*, Bloomington, Ind., 1984.

9

In Quest of
the Elders of Zion

It would have been surprising indeed if immigration on so great a scale did not produce a reaction among the native populations of England and America. Despite ample evidence of popular unease, employers in the United States nevertheless encouraged the movement westward. With lots of steerage space to fill, the shipping companies activated hundreds of travel agents in Europe to ensure their share of the lucrative passenger traffic. In this they enjoyed the fullest co-operation of industrial interests, keen to replace their recalcitrant Irish workers, who gave them so much trouble in the 1870s, with more docile labour. But that was the attitude of big business, not exactly the working man's friend. 'Nativism' is an American sentiment applied more to the workbench, and in districts where leisure was spent on the street corner and in the saloon. The Jews did not fit in as they ought.

The Irish, and the Italians who followed, at least kept faith with the redeeming custom of putting on a fresh set of clothes every Sunday and attending church – papist to be sure, and not the kind of place to induce fraternity in the average Anglo-Saxon breast, but a church nevertheless. And they tended to spread a little, out of New York, while remaining fixed in the lower occupational strata just a step or two above the blacks. Hostility towards them was tempered by anticipation of their eventual adjustment. The Jews on the other hand appeared as survivors of an extinct civilisation. Their faith kept them strictly to themselves, and yet they disconcertingly prodded around the economy to find a soft entry point. In England they disgorged from the London docks as a more conspicuous entity, the first compact and wholly foreign element for centuries to settle in this virtually homogeneous society.

Unlike Britain, America welcomed immigration as a doctrine,

what with wide underpopulated regions and the insatiable demand for working hands to keep the Reconstruction era booming. But were these the people to fill the need? Southern Europeans came from peasant stock and were prepared for toil during all the hours of daylight. The Jews were incurable city-dwellers, almost exclusively associated with trade, hardly known to till a field or build a road or descend a coal-mine. Moreover, they had been preceded by their stereotype. The unsavoury figure of Shylock permeated prejudice as a universal *idée fixe*. Even people who had never encountered a Jew knew he was arrogant, cunning and enslaved to gold. Paddy was stereotyped too, as stupid, drunken and good for little except as a workhorse, while the Italian conveyed a picture of good-humoured servility, without interest in education, few aspirations beyond the ice-cream counter, bound eternally to mama. None of these could be conceived as ever qualifying for the status won by America's pioneer breed. But of them all the Jew was preferred the least.

Curiosity brought visitors down to the East Side of New York, and the East End of London, to inspect the newcomers. If hostile, they had little difficulty in fastening distasteful attributes upon the Jews. In the first place, they stank. 'They are utter strangers to soap and water', reported the *New York Herald* in September 1882, 'and take only one bath a year.' As to their fecundity, more bad news: they multiplied like rabbits. Their children made bedlam of East Broadway, choking the streets and impeding the traffic. One sanitary official declared they kept chickens in their rooms, frequently under the bed. Thievery too was evidently a Jewish characteristic, especially among the Polish immigrants. Jacob Riis, a generally sympathetic observer, wrote that 'their greed was such that life itself was of little value compared with even the leanest bank account'.[1]

America had prospered from coolie and slave labour in the past, but these newcomers refused to stay in their designated station. Henry Adams, philosopher, historian and grandson of a US President, watched from the new Brooklyn Bridge and found his patrimony sinking beneath the sheer weight of alien humanity

[1] Reports cited by Irving Howe in *World of Our Fathers*, New York, 1976, published in London as *The Immigrant Jews of New York*, pp. 396–7.

crowded upon Manhattan island. Henry James went so far as to sample the Yiddish theatre; he came away with a painful sensation of dispossession. The fastidious British felt precisely the same in the 'annexation' of London by those unsightly foreigners inhabiting the agglomeration of East End slums (presumably well-scrubbed, model housing estates before the Jews' arrival) with their ever-proliferating tailoring sweatshops. In both countries public figures voiced a dread of the mongrelisation of the race. No one who cared for his people would wish to intermarry with these fugitives from the East European ghettos, of this they were convinced, but without restraints from above the possibility hung ominously about the big cities.

On the other hand, danger lurked in the Jews' own refusal to mix. In 1905 Arthur James Balfour, then British Prime Minister, told the Commons:

> A state of things could easily be imagined in which it would not be to the advantage of the civilisation of the country that there should be an immense body of persons who, however patriotic, able and industrious – however much they threw themselves into the national life – still by their own action remained a people apart, and not merely held a religion differing from the vast majority of their fellow-countrymen but only intermarried among themselves.[2]

A familiar charge, heard throughout the centuries. To Jewish ears Balfour spoke with the tongue of Haman.

The lesson was clear. The Jews constituted a species deserving of every support in their struggles for equal rights elsewhere; but one's own country, vaunted as hospitable by tradition, famous as a shelter for victims of persecution, could, when put to the test, precisely register its limits of tolerance. The French too revealed these instincts: love of freedom in theory for all peoples, if kept at arm's length; otherwise, contempt, hostility, fear of contamination. Jewish arrivals in Paris concentrated in the third and fourth *arrondissements*, off the rue de Rivoli, and were described by the newspaper *La Cité* as people 'who scarcely work, but plunder

[2] House of Commons Report, 10 July 1905.

each other ... Fathers marry their daughters, brothers their sisters. In infected slums entire families swarm in promiscuity, and their exotic quarter in the heart of Paris has a veritable cut-throat look.' And just as the Member of Parliament for Stepney in East London was a founder of the anti-alien British Brothers' League, so in Paris the municipal councillor representing the fourth *arrondissement* enjoyed prominence in the League of French Patriots and had the enthusiastic support of Drumont's *Libre Parole*.[3]

Immigration raised a leviathan, planting anxieties in the hearts of all decent people. America had earlier been preoccupied with another kind of intruder, from the Far East. Chinese coolies accounted for a third of California's population by 1882, for the law of the land granted unrestricted entry from any quarter until that year. Then, finally, agitation on the West Coast compelled the US Congress to close the gates against the Chinese. This condemned thousands of families to permanent separation, as the men could no longer send for their dependants once they had established themselves. Japanese settlement was contained in less Draconian a manner, by means of a gentlemen's agreement between the respective governments. Thus the Jews, so substantial a proportion of the European immigration, could have no cause as yet for complaint. Resentment against their coming waxed furiously, but did not result in amendment of the immigration rules until the end of the First World War.

One reason for this lay in the remarkably swift adaptation of the Jews to American conditions, facilitated by their charitable agencies and the anxiety of the indigenous Jewish population to keep their people off the welfare rolls. Until the era of the Russian pogroms, American Jewry consisted in the main of German-speaking arrivals from earlier in the century (their own precursors, Sephardic 'founding fathers' of Jewish America, having by then substantially diminished through assimilation). The Germanic Jews blended into a unique social cocktail, as the writer Stephen Birmingham so graphically explains in his *Our Crowd*.[4] They managed to remain German and Jewish and American all

[3] Paula Hyman, *From Dreyfus to Vichy*, New York, 1979, p. 66.
[4] New York, 1967.

at the same time, the only doubly hyphenated minority in the country. Many of them started out willingly in the New World as pedlars, even though their occupations might well have been rather more elevated in their countries of origin. They spread across America hawking everything from men's pants (like Levi Strauss, whose garment, originally for cowboys, now covers the legs of all humanity) and *Bratwurst* to scrap metal. Their transformation into contractors to the opposing armies during the Civil War required but a short stride. Connections discreetly maintained with the old country turned their more successful members to international banking, so that by the 1880s they had ascended heavenwards as an oligarchy of wealthy families headed by the Schiffs – never of course pedlars – powerful in finance and commerce, owners of great newspapers and names to reckon with in the judiciary, civic affairs and as patrons of the arts.

To say they experienced a *frisson* as the East Europeans swarmed over New York underplays their reaction somewhat. In fact they were appalled: men and boys still sporting side-curls; tiny shop-windows cluttered with praying shawls and Bibles and candlesticks advertised at bargain prices; newspapers printed in Oriental script. It struck them as a travesty of all they had sought to create in this free, wonderful America. The newcomers spoke Yiddish, a language the established settlers abhorred. They had barely been able to tolerate such people in the old days in Europe, when refugees from Poland and Russia filtered into Frankfurt, Berlin and Vienna. Now, here!

Fearing a native American backlash, the community leaders leapt into action. They had better get the greenhorns adjusted without delay, show them the American way and introduce them to an Anglicised form of worship in which the synagogue breathed the atmosphere of an Episcopalian church. Needless to recount, the old Italian families, largely from northern Italy, suffered similar spasms of insecurity with the multitudinous arrival of primitive southerners.

The Jewish community leaders had been playing it safe ever since their discovery of America, and with justification. They had themselves encountered the chillest of breezes during the Civil War, when some 10,000 Jews, nine of them generals, had fought on the opposing sides and yet were suspected of all manner of tricks, including draft-dodging and profiteering. Ulysses Grant, in his notorious General Order No. 11 of December 1862, tried to expel them all from the areas under his command. The incensed Hebrews, serving as faithfully as any Americans, sustaining casualties along with the rest, appealed directly to Lincoln and had the order revoked. Jews indeed felt completely integrated in this nation, adjusting to every regional difference. During the fierce controversy over Negro slavery those domiciled in the South held firmly against abolition, while in the North they campaigned for the slaves' freedom. Rabbis experienced little difficulty in citing biblical and Talmudic authority for diametrically opposed viewpoints, while a leading cleric in a border state entirely refrained from taking a position, as likely to incur offence whatever his stand.[5] And while they felt that here, at last, all men were equal, in reality they were not. Many fashionable hotels and clubs, even complete townships, barred Jews – an exclusion befalling no less a dignitary than the government banker, Joseph Seligmann, when he requested a room at the Grand Union Hotel, Saratoga Springs, in 1877.

Nevertheless the United States came as close to paradise as any Jew might achieve on this earth, and they did not intend to have it disturbed. But the latecomers from Eastern Europe would travel only part of the way with such leaders. Night-schools, youth clubs, yes. Abandonment of their old cultural equipment, decidedly no. Moreover, their proletarian mentality, nurtured in Bundism and resulting from generations of discrimination, instilled a profound distrust of capitalist authority. Those other Jews in their fine residences, bastions of the system with their banks and department stores, belonged to the enemy camp. Every Yiddish newspaper published on the East Side and elsewhere in America preached Socialism, sometimes anarchism. In time, after much internecine conflict, the immigrants would change, but in any case they preferred to Americanise themselves in their own way. And that, incidentally, proved quite acceptable to the Tammany bosses, heavily Irish, who dominated the scene and locked up Jewish support by readily donning a skull-cap for a

[5] See David Brion Davis, *Slavery and Human Progress*, New York, 1984, pp. 82–101.

local worthy's funeral or a barmitzvah. In the meantime the Jewish East Side took over as the pace-setter of militant trade unionism. So far as national politics interested them they acclaimed the Marxist Eugene V. Debs; one day they would adopt his initials as a calling signal for their Yiddish radio programme. Such a political outlook also had the effect of drawing them closer to the most exploited group of all, the blacks.

This advanced radicalism, which served the Jewish masses as a surrogate religion – East Side synagogues rapidly assumed a forlorn, neglected look – struck average America as brazen ingratitude. Opposition to the open-door policy, first a muttering, rose to a clamour. Discrimination in white-collar employment, the branding of Jewish politics as unAmerican, fist fights in Union Square during the long hot summers: 'We fared no worse under the Tsars', declared the cynics. A truce of sorts came into operation with the outbreak of the European war in 1914, for immigration dropped to an insignificant figure anyway, but Madison Grant could still, in 1916, publish a book, *The Passing of the Great Race*, that told of the degeneration of America in the grip of Judaism. It was a portent.

American Jewry, by this time nearly four millions strong, shared the general mood in the United States of thankful, isolationist neutralism towards the war raging on the other side of the Atlantic. In so far as it would express a preference for either side it was for Germany and the Central Powers. Abe Cahan, spokesman of the masses, editorialised in his Yiddish paper *Forward*: 'All civilised peoples sympathise with Germany, every victorious battle against Russia is a source of joy.' The East Europeans detested their former homeland and naturally wished disaster upon Russia, while the German-American Jews, along with gentiles of like provenance, also gave their moral support to the erstwhile *Vaterland*. Naturally, the Irish were with them to a man. One bleak day in 1916 the British ambassador in Washington, Cecil Spring-Rice, notified London that 'all the enemies of England have been marshalled against us, and the Irish have lent their unequalled power of political organisation to Jews, Catholics and Germans'.[6] That could hardly be the attitude of Jews in

6 Stephen Gwynn (ed.), *Letters and Friendships of Sir Cecil Spring-Rice*, Vol. II, London, 1929, p. 309.

Britain. How could they exult in the catastrophes of the tsar's armies, who were gallantly holding a line on the Eastern Front as their allies in the conflagration!

It had been no primrose path, their adjustment in Britain. Nor had they encountered an open-hearted welcome, as witness the statement of Prime Minister Balfour quoted above. This nation, stratified by class as none other in the English-speaking world, xenophobe by instinct, had nevertheless kept faith with its liberal tradition when the Jews began pouring in from across the Channel in the 1880s. But after twenty years? In 1903, with some 50,000 foreigners crammed into one corner of an already overpopulated island, and more arriving by the shipload, and subsequent upon a costly war almost lost against the Boers in South Africa, the strain was beginning to tell.

In most respects, apart from the more formidable economic problems intrinsic to a less endowed society (for the working classes, that is, not the gentry) the Jewish experience in England mirrored the American pattern: concentration in the slum areas, the helping hand of a well-established, Anglicised 'aristocracy', a predilection for Socialist, or at least, Tolstoyan, philosophy, absorption in the garment trades and a determination, by frugality and schooling, to improve themselves at all possible speed. This supposes a somewhat idealistic picture; but, as in the case of the United States, Anglo-Jewry had indolents and do-nothings enough to pack any charity queue, and gamblers galore. Native reaction too was the same, except that in England this developed more promptly than in heterogeneous America. Also, it led indirectly to an outcome of historic moment for the future of the Jewish people as a whole.

Pressure for the stoppage of immigration, led by the MP for Stepney, William Evans-Gordon (he of the British Brothers' League), had in 1902 forced the government to appoint an Aliens Commission to enquire into the problem. 'Aliens' in England at that time could signify only the Jews. Few other foreigners settled in the country, while the Irish were British citizens anyway whose right of residence could not be questioned. Balfour, aesthete and philosopher-politician, succeeded his uncle Lord Salisbury as Prime Minister the same year.

Anti-Jewish sentiment drew its rationale from the people's

apparent reluctance to assimilate, their alleged tendency to undercut the Englishman's wages and thus usurp his employment, exploitation in the airless sweatshops and the dangers the Jews presented for the proper observance of the Christian Sunday. An imposing indictment. The Aliens Commission comprised important names, including Evans-Gordon himself, and Lord Rothschild, the acknowledged leader of Anglo-Jewry and first of the tribe to be elevated to the peerage. His membership of the commission,[7] warranted by his expertise in the affairs of his people, vouchsafed justice for the alien.

It proved a thorough enquiry. Evans-Gordon undertook a personal tour of the Russian and Polish ghettos to study the problem at its source. While in Pinsk he enlisted as guide the young Chaim Weizmann, already active in Zionism.[8] Most significantly, however, and much to Rothschild's displeasure – subsequently assuaged – Theodor Herzl came to London to appear before the commission and avail himself of this important forum, heaven-sent, to plead for a homeland: not Palestine necessarily, the Turks remained hostile to the idea, but Britain possessed an enormous empire of its own. Herzl seemed incidental, or accidental, at this particular investigation, certainly irrelevant. Yet from his presence flowed a succession of events tying Great Britain to the Jewish question as a world problem, and ripening to the advantage of both in the 1917 Balfour Declaration, Jewry's 'charter' for settlement in Palestine won at last.

In its conclusions the Aliens Commission found itself unable in conscience to fasten upon the Jews the catalogue of evils embraced in the propaganda of the British Brothers. A case could not be established for the exclusion of immigrants, partially or totally. Housing constituted a problem, indeed it had been so since the Industrial Revolution, but could be ameliorated through stricter enforcement of existing by-laws. Perhaps certain districts in the larger cities should be declared prohibited areas to

[7] Its Report, with Minutes of Evidence, was published as Command Paper 1742, in 1903.
[8] Evans-Gordon subsequently wrote to Weizmann: 'The inrush of people from Eastern Europe and the consequent displacement of the native population is causing a steadily increasing bitterness of feeling against the Jews – some day or other this feeling will culminate in an outbreak.' See Weizmann, *Letters and Papers*, Vol. II, 1971, p. 87.

aliens – a recommendation highly problematic in application. The only development of substance to come out of the enquiry was an Aliens Act (1905) authorising the repatriation of criminals, prostitutes, idiots and other undesirables, because of a likelihood of their becoming a public charge.

So characteristically English, the commission had constituted a mock trial serving as a sop to public opinion, a substitute for distasteful action. The Aliens Act held no dangers for the Jews. Immigration was reduced by not more than a marginal figure, refugees continuing to arrive virtually without hindrance. Since they were not of course in the habit of scrutinising Acts of Parliament, the debate preceding the measure in 1905 sufficed for many Jews to impute antisemitism on the part of the Prime Minister, particularly as the situation of their co-religionists abroad deteriorated afresh and relatives wanted their families safe in London. However baseless, the charge left Balfour under a Jewish cloud. Winston Churchill could not refrain from exploiting the issue among the Jewish voters of Manchester during the general election early in 1906, which resulted in Balfour's defeat in the same city and the fall of his Conservative government.[9] As reported in the ghettos of Eastern Europe, the Aliens Act hinted at difficulties of entry into England, to cause some prospective newcomers to divert to France. Yet Britain vindicated itself as a haven for refugees, both during the Great War and subsequently, though to certify this country as free of antisemitism would err in generosity. In truth the 'undesirable alien' became permanently lodged in the Englishman's psyche.

The subject of Jewish homelessness hovered over the deliberations of the Balfour Cabinet in Downing Street throughout the term of the Aliens Commission's existence. As already indicated, Herzl's presence in London had not been in vain. In October 1902 the Colonial Secretary, Joseph Chamberlain, suggested to him a settlement project in the region of El Arish, a hop away from Palestine within Egyptian territory, and therefore under British control. Months passed in investigation of the proposal, only to prove fruitless. Water resources were considered inadequate

[9] Churchill sought the help of Weizmann, among others, to influence the Jewish vote. See Weizmann, *Letters and Papers*, Vol. IV, 1973, p. 216.

without excessive diversion from the Nile, and problems of suzerainty over the area proved intractable. However, El Arish could not exhaust all the possibilities in London's fee, and sure enough the British were soon ready with an alternative: an area of Kenya, then falling within the East African colony of Uganda. It would have been unimaginable a generation earlier, such recognition by the world's greatest power of the Jews' entitlement to a territorial solution of their problem on quasi-national lines. Herzl brought the offer triumphantly to his Zionist Congress in 1903. Not merely was this a concrete demonstration of Britain's goodwill; it gave his organisation the credibility as an international body it had not hitherto earned, even from the Jews themselves. But was this Zionism? Uganda? Few Jews in Eastern Europe had ever heard of the place.

The year 1903 was the year of Kishinev, the Easter pogrom that cost forty-three lives and sent thousands of Jews packing, as fast as their legs could carry them. Yet the idea of an East African haven threw the 600 delegates at the Zionist Congress into a whirl of anger and doubt – particularly the Russians among them, who were in the majority. Africa was not Zion, Herzl conceded, and could never be Zion, but in these critical times how could the Jews turn the offer down? The British gesture represented a unique act of statesmanship, he said, and deserved their profoundest gratitude. Despite six years of tedious lobbying in the chancelleries of Europe, beginning with the creation of the Zionist Organisation, Palestine still eluded them. Surely Uganda was at least worth a try! Herzl also hoped for a word of appreciation to himself, a man in fast-failing health. None was forthcoming.

His principal lieutenant, the writer Max Nordau, in those days almost a household name in the book world, took up the plea. Let them regard Uganda as an emergency resting-place for the tired wanderers, a *Nachtasyl*, overnight shelter. The East European delegates (some were from the stricken city of Kishinev) would not have it. Uganda could never belong to the dream they had clung to since the Dispersion. Their tragedy throughout history was punctuated by such overnight shelters, temporary lodgings reluctantly provided in other people's lands. The congress split into rival factions and dissolved in an atmosphere of recrimination. According to Weizmann, Herzl muttered to his supporters during an interlude in the prolonged debate: 'These people have a rope around their necks, and still they refuse!'[10]

In one respect Herzl and the 'Ugandists', many of them following him solely out of loyalty, got their way. A team of colonisation experts would proceed to Africa and survey the area of possible allocation – nothing was definitely promised – and report on its potential to the next congress, two years hence. It was a holding operation, poorly disguised. In the meantime the knives were out. Herzl, but lately regarded as their prince, was now condemned by delegates from the Pale of Settlement as a posturing amateur. This man a leader? In Jewish terms the Viennese journalist struck them as a cultural illiterate.

Stage two of the Uganda project: Herzl's sudden death, at the age of forty-four, in 1904. This left the ship without a pilot. The formal rejection of the proposal, following an adverse report by the fact-finding commission and a failure of will on the part of suitable Western Zionists, Nordau among them, to assume Herzl's mantle, marked stage three. Zionism, nonplussed, now stumbled along the old diplomatic road with halting step. When Herzl began his mission, in 1897, no one really knew how to get the crusade started. Now he was dead, no one knew how it could be stopped. Over in Palestine itself young men and women of a practical bent worked quietly, even surreptitiously, to build the Jewish presence stone by stone and acre by acre, there being no legal objection on the Turkish side provided the pioneers acquired land through purchase and did not evince ambitions of making this corner of the Ottoman Empire their own. He was a knowledgeable Jew indeed, on the outbreak of war in 1914, who could put a name to the leader of their national movement.

Zionist groups existed in all the countries on opposing sides of the firing lines, and in neutral America. They faced a bleak future, at best in utter disarray, at the worst brother fighting brother, Jew against Jew. Everything depended on one's passport. Chaim Weizmann, born in the Pale of Settlement, educated in Central Europe, domiciled in Manchester, happened to be a British citizen. He recalled the Uganda crisis as political and ideological

[10] Chaim Weizmann, *Trial and Error*, London, 1949, p. 115.

257

bankruptcy. While a junior lecturer in chemistry during the election campaign of 1906 he had discussed Zionism with no less a figure than Balfour himself. Weizmann frequently returned to his parents' home in Russia to witness the penury of the masses, sharing their fears of recurring pogrom. He had observed the Jewish population of Europe transplanting itself to the New World, by his doctrine a negative path leading to ultimate disappearance. And he had seen the movement of which he was an early member disintegrate as, decapitated, it awaited some sign from Turkey. Chaim Weizmann now decided, entirely on his own, that as regards the Jews and Palestine this was Britain's hour.

The process by which Weizmann turned events in his favour falls beyond the scope of our subject; regrettably so, for here was one of Britain's many 'undesirable aliens' who encountered in that country not hostility, which is most directly the theme of this book, but respect and, at times, veneration. True, luck stayed obedient to him. Turkey's entry into the war on Germany's side late in 1914 told him to gamble on Constantinople's eventual defeat. Therefore Zionist planning should now forget the Porte. British armies stood in force on the Nile; one day they would have to move northward. Palestine lay in their route of conquest. The Jews had an ally for the asking.

Weizmann's fellow-Zionists across the world did not share his view – quite the contrary. In Berlin, the movement's headquarters, none could conceive of the war's conclusion without a German victory; it was self-evident truth, beyond argument. In France, Zionists were rare creatures indeed, but every French Jew identified with his country's traditional role as the power *en premier lieu* in the Levant since the Crusades. The East European Zionists on their part saw indications all around them that Russia would collapse in this war, and deservedly, so in alliance with such a broken reed what indeed were Britain's prospects of triumph? Most incensed of all at Weizmann's machinations stood a formidable group of American Zionists. They intended taking the movement into their hands and holding it in safe, neutral keeping until the end of hostilities. They worried for the welfare of the Jews already in Palestine – some 80,000 in 1914 – and studiously maintained good relations with Constantinople through the US ambassador there, Henry Morgenthau, one of those model German-American Jews without a shred of Zionist sentiment in his soul. In England itself Weizmann encountered obstruction from his own people at every turn. As British Jews they would fight for their country. As Zionists they must stay outside the struggle.

Undeterred, he pressed forward. At first British public figures appeared far from eager to endorse Weizmann's ambitions, carefully enunciated by him, for a Jewish home in the Holy Land under their suzerainty. The plan bristled with difficulties: religious, racial, international. British thinking had not advanced so far as to contemplate piling Palestine on the heap of their already excessive overseas responsibilities. Since the South African War, calamitous for Britain's standing among other European powers, the mood of the Liberal Party, then in office, tended towards unburdening the country of empire, not adding to it. A non-Zionist co-religionist of Weizmann's, Herbert Samuel, member of the government and the first professing Jew to achieve a place in the Cabinet, had in fact already mooted the question of an Anglo-Jewish Palestine. On submitting a scheme to his Prime Minister, Herbert Asquith, he received a dusty answer.[11]

War, however, feeds the appetite even while the spectre of possible defeat haunts the mind. Weizmann played equally on British hopes and fears among his political contacts. A biochemist of distinction, he discovered a fermentation process for producing acetone when the usual overseas sources of supply were being denied Britain by the German blockade. Acetone was the missing ingredient required to blend the three constituents of cordite so as to render gunpowder smokeless, essential to conceal the position of heavy guns. The discovery brought him to Lloyd George, who in December 1916 succeeded Asquith as Prime Minister. By this time Britain and France were secretly dividing

[11] Asquith wrote, *inter alia*: 'I have just received from Herbert Samuel a memorandum entitled "The Future of Palestine". . . . It reads almost like a new edition of *Tancred* brought up to date. I confess I am not attracted by this proposed addition to our responsibilities, but it is a curious illustration of Dizzy's favourite maxim that "race is everything" to find this almost lyrical outburst proceeding from the well-ordered and methodical brain of H.S.' See Earl of Oxford and Asquith, *Memoirs and Reflexions*, Vol. II, London, 1928, p. 59.

the spoils to be anticipated from eventual victory over the Turks.

Theirs was hardly a *union sacrée*, especially in regard to Turkey's possessions in the Near Eastern Arab world. Advised by historians, coaxed by theologians, driven by greed, they marked out respective spheres of interest on the maps as though dividing a cake brought by a favourite aunt. France remained cool towards Zionism's aspirations, but Britain began warming to them, and this despite certain undertakings of independence it gave to the Arabs, led by Shereef Hussein, ruler of the Hedjaz, for support against their Turkish overlord. The future status of Palestine remained ambiguous both in the Allied plan for the Levant and in Britain's negotiations with the Arab leader.

Meanwhile, to strengthen his own legitimacy, Weizmann organised himself into the presidency of the English Zionist Federation (not a difficult manoeuvre; it barely existed except on paper) and enlisted some influential friends, the second Lord Rothschild among them. He also made important enemies, not personally, but because of Zionism: a section of the old Anglo-Jewish gentry, for a start, and then two powerful figures in the Lloyd George coalition government, Lord Curzon and Edwin Montagu (the latter Herbert Samuel's fanatically anti-Zionist cousin). Balfour, now Foreign Secretary, equivocated.

Europe was dragging a weary course through its third year of war, with Palestine still in Ottoman hands, when, in the spring of 1917, Weizmann worked two dramatic developments to his advantage. (Nothing had so far been clarified, by any party to the discussion, as to Zionism's true aim: whether Palestine should become a Jewish state or a 'national home', whether the whole of Palestine was envisaged or an entity within it; nor indeed the area comprised by the term 'Palestine', for the region was ill-defined. No such place appeared on the maps of the Turkish Empire, and biblical sources were unhelpful.) The first development, tsarism's collapse in Russia, placed in jeopardy that country's continued participation in the war. As against the depressing eventuality of Russia's signing a separate peace, America came in, reluctantly, on the side of the Entente, though without declaring war against Turkey. The Allies stood near to exhaustion as the conflict spread to other continents, and millions of tons of shipping lay at the bottom of the ocean. How effective, and how swift, would be the succour from across the Atlantic? Britain needed every friend it could find.

Weizmann operated on two levels, as scientist and Zionist leader. In the former capacity he was a valued technical expert, in the latter he negotiated as the representative (in England only, be it emphasised) of the Jewish people. He put it to the government that an early British statement in favour of Jewish aspirations in Palestine would at a stroke win over the Jews of the United States to the point of persuading President Wilson to declare war on Turkey while simultaneously encouraging the Jews of Russia, now free and equal citizens, to agitate for continuation of the struggle on the Eastern Front. He laid these hopes of powerful Jewish support before Lloyd George and Balfour at a meeting in July 1917, with the additional enticement that American Jewry, electrified as it were by a British undertaking to support Zionism, would rush to enlist and participate in the forthcoming Palestine campaign.[12] This was whistling in the dark, for no important Zionist in either Russia or America (where they were led by Justice Louis Brandeis, a man close to Wilson) had authorised Weizmann to speak in such terms on their behalf. But Lloyd George particularly wished to believe it. He required arguments upon which to justify his country's exclusive control over Palestine, a subject on which the British and French differed violently.

As for the Arabs, now represented by Shereef Hussein's son Faisal, they would no doubt be propitiated with nominal independence in strictly Arab lands, 'protected' by the two Western allies according to the secret plan, known as the Sykes–Picot Treaty, worked out in 1916. For the present the Arabs could be disregarded.

But the Jews? Here they were, according to Weizmann, strong influences upon the policies of those two enormous nations, the United States and Russia, and prepared to put their weight behind Britain. Lloyd George, against Balfour's doubts, and despite the Curzon–Montagu opposition and French charges of hypocrisy, now acted. The declaration of his government supporting the Zionist endeavour, bearing the signature of Foreign Secretary Balfour, was made in November 1917. As with other

[12] See Weizmann, *Letters and Papers*, Vol. VII, 1975, pp. 441, 480–1.

statements issued in the heat of war, this one was susceptible to various interpretations and so resulted in endless controversy. Further, it failed to keep Russia in the war, or bring the Americans to fight against the Turks. From the military point of view it was futility itself. Yet it must count as a masterpiece of draftsmanship.

The Balfour Declaration said:

> His Majesty's Government view with favour the establishment in Palestine of a national home for the Jewish people, and will use their best endeavours to facilitate the achievement of this object, it being clearly understood that nothing shall be done which may prejudice the civil and religious rights of existing non-Jewish communities in Palestine, or the rights and political status enjoyed by Jews in any other country.

Opponents of Zionism have sought to read as little as possible into the Balfour Declaration, supporters as much as its language will stand. Weizmann confessed to profound disappointment on first sight of the text.[13] No doubt, for experience had not yet reined his imagination to the realities. Nevertheless the British statement gave to the Jews a twentieth-century, secular legality for the return to the Holy Land, when hitherto that legality rested only on an ancient presence, a majestic literature and a mystical idea. They took the Balfour Declaration as their signal, when war ended with three battalions of the British Army enrolled under Judean colours, to launch an intensive development of Palestine detached from the Arab factor. Britain quoted the declaration to extract from dubious France, and then from the entire League of Nations, the Mandate to control and administer the country as a British possession, for how long (eternally?) no one could state or foretell.

Herbert Samuel arrived in Jerusalem as the first high commissioner, and the auguries for Zionism looked promising. But storm clouds soon appeared on the horizon. Far from eliminating the root cause of antisemitism by laying the curse of Jewry's collective homelessness, Zionism gave a new, ironic twist to the

[13] *Trial and Error*, p. 204.

problem. An old paranoia came to the surface: the Jews as a power hostile to Christendom, in conspiracy with Satan. Yes, they had a plan to assume mastery of the entire world. Long germinating, secretly passed down the generations, the Jewish plot now, in the twentieth century, approached its consummation. The last diabolic act of this Manichaean drama had been initiated by Theodor Herzl and would be completed by Chaim Weizmann. Well, why not? Anyone with a searching eye could put the fragments together.

By establishing the Zionist Organisation in 1897 Herzl had created the first international political instrument in Jewish history. Such was the measure of his achievement. Jewish bodies, religious and secular, already abounded. Some of them enjoyed considerable prestige, such as the Alliance Israélite Universelle in Paris, the Board of Deputies in London and the B'nai Brith ('Sons of the Covenant') in New York. But they were organisations like all others, composed of specific interest groups and subject to the laws of their country of location. Their concerns – personal status, charity, education, the rebuttal of antisemitism – lay beyond public controversy or political intent. Only a British Jew could have membership of the Board of Deputies, only a French *israélite*[14] of the Alliance. The Zionist Organisation, on the other hand, brought Jews of any and every nationality together and, despite the misgivings of those other bodies, avowed to speak for the Jewish people as a whole. The claim carried no force in law, national or international, and indeed enjoyed little recognition until Weizmann utilised the Zionist name in his wholly personal mission. The Jewish intelligentsia, except for transient interest by a few who abstained from total commitment to the ideal, studiously avoided involvement in the movement.

Nevertheless the Zionist Congress, meeting regularly in Europe, offered a constant temptation to those in search of arguments to denounce the Jews as an international power beyond the reach of man-made laws, and belonging to the forces of the Antichrist. The true deliberations of the Zionist Congress, according to these antisemites, were guarded by an anonymous

---

[14] The Jews of France spelt *israélite* with a small letter to emphasise their description as a religious and not an ethnic group.

conclave of rabbis and remained secret. In 1903 a St Petersburg newspaper, *Znamia* ('The Banner'), published material purporting to be summarised from their transactions, *The Protocols of the Learned Elders of Zion*. They bore the signature of a council described as 'the Representatives of Zion of the 33rd Degree'.

For those to whom such matters are a mystery, the designation 33rd Degree appears in Freemasonry, and is ascribed in the original Scottish rite as an 'honorary degree' given to the Sovereign Grand Inspector-General. We are thus introduced to the Judeo-Masonic connection, ostensibly dating from the construction of Solomon's Temple, where the mesmeric procedures disguising the Jews' ultimate ambitions were laid down.

These *Protocols* told of only a short distance to traverse before

> the cycle of the Symbolic Serpent – that badge of our people – will be complete. When the circle is locked all the states of Europe will be enclosed in it, as it were by unbreakable chains . . . We intend to appear as though we were the liberators of the working man come to free him from oppression, when we shall suggest his joining the ranks of our armies of Socialists, anarchists and Communists . . . Our strength lies in keeping the working man in perpetual want and impotence; because, by so doing, we retain him subject to our will. In his own surroundings he will never find either power or energy to stand up against us. Hunger will confer upon Capital more powerful rights over the labourer than ever the lawful sovereign could confer upon the aristocracy . . . When the time comes for our World Ruler to be crowned we will ensure that by the same means – that is to say, by making use of the mob – we will destroy everything that may prove an obstacle in our way.

And further:

> Now I will deal with the manner in which we will strengthen the dynasty of King David, in order that it may endure until the last day . . . Only such men as are capable of governing firmly, although perhaps cruelly, will be entrusted with the reins of government by our Elders . . . The King's immediate plans, and still more, his plans for

the future, will not even be known to those who will be called his nearest councillors. Only our Sovereign, and the Three who initiated him, will know the future ... According to the records of secret Jewish Zionism, Solomon and other Jewish learned men, in 929 BC, already thought out a scheme in theory for a peaceful conquest of the whole universe by Zion.[15]

This farrago, much amplified in several columns of print to elaborate the methods by which the Jews would subvert the righteous peoples of the earth, did not arrive accidentally in the bureau of *Znamia* in 1903. The editor was none other than Pavel Kruschevan, whose other newspaper, the quasi-official *Bessarabetz*, fomented antisemitism in Kishinev and inflamed the mob to pogrom there during the preceding Easter. Kruchevan had long peddled anti-Jewish libels, including the allegation of human sacrifice in the rituals of the Jewish faith. How he received the bizarre *Protocols* makes a story of fantasy and forgery in itself.

As is abundantly evident from history, man's credulity, and his wonderment at the forces controlling human destiny, never ceased to manufacture fears of global domination by anonymous forces operating with the connivance of a netherworld. This principle lay at the root of conflict between Catholic and Protestant before politics and religion became detached from each other – if indeed this has ever been the case. What army has not recruited God to explain its victories, or to impose retribution upon the defeated? Human strife will perhaps never be free from the associated hypocrisy of limitless good versus limitless evil. Our story so far has not been lacking in examples.

In the eighteenth century the conspiracy myth began in Catholic countries to be attached to the Freemasons. Some recognised in Masonry the true authors of the French Revolution, although hundreds of them were guillotined during the Terror. Soon the Jews became linked with Freemasonry as partners in the Devil's work, particularly when Napoleon convened his Sanhedrin in 1806. There was no dearth of heirs to the power of the French emperor, suspected of carrying the plot forward

[15] For a comprehensive history of the *Protocols*, see Norman Cohn, *Warrant for Genocide*, London, 1967.

and perfecting the occult web of intrigue, deceit and subversion:
Lord Palmerston, Prime Minister of England, for example, and
Giuseppe Mazzini, whose writings on revolution fill some forty
volumes. Disraeli of course had the arrogance to slip evidence of
the conspiracy into his novels as he dilated on the superiority of
the Jewish genius. Somewhere in Europe an organisation, the
most secret of all secret societies, was at all times invigilating the
conquest of Christendom and the creation of that universal chaos
which must inaugurate its rule. The theme was rarely absent
from the important Jesuit periodical close to the Curia, *La
Civiltà Cattolica*, ever since its foundation in 1850.

In 1868 a German writer, Hermann Goedsche, described in a
long novel, *Biarritz*, how the leaders of Judaism conducted a sort
of black sabbath in the Jewish cemetery of Prague, to review
progress and confirm plans and strategies. The Devil, literally
rising from one of the graves, presided. Extracts from the little-
noticed novel, whose author hid behind the pseudonym Sir John
Retcliffe, appeared in Russian translation during the following
decade. Versions differed between St Petersburg and Odessa, as
subsequently between others published in Prague and Paris. The
name Retcliffe occurs in conflicting guises, on occasion as a Jew,
Chief Rabbi John Readcliff, or an Englishman, and even as a
Christian martyr. Doctored texts, necessary to the conditions of
individual countries and to absorb references to contemporary
events, competed for attention. In this the French excelled, particularly in binding Freemasonry to the Jewish plan.

Admittedly, the Freemasons availed themselves of a mishmash
of symbols from various religions, and they mined deeply in
Jewish cabbalistic literature, itself a pastiche. The connection
inspired a Catholic aristocrat, Gougenot des Mousseaux, to
publish a work which has since been described as the Bible of
modern antisemitism: *Le Juif, le judaïsme et la judaïsation des
peuples chrétiens*.[16] Almost every sect not absolutely acceptable
to Catholicism, this author wrote, owed allegiance to the Jews.
Soon that race would be ready to announce its governance over
the world, and be defeated only with the Second Coming and the

---

[16] Published in Paris on the eve of the First Vatican Council, 1870. The Pope
blessed Gougenot for his courage. See Heer, *God's First Love*, p. 152.

Last Judgement. Doubtless Gougenot could find ample support for his thesis in the New Testament concept of a final struggle against the Antichrist, who of course had France, eldest daughter of the Church, in his sights as the prime target for destruction. Drumont would shortly take up the cry, bringing in the Rothschilds, the Panama scandal and, finally, Dreyfus. The Zionist Congress did not as yet exist, but pending its arrival on the scene fanatical antisemites applied the Judeo-Masonic concoction to the Alliance Israélite Universelle, whose fame thus spread as a sinister force across Europe.

Within Russia both the Holy Synod and the secret police, long receptive to the theme of Jewish subversion, enjoyed the co-operation of a baptised member of the tribe in disseminating these fantastic tales. Joseph Brafman doubled as professor of Hebrew at a Minsk theological seminary and zealous police agent. He knew how to break the hidden power of the Alliance Israélite – by the conversion of all Jews to Christianity. In the meantime he deemed it his sacred task, through his major writings *The Book of Kahal* and *Local and Universal Jewish Brotherhood*, to warn mankind of the tightening net. It thus transpired that in 1897 Theodor Herzl, by inviting the Zionists to Basle to discuss the revival of Jewish nationhood, inspired a title for the conspiracy literature already circulating in a variety of forms among the *cognoscenti*. Excerpts were stitched together, embellished with contributions from many hands, and became *The Protocols of the Learned Elders of Zion*. When Pavel Kruschevan secured his version for *Znamia* in 1903 a full text had not yet been published, but a manuscript lay pigeon-holed at the headquarters of the Russian censorship department. No doubt it was from this text, a ludicrous combination of political propaganda and impenetrable mysticism, authored by one Sergei Nilus, that Kruschevan borrowed his material. The Nilus original in fact did appear in print, in 1905, and extracts were ordered by the Metropolitan of Moscow to be read in all the churches under his jurisdiction.

One might well ask, how could so confidential a document, a blueprint for global domination no less, have escaped from the 'elders' of the Zionist Congress? Solutions to that particular mystery were not in short supply. The *Protocols* were obtained by a Russian agent who infiltrated the congress; no, they were stolen by a woman from a leading Freemason after a meeting of the elders in France; again, they were in the charge of a Jew on his way from Basle to the Masonic lodge in Frankfurt, when he was bribed to divulge their contents. As late as 1922 an American lady, married to a White Russian, averred they were the work of the Hebrew author Asher Ginsburg (an opponent of Herzl better known by his pseudonym Ahad Ha'am – 'One of the People'). He was presumed to have written the *Protocols* in 1890, then put them in the trust of the Alliance Israélite in Paris for future submission to the as yet non-existent Zionist Congress.

Despite an expanding literature in the genre, the *Protocols* attracted no great attention until the Bolshevik Revolution of November 1917. Lenin's coup, taking Russia out of the war in a memorable peace which ceded vast territories, including White Russia, the Ukraine and Poland to the Central Powers, exposed the remaining Allies to the full force of German might on the Western Front. Russia, but yesterday a gallant, hard-pressed comrade-in-arms, was metamorphosed overnight into an atheistic ogre, with at least one of its leaders, Leon Trotsky, advancing a theory of permanent, universal revolution.

Trotsky's original name, Lev Bronstein, testified to his racial forebears. In fact he was the most important Jew among many in key positions of control within the new regime. Furthermore, the downfall of tsarism brought to Jews everywhere, not only of the working classes, a sense of relief and gratitude, signifying as it did the end of state-supported antisemitism in territories containing two-thirds of their world population. In the United States the majority of Jews received the Balfour Declaration, also of November 1917, with little enthusiasm. Indeed, many of them were bitterly against it, to the degree that President Wilson, though personally in favour, refrained from giving public endorsement to Britain's pro-Zionist statement.[17] On the other hand, the Communist Revolution sent a charge of passionate approval through the East Side of New York, and Jewish radicals even spoke of returning to their old homes; an estimated 15,000

---

[17] See, e.g., David Goldblatt, 'The Impact of the Balfour Declaration in America', *American Jewish Historical Quarterly*, June 1968, pp. 455–95.

actually did so. Some Yiddish-language schools in America placed the date of the revolution in their holiday schedules, along with Passover and the Paris Commune.[18] Wasn't it *their* Trotsky, so recently sharing a glass of tea with his Jewish friends in the Second Avenue cafés, who fashioned the heroic Red Army?

Anger in the West at Russia's defection from the alliance gathered fuel from fear of the revolution's spreading beyond the boundaries of the Soviet Union. The Bolsheviks made no secret of their dream to plant their doctrine round the world. And who were their leaders anyway? Grigori Zinoviev had travelled with Lenin in that famous 'sealed train' from Switzerland to engineer the revolution, and was now organising the Communist International; Lev Kamenev, editor of the underground *Pravda* in tsarist times, came to the fore as chairman of the Moscow Soviet; Lazar Kaganovitch, close to Stalin, belonged to the inner apparatus; and Karl Radek, also enclosed with Lenin on that train journey to power, had most of the foreign propaganda activity in his charge. Adolph Joffe had opened the peace talks (completed by Trotsky) at Brest-Litovsk and now emerged as Soviet ambassador in Berlin, while Maxim Litvinov, married to an Englishwoman, was their diplomatic agent in London. Jews all of them, and the list seemed endless, with Jacob Sverdlov as chairman of the All-Russian Central Executive Committee, and a new secret police force, the Tcheka, headed by Moisey Uritsky. The conclusion seemed inescapable: Russia demonstrated beyond doubt the truth of the message in *The Protocols of the Learned Elders of Zion*.

The final, desperate months of the Great War, bringing all its European participants to their last martial gasp, took the form of a mighty duel of wills between Ludendorff and Foch. This simplified the issues for those hanging upon the outcome. It was true, was it not, that the Polish Jews had welcomed the German stampede through their country, greeting the Hun as liberator? And hadn't their American brethren blatantly encouraged Germany in the days of their so-called neutrality? Now Russia suffocated in the grasp of an irreligious Jewish cabal. Clearly, here was evidence enough of a widely ramified conspiracy

---

[18] Howe, *World of Our Fathers*, p. 358.

against true civilisation. Perhaps the *Protocols* were not entirely true, but how could they be entirely false? And to complete the circle, General Allenby was expending precious Christian blood in Palestine to release the most sacred place from its old masters and hand it on a platter to the Jewish race.

What had begun that fateful August four years earlier as a struggle between rival patriotisms ended starkly with a complete generation of young men wiped out, and faded hopes for all: the horrors of starvation in Europe, mutual resentments among the victors, unemployment, restlessness and recrimination pervading the continent. The atmosphere, ideal for the flowering of prejudice, heartlessness, special pleading, inevitably raised to the surface the latent antisemitism in all nations. Germany, declared Ludendorff, had been brought to grief by the insidious power of Jewry allied to Freemasonry. The triumph of Russian Bolshevism revealed their hidden hand. Britain and France, according to spokesmen of ultra-right-wing politics in both countries, had been duped by the same force, while America alone, where Jews stood supreme, had enriched itself. Whatever the argument, it matched the theory. Within the space of three years translations of the *Protocols* appeared in English, French, Polish, Hungarian, Italian and Latvian, besides new Russian versions distributed by émigrés far from their homeland and by the White Russian armies operating in the interior with Western assistance against the Communist regime.

If the world was coming within Jewish power, this was now revealed as a most peculiar force. Zionism soon suffered setbacks in Palestine, where progress languished through lack of funds, a pronounced reluctance on the part of Jews to settle there, the animosity of the Arabs and conflict with the British. Disillusionment stretched ahead for any but the hardiest of the pioneers. In the Ukraine disaster befell the Jewish masses, for hunger stalked as terror reigned. Many thousands perished; some put the figure as high as 300,000, though Simon Dubnov, who then lived in Russia, estimated 60,000 in his sober *History*. Whatever the number, it was a tragedy of epic dimension. The anti-Communist, separatist forces in the Ukraine, under the counter-revolutionary general Anton Denikin, fought a hopeless war against the Red Army, and in defeat and withdrawal turned into a wild rabble, resorting to pillage and massacre.[19] To complete a sorry picture of the Jews' inability to foster their own interests, nativist agitation in the United States grew to such a pitch as to make the closure of American gates inevitable.

In the immediate post-war world the Jews suffered anguish enough from their collective impotence, though not in the eyes of some Christian observers. There is much evocative of the *Protocols of Zion* in a description by Winston Churchill when he put pen to paper on the theme of Bolshevism and Zionism. Churchill, who claimed to be the Jews' friend, wrote of them as

> the most formidable and the most remarkable race which has ever appeared in the world . . . It would almost seem as if the gospel of Christ and the gospel of Anti-Christ were destined to originate among the same people; and that this mystic and mysterious race had been chosen for the supreme manifestations, both of the divine and the diabolical.

And, to indicate the character of the 'world-wide confederacy for the overthrow of civilisation and for the reconstitution of society on the basis of arrested development, envious malevolence and impossible equality', Churchill listed revolutionary leaders of Jewish origin in Russia, Hungary, Germany and the United States: Trotsky, Bela Kun, Rosa Luxemburg and Emma Goldman.[20]

That France gave a respectful hearing to antisemitic exponents of a particularly subtle kind, civilised to the point, like Churchill, of dressing their views in tones of confused innocence and feigned admiration, should occasion no great surprise. Still haunted by the trauma of Dreyfus, the French ultra-Right could not forgive the man, nor his people, for the collapse of pride and reputation caused to their beloved land. The war merely confirmed their suspicion of Judaism as a more sinister form of Protestantism, with its power-base across the Rhine. To admirers of Charles Maurras, Léon Daudet and Maurice Barrès, all of

[19] The Ukrainian national leader, Simon Petliura, disclaimed responsibility for the pogroms while an exile in Paris, but he was nevertheless assassinated by a Jew in 1926.
[20] *Illustrated Sunday Herald*, London, 8 February 1920.

them important writer-politicians, Judeo-Bolshevism was less immediate a menace than Judeo-Germanism. The influence achieved by Action Française, which this trio of specialists in verbal assault had founded as a racist, royalist movement as well as a newspaper, expanded enormously in the war's aftermath. Clemenceau had been too easy with Germany, the trio charged. The 'Tiger' who had dominated the Paris Peace Conference, though personally not enamoured of the *israélites*, had conducted himself as their champion during the *Affaire* and had included five of them in his post-war Radical government. This sufficed for Maurras to claim that in reality the great republican was a Jewish pawn. Later we shall find the same Action Française group enunciating the philosophical basis for French Fascism and in Vichy times standing solid with the most obsequious pro-German collaborators.

Britain had its replicas of Maurras and Daudet in those eminent adornments of English letters, the Catholic writers Gilbert K. Chesterton and Hilaire Belloc. Anti-democratic romantics, they alone glistened in an otherwise banal upper-class league comprising propertied aristocrats, superannuated generals and right-wing journalists. They gave a distinct antisemitic coloration to the Conservative Party, which in those days won little support from Anglo-Jewry. Accepting the *Protocols* as literal truth, Belloc, Chesterton and their small though highly articulate coterie detected the many heads of the hydra in all the capitals of the world, except Rome. Mussolini's accession to power in 1922 completed their admiration for Italy and gave them hope that such a saviour would one day emerge in their own land to rid it of that nefarious coalition of international financiers, Jews and Communists.[21] For them the arch-conspirator was Chaim Weizmann, as we shall see.

Antisemitism, by no means restricted to the Conservative fringe, ran through every class in Britain. It was the reflex of an insularity which regarded all foreigners as social deviants. As Kipling put it:

> The stranger within my gate,
> He may be true or kind,

[21] See Richard Griffiths, *Fellow-Travellers of the Right*, London, 1980.

> But he does not talk my talk,
> I cannot feel his mind.
> I see the face and the eyes and the mouth
> But not the soul behind.
> The men of my own stock
> They may do ill or well
> But they tell the lies I am wonted to,
> They are used to the lies I tell.[22]

And generations born of foreign stock in Britain remained always as strangers. It was virtually impossible before the Second World War for a Jew bearing a foreign name to gain employment as a bank clerk or even a postman, jobs for which he would have to compete, during heavy unemployment, against the 'English' worker on his own terms. Discrimination forced many into tiny one-man businesses as tailors, cabinet-makers and shopkeepers (which, incidentally, were better rewarded) and their children to seek immunity from prejudice through higher education. But in no sense did the prejudice translate into governmental restrictions more severe than those embodied in the Aliens Act of 1905. In the United States, however, a very different situation now prevailed. An anti-Jewish crusader of immense prestige, personification of the American dream, stepped out of his automobile factory in Detroit. Henry Ford, the one-time machine-tool apprentice, now a billionaire, bethought himself of affairs of state, and the ruin in store for his beloved country.

The year 1914 had brought another huge influx from Eastern Europe to the United States, some 140,000, but the war called the immigration traffic almost to a halt until 1920. Then the unwanted populations of the old continent, still in large proportion Russian, Polish and Romanian Jews, started to move once more. Thousands of them took thankful leave of the Soviet Union, a country they were presumed to control, while the border still remained open. The neighbouring countries likewise gave their brethren little encouragement to stay. Poland, independent of Russia at last, found itself with an exceptionally large Jewish minority, as always indigestible in this fervidly Catholic

---

[22] From his poem 'The Stranger'.

climate. In Romania, now much expanded in territory, the Jewish poverty of the old regime was perpetuated in the new. Ostensibly, both countries were bound by undertakings given in the minority treaties written into the Paris peace settlement. It did not work out in practice. Discrimination in education and economic activity became the norm, at least for the mass. Hence the compulsion to depart. They crossed the Atlantic along with multitudes of southern Italians, Greeks and refugees of every class and nationality.

Feeling ran strong in America that the divine blessings (Protestant, naturally) which had spared God's own country from the calamities of the Old World seemed about to expire in a cacophony of languages and a discord of tribal customs. The anxieties of Madison Grant, H. L. Mencken and other writers concerned for the Anglo-Saxon character of their nation penetrated to the heartland: they were being taken over. Talk of the 'Jewish peril' found a ready response among farming folk, who nurtured a grievance alleging their exploitation by city bankers and 'New York liberals', a handy euphemism signifying the Jews.

Though much devalued today as an aspiration, America still gave lip-service to the 'melting pot' theory, anticipating the dissolution of ethnic and social divisions among the white components of the nation, with the blacks of course relegated as a race apart. But the Jews, despite their rapid acculturation to an English-speaking society, remained a highly individual, urban element. Their noisy radical wing had them eternally on the march, demonstrating, debating, going on strike. Everybody read, or was told, of the pronounced Jewish element in the Soviet hierarchy. Now the 'Red Scare' seized hold of the United States. Even the Jewish-owned *New York Times* took up the cry.

Henry Ford had made Detroit a focus of good industrial relations, pioneering the eight-hour day and profit-sharing in his mighty business. When he spoke, millions listened. An austere patriot who had risen, thanks to all the puritan virtues, from a humble background, he now raised his voice in warning against the Jewish peril. Europe had fallen to the Judeo-Bolshevist conspiracy. America must cleanse its house while time still allowed. Ford railed like an Old Testament prophet against complacency. G. K. Chesterton wrote of him: 'If a man like that has discovered that there is a Jewish problem, then there is a Jewish problem. It is certainly not due to prejudice.'[23] Ford's private newspaper, the *Dearborn Independent*, began publishing extracts from the *Protocols* in May 1920, and by the following October he had drained from that congested prose virtually every assertion of the mystical power that intended the enslavement of America. He introduced his own variations, more closely applicable to transatlantic susceptibilities, as of a secret agreement between Great Britain and international Jewry which gave the latter control of the world's largest fleet to protect its trade. The American Civil War, in fact, had been engineered from the same quarter, Abraham Lincoln had died by a Jewish hand, and a subtle plan existed to demoralise the young, as in Russia, through the introduction of sex education in the schools.

The *Dearborn Independent*, hardly the kind of paper purchased by the average American at the street corner, secured its distribution through Ford's automobile dealers, each of whom was generously apportioned a quantity. But newspapers are ephemeral, so Ford put large extracts between the covers of his book *The International Jew*. This was translated into several European languages, and it so entranced Hitler that in 1924 the future German dictator dispatched a fund-raising emissary of his National Socialist Party to its author – pointlessly, as it happened.[24] Ford did not exactly take America by storm with his violent antisemitic tirades, for their naïvety advertised the limits of the man's perceptions. Yet many saw him as the salvation of the nation, and a future President. He was convinced the Jews had the White House in their web, and he organised an intelligence service to spy on prominent members of the community, to catch them in the act of sending Washington their instructions.

'Every influence that leads to lightness and looseness in gentile youth today heads up in a Jewish source', Ford wrote in *The International Jew*:

> Did the young people of the world devise the 'sport clothes' which have had so deleterious an effect on the youth of the times? . . . Children are hardly free to play

---

[23] *What I Saw in America*, London, 1922, pp. 139–40.
[24] See Alan Bullock, *Hitler: A Study in Tyranny*, London, 1952, p. 76.

nowadays, except under play-masters appointed by the State, among them, curiously enough, an astonishing proportion of Jews manage to find a place . . . All this focuses up to the World Plan for the subjugation of the gentiles.

Such effusions were significant only in their reflection of a particular mood, which allowed a sanitised racialism to gain respectability in America, under the pseudo-scientific designation of 'Eugenics'. The Ku Klux Klan, once restricted with its ludicrous regalia to keeping Negroes 'in their place', now revived as an anti-Catholic, anti-Jewish vanguard, and won some five million adherents. Of course, the Jewish organisations were not taking all this lying down. The B'nai Brith had formed a specific Anti-Defamation League in 1913, and this struck back with the enlightenment of public opinion on the role the Jews played in advancing the prosperity of the nation, in non-sectarian charitable works and in their contribution to the cultural commonweal. Pride in the American-Jewish ethos rose enormously during the war and proved no mean adversary against Ford and the proto-Fascist groups which flooded the mails with their antisemitic literature. The Jewish leaders, still of the old German establishment, nevertheless worried over the militant East Side garment workers and their firebrand spokesmen. Five Yiddish dailies were still being published in New York at the end of the war, their columns resounding with revolutionary thunder. The middle-of-the-road labour organisers, of Bundist tradition, watched with increasing concern as the Communists attempted a take-over of the unions. It was just as well, many Jews told themselves, that Henry Ford did not understand Yiddish. Their leaders begged for a moderation of the strident revolutionary tone. Yes, they were citizens equal to all others, with freedom of expression, but deference to American susceptibilities was called for.[25] It was the kind of admonition on the lips of assimilated Jewish gentry everywhere towards the more recent arrivals.

But American Jewry was forced in 1921 to bow to the

[25] For Communist penetration of the Jewish trade union movement, see Will Herberg, 'The Jewish Labour Movement in the United States', in *American Jewish Year Book*, 1952 edition.

inevitable – perhaps not with total reluctance. The US Congress applied a rigorous quota upon immigration: three per cent annually of the number of people from each country residing in the United States in 1910. The law favoured those nationalities which until that date comprised the large majority of the population – British and Irish, Germans, Scandinavians – who would never fill their quotas anyway. The law cut the numbers down drastically from Eastern and Southern Europe, and the 'Nordic' purity of America was saved. This still did not satisfy the nativist mood. In 1924 the quota was reduced from three to two per cent, with 1890 as the basic year. Masses of Jews had been awaiting visas, but reaching America now involved years of uncertainty, endless frustration and the odd lucky stroke of fortune. For the many Jews who still needed to escape from Europe thoughts turned for the first time to Palestine, which received candidates in quantity for the pioneering life at last. But America's hostility was not yet done: in 1929 the total immigration figure for any single year was reduced to 153,000 – this in a subcontinent of immense uninhabited space. It practically barred everyone not originating from the favoured nationalities. Strangely, these restrictions have been largely turned on their head in accepted American-Jewish thinking today. The principal character in Neil Simon's popular stage play depicting the 1930s, *Brighton Beach Memoirs*, on learning of his brother's arrival in America from Poland, exclaims in wonderment, 'He's got out!' In reality the problem for Jews in those days was not getting out, but getting in.

Those Ivy League temples of learning, including Columbia, Harvard and Yale, had observed with growing misgiving the Jewish penetration of their campuses. Evidently City College in New York, where entry was free, could no longer contain the aspirations of the younger generation, now mostly American-born; graduation from that dilapidated institution could be the reverse of a recommendation for employment in the higher professions. Unrestricted the Jews threatened the Anglo-Saxon tradition of the more eminent establishments. 'The alien and unwashed element', in the phrase of Yale's head of admissions, had to be reduced. A limitation, long applied unofficially in the prestigious colleges, was formalised in 1922, reminiscent of the way Russian universities stemmed the Jewish tide during the era of the tsars. The medical faculties put up a particularly discouraging front, compelling hundreds of students to leave mom and pop in their Seventh Avenue workshops and East Side delicatessens and find a more hospitable home for their microscopes and anatomy books overseas.[26]

Until 1921 *The Protocols of the Learned Elders of Zion* retained their bogus authority, conveying a truth self-evident as when men believed the earth was flat. No one had as yet discovered their true origin, nor subjected them to methodical examination, which would easily have exposed them as a tissue of extravagant meanderings. The propaganda required a certain amount of stimulation by interested parties: noticeably, the *Protocols* owed their survival to the industry of White Russian émigrés who feared that Western governments would abandon their anti-Soviet cause. Perhaps this indicates how small was the initial impact of the *Protocols* upon opinion as a whole. Then, early in 1920 a so-called official translation, entitled *The Jewish Peril*, made a highly publicised appearance in England and received a long and imposing review in *The Times* of London. Compared to a pipsqueak of a newspaper like the *Dearborn Independent*, *The Times* spoke with the voice of irrefutable omniscience. Nothing in its columns could be ignored, and certain classes of Englishmen revered the paper as did Jews their Torah.

Britain's leading daily was then in the ownership of the capricious Lord Northcliffe, who had brought sensationalism to the British press and turned the *Daily Mail* into the country's first mass-circulation newspaper. Northcliffe, assisted by his brother Lord Rothermere, made the 'press baron' in Fleet Street a synonym for vanity, excessive power, oversimplification and ruthlessness in the race for circulation. When he embraced *The Jewish Peril* his mental balance was gravely disturbed – the beginnings of a terminal illness.

Reviewing *The Jewish Peril*, *The Times* arrived at no absolute conclusion regarding the *Protocols'* authenticity. But, the article stated, much of the prophecy, if such it was, had been fulfilled. Had therefore the British Empire, 'by straining every fibre of its

---

[26] Yale maintained restrictions until the early 1960s. See Dan A. Oren, *Joining the Club*, New Haven, 1986.

national body, escaped a "Pax Germanica" only to fall into a "Pax Judaica"? The Elders of Zion, as represented in their "Protocols", are by no means kinder taskmasters than William II and his henchmen would have been.'[27]

The message was taken up in other papers, most enthusiastically by the Tory *Morning Post*, which went overboard with eighteen articles on the Judeo-Masonic conspiracy. Antisemitic charges in one weekly, owned by Lord Alfred Douglas, claimed that Winston Churchill, on instructions from his Jewish paymasters, had facilitated the escape of the German fleet after the Battle of Jutland in 1916.[28]

The campaign flourished in this vein for a year or so, when suddenly *The Times*'s correspondent in Constantinople, Philip Graves, notified his editor of important news, for which he required ample space. Graves was allocated three articles on successive days in August 1921, to expose the *Protocols* as a work of plagiarism and forgery. He had discovered the source: a satire against Napoleon III by a French lawyer, Maurice Joly, first published in 1864 as *Dialogues aux Enfers entre Montesquieu et Machiavel*. Graves was put on the scent by a White Russian émigré in Constantinople who had obtained the original from a former agent of the tsarist secret police. This work consisted of twenty-one so-called dialogues illustrating the tactics by which the French ruler had returned to France from his English exile in 1848 and, to universal stupefaction, stolen power. Almost half the document corresponded word for word to passages of the *Protocols*, as was verified by comparison with a copy of Joly's original discovered in the library of the British Museum. The author had suffered fifteen months' imprisonment for his lampoon against the Napoleonic regime, with all available copies of the work confiscated and destroyed.

The Times published a full retraction of its allegations against the Jews, but this did not deter Henry Ford, nor other interested parties, from continuing to foster the idea of an international Jewish conspiracy. *The Times* itself changed tack: not a conspiracy by many Jews, but a heinous plan by just one of them to lock the British Empire into his schemes. Guilt pointed to Chaim

[27] *The Times*, 8 May 1920.
[28] Cohn, *Warrant for Genocide*, p. 155.

Weizmann. He had ensnared Britain in his sinister Zionist ambitions to secure Palestine. Rioting between Jews and Arabs had resulted, with the innocent British army caught in the middle. Britain should get out, 'bag and baggage'.

The Northcliffe papers spoke out loudest, but almost the whole of the right-wing British press took up the cry. The *Daily Express* headlined one story: 'Mystery of the Great Chaim: Last of the Foreigners who Meddle with British Affairs: Palestine Morass: The Genius that Lured and Keeps Us There'. The front-page article continued:

> Zaharoff and Venizelos have gone, and their secret influence has been cut out of our Government. But a more powerful foreigner remains . . . The last of the foreigners surpasses them both in his genius for exerting a hidden mastery over the minds of our simple British politicians. His name has never been whispered in the ears of the electors. They are hardly aware of his existence . . . Who is this man of mystery? His name is Dr Chaim Weizmann. He is president of the Zionist Organisation. His genius it was that lured us step by step into the morass of Palestine. His genius keeps us there and will keep us there until we sink up to the neck in irretrievable disaster. The Great Chaim is one of those master-minds who dominate the destinies of nations . . . He is one of the greatest chemists in the world. He is also a political chemist of the highest order. He has established his ascendancy in the heart of our Foreign Office and in the core of our Government . . . Let us have no more of the Great Chaim and his Palestine State subsidised by British money and based on British bayonets.[29]

This concerned a live political issue. Many British people doubted the wisdom of their country's accepting the Mandate over Palestine – in fact the House of Lords had voted against the proposal. Problems were mounting in the Middle East as a whole, because of disappointed Arab expectations in the kind of independence meted out to them by the Western powers. Arab

[29] *Daily Express*, London, 28 October 1922. Its editor was R. D. Blumenfeld, an American Jew.

nationalism, a sentiment only recently awakened, was on the increase. But the 'Great Chaim' is not described as a political leader; he is a devilishly clever intriguer – 'one of the greatest chemists in the world'. The subject-matter related to British politics; the tone was reminiscent of the *Protocols of Zion*.

Despite their exposure as a fiction, the *Protocols* continued to circulate in new editions throughout the world. Indeed, the printing has never ceased, and even in England specialist bookshops stock versions to this day. But what of Henry Ford? In 1927, following a libel suit, he wrote a full retraction and apology to Louis Marshall, president of the American Jewish Committee. Explaining that he was never fully conversant with the contents of either the *Dearborn Independent* or *The International Jew*, he had now had all copies destroyed:

> To my great regret I have learned that Jews generally, and particularly those of this country, not only resent these publications as promoting antisemitism, but regard me as their enemy ... I confess that I am deeply mortified that this journal, *The Dearborn Independent*, has been made the medium of resurrecting exploded fictions, for giving currency to the so-called *Protocols of the Wise Men of Zion*, which have been demonstrated, as I learn, to be gross forgeries, and for contending that the Jews have been engaged in a conspiracy to control the capital and industries of the world, besides laying at their door many offences against decency, public order and good morale.
> ... I am fully aware of the virtues of the Jewish people as a whole, of what they and their ancestors have done for civilisation and for mankind towards the development of commerce and industry, their sobriety and diligence, and their unselfish interest in the public welfare.[30]

---

[30] Charles Reznikoff (ed.), *Louis Marshall: Selected Papers and Addresses*, Philadelphia, 1957, pp. 376–9.

10

Fascism Triumphant

Probably no epoch in modern history can compare with the 1930s for cynicism, myopia and self-destructive statecraft. Few nations are not ashamed of their record during that decade of disgrace. Even if the culmination of the period by the Second World War, its condign penalty, could be eliminated from our retrospective judgement, the epoch would stand condemned for the banality of national leadership and the spurious philosophies of the intelligentsia, not to mention the sickening mindlessness of people in the mass.

Europe did not bear the totality of guilt for the 1930s. The disease of the times, its contagion a political Black Death, spread to the nations which Europe fostered across the globe. Latin America and the vast English-speaking communities were not immune. Our present preoccupation with the Jews does not permit amnesia in regard to the oppression and squalor engulfing other peoples. This was still a world exclusively controlled by the white man as he had created it for his purposes. Countless numbers among his subject races suffered as well as the Jews, though in silence, their miseries to go largely unrecorded until they could find voices of their own.

But the Jews were the selected sacrifice of the decade in Europe. The Spanish people, victims of a proxy war fought by clashing ideologies, and the Russians under a tyrant who promised a society of humanity and equality yet gave his anonymous millions little except unspeakable ordeals, stood at least on soil to which they held ancestral title. The Jews, denationalised, had no such basic right. And this despite their quantum leap into contemporary society, and their forceful representation in science, commerce, politics and the arts.

What happened in the 1930s to take them to the European

abyss into which they had to fall, as a specific ethnic fate, during the Second World War? All the recurring features of their history – economic marginality, social alienation, contempt – coalesced in that decade with their perennial landlessness, and led to the ultimate catastrophe of extermination. The desire of many Jews for total assimilation collided against a Christian instinct to turn them away. Admittedly, all was not harmony within the fold itself. They were a divided as well as a dispersed people. The growing prestige of Zionism told some of them to reject assimilation as a hopeless cause, while a visceral distrust of the gentile, to the point of hatred, kept a large proportion of the religiously devout out of the mainstream of national life. Despite all this, the question 'Why the Jews?' worries every examination of the human condition of those days.

A glance at their numerical distribution will illustrate how, by the beginning of the decade, the United States already contained the greatest, and most assured, Jewish settlement of all: some 4,300,000 resided there, about 3.2 per cent of the American population. What they lacked in cohesion they enjoyed in the unity of a subcontinent without frontiers. Within Europe, Poland now had the largest number, a little over three million Jews, ten per cent of a nation where minorities, each of them jealous for its identity, coloured the attitude of the whole. The 1926 census in the Soviet Union produced a figure of 2,600,000 in European Russia. Already by the early 1930s this two per cent of Russia's population retained only tenuous links with the rest of their people, while their legal status as a recognised nationality within the USSR carried ambiguities that are still unresolved. Next in size came Romania, whose Jewish citizens had swollen in number because of Romania's expansion since Versailles at the expense of Russia and Hungary. There were 800,000 Jews in a total Romanian population of 18 millions. Hungary, now truncated, had 400,000 (total 8.6 millions), and Germany half a million within its 65 millions.

These comprised the largest concentrations in 1930, for in Great Britain the Jews calculated themselves to be just 300,000, and in France 260,000. We have thus accounted for something in excess of 12 millions in a world estimate of 16.5 millions of Jews. So approximately another four and a half millions were spread thinly over the rest of the globe, with small numbers in most countries, including 175,000 (seventeen per cent of the total population) in Palestine and perhaps 370,000 in the three constituents of French North Africa.

All such statistics are estimates. Many governments did not require particulars of religion or ethnic origin in the census. Jewish communities making their own calculations would have excluded the baptised (or they excluded themselves), and no one knew how many defectors 'passed over' to the faiths dominant in their country of residence. The great majority of Jews inhabited large cities, usually capital cities. Over two millions resided in metropolitan New York alone. We must therefore take note of such cities' characteristics. The metropolis in any country would always lead in social change and religious tolerance, besides permitting the most relaxed sexual mores. It also offered the best educational, professional and economic opportunities. It exerted a magnetism for those people leaning towards artistic experimentation and radicalism in politics. Jews may have been small minorities numerically, but their strong representation in capital cities rendered them prominent in the activities which such centres inevitably nurtured. If you hoped to make a name for yourself, you were attracted to the capital; if you desired anonymity, likewise.

Those seeking an explanation for the Jews' disproportionate contribution to intellectual Europe in the earlier part of this century frequently cite devotion to religious study as a kind of mental gymnastics that stimulated Jewish abilities in pursuits remote from the spiritual. Poring over the Talmud exercised the mind in logic and dialectics, it is claimed, for the sages who compiled that huge literature resorted to an infinity of subtleties in debating the finer theological points.[1] Whether this was indeed the case must be reckoned as self-serving conjecture, to say the least. Few of the major Jewish figures in modern times cared enough for the Talmudic works to acquire significant

[1] Thus Cecil Roth, an eminent historian: 'There is obviously a high degree of intellectuality and an unswerving determination to follow processes of thought to their conclusion, a heritage of the long Jewish absorption in study in the ghetto period.' Preface to *The Jewish Contribution to Civilisation*, London, 1956, p. xv.

acquaintance with them, while those most faithful to the tradition adhered closely to its rules and absolved themselves from identification with the profane daily world. It is likewise perilous to speculate, in the case of the Jews, on a process of natural selection whereby genetics gave them an inherited superiority.

More prosaically, Jewish achievement was an index of their physical concentration in the centres of challenge and change, those capital cities. This also facilitated the growth of an exceptionally large middle class, the reward of specialisation in commerce and trade. One hardly needs an economist's training to comprehend that more money is likely to be made in buying and selling than in descending a coal-mine or working a sewing-machine. Even among the poor the owner of the miserable corner grocery would probably be the only one in the street with a bank account. Higher education, for long a privilege of young people drawn from families in the upper income groups, particularly benefited the Jews, and this despite restrictive quotas in many institutes of learning. The people as a whole derived prestige from the attainments of the few. And while a large segment constituted a proletariat, they all shared a proprietory interest in Einstein and Freud, names arising in working-class Jewish conversation as frequently as Disraeli and Al Jolson.

Be all this as it may, if we take the year 1930 as pivotal to its destiny, we encounter European Jewry at its zenith of achievement. To discuss the people's subsequent fate without due reference to this creative climax would deny full comprehension of antisemitism at its moment of deepest impact.[2] In the world of art, for example, they had breached every restraint, religious and social, that obstructed Jewish participation in the great schools of previous ages and, besides hundreds of less-acclaimed painters, numbered among the eminences of the École de Paris. Pissarro and Modigliani had by this time come and gone, but Pascin, Soutine, Chagall and Mané-Katz, with Jacques

---

[2] Hannah Arendt (*The Origins of Totalitarianism*, New York, 1973, p. 52): 'The crowding of Jewish sons of well-to-do parents into the cultural occupations was especially marked in Germany and Austria, where a great proportion of cultural institutions, like newspapers, publishing, music and theatre, became Jewish enterprises.'

Lipchitz in sculpture, commemorate the last golden summer of Montparnasse as the forcing-house of experimentation before Europe's winterset. Not that they formed a school of 'Jewish art' – assuming the validity of such a term – for with important exceptions, notably Chagall and Mané-Katz, they worked as unaffiliated inhabitants of their own cultural universe. Max Liebermann, a Berliner, introduced a much-needed progressivism into German art (the Sezession) and became president of the Berlin Academy of Fine Arts. He occupied this position from 1919 until Adolf Hitler's accession to power in 1933, when he went into oblivion. Jankel Adler would suffer a similar fate in Germany, and excoriation as an exponent of 'degenerate art'. Adler would find shelter in Britain, not then the most congenial of artistic environments although out of it rose those leading modernists Mark Gertler, David Bomberg and Bernard Meninsky.

In contrast with the majority of Jewish artists, mainly of East European origin and thus cultural strangers in the West, writers interacted closely with the corresponding national traditions. In France the Halévy family (see page 204) and Marcel Proust (Jewish on his mother's side) had already set a pattern of total Gallic assimilation. By the year 1930 no aspect of French literary activity lacked its Jewish participants, some of them baptised. André Maurois, Georges de Porto-Riche and Joseph Kessel, biographer, playwright and novelist respectively, would each receive election in time among the 'immortals' of the Academy. A much more numerous group chose to embrace left-wing politics and plunge into the ferment which, between the wars, gave to Paris its reputation as the capital with the most intellectuals committed to libertarian ideals. Their inspiration came from what they took as the example shining out of Soviet Russia. Revolutionary novelists, essayists and editors of the rank of Jean-Richard Bloch, Julien Benda and Emmanuel Berl would come properly into their own with the rise of Hitlerism and the Spanish Civil War, when their conviction that Russia alone barred the way to armed conflict over the body and soul of Europe hardened into dogma. Ilya Ehrenburg, *Izvestia*'s Jewish correspondent in Paris and Stalin's unofficial commisar, zealously encouraged the anti-war, pro-Soviet mood that caught these writers in its spell.[3] Of course, there sparkled in this constellation of Jewish talents others without strong political commitment, such as Alfred Savoir and Henri Bernstein in the theatre and Max Jacob in poetry. Above and beyond them all stood Henri Bergson, the philosopher of 'time and duration'. He won a Nobel prize in 1928, by which time the occurrence of Jewish laureates was already a commonplace.

Bergson, together with Freud, Einstein and Martin Buber, gave a specific Jewish resonance to the advancement of European thought as the fateful decade dawned. Merely to list them, without attempting a discussion of their ideas and influence, violates their memory; but our subject allows for little here except a catalogue of names. They varied widely in Jewish commitment — Bergson acknowledged none at all and was on the point of baptism when the Nazi occupation of Paris beckoned his conscience back to his roots; while Buber, collaborator of the inspired metaphysician Franz Rosenzweig, took Judaism as object of both lifetime study and spiritual devotion. Freud, whose father came from a Hassidic background, tussled ambivalently with his origin in discussing the nature of religion, a conflict still left unresolved with his last work, *Moses and Monotheism*, written in English exile at the age of eighty. Einstein, by contrast, encountered no problem in reconciling his humanist *Weltanschauung* with the Jewish heritage.

For self-expression in art we have turned inevitably to the émigré world of Paris. Literature, music and science, however, offered their most impelling attractions within the Germanic triangle formed by Berlin, Vienna and Prague. These cities, their history and culture interwoven as the spirit of the extinct Habsburg Empire lingered, created a psychic challenge for the Jews. The German language gave them a common denominator to compensate for their exclusion from Central Europe's diversifying national movements. The Jewish intelligentsia of Budapest, on the other hand, chose complete Magyarisation, as in the case of Ferenc Molnar (*Liliom*, translated to music as *Carousel*). Within the Germanic triangle no barriers could hold against excellence of accomplishment, which was supranational. Thus

[3] For a graphic description, see Herbert Lottman, *The Left Bank: Writers in Paris from Popular Front to Cold War*, London, 1982.

ambition sharpened. Reward seemed limitless in 1930 for those who could compose a melody, stage a drama, write a satire or extend the frontiers of knowledge. Explore any field of activity and there were the Jews, eager, resourceful and prolific.

Franco-Jewish intellectuals held the Revolution's compact with their people as individuals to be sacred. Many went to the extreme of suppressing every surviving trace of their ancestral nature. Writers in German were more relaxed, despite the existence of a school of fanatical assimilationists, fathered by the philosopher Otto Weininger (died by his own hand in 1903, at the age of twenty-three), that led its adherents virtually into the ranks of antisemitism. Weininger had classified all women as sexual instruments, all Jews as biologically nihilist.[4] His Jewish disciples included other 'self-hating' Jews: Karl Kraus, poet, satirist and champion of linguistic purity; and Kurt Tucholsky, like Kraus a satirist, like Weininger a suicide. The dramatist and revolutionary activist Ernst Toller, yet another suicide, fell into the same category. They were Judaism's own anti-Jews; every epoch has produced them.

In general Central European writers easily balanced their Germanity with their Judaism, pace Kafka and that quandary over identity taking him to the depths of pessimistic fantasy. Some of the 1930s writers could still recall with admiration Theodor Herzl in his journalist's persona as features editor of the Viennese Neue Freie Presse; even Kafka, who died in 1924, was drawn to Zionism and took lessons in Hebrew. Kafka's friend Max Brod (Unambo) and Arnold Zweig (The Case of Sergeant Grisha, The Axe of Wandsbeck) chose Palestine for their exile under Nazism, the latter subsequently transferring to a Communist paradise in East Berlin. It was the period of Jakob Wasserman, Arthur Schnitzler, Stefan Zweig, Franz Werfel, Lion Feuchtwanger, Richard Beer-Hofmann, Hugo von Hofmannsthal and Nelly Sachs – truly, the Jews had found Parnassus. Max Reinhardt, the first director to stage Hamlet in modern dress, dominated German theatre, as did Otto Klemperer and Bruno Walter the concert halls. Kurt Weill was already renowned as the composer of The Threepenny Opera.

[4] See D. Abrahamsen, The Mind and Death of a Genius, New York, 1946.

We are still in the Germany of the Weimar Republic, which owed so much, faults as well as virtues, to the engineer-statesman Walter Rathenau. He had led his country out of the trough of Versailles as minister of reconstruction and was Foreign Minister, with a pan-European outlook, when an anti-republican assassin struck him down in 1922. Eight years later Germany appeared on the mend, despite its millions of unemployed. It was also the moment for Max Horkheimer to recruit Theodor Adorno, Walter Benjamin and Herbert Marcuse to his Frankfurt School, so characteristically Jewish and yet agnostic, intensely German yet universalist. They formed a neo-Marxist battalion of sociologists applying Hegelian idealism to the criticism of art and music. Today we can look back to such forerunners of the New Left as delineating an age of innocence.[5]

Still, shadows had already fallen across these Elysian Fields, in the shape of populist, militant nationalism, the glorification of historical tradition and the ethos of *patrie* – in a word, Mussolini's Fascism. It would be embraced as the sure panacea for every political *malaise*, the only real alternative to advancing Communism. And although Mussolini, that paradigm of demagogic leadership, long rejected antisemitism so that Italian Jewry fared better than the people elsewhere on the Continent, the export of his doctrine meant the inevitable deployment of Europe against them.

Now that the Italian dictator has descended into history as a figure whose inflated pretensions brought disaster on his country, we have some difficulty in recalling how much Mussolini was courted and admired between the wars. Italy barely rated as a European power when he won control in 1922. The country's feeble military contribution to Allied victory had earned it only a

---

[5] See Martin Jay, *Adorno*, London, 1984, for an abbreviated account of the Frankfurt School. By one of those Jewish ironies, it struggled on elsewhere in Europe to maintain its academic detachment from the Jewish crisis after the arrival of Nazism, only to be compelled into reluctant employment in the United States by the American Jewish Committee (except for Benjamin, who committed suicide). Adherents of the Frankfurt School received a commission in New York to analyse the roots of antisemitic prejudice, which they accomplished, to their own satisfaction at least, in five volumes. Horkheimer re-established his school in Germany at the first opportunity after the war and was followed by Adorno, who returned to his Chair of Sociology in Frankfurt.

minor role at the Paris Peace Conference, from which it departed disgruntled with insignificant gains. Strikes paralysed government, citizens were compelled in droves to seek low-prestige employment beyond Italy's frontiers, penury and illiteracy were rife. Mussolini imposed his Fascist order through strong-arm tactics. Suppressing all opposition, he inspired thousands of young men to march through the streets in their black shirts, and made flamboyant orations connecting his regime with the glories of the ancient Roman Empire, whose raised arm salute he revived. By 1930 the Duce, having given a livelihood to millions in public works, taken Austria under his protection, expelled unfriendly foreign correspondents and bribed the sycophants, had produced the façade of a virile nation commanded by a leader of personality and vision. Soon the world became generously endowed with potential Mussolinis delivering speeches of blood and fire, all surrounded by followers in variously coloured uniforms. Adolf Hitler's wore brown though he distinguished his personal élite corps, the Schutzstaffel (SS), by putting them in black.

Democracy looked effete in contrast, apologetic. And while it strove to justify itself, elected governments began to reckon with Fascism as a growing factor in international affairs, though not necessarily a hostile one. But Stalin, after a momentary flirtation with Mussolini in 1932, regarded Italy as a menace, specifically directed against the Soviet Union. Preoccupied with its own dire agricultural and industrial backwardness, the Soviet Union betrayed no ambitions for a world role in those days. It did not achieve membership of the League of Nations until 1934, after Stalin had, as it were, abandoned the policy of 'world revolution' and replaced it with 'Socialism in one country'.[6] In the diplomatic scheme of things Russia counted for little, and could be ignored.

Hitler created a far more disturbing impression than Mussolini on his accession to power in 1933, by introducing the racial dimension to Fascism. When he spoke of Bolshevism it was in the same breath with which he berated 'international Jewry'. Yet Hitler found apologists just as speedily as his fellow-dictator

---

[6] With a ruthless collectivisation process involving genocide of the kulak peasantry. See, e.g., Robert Conquest, *The Harvest of Sorrow*, London, 1986.

across the Alps. People who could not really abide Hitler's trumpetings about the Jews, and the primacy of the Aryan race, took heart from the rise of a new ally against Bolshevism. The unemployed in the democratic states were falling fast into the arms of left-wing revolutionaries, and anti-Communism needed all the friends it could get. Observers failed to realise that it was no mere rhetorical extravagance when Hitler charged the Jews with master-minding Bolshevism's infiltration of every country in Europe.

He went still further. The purposes of the Judeo-Bolshevik alliance, he declared, were served also by modern art, ungodly literature, cosmopolitan science and the bankers of London and New York. His version of totalitarian discipline was offered as the sole bulwark against an all-pervading European decadence. The Nazi leader discounted any considerable contribution by the Duce in this regard, his respect for Mussolini being diluted by his contempt for Italy. Hitler claimed for Germany the unification of the *Volk* and the restitution of territory forfeited in Europe – for the present no more – while Mussolini demanded space in Africa. So the two could well go their separate ways, in neither friendship nor enmity. Conventional statesmen in England and France dismissed these respective territorial aspirations as bombast: between them they controlled the League of Nations, where manifestly such problems would be peaceably argued out.

As to the Jews, Hitler's intention to liquidate their presence in Germany had long been established, through his turgid ideological dissertation *Mein Kampf*, first published in 1925. The term most frequently arising is 'removal' (*Beseitigung*), which ambiguously embraces the simple literal definition but could also imply a much more radical fate. Nowhere does *Mein Kampf* spell out proposals for the solution of the Jewish question by a process of physical annihilation. Perhaps the printed record imposed its inhibitions, for there can be no doubt that Hitler's imagination did not exclude such a possibility. Throughout his book he refers to the Jews with a pathological loathing.

Thus:

> With satanic joy in his face, the black-haired Jewish youth lurks in wait for the unsuspecting girl whom he defiles with his blood, thus stealing her from her people.

With every means he tries to destroy the racial foundations of the people he has set out to subjugate. Just as he systematically ruins women and girls, he does not shrink back from pulling down the blood barriers of others, even on a large scale. It was and it is Jews who bring the Negroes into the Rhineland [the French employed Senegalese troops in their occupation force, 1919–30], always with the same secret and clear aim of ruining the hated white race by the necessarily resulting bastardisation, throwing it down from its cultural and political height, and himself rising to be its master... In Russia he killed or starved about 30 million people with positively fanatical savagery, in part amid inhuman tortures, in order to give a gang of Jewish journalists and stock exchange bandits domination over a great people.[7]

Naturally, Hitler accepted the authenticity of what had been conclusively demonstrated as a virulent antisemitic hoax:

To what an extent the whole existence of this people is based on a continuous lie is shown incomparably by *The Protocols of the Learned Elders of Zion*, so infinitely hated by the Jews. They are based on a forgery, the *Frankfurter Zeitung* moans and screams once every week: the best proof that they are authentic. What many Jews do unconsciously is here consciously exposed.[8]

Jewry had already subjugated Germany in pursuit of its own insatiable ambitions:

The leadership of our destinies has, since the end of the War, been quite openly furnished by Jews ... Conscious purpose is destroying our nation. And once we examine the apparent madness of our nation's leadership in the field of foreign affairs from this standpoint, it is revealed as the subtlest, ice-cold logic, in the service of the Jewish idea and struggle for world conquest.[9]

[7] Tr. Manheim, pp. 295–6.
[8] Ibid., p. 279.
[9] Ibid., p. 611.

Ranging over Germany's misfortunes, Hitler's mind visualised death as exemplary punishment for Jews by a method that today carries a hideous retrospective resonance: 'If at the beginning of the War and during the War twelve or fifteen thousand of those Hebrew corrupters of the people had been held under poison gas, as happened to hundreds of thousands of our very best workers in the field, the sacrifice of millions at the front would not have been in vain.'[10]

The author of these sentiments assumed the chancellorship of Germany on 30 January 1933 quite legally, for at the elections the previous November his National Socialist German Workers' (Nazi) Party achieved 33 per cent of the vote, the Socialists 20 per cent, the Communists 17 per cent and the Catholic parties together 15 per cent. President Hindenburg acceded to his demand for dissolution of parliament, emergency decrees and new elections, on the grounds of the Communist danger to the democratic order. Hitler thereupon increased his vote to 44 per cent, still not a majority, and immediately embarked upon the rooting out of all opposition. Many Socialists and all known Communists were arrested, including some elected to the Reichstag. The first concentration camp was opened in the grounds of a former gunpowder factory at Dachau, near Munich. In July 1933 the Nazi Party became the only one sanctioned by law, and so a Fascist revolution was silently achieved.

Jewish storekeepers saw no immediate cause for panic. They did not put up their shutters, though attempts to boycott them had already begun, while SA members, the stormtroopers of the Sturmabteilung, exceeded Hitler's own orders by dragging Jewish judges from the courts and molesting individual teachers and pupils in the schools. The nation followed these developments in a political stupor, as illustrated by the plebiscite conducted in association with fresh elections on the single party list and a programme of withdrawal from the League of Nations. This gave Hitler the endorsement of 92 per cent of the electorate. The freedom of the election may be gauged by the astounding result in the Dachau concentration camp: 2,154 of its 2,242 inmates voted for the government.[11] A million and a half copies of *Mein Kampf*

10 Ibid., p. 620.
11 William Shirer, *The Rise and Fall of the Third Reich*, London, 1964, p. 265.

were sold in 1933, and the following year the Führer's thoughts entered the educational curriculum as compulsory reading in the schools. This progressive consolidation of power was accomplished by warnings to the Jews beyond Germany's borders to stay out of the country's affairs.

Certainly, they had been staging protests against the regime and the dangers it portended – for the Jews, for the future of Germany, for the peace of Europe. Christian leaders and other public figures readily joined their demonstrations. But this found no echo in a Jewish reaction within the Reich itself. Warnings that they had better keep in line, and the fear of new excesses against them, contributed of course to their silence. Stronger in its effect, however, was the persisting naïve hope that what had so far transpired represented a momentary aberration, an outburst of emotion uncharacteristic of the German personality. Anti-Jewish violence was the work of undisciplined thugs: hence the community's urgent appeals for restraint to their coreligionists abroad. They could not recognise the ravings of the petty agitator of *Mein Kampf* in the statesmanlike speeches of Hitler in office. His programme outlined to the Reichstag late in March 1933 struck some German Jews as a rational approach to the country's problems. A prominent German Zionist, hearing the address on the radio in Palestine, described it as 'significant, interesting and absorbing'.[12] Talk of emigration fell from many lips, but not enough to dissipate the illusion that life could still be bearable under the Nazis. And this despite the methodical expulsion of Jews from official positions in the civil service, the universities and the bench, besides the revocation of citizenship of those naturalised under the Weimar Republic. Old-established German Jewry argued that such measures applied mostly to *Ostjuden*, recently arrived, poorly adjusted and without their own sterling patriotism. Moreover, they noted, Jews were by no means the only victims; liberals of the Christian faith, including some in holy orders, were also being forced out of public life.

On 10 May 1933, at midnight, an eerie ceremony, reminiscent of the spirit of the Middle Ages, took place in the centre of Berlin and in many other cities besides: the burning of the books. The

[12] Arthur Ruppin, *Memoirs, Diaries, Letters*, London, 1971, p. 263.

test as to which authors should be made a sacrifice at this cultural *auto-da-fé* seemed to be a matter of individual whim. But without exception the writings of known Jewish authors were given to the pyre: the scientific works of Einstein and Freud, the speeches of Walther Rathenau, the fiction of Feuchtwanger, Wassermann, Schnitzler, Arnold and Stefan Zweig, Proust, the popular biographies of Emil Ludwig. Also non-Jewish authors, German and foreign, calculated to corrupt the mind: Thomas and Heinrich Mann, Karl Kautsky, Erich Maria Remarque, Jack London, Upton Sinclair, H. G. Wells, Havelock Ellis, Émile Zola, André Gide. Culture as translated into *Kultur* would now be accorded a definition consonant with the virtues, dignity and disciplines of the master race. Thus orchestras could no longer play the works, classified as Jewish, of Mendelssohn and Schoenberg, nor of Hindemith, exponent in music of the *Neue Sachlichkeit* (neo-realism) expressed in art. The denunciation of modernism led to the disappearance of 16,000 paintings, drawings and pieces of sculpture from the public galleries. Stupor in politics evidently needed reinforcement in a stupor of the spirit.

And so it was. The man who could command the support of only a minority of his people while elections were free now had the acclaim of the Church, the army, the judiciary, the broad mass of intellectuals, the great capitalists of heavy industry. This was a national leader indeed: at a stroke he had wiped from the memory the puppets and intriguers of yesterday's republic. Nullification of the Versailles diktat, restoration of pride, economic revival, elimination of corruption, everything he promised the German people surged into the sphere of practical objectives. Also, to court the goodwill of the outside world Hitler exerted restraint over his followers' public attacks upon the Jews; in due course that unwanted race would realise the country had no place for it and they would all depart.

By the end of 1933 some 50,000 Jews had reassessed their situation and indeed emigrated – ten per cent of their total, together with another 10,000 Christians of non-Aryan descent (i.e. converts or part-Jews) as well as others regarded as enemies of the state. Those remaining still clung to a belief that, despite the painful adjustments involved, they might continue their lives on the soil they worshipped. Who is not reluctant to abandon his home, his language and culture, and in many cases his fortune, to go forth as a stranger in an alien world? By a supreme effort of self-delusion the majority of those describing themselves as authentic Germans, with medals earned and casualties suffered in the Great War, placed their trust in the civilisation of their heroes, Bismarck, Goethe and Beethoven. Decency, they knew, could not be dead. Even old soldier Hindenberg, the State President, was moved by the shame of dismissing war veterans from their posts. He had protested to his Chancellor:

> In the last few days a whole series of cases has been reported to me in which war-wounded judges, lawyers and civil servants in the judiciary, with unblemished records of service, have been forcibly furloughed and will later be dismissed simply because they are of Jewish origin. For me personally, revering those who died in the war and grateful to those who survived and to the wounded who suffered, such treatment of war veterans is altogether intolerable ... If they were worthy to fight and bleed for Germany then they should also be considered worthy to continue serving the fatherland in their professions.[13]

Hindenburg was then eighty-six. Hitler sent him a conciliatory reply, though of course nothing changed.

While German Jews in the main clutched at any straw, those beyond the shadows recognised in Nazism a plague which, uncontrolled, could engulf them all. Demonstrations served for little. Direct, immediate action was required. They called for an embargo on Germany's trade, pronouncing it a moral offence for Jews to buy goods manufactured in that country. This flexing of economic muscle had a perceptible impact initially, Germany being starved of foreign currency. But soon it dwindled to a mere gesture, and difficult to sustain at that, except in such industries of Jewish preponderance as furs and diamonds. Far more significant than practical action was the psychological response to Nazism.

Jews everywhere suffered the shock of discovery that as a

[13] Lucy Dawidowicz, *The War against the Jews, 1933–45*, London, 1977, p. 86, citing *Dokumente der deutchen Politik und Geschichte*, Vol. IV, pp. 147–8.

people they could no longer take the status they had won for granted. If a country like Germany, unequalled for its splendid cultural tradition, so admired for its philosophy and scientific attainments, its Jewish community brilliantly adjusted after centuries of unbroken residence, could succumb to an antisemitic tyranny, were the Jews safe anywhere? Spellbound by Hitler the Germans could understandably be, but some public figures of other nations were speaking of this upstart of a dictator with grudging admiration, accepting him as a statesman with no ambition more heinous than to remedy the injustices of Versailles. In London *The Times*, during July 1933, published extracts from *Mein Kampf* that omitted all Jewish references. The passages were carefully selected so as to convey a favourable impression of the man, his policies for Germany and his attitude to Great Britain.

Hitler's greatest achievement in those early days, little realised at the time, was to change the mentality of the Jewish people as a whole. Historical assumptions were abandoned overnight. They scrutinised their neighbours for enemy or friend. They took their first moves towards the internationalisation of their institutions. They pored over their newspapers for a sign that the world's leaders intended some co-ordinated quarantine against this man of ruthless intention. There appeared no such desire. To the gentile mind, the Jews were resorting to their customary exaggeration in speaking of Nazis atrocities.

Another disturbing revelation: no other country extended an open invitation to the victims of persecution. Naturally, visas existed in abundance for the eminent. Competition waxed furious among the world's universities for celebrated writers and scientists. Everyone wanted the Nobel laureates—Einstein, Fritz Haber, Richard Willstaeter (the last-named, dismissed from his Chair of Organic Chemistry at Munich, refused to leave the country). Max Reinhardt, Conrad Veidt, Elisabeth Bergner, Richard Tauber and their kind had the world's theatre at their feet. And, *faute de mieux*, foreign institutions accepted the not-so-eminent. Needless to say, money too could speak all languages. But ordinary doctors and teachers, skilled workers, single unattached women, orphaned children, the anonymous applicants queuing outside the consulates, these encountered difficulties. Economic depression characterised the time. All governments took recourse in the excuse of their own unemployed and the fear of competition in the labour market.

As a consequence, the significance of Palestine soared in the people's calculations. Hitherto Zionism had aroused no great enthusiasm in Jewry. Just a tiny minority were wholly committed to the ideal, although this few spoke as if it had the entire race behind it. The movement's leaders waged a constant struggle to finance their work in Palestine, with many benefactors giving in charity, uninterested in how their money was spent. Western Europe and America might provide stewardship for Zionism, but the immigrants they sent to the Promised Land came almost exclusively from the tribal stock in Poland and Romania. It now emerged with startling clarity, even to Jews regarding themselves as totally assimilated, that as a haven of last resort no true homeland existed except in Palestine. Deny it the Arabs might, but only to that place could the people go, in a memorable phrase of Winston Churchill's written into a British statement of policy, 'as of right and not on sufferance'.[14]

In 1931, before the advent of Hitler, 254 delegates attended the Zionist Congress. In 1935 the number had swollen to 463, the new faces including some who had all their lives looked upon Jewish politics with boredom, or detachment, or distaste. Chaim Weizmann and his Zionists came into their own as the sole effective arm of Jewry in crisis. They had laboured to bring Palestine into the Jewish perception as the home of first, not last, resort, but they nevertheless welcomed the late converts who now flocked to help – among them men and women carrying political influence in their own countries of residence. Jews learnt to lobby their governments, bombard newspaper editors with their propaganda and canvass for funds as never before.

Immigration to Palestine leapt to dramatic figures. While less than 10,000 arrived in 1932, the 1933 total exceeded 30,000, in 1934 42,000, and in 1935, the record year under the British Mandate, 61,000 arrived. But here a wry note: Germany's emigrants preferred, in large measure, to settle elsewhere.

---

[14] White Paper of June 1922, Cmd 1700. Churchill had been Colonial Secretary.

Weizmann's prestige as a Jewish spokesman, the impression he created of moderation, gained him the ear of prime ministers and presidents throughout the world. He seemed to be leading a government-in-exile. Only one country could be reckoned unconditionally hostile to Zionism: Soviet Russia. Despite the large Jewish representation in the upper reaches of the apparatus, or more likely because of it, the Palestine solution was classed as anti-Communist, a tool of British imperialism, and Soviet citizens subscribing to the cause faced penalisation for the crime of bourgeois deviationism. As early as 1928 it was estimated that 775 Zionists were in prison or internal exile.[15] (Poland, on the other hand, actively fostered Zionism to the length of financing its activities as opportune for ridding its soil of this people.) But the USSR did not forfeit foreign Jewish sympathies as a result. Russia proclaimed antisemitism to be a criminal offence under the Soviet constitution, and condemned racial persecution as an imperialist device to divide the proletariat. Jews were by no means singular in their conviction that if any statesman revealed a determination to stop Hitler and halt the slide to war he was Josef Stalin. It was a view shared by many millions throughout the world.

This conviction enormously increased the drift among Jews towards the radical Left, and especially so when Mussolini began making common cause with Hitler. Italian Fascism, superimposed on German Nazism, rippled through Europe as an attractive option for emulation by the conservative Right. The implications of Fascism as a creed of racial nationalism left the Jews with no political alternative but the opposite camp, for liberalism was a dying force and they had nowhere else to go. Zionism too became infected by the trend towards polarisation. It had its own Left and Right wings shading into a Jewish quasi-Communism and quasi-Fascism. Out of the ultra-Right a leader, Vladimir Jabotinsky, emerged who was much taken with the rejuvenating effect Fascism exerted over a disheartened people. He modelled himself on Mussolini. In Eastern Europe, where Jabotinsky was strongest, his supporters paraded, like Hitler's SA, in brown shirts.

[15] J. B. Schechtman, in Lionel Kochan (ed.), *The Jews in Soviet Russia since 1917*, London, 1970, p. 108.

Meanwhile, politics had been travelling along a path all their own in the United States, specifically among the Jews of New York City. As we have noted, here they were more numerous, enjoyed greater freedom and experienced fewer inhibitions than anywhere else. Within that kaleidoscope of ethnic diversity ideologies assumed a European hue refracted through the prism of distance. Some Italian Americans decorated their restaurants with portraits of the Duce, while German Americans beyond Jewish earshot confessed to their admiration for Hitler. The Communist doctrine fertilised most easily in the districts inhabited by Jews. Their militancy did not operate so much in the national arena as in the powerful unions of the needle trades, the International Ladies' Garment Workers' Union (ILGWU) being the second largest labour organisation in the country. Conflict between the radical Left and middle-of-the-road Socialists, a bitter vendetta conducted, be it noted, mainly in the Yiddish language, continued violently throughout the 1920s and deep into the 1930s. The adversaries enlisted rival gangs to break up each other's meetings, till the union leaders reluctantly called in Arnold Rothstein, 'absolute boss of the New York underworld',[16] to forestall an incipient Jewish civil war. Schism succeeded schism, Trotskyites battled with Stalinists, and the anarchists eternally clamoured for a general strike.

Ultimately the moderate labour leaders, heirs to the European tradition of their Bundist past, fought their way back with a network of political groups that developed into the American Labor Party. They offered fealty to the State Governor, Franklin D. Roosevelt, and placed their considerable weight behind his bid for the presidency. The architect of the alliance, David Dubinsky of the ILGWU, persuaded the factory workers that in America the term Democrat really meant what it said. Roosevelt had proved a popular Governor among the immigrants. Dubinsky, the former Polish pastry-cook, earned a degree of immortality for his achievement in delivering the solid Jewish vote that stayed faithful to Roosevelt and the Democratic Party for a half-century. Roosevelt's New Deal captured the Jewish heart as the authentic answer to Fascism. Whatever might befall

[16] Howe, *World of Our Fathers*, pp. 330–47.

Europe, even to the point of a Fascist supremacy over the entire continent, the presence of Roosevelt in the White House would keep America safe. Thus the old German-Jewish aristocracy and the East European proletariat united in a Democratic phalanx. That phalanx of Jewish votes eludes complete demolition by the Republicans to this day.

Through the gravitation of the American electoral system, New York, as city and state, assumed crucial importance in the quadrennial heavyweight contest for the White House. Roosevelt, in gratitude for the near totality of his Jewish support, and with Jews prominent in his famous 'Brain Trust' that set about curing the Depression,[17] might reasonably have endeavoured to secure a relaxation of the immigration rules and afford sanctuary in significant number to the Jews who, slowly but ineluctably, were finding life in Hitler's Reich intolerable. He failed to budge on this sensitive question. He suffered no strictures from his vast Jewish constituency for his heartlessness. None of his Jewish officials resigned. Such was the degree of their infatuation with the President. France did better in granting early emigrants a refuge, though purely on a temporary basis and without work permits, chivvying them to move on.

Obviously, the problem demanded organisation on a global scale, but no country would take the initiative. Action was left to the Jews themselves. Late in 1933 the two major organisations of relief, the Central British Fund in London and the American Jewish Joint Distribution Committee of New York, put up the finance for a High Commission for Refugees under the auspices of the League of Nations. Weizmann, representing his Zionists, and Lionel de Rothschild, the non-Zionist philanthropist, heaved this body into existence with the appointment of James G. McDonald as High Commissioner. Formerly chairman of the Foreign Policy Association in America and an expert on the workings of the League (which, of course, the USA had not

[17] Jews close to Roosevelt included Anna M. Rosenberg and Sidney Hillman of the National Recovery Administration; Samuel Rosenman, presidential counsel and speech-writer; Benjamin V. Cohen, who drafted legislation; Bernard Baruch, economic adviser; Supreme Court Justice Louis D. Brandeis; Felix Frankfurter, Harvard professor, later a Supreme Court Justice; Stephen S. Wise, a leading rabbi; New York Governor Herbert Lehman; and Secretary of Treasury Henry Morgenthau Jr.

joined), McDonald rightly viewed his task as the succour of all refugees, Jewish and gentile.

The emphasis in the High Commission's directives was British rather than American. Lord Cecil of Chelwood accepted the office of chairman of its governing board, and the post of Deputy High Commissioner went to the Londoner Norman Bentwich, earlier the senior law officer of the Palestine Administration and a Weizmann nominee. Distinguished Anglo-Jewish personalities, notably Herbert Samuel and Simon Marks (head of Marks & Spencer stores), visited the United States periodically to quarry funds out of their American brethren for the activities of rescue.[18] It did not go unremarked by his critics that Weizmann observed the German catastrophe from his distinctly subjective standpoint as a Zionist purist. He needed to strengthen the Jewish presence in Palestine, so who better than those industrious Germans, many of them with substantial savings and technical skills vital to the development of the national income? As pioneering material what a contrast they would make to the Poles, who required subsidising all the way and threatened to turn the main thoroughfare of Tel Aviv into a replica of Warsaw's extended street market, the Nalevki!

As it happened, the German-Jewish crisis appeared in 1934 to be close to solution. Emigration remained at constant, manageable levels, with Great Britain now the principal immediate refuge, if not topmost as ultimate destination. Most of the Jews intent upon leaving Germany were getting away, thanks to the intercession of the rescue organisations, not all of them Jewish. Britain behaved more creditably than others, to be sure, and one should not detract from the humanitarianism of its citizens. But other factors contributed to force their government's hand. Britain's pre-eminence in Europe carried special obligations to serve as an example, to which may be added the importance of the local Jewish community, which at that time was the best organised in the West and more influential in world affairs than its isolationist American counterpart. Thus Britain was the point of most effective thrust. More substantially, however, Britain felt uneasy in its role as the trustee of Palestine with a particular

[18] For a comprehensive account of the work achieved, see Bentwich, *They Found Refuge*, London, 1956.

concern for encouraging the national home. This made London the focus of attention, for Palestine, in the eyes of the world, was surely the obvious destination for Jewish refugees. Ah, but this argued without the vexing complication of the Arab community in that country, a concern that troubled other governments not one whit.

Discontent had long simmered in the Holy Land. Only recently, in 1929 and before the arrival of Hitler, it had exploded in communal violence when an extremist Arab leader, Haj Amin el Husseini, goaded his people to open revolt. In his capacity as Mufti of Jerusalem, Husseini combined religious authority with substantial political strength. He now observed the Jews stream-ing into Palestine, and from the mosque harangued his people (innocent, as he reminded them, of the sins of antisemitic Christ-endom) on the impending loss of their patrimony: with the con-nivance of the British government these people, well financed, efficiently organised, influential in the world's capitals, bade fair to usurping the land from under their noses. The Mufti agitated for an independent Arab Palestine, threatening the direst conse-quences of delay. In the meantime all Jewish immigration must cease, except by sanction of the indigenous inhabitants.

Immigration did not cease. On the contrary, it increased very substantially, as we have shown – not enough to satisfy the Jews, far too much to assuage the Arabs. And yet, hoping to stem disquiet on both sides, and much to Jewish indignation, Britain was placing limits upon certain categories of Palestine immig-rants. Those with an acceptable minimum of capital could come in without restriction, but the number of worker immigrants was kept low. Simultaneously, to arrest criticism on this score the British opened the gates of their own island slightly wider. Neither Jew nor Arab was appeased, but this would ever be in the nature of the Palestine imbroglio.

Some legitimacy to Arab grievances is warranted. But Palestine apart, no country receiving Jewish refugees suffered thereby, unemployment and economic slump notwithstanding. For initial subsistence, when necessary, they looked to their own without lengthening the welfare queues. They introduced branches of learning, such as psychiatry, pure mathematics and the history of art, to countries where these disciplines were still rudimentary.

For the techniques of colour printing Germany had been leading the world, now no longer. In Britain alone the Board of Trade listed 163 new enterprises bringing jobs to regions of special distress, notably South Wales and Northern Ireland, through the agency of newcomers.[19]

Without entering into the sincerity, or lack of it, attending Germany's stated foreign policy, it should be noted that Hitler specifically renounced claims to Alsace-Lorraine. This was received in France with gratification and relief. France could now join more readily with Britain in viewing the new Germany as a power that need not inevitably encroach upon its own interests. And this despite German rearmament and withdrawal from the League of Nations. Such complacency served only to increase Moscow's suspicions of the West. To Russia it signified collusion between all three in Western Europe, a conspiracy directed against the Soviets. Stalin watched and waited. This evolution of Nazi 'respectability', coupled with Mussolini's invasion of Ethiopia, kept the Jewish question at a low priority. The Jewish organisations were themselves deceived. They debated whether to suspend their efforts on behalf of German Jewry and switch to the critical situation growing for their people in Poland.[20] In reality, all was coming to the boil, with repercussions spilling over to almost every country in Europe.

While people of goodwill preferred to excuse Hitler his early excesses against the Jews, regarding the subject as concluded, the Führer engaged in more radical steps to drive them out of the Reich. The idea of compromise on this score could never be entertained. by the man who, as early as 1922, had advised Germany that the nation could not survive with a Jewish presence, for 'the Aryan alone can form states and set them on their path to future greatness ... The Jew is seeking to disintegrate the national German spirit.'[21]

Now, in 1935, had come the moment to act. Summoning the Reichstag to Nuremberg that September, Hitler had a rubber

[19] Association of Jewish Refugees, *Britain's New Citizens*, London, 1951, p. 25.
[20] Bentwich, *They Found Refuge*, p. 27.
[21] Norman H. Baynes (ed.), *The Speeches of Adolf Hitler 1922–39*, London, 1942, p. 21.

stamp placed on racial decrees which were without precedent in European civilisation, though the Middle Ages came close. These decrees were mainly embodied in the Law for the Protection of German Blood and Honour. Marriage between Jews and 'nationals of German kindred blood' was henceforth forbidden, along with extramarital relationships. Subjects of the Reich (*Staatsangehoerigen*) and citizens (*Reichsbuerger*) were to be rigorously separate categories. The former enjoyed the protection of the Reich, to which they were obligated, but citizenship would apply exclusively to those of German or 'cognate' blood. Jews, falling into the first category, could not employ female staff below the age of forty-five, nor could they fly the German flag. The designation 'German Jew' no longer existed. Of course, any employment requiring citizenship was closed to them, forcing them back to the ghetto. Everything German belonged to the *Volk*.

But who was a Jew? A good question in this land of steady intermarriage since the late eighteenth century. A person with at least three Jewish grandparents, whatever his professing religion, now found himself classified as a Jew. So were those with two Jewish grandparents if they belonged to the Jewish community on 15 September 1935, or who joined it later, and had married a Jew, or were the offspring of such a marriage, or would be born out of wedlock through extramarital relations with a Jew. But the descendant of only one Jewish great-grandparent received all the entitlements of a German. (This concession spared not a few in the Nazi Party.) Then came the partly Jewish *Mischling*. Two Jewish grandparents, and no connection with the religion, signified a *Mischling* of the first degree; one Jewish grandparent and that person counted as a second-degree *Mischling*. Their destiny awaited further examination of the blood factor in German society. *Mein Kampf* was thus written into the statutes of the Reich.

Dürer's beautiful city, already degraded by publication there of Julius Streicher's pornographic, antisemitic periodical *Der Stuermer*, now doubly earned its place of revulsion in the Jewish consciousness. High Commissioner McDonald read the Nuremberg laws and awaited a response from the League of Nations, some gesture perhaps of international protest. None came. The exit of Jews and half-Jews, despairing now of ever recovering a tolerable position under the regime, welled into a flood. The world's indifference left McDonald isolated and nonplussed. He dispatched a letter of resignation to the League Council to mark at least one man's stand against Germany's criminal debasement of the standards of civilisation:

> Relentlessly, the Jews and 'non-Aryans' are excluded from all public offices, from the exercise of the liberal professions, and from any part in the cultural and intellectual life of Germany. Ostracised from social relations with 'Aryans' they are subjected to every kind of humiliation ... More than half of the Jews remaining in Germany have already been deprived of their livelihood. In many parts of the country there is a systematic attempt at starvation of the Jewish population ... The moral authority of the League of Nations and of State Members of the League must be directed towards a determined appeal to the German government in the name of humanity and of the principles of public law in Europe ... Pity and reason alike must inspire the hope that intercession will meet with response. Without such response, the problems caused by the persecution of Jews and the 'non-Aryans' ... will continue a danger to international peace and a source of injury to the legitimate interests of other states.[22]

To Europe's shame, Fascism advanced still more rapidly throughout the continent after the Nuremberg laws than before. True, the argument ran, the achievements of the two dictators were accompanied by persecution, imprisonment and the silencing of every independent voice. But what successful operation did not entail radical surgery? And what could the democratic powers offer as alternative to their dynamic? France languished in disarray, six of its governments having collapsed during 1933–4. The country's parliamentary system shook to its foundations into the bargain (see below, page 312) on account of a scandal too reminiscent of the Panama affair for comfort. While Hitler took

[22] Bentwich, *They Found Refuge*, pp. 28–9.

his nation in hand, and Mussolini planned to avenge an old Italian humiliation with the conquest of Ethiopia, a French enquiry was painfully uncovering the involvement of ministers and other parliamentarians in the fraudulent adventures of Alexandre Stavisky, an East European Jew. England made an equally sorry spectacle: a divided society perpetually stopping for tea, and led by Ramsay MacDonald, Socialist renegade in decline, who was partnered by an old-fashioned Tory country gentleman, Stanley Baldwin.

Such, at any rate, was the widely held view. The succession of foreign admirers come to pay their respects to Hitler proved the point. They applauded the discipline of the younger German generation, the magnificently orchestrated devotion revealed at the Nazi rallies. Even British figures fell over each other in their obeisance. From the 'Mother of Parliaments' in the land where personal freedom ostensibly counted above life itself, there arrived Lloyd George and a string of other political celebrities. The newspaper magnate Lord Rothermere and Lord Londonderry – a sometime Cabinet minister – were regularly welcomed at Berchtesgaden. George Lansbury, former leader of the Labour Party, joined the queue. Hitler greeted these encouraging gestures of friendship with appreciation, on his part affirming undying admiration for Great Britain. Among the duped were the eminent historian Arnold Toynbee and the Duke of Windsor, together with the lady for whose love he surrendered an empire – some indication of the type of courtier who advised him.

The Fascist leaders emerging in Europe's swing to the Right during the 1930s were not, all of them, outright antisemites. In the Jews' eyes, however, they were guilty of the disease by association. The respectful attention they sought from the dictators, the adoption of their political styles and the acceptance of their financial support all gave the Jews cause for profound anxiety. In what direction, then, could they look for salvation? Zionism might offer a solution, but the great majority of Jews, while recognising its virtues for some other fellow, refused personal surrender to an ideology with an infinity of complications and a nigh-insurmountable psychological barrier. Zionism instilled in them the fear of return to a cultural ghetto. It could only be an escape, never a choice. And even if the Arab problem could be surmounted (a remote possibility) the prospect of turning the Jewish clock back two thousand years to nationhood in Palestine appealed just to a few.

No. Their response as Jews could reside only in the defeat of Fascism, together with the ultra-conservative forces travelling with Fascism, throughout Europe. Again and again, just one important leader spoke that language: Stalin, through the machinery of the Comintern. Despot he might be (though many fiercely disputed this), he stood against the tide. Purges of the old faithful were sending thousands to their death or to indefinite exile in Siberia, among them many Jewish builders of the revolution hitherto described as heroes, civil and military – Kamenev, Zinoviev, Radek, Tomsky, Yakir, Feldman, Schmidt, names that could be multiplied countless times over. But an internal struggle against Trotskyism and reaction necessitated such measures, the Left maintained, for Stalin was remote from antisemitism. The Jews' trust in Russia held, to be exemplified in that English creation the Left Book Club, which grew into a movement with 60,000 members enrolled in seminars throughout the country. Of the three intellectuals who ran the club, two were upper-class Jews, Victor Gollancz and Harold Laski. The editorial board of a rival Right Book Club, on the other hand, contained no Jewish members.

In their dread of another European war Britain and France played for time while ceding the initiative to Italy and Germany (and, in the Far East, to Japan). Ill-equipped both militarily and mentally, the Western democracies hoped to contain the ambitious dictators by allowing them fulfilment of 'reasonable' demands. As regards Italy, the Jews had no specific objection to its policy, for they had no direct quarrel with Mussolini. Indeed, their community in Italy and its North African colony declared its wholehearted enthusiasm for the Duce.[23] But their very survival in Europe depended upon Hitler's destruction. We are in 1936, the year of the Berlin Olympic Games, that Nordic pageant which told of the *judenrein* blessedness to come. It was also the year of Léon Blum's Popular Front government in Paris. Blum, the first Socialist and the first Jew to lead a French

[23] The chief rabbi of Tripoli issued a statement affirming the Jews' profound faith in 'our Fascist fatherland'. *Jewish Chronicle*, 8 January 1937.

administration (and he could do so only by courtesy of the Communists, who declined his invitation to enter the coalition), had his freedom crippled by financial crisis, with factories at a standstill and the full range of Catholic hostility against him. 'To think of our old Gallo-Roman country being governed by a Jew!' cried Xavier Vallat, later Marshal Pétain's Commissioner for Jewish Questions, in the parliamentary chamber. Blum! That enemy of morality notoriously recalled for his early book *Du Mariage* advocating experimental pre-marital sex. France lay folded in the bonds of its inertia. It manufactured thirty-eight aeroplanes each month while Germany produced more than a thousand.[24]

Stalin proved his intentions by vicariously engaging the dictators on a battlefield immediately available – Spain. When General Franco rose against the liberal republican government of Madrid, in a crusade ostensibly to forestall a drift to atheistic Socialism, Blum and his opposite number across the Channel, Stanley Baldwin, settled for a policy of non-intervention. Not so Hitler and Mussolini. They sent Franco the Condor Air Legion and 50,000 Italian troops disguised as volunteers. Stalin responded with arms, technicians and advisers, keeping his Red Army at home while left-wing sympathisers from other parts of the world arrived to stand in line with the Spanish government forces. They flocked to the International Brigades both because of Stalin and despite Stalin, though no doubt the Communists in the force outnumbered all the others put together.

Of the 40,000 foreign volunteers in the International Brigades, the Jews constituted the largest group, perhaps a quarter. Of the 5,000 comprising the Polish detachment, all of them exiles from a country then on close and friendly terms with Germany, almost one-half were Jews; a company of two hundred was formed entirely of Yiddish speakers. Of the 2,000 Britons, 214 were Jews. In the battalions which crossed the Atlantic as the Abraham Lincoln Brigade, a thousand members, one-third of the total, admitted to being Jewish. They included the highest ranking American, Colonel John Gates (originally Sol Regenstrief). People would think in those days that every Jew in Palestine was

---

[24] André Maurois, *Why France Fell*, London, 1941, p. 13.

a Zionist, and yet four hundred men from that small community, all Communists, went to Spain, one of them a combat pilot in the André Malraux squadron. Anti-Nazi Germans of the large Thaelmann Brigade contained a substantial Jewish complement, as did the Paris Commune Brigade from France, though in neither case is the actual number known.[25] A Jew destined to win fame for his contribution to the literature of Communist disillusionment operated on the intelligence front behind the Franco lines: Arthur Koestler. On capture he escaped death in an exchange of hostages. One may well ponder on the strange turns history can take when descendants of the people exiled from a heartless Spain in 1492 could return eagerly to take up arms in defence of the integrity of that same country three and a half centuries later.

Their role over, the survivors wandered, many of them homeless and psychologically scarred, having lost their faith in Stalinism without regaining an anchor in Judaism. The many gentile intellectuals could return to their roots to finish their studies, write their books, glow in the prestige earned from active service on the front line against Fascism. England had its Orwell, France its Malraux. Who valued an expatriate Polish-Jewish ex-Communist tailor sufficiently to grant him a visa?

Hunting for immigration visas had now assumed the character of a major Jewish industry. A nervous nationalism was twisting a xenophobic screw everywhere, including the tolerant Western democracies. In France, Action Française, an overtly antisemitic force, represented large numbers of ordinary citizens with all the decent, patriotic qualities of the bourgeoisie, qualities which by French definition encouraged the violence of the Croix de Feu and Camelots du Roi, both of which took Fascism on to the streets. When banned just before the election to office of Blum (who had his motor-car windscreen smashed amid cries of 'À bas le détritus humain!')[26] they camouflaged themselves as orthodox political parties. British newspapers were simultaneously filled

---

[25] Albert Prago, 'Jews in the International Brigades' (*Jewish Currents*, New York, February 1979), citing 'Judios en la Guerra de España' by Alberto Fernandez in *Tiempo de Historia*, Madrid, 1975. Fernandez calculated the Jewish percentage in the brigades as 22 to 25 per cent.
[26] Lottman, *Left Bank*, p. 80.

with the exploits of Sir Oswald Mosley, whose British Union of
Fascists, subsidised from abroad by Mussolini and at home by
the press baron Lord Rothermere and the industrialist Lord
Nuffield, introduced a thug element for the first time into docile
British politics. Attired in black shirts, Mosley's followers
marched through districts of heavy Jewish concentration, while
other working-class thoroughfares proved a hazard many Jews
were not prepared to risk. Smaller groups clustered to the right of
the BUF. Among them the Imperial Fascist League, led by the
so-called 'camel doctor' Arnold Leese (he was a veterinary
surgeon), travelled all the fanatical way in antisemitic ideology,
to the extent of making *The Protocols of the Learned Elders of
Zion* members' required reading and repeating the hoary allegations of ritual murder.

Mosley, formerly a minister in the Labour government of
Ramsay MacDonald, attracted considerable support from his
patrician *confrères*, to whom he registered as a serious politician,
as well as in the working class. But unlike Charles Maurras of
Action Française he gathered no middle-class moss. However,
Streicher's Nazi weekly *Der Stuermer* hailed the English Fascist
as 'a hero of the new age'.[27] The leaders of Anglo-Jewry counselled their people to avoid his public demonstrations (an Anglo-
Jewish version of the 'silence of contempt' offered in Paris during
the Dreyfus Affair), and allow the Blackshirts to die from lack
of publicity. This advice they chose to ignore. Self-appointed
bands of vigilantes, Communist in the main, sought confrontation in the streets, striving to break up Mosley's meetings. One
result was the 'battle of Cable Street', when the slums of East
London resounded with the slogans of Madrid as the local
inhabitants, reinforced by volunteers from other areas, confronted an 'invasion' by Mosley's little army, and the police had
difficulty in keeping the adversaries apart.

Mosley married as his second wife Mrs Diana Guinness, like
her sister Unity Mitford notoriously bewitched by Hitler. The
ceremony took place secretly in Berlin. Mosley excused every
German excess, not omitting the 'night of the long knives', 29
June 1934, when Hitler had some leading conservatives assassi-

27 Quoted in *Jewish Chronicle*, 22 January 1937.

nated and cut down the power of the stormtroopers in the Nazi Party by executing Ernst Roehm and some eighty-five others. Such operations were unavoidable on the path to Germany's regeneration, Mosley contended, precisely as the Left took Stalin's purges in its stride with similar arguments applied to the 'road to Communism'. Mosley charged 'international Jewry' with a plot to drag Britain into war with Germany, a sentiment with which not a few retired generals and admirals concurred.

Given all the stern alarums, the British Union of Fascists' attempts to scare the country with the Jewish menace represented little more than a social nuisance. In fact, the United Kingdom during the 1930s stood as the only European country west of Russia without a Fascist party of any significance, or an antisemitic movement capable of political impact. Perhaps it was this exception to a general rule that ultimately proved the continent's saving grace. Mosley won few supporters in Parliament or the universities, and his paramilitary posturings received a punishing blow late in 1936 when a Public Order Act banned the use of political uniforms in Britain.[28] No one sporting a Fascist *cocarde* in a parliamentary or municipal election won anything but a trivial number of votes. Yet a certain durability characterised the Mosley movement. It went into repose during the Second World War as Mosley himself was interned under Defence Regulation 18B. On its subsequent sanitised revival the movement hastened to shed its antisemitic penumbra, dropped the term 'Fascist' from its name and concentrated, in vain it transpired, on achieving respectability in the cause of European unity.

Oswald Mosley's career proved the utter barrenness of antisemitism as a platform in British politics. France was different, as may be gauged by the fury of the ultra-Right's street offensive against the Palais Bourbon, consequent upon the Stavisky scandal, that February day in 1934. Action Française, reinforced by the Croix de Feu, battled long against the police to leave seventeen persons dead and 2,400 injured, whereas Cable Street, on the

---

[28] The Preamble: 'An Act to prohibit the wearing of uniforms in connection with political objectives and the maintenance by private persons of associations of military or similar character; and to make further provision for the preservation of public order on the occasion of public processions and meetings in public places' (18 December 1936).

other hand, ended with a few bloody noses. Action Française was attempting a virtual *coup d'état* and succeeded at least in compelling the resignation of Édouard Daladier's Radical government. At the Sorbonne, Jean Zay, Minister of Education in a later administration, was assailed by howls of 'France for the French, down with the *métèque*!'[29] This was in 1937. To think of the beloved university of the venerated Émile Durkheim, the greatest name in sociology and equally a *métèque*, as an antisemitic stronghold!

Fascist uniforms made a rainbow of colours in the spread of a doctrine promising grandeur to any country if homogeneous, authoritarian and purified of Judaism. Christianity itself sometimes assumed a racialist complexion, for Hitler's imitators could borrow from Italy what they missed in Germany. Vienna, Warsaw, Budapest, Prague, Vilna – no city was free from the stamp of marching feet and the hoarse demagogy of a local Mahdi. Some of them had taken their cue from Mussolini well before Hitler's arrival, as for example Cornelius Codreanu in Romania, proclaiming a quasi-religious mission founded on ethnic pride. As early as 1927 Codreanu, still in his twenties, mobilised the green-shirted Legion of the Archangel Michael as centurions of the Fascist Iron Guard. The archangel had visited him in a vision and ordered him to restore Christianity to the fatherland: an effective ploy, for by changing the name of his legion to 'All for the Fatherland' Codreanu helped the Iron Guard in 1937 to win sixty seats in the shackled parliament of the dictator king, Carol II.[30]

Romania cherished no territorial ambitions, having expanded in the 1919 peace settlement beyond its wildest hopes. But it was poor, desperately so. The Iron Guard pin-pointed the Jews as the cause: they were not only alien, not only loyal to a different cultural tradition, they were substantially lower middle-class in a predominantly agricultural economy. The Iron Guard spread terror among the Jews, demanding their eviction from the universities and their exclusion from the professions, not to mention all branches of commerce.

[29] *Jewish Chronicle*, 19 November 1937.
[30] See the contribution of Z. Barbu, in S. J. Woolf (ed.), *European Fascism*, London, 1968.

'Send them back to Palestine!' Codreanu and his political mentor, Professor A. J. Cuza, made as their slogan. Some took the hint. They paid extortionate rates for a berth in the ships attempting to breach the British immigration regulations into Haifa, only to end up in a British internment camp. Under a variety of banners Codreanu's legionnaires, mounted on white horses, swept through towns and villages, burning a cross on the model of the Ku Klux Klan. They posed a threat to the king him-self. Carol defended himself by conducting a purge of Stalinist dimensions. Struggling to keep his autocratic powers as well as his Jewish mistress, Magda Lupescu, while he played off Britain and France against Germany (the former being his territorial benefactors, the latter the best customer for Romanian oil), the king ordered the execution in 1939 of Codreanu and 1,200 of his followers. The slaughter availed him nothing, for it neither destroyed the antisemitic movement nor saved the throne. When war came the Iron Guard returned in strength to join a coalition government with General Antonescu as Hitler's ally.

Across the border in Hungary the green shirt was in evidence again, worn by members of the Arrow Cross, another openly Nazi organisation commanded in 1937 by Ferenc Szalasi. Army officers joined in droves. They hoped for a Catholic kingdom under the patronage of their royal saint Stephen, monarch of the realm in AD 1000. The Arrow Cross embraced some 20,000 members, and was growing. National Socialism was an acceptable Magyar ideology, Admiral Horthy, the regent, being the first political leader in office to make a pilgrimage to Hitler. Racial laws after the pattern of Nuremberg, encouraged through the upper chamber by a speech from Cardinal Serédi, Archbishop of Budapest and Hungarian Primate,[31] were enacted in 1938. Hungary of course had its Judeo-Bolshevik memory in the short-lived 1919 regime of Bela Kun, whose consequence was the 'White Terror', against Jews, liberals and Communists, and the institu-tion of Horthy rule. Still, antisemitism had no easy passage in Hungary until the war. An underlying conviction in its immunity from German Jewry's fate lulled the community, and almost until their deportation to Auschwitz assimilated Jews continued

[31] He personally demurred only in the case of baptised Jews. See Heer, *God's First Love*, p. 339.

to write their Magyar poetry, conduct their journalism and pursue their business interests in Budapest – or retain their separate eighteenth-century ways in the Hassidic fastness of eastern Hungary; and all on the basis of a studied compromise with Fascism. Call it blindness perhaps, or their accommodation to a situation without alternative. They rejected any comparison with Poland to the north, where the politics of race placed the Jews in a condition of perennial ferment.

This ferment owed little to antisemitic laws, or Catholic hostility. Anti-Jewish violence was uncommon in Poland, no pogrom having occurred there since the outbreak in Warsaw in 1881. The problem was the more fundamental one of overpopulation: 3,200,000 Jews (1931 census) constituted an unassimilable factor for the size of the country, as recognised by the Jews themselves. In 1936 two prominent Zionists, Isaac Gruenbaum on the Left (a member of the Warsaw parliament) and Jabotinsky on the Right, spoke of one million or more Jews too many in Poland. They of course dreamed of a wholesale departure in order to reverse the tribal proportions in Palestine, an eventuality much desired also in Polish government circles (though for different reasons). It would have been a hollow demand if Palestine were tranquil, so how much more so while a huge British army was bogged down keeping an Arab rebellion under control.

In agitating against the immigration restrictions operating in the Holy Land, the Zionists were making great play of Jewish hardship in Poland during this, the post-Pilsudski era. And truly, the weak triumvirate that followed Pilsudski allowed the National Party, the Endeks, ample freedom to force segregation in the universities – the notorious 'ghetto benches'. Yet there could be no basis for a 'Poland for the Polish' call; the country would dwindle by its achievement, vast areas being occupied by so many other resentful ethnic minorities. To this day the general impression of a poverty-stricken Jewish community, as a by-product of antisemitism in pre-war Poland, is given unjustified currency. A book of photographs depicting the Jews as existing in the most wretched circumstances became a best-seller worldwide in 1983 and earned its creator the honorary citizenship of New York.[32] The camera focused largely on beggars and the

---

[32] Roman Vishniac, *A Vanished World*, New York and London, 1983.

geriatric poor. Poland certainly had them, but to generalise from this economic premise made a travesty of the true nature of Polish Jewry. Within the objective limits of the time it flourished as much as any other community. It boasted important institutions, great industrial enterprises and a rich artistic life. As the Polish scholar Rafael Scharf wrote in a review: 'The notes and captions distort the perspective and blemish *A Vanished World* as a source of information. The Polish government and population have enough to answer for without being accused of things they did not do and could not help.'[33]

This judgement is endorsed by another writer with deeply researched knowledge of Polish-Jewish conditions;

> Most Jews were better off than most Poles. Polish efforts to strike at the Jews' economic well-being through such means as the Sunday rest laws, étatism, numerus clausus, boycott, etc., were ineffective. Even in the late 1930s the Jewish middle class and lower middle class were holding their own ... Jewish strikes against Jewish-owned enterprises were more damaging to the Jewish economy than Polish state-sponsored measures. The real problem was Polish poverty and Jewish over-population ... Discrimination only added marginally to their poverty.[34]

As the strongest personality in the Polish ruling triumvirate the Foreign Minister, Colonel Josef Beck, regularly made the rounds of European capitals. With his country locked inside a continent that wanted no truck with the Jews he searched wildly for some outlet to relieve the pressure. At the departure rate then obtaining – a thousand visas here, a hundred there – an eternity would elapse before any significant inroad would be effected. So far as Britain and France would relent, priority went to Jews of German rather than Polish provenance. The United States refused to modify its immigration laws, in fact never even fulfilled its declared quota. Palestine, the so-called national home of this rejected people, lay in an embattled present while its future was

[33] *Jewish Quarterly*, London, autumn/winter 1983–4.
[34] Joseph Marcus, *Social and Political History of the Jews in Poland, 1919–1939*, New York, 1983, pp. 210–40 *passim*.

shrouded in a political mist.[35] Canada? Its millions of square miles sustained a population hardly greater than London's, but it could find space for less than a thousand Jews annually, and all the while an antisemitic movement led by Adrien Arcand in Quebec campaigned for separation from British and Jewish 'profiteers' alike. South Africa had formerly been open, but the Boer nationalist leader Daniel Malan, together with a grey-shirted Fascist party, forced General Smuts in 1937 to deny further entry to Jews. Australia and New Zealand offered a home to any Britishers who cared to come (begged for them, rather) but to practically no one else.

Mexico, boasting a Fascist party in gold shirts, accepted one hundred refugees a year. Argentina had granted 40,000 Jews settlement on its empty pampas (every acre purchased by the Baron de Hirsch) in previous decades, along with others in the towns, and now felt overcrowded. Brazil remained virtually deaf to reports of European persecution. Back in Europe the antisemitic temper was now rising to a peak. Holland's Nazi Party claimed 30,000 members, Belgium produced a Rexist Party under a prospective Führer named Léon Degrelle. Czechoslovakia faced disintegration in 1937: Konrad Henlein's Nazi irredentists in Bohemia, Father Andrej Hlinka's fiercely anti-Jewish Catholic following of separatists in Slovakia. What of the Soviet Union, which proudly proclaimed its abolition of antisemitism? Stalin accepted no immigrants, assuming any would have elected to go there. But he permitted trans-Siberian transit to some 17,000 with Japanese visas for occupied China, including Shanghai – a traffic destined to cease after 1941 and Pearl Harbor.

Chaim Weizmann, pleading for his people before a British Royal Commission investigating the Palestine situation, cried in a wilderness when he said: 'Almost six million Jews are doomed to be pent up in places where they are not wanted, and for whom the world is divided into places where the Jews cannot live and places into which they cannot enter.'[36] Still undeterred, Colonel

---

[35] Palestine nevertheless saw a greater immigration than any other country, despite the reduction after 1935 consequent upon the disorders. Some 80,000 Jews arrived between the years 1936 and 1939 inclusive. Illegal immigration added a few thousand more.

[36] Palestine Royal Commission, Minutes of Evidence at Public Sessions (Colonial No. 134), London, 1937.

Beck of Poland lodged a claim with the League of Nations for a colony anywhere to decant his Jewish surplus. This proposal was received in stony silence. But he had discovered an island, Madagascar. It was a French possession containing few Europeans. Léon Blum's government expressed interest, without for one moment contemplating a substitution of sovereignty. In 1937 a provisional agreement was reached, though ever so vaguely worded. The number of Jews to be accepted in no degree approached the figure – perhaps Jabotinsky's million – in the mind of Colonel Beck.

The cautious French slowed down negotiation of the details. The Jews, in their imagination fearing banishment to a sort of Devil's Island in the Indian Ocean, remained unenthusiastic. The international situation deteriorated. Nothing concrete emerged from the talks, assuming of course that a compulsory evacuation of Polish citizens to that *terra incognita* could have been smoothly executed. The Madagascar scheme was revived in 1940, following the fall of both Poland and France, by none other than Heinrich Himmler, German police chief. One year later it still appeared to be under active consideration by Hitler's Foreign Minister, Joachim Ribbentrop, with a project to remove four million Jews from European soil. But by then the 'Final Solution' began taking its apocalyptic form.[37]

The plight of the Jews in Europe touched new depths in March 1938 when Hitler, breaking every agreement he had made with Austria, swept across the border and took possession of his little neighbour. Now another 200,000 were confronted with notice to quit. And in this case that same smiling Austria, unbelievably, turned overnight into a snarling, hate-filled nation against which Germany itself appeared restrained and tolerant in contrast. The *Anschluss*, ardently anticipated by many Austrian bishops since 1933,[38] induced a wave of antisemitic hysteria hitherto unparalleled. Reports of Jews dragged from their homes to scrub the streets of Vienna on hands and knees made the front pages of the world's press. Eager foreign universities and hospitals scooped up dozens of distinguished scientists who now found themselves

[37] Cf. Michael R. Marrus and Robert O. Paxton, *Vichy France and the Jews*, New York, 1981, pp. 60–2.
[38] Heer, *God's First Love*, pp. 272–3.

unemployed, Sigmund Freud being among the first to go.

During the two months following the *Anschluss*, 578 Viennese Jews committed suicide, while thousands more were sent to Dachau concentration camp. Still more, Polish and Czech nationals, received deportation orders to return to their countries of origin. Poland at first refused to admit the largest part, claiming that their residence abroad had cost them their citizenship. Colonel Beck left them suspended in homelessness until an international outcry forced his hand. A ship with fifty-one Jewish passengers drifted up and down the Danube for four months in search of a landing-place. One day soon the Nazis would recall this almost universal rejection and draw from it the most horrifying conclusions. Yet it was reported that Adolf Eichmann, the SS officer responsible for Austrian Jewry's emigration, intervened to forestall the eviction of a great number from their homes on the eve of Yom Kippur, October 1938.[39]

If this was intended as an act of humanity, it did not impede Eichmann's efforts to drive the Jews out of Austria entirely. He performed diligently in this regard, in close liaison with the Zionist and other Jewish organisations. Unlike their German brothers, the Jews of Austria bowed at once to the inevitable. And while many in Germany had been lingering perilously for years in hope of a sea-change, here they reacted with fatalistic speed. They would accept any haven on offer. In the event, most of them managed to reach England, the United States or Palestine, so that two-thirds of the community saved themselves. Though not before *Kristallnacht*, that night of terror, 10 November 1938.

The Germans officially described it as a spontaneous eruption of Aryan anger. Three days previously, a seventeen-year-old Polish Jew, Herschel Grynszpan, had walked into the German embassy in Paris with a revolver and killed the first man he encountered. He happened to be a third secretary, Ernst vom Rath.[40] The pogrom of the 'Night of Splintering Glass' ostensibly followed as a result. According to German sources 195

---

[39] See the contribution of Otto D. Kulka, in *Encyclopaedia Judaica*, Vol. III, col. 899.

[40] Grynszpan's father had been one of those expelled to Poland. The incident inspired Michael Tippett's oratorio *A Child of our Time*.

synagogues in Germany and Austria were set on fire, with 76 of them completely gutted. Several thousand shops and houses also went up in flames; 20,000 Jews were arrested; thirty-six others died. For these crimes perpetrated against them the Jews themselves received a collective fine of a billion marks, a third of which had to be raised in Austria.

The casualty figures, and the particulars of damage sustained, are false, having been played down on instructions subsequently given by Hermann Goering. For there was nothing spontaneous about *Kristallnacht*. Captured Nazi documents submitted to the Nuremberg Trials revealed the truth.[41] The atrocities were organised by Reinhard Heydrich, the sadistic Reich security head and deputy chief of the Gestapo, on the command of Propaganda Minister Josef Goebbels. The instructions Heydrich gave detailed how the arson was to be committed without endangering German life and property. No looting of Jewish establishments would be tolerated; the police were not to impede the demonstrators; as many Jews, particularly the rich, to be arrested as could be accommodated in the prisons, and then transferred to concentration camps. The billion marks' fine was intended in part to reimburse the German insurance companies, which filed complaints of likely bankruptcy should they be liable, and forfeiture of confidence by the international insurance market should they default. Just two months had elapsed since the Munich Agreement, by which those great powers Britain, France and Italy granted the Nazi Chancellor the satisfaction of a diktat without the cost of a single German soldier. The brown shirt proved its superiority over the swallowtail coat, with a giant stride towards a *judenrein* continent by the cession to Hitler of the Sudetenland in Czechoslovakia.

Now, finally, every Jew trapped within the German orbit knew that any future for his family hung upon his departure. As always, escape depended upon money, or influence, or the efficacy of Jewish organisations overseas. Even children required, each of them, a guarantee of sponsorship and support from a citizen in the country of their reception (lest they take the bread from another child's mouth?). Germany did well out of

[41] Nuremberg documents *Nazi Conspiracy and Aggression*, Washington, 1946, Vol. IV, pp. 425–7, and Vol. V, pp. 797–801.

such arrangements. It should not be assumed that the Nazi authorities shrank from business intercourse with Jews. They had long serviced an agreement with the Zionists whereby Germany permitted the export of Jewish blocked capital in the form of merchandise which was later encashed by the Jewish Agency in Jerusalem. On the one side the German economy gained; on the other refugees with means were encouraged to choose Palestine. Many Jews bitterly opposed such infringements of the trade boycott against the enemy; it made bad blood between Zionists and non-Zionists, particularly in America. It was also common knowledge that the Gestapo fostered the illegal immigration into Palestine (i.e. for those without British entry certificates). The Hamburg–America Line openly advertised for passengers in its Mediterranean freighters otherwise awaiting the breaker's yard.[42]

Thus the refugee situation in 1938 assumed the proportions of a grave international crisis, as James McDonald had predicted. Public opinion seemed aware of its magnitude well before the world's statesmen. A clamour for action arose which at last reached the ears of the President of the United States. Roosevelt summoned a conference; the nations seated together could not hope to change Germany's policy but perhaps they could mitigate its worst effects by providing shelter for the persecuted. Thirty-one countries, large and small, sent representatives to the conference in July 1938, at Evian on Lake Geneva. This appeared a turning-point. Poland and Romania submitted memoranda advancing the urgent need for consideration of their own Jewish minorities in the discussions, but the agenda excluded matters not strictly related to Greater Germany. A notable absentee was the Soviet Union. The British participated, though with a qualification that was to shatter the entire enterprise: Palestine must remain outside the debate. Britain was at that time working laboriously towards a round table conference of Jews and Arabs in London to solve that particular conundrum.

Evian concluded with the establishment of a body to combine with the machinery of the League of Nations High Commission

---

[42] Mark Wischnitzer, *To Dwell in Safety*, Philadelphia, 1948, p. 214, citing an on-the-spot report in the *Saturday Evening Post*, 9 August 1939.

for Refugees – *mirabile dictu*, that office, upon which McDonald
had turned his back in disgust in 1935, still functioned. This was
the sum total of Evian's achievement, mocking the problem. For
time lapsed in reporting back to home governments, then more
time in preparing schedules, then, as it transpired, to the manufacture of excuses. Discussion resumed at leisurely pace in
London. Only one country, secluded inconspicuously in the
Caribbean, evidenced any real willingness to deal seriously with
the subject. The Dominican Republic (part of Christopher Columbus's Hispaniola) shamed all the others with an offer to
accept 100,000 refugees for settlement in agriculture.[43] The rest
lodged their customary alibis: lack of finance, Germany allowing
each refugee to take out only ten marks in currency; unemployment; the world crisis. Australia, two thousand times the
Dominican magnitude in area and riches, opened its heart, after
long deliberation, to 15,000 – to be spread over three years. South
Africa, whose Prime Minister Smuts was revered by the Jews of
Johannesburg no less than Roosevelt by their co-religionists in
New York, was not even represented. Myron C. Taylor, American delegate and chairman of the proceedings, had instructions
to concede nothing for the United States beyond the niggardly
immigration quotas, which were still not being honoured. Great
Britain's gesture was to hint at allocating some land for settlement in its Guiana colony. Offers by others represented at Evian
aggregated to a pathetic few thousand.

If this revealed the moral bankruptcy of governmental
thought, that verdict must embrace also in its condemnation the
conduct of highly influential Jews, primarily but not exclusively
those of America. Their representatives haunted the corridors at
Evian and the subsequent London meetings, though they were
excluded from the discussions. They reassured delegates of the
ample funds available from their charitable bodies to finance
whatever settlement schemes emerged. But not one of them had
the courage to canvass substantial immigration to the USA.
Thousands of orphan children in Greater Germany lacked
affidavits for their rescue by sponsorship of private families. The
British declared their quota into Palestine for this category to be

---

[43] Only a few hundreds reached that country by the outbreak of war.

filled. Yet the Jewish spokesmen of the United States lent no weight to any effort to give the children homes over there.

A Bill introduced to Congress by Senator Robert F. Wagner of New York and Representative Edith N. Rogers of Massachusetts to bring in 20,000 of them failed miserably. White House apathy, nativist antisemitism and the opium of isolationism (stimulated by, among others, the Daughters of the American Revolution) killed the measure. American Jews were no less generous than any other, yet they allowed the burial to proceed with barely a murmur. What could they have feared? William D. Pelley and his paltry 'Silvershirts' on the West Coast? The Nazi German-American League and its Führer Fritz Kuhn? Father Coughlin, the radio priest of Michigan and his crude tabloid embellished with the *Protocols* and long extracts of Josef Goebbels's speeches?

Perhaps a clue to their inertia could be traced in a reluctance to weaken the Zionist case, conducted so energetically by Weizmann and his pugnacious colleague David Ben-Gurion, for the transfer of all Jewish refugees to their rightful, welcoming home. In the event, 288 children were carried to safety to foster-parents across the Atlantic, ten more than to Sweden. Britain itself, from a combination of humanitarian motives and to avoid obloquy resulting from its Palestine ruling, took in no less than 10,000.[44]

On 13 May 1939, the Hamburg–America luxury liner *St Louis* sailed for Cuba with 930 passengers, of which two were Gestapo agents on a mission of German intelligence and the rest Jewish refugees. Except for a few, their entry visas had been acquired through the bribery of Cuban consular staff in Germany. Some of the Jews had ongoing permits for the United States, though of a low priority according to the system of sequence operating in

---

[44] For the American attitude, see David C. Wyman, *Paper Walls: America and the Refugee Crisis 1938–1941*, Amherst, Mass., 1968; Henry Fairgold, *The Politics of Rescue*, New Brunswick, NJ, 1970. The British waived passport regulations for the 10,000 children, of whom one thousand were Christian 'non-Aryans'. They reached England in a succession of convoys, the last arriving a few days after the outbreak of war. Sir Samuel Hoare, Home Secretary, appealed in a House of Commons speech to 'my fellow-countrymen to take the young generation of a great people ... a chance of mitigating to some extent the terrible sufferings of their parents and friends.' House of Commons Report, 25 November 1938.

that country. To the St Louis captain, Gustav Schroeder, these were passengers to be treated as courteously as any in his long career of pleasure-cruising, and he had the first-class saloon adapted for their use as a synagogue. Half-way across the Atlantic he was radioed as to possible disembarkation difficulties in Havana. Schroeder pressed on.

Arriving at Havana, twenty-two passengers were permitted to land. The rest were informed of complications regarding their visas, but given reassurance nevertheless that all would be well. Discussions were in train between local representatives of the American Joint Distribution Committee, not an insignificant organisation, and the Cuban authorities. Days passed in growing suspense, the passengers grew fretful, and the captain needed all his authority to prevent the Gestapo agents from usurping his command. News and rumours intermingled on board until the truth came out: the Cubans were prepared to overlook irregularities in the visas in exchange for money. The officials of the American Joint were quoted a figure of 500,000 dollars in cash, an astronomical sum in those days, which rapidly increased to 650,000 dollars. Soon the Havana dockside became a focus of keen international attention. Higher officials of the American Joint flew down from New York. Reporters descended upon the scene and quickly hired launches to interview the passengers through megaphones.

A ransom of such magnitude perhaps indicated a game of bluff, and the American Joint played for time. Suddenly Cuba ordered the St Louis out of its territorial waters. Schroeder received instructions from Hamburg to return home, but he knew what this implied for his passengers, some of whom were now threatening suicide. He too played for time. Meanwhile negotiations were proceeding at diplomatic level, involving the State Department in Washington, US ambassador Joseph Kennedy in London, Cuba's President Bru, his strong man Colonel Batista and refugee organisations on both sides of the Atlantic. Then all seemed lost: Cuba refused a deal. Word of the Dominican Republic's readiness to take the refugees at a price reached the American Joint, but soon afterwards the contact went dead. Schroeder started his engines as though in preparation for the return voyage. He was convinced that if all else failed

America would surely take the Jews, for wasn't President Roosevelt this people's friend?

The captain therefore decided to sail northwards, to Miami, fully expecting permission to give the order to disembark. None came, and soon the *St Louis* was surrounded by police vessels lest any passengers should dare to make a swim for it. They had been at sea for three weeks. The American Joint had evidently played the last of its cards, and the silence from New York was deafening. Schroeder therefore took a desperate decision in order to prevent his passengers from falling back into German hands. He would return to Europe as ordered, but sail towards the English coast and scuttle his ship close to shore. He knew a convenient place, Beachy Head near Eastbourne. There he would set the *St Louis* ablaze, leaving the British with no alternative than to rescue the passengers. It was now 10 June. The representative of the American Joint in Paris, Morris Troper, had been on the telephone for days to all his contacts in Western Europe. At length he received a reply from Brussels: Belgium offered sanctuary to 214 *St Louis* passengers. Troper telephoned London, and the news precipitated action elsewhere. Britain agreed to accept 288, France 224, Holland the remainder, 181. The last Jew stepped ashore at Southampton on 21 June. So it had been another forty days and forty nights before this twentieth-century Noah's Ark could touch dry land.[45] However, for many of those people the refusal of Havana to admit them signified a sentence of death.

And so we reach this decade's conclusion, when inaction towards saving the Jews found a more valid alibi, though not wholly valid, in action to save civilisation. Germany swallowed what remained of a free Czechoslovakia, so drawing from the British Prime Minister the confession of his disillusionment with Hitler. It was time to begin dispositions for a probable European war. Mussolini pronounced the Mediterranean Italy's *mare nostrum*, thus awarding himself fishing rights in those troubled waters as far as the shores of tormented Palestine. Let the Arabs not despair, for the Duce had nominated himself their protector. Britain therefore realised only too keenly that in the event of war

---

45 The full story in Gordon Thomas and Max Morgan-Witts, *Voyage of the Damned*, London, 1974.

the Middle East could form part of the conflict. It therefore urged compromise on Jews and Arabs, but the London Round Table Conference of 1939, at which the opposing sides never met face to face, collapsed amidst its lost opportunities in tales of betrayal.

Appeasement of Hitler had failed ignominiously. Appeasement of Mussolini held little prospect of greater success. The British Prime Minister, Neville Chamberlain, now tried appeasement of the Arabs, for the Jews in Palestine numbered a bare half-million while the Muslim world stretched to India and beyond. He ruled that a maximum of 75,000 Jews could enter Palestine during the next five years, and they must settle only in a circumscribed space which, the Jews protested, would turn their national home into a Middle Eastern ghetto. Further, announced Chamberlain, Palestine could not accept Jews beyond that figure except by Arab agreement, and never attain to more than one-third of the country's total population. Independence was contemplated for Palestine within ten years. This policy, incorporated in a White Paper,[46] was produced as the one possible solution that did a minimum of injustice to either side. Instead, it initiated a painful new chapter in Palestine's melancholy story, and a regional conflict that is still with us.

The White Paper virtually sealed Europe against Jewish escape. So where did comfort for this people lie as the continent wilted beneath Hitler's rhetoric? Still, not a shot had been fired. On 20 April 1939 the Führer celebrated his fiftieth birthday; among his telegrams was one from the Pope. And what of Stalin? He had not complained of too many Jews. No Fascists in red shirts marched along the Nevsky Prospekt shouting 'Death to Judah!' Suddenly, in the most momentous policy reversal of modern history, Moscow signed a pact with Berlin. Hitler's war against the democracies was about to begin. His war against the Jews was already won.

[46] British Statement of Policy, known as the MacDonald White Paper, Cmd 6019, May 1939; Palestine Land Transfer Regulations, Cmd 6180, February 1940.

11

Holocaust

During the Second World War the present author served in the British armed forces from January 1940 until the termination of hostilities, for the major part of that time overseas: in France until the Dunkirk evacuation at the end of May 1940, and then in the Middle East theatre. He was captured by Rommel's Afrika Korps in the Libyan desert in May 1942, and thereafter lived out the war as a prisoner. It was to Upper Silesia that he was transported, along with most other British prisoners held in Italian camps, in September 1943 following the collapse of Italy as Germany's ally. Thus he was enabled to witness at first hand, albeit from a severely restricted angle, the degradation of captive Jewish civilians in the region of Upper Silesia, where large numbers of them were concentrated.

The author had occasional personal contact with some of those Jews. They were brought into his prison camp for various tasks, such as shifting bricks and lumber, tasks which for reasons known only to the German authorities were not allotted to uniformed prisoners, who worked regular hours on outside construction sites. The author encountered other Jews at the huge building complex known as Blechhammer. During transfers from camp to camp, or for hospital attendance in two large towns, Gleiwitz and Kattowitz, he was able to observe more Jews shuffling along the streets under escort. Without exception all such people were fearfully diseased, their legs and feet swollen, sores covering their skins and clothed in rags – the yellow Star of David (bleached dirty white by now) on their backs. Any onlooker would have perceived that these people, not part of a war fought under recognised rules, had been reduced, through hunger, medical neglect, ill-treatment and lack of hygiene, to total dehumanisation. Death could not have been far away. One of them, to whom this writer was able to speak briefly, told him they carried on working lest they be 'ausgeschwitzed'. He had used a term derived from the name of a place, Auschwitz, of which the writer had never heard, though he must often have been within a few miles of it.

All this is stated here because of the astonishment sometimes expressed, *inter alia* by Hannah Arendt in her *Eichmann in Jerusalem*, that the Jews in the main went to their slaughter fatalistically, without protest. If the Jews encountered by the present writer were typical examples at that stage of the war, then any idea of resistance was already beyond their mental and physical capacities. He saw other foreign workers, Polish and Ukrainian, in Upper Silesia, but none of these had been brought down to so lowly a condition. They, evidently, were adequately fed and sheltered. French workers fared best of all. Many were volunteers, frequently demobilised POWs recruited by the Germans through newspaper advertisements, and regularly returning to France on leave. Russian POWs, however, observed in their segregated though adjacent camps, appeared to be suffering treatment similar to the Jews. In fact death claimed five million Russian soldiers in captivity. Hitler, before his attack on Russia, reminded his generals that Russia was not a signatory to the Hague Convention and had no rights under it.[1]

Doubtless other Jews trapped within this seventh circle of Nazi hell were more fortunate, or had not yet sunk to that ultimate depth. So it is appropriate to recall that the first co-ordinated uprising in the whole of Europe (except for Tito's irregulars operating in the unconquered Yugoslav hills) during the German occupation was indeed a heroically fought though hopeless Jewish resistance in the Warsaw ghetto. They made their desperate stand in April 1943, one and a half years before the general Warsaw revolt of 1944. They fought alone, with minimal supplies of arms from Poland's underground Home Army, possessing just a few home-made explosives and smuggled weapons. Much has been written, and romanticised, concerning resistance in Europe. Many individual acts of defiant courage indeed took place. But nowhere did a civilian population make a significant

[1] Affidavit of General Franz Halder, 22 November 1945, in Nuremberg Documents (ND) NOKW 3140.

stand against overwhelming odds before the Jews of Warsaw.

Moreover, Jewish resistance by no means began and ended in the Polish capital. A month earlier the ghetto of Bialystok attempted a revolt, lacking though it did even the meagre preparation and semblance of unity achieved in Warsaw for a confrontation with the Nazi murder squads; in Cracow, Vilna and Minsk earlier still. Jewish partisans later gathered for action in the forests of Eastern Europe despite the reluctance of many Polish and Ukrainian bands to accept their help. (Some rejected it entirely.) Isolated groups of Jews made a last desperate stand in the extermination centres themselves, notably at Treblinka, Sobibor and Auschwitz, before entering the gas chambers.[2] Stripped of its fiction, the French Résistance barely existed before the middle of 1943, and certainly no Communist, Jew or gentile, offered the Germans any opposition until the Russia he glorified was invaded in June 1941. Still, Jews were the earliest to strike back in France, bringing a ready-made Organisation Juive de Combat to the overall Conseil National de la Résistance when finally this body emerged in May 1943. The last transport to leave France on its journey to death carried ten young Parisian Jewish leaders surprised at a meeting in the rue de la Pompe.

The Second World War erupted on 1 September 1939, just a few days after Germany and the Soviet Union signed the non-aggression pact which joined Communism to Fascism. Two weeks elapsed and a pulverised Poland could be dismembered. Stalin then contrived to bring the Baltic states of Estonia, Latvia and Lithuania within the Soviet system and, after a fierce struggle, to subdue Finland. Hitler now held his hand until April 1940 when, in a six weeks *Blitzkrieg*, he took possession of Norway, Denmark, Belgium, Holland and Luxembourg, soon afterwards crushing France and subjecting a British Expeditionary Force 350,000 strong to ignominious flight. This first phase of the land war concluded with the Führer virtually master of the continent. The British fought on, though except for isolated commando raids on the periphery they were restricted to naval and aerial battles. They visualised a long conflict before their *reconquista*. As to the final outcome, they had no doubt.

[2] For the most comprehensive treatment of this subject, see Reuben Ainsztein, *Jewish Resistance in Nazi Occupied Europe*, London, 1974.

Russia and the Baltic states, with Yugoslavia and Greece, had not as yet been swept up by the Nazi tidal wave. But already some four million Jewish non-combatants swirled in it, for we must include those of Hungary and Romania, countries readily genuflecting to the warlord. To the outside world these Jews at first dissolved among an entire continent of hostages. Were they not, all of them, equal victims of the losing (not lost) struggle? It was an assumption innocently made, for who could live contentedly under a tyranny such as Hitler exerted, a tyranny reinforced by a great army obedient to his will and at its core a nation solidly behind him? Gentile and Jew were surely sharing a common fate.

So it was assumed. In fact the outside world might have known better. The representatives of neutral countries continued ensconced in their diplomatic and commercial missions as before. Truth to tell, they preferred not to look. Of the captive nations the ordeal of the Poles ranked as the most painful, while the French, on either side of the divide between Marshal Pétain's Vichy and the occupied zone, came through scarred the least. The Poles, pressed between two inhuman despotisms, endured the scorn and oppression of them both; personal survival depended on the alacrity with which one jumped to orders, no matter how barbarous. The French, on the other hand, could adapt philosophically to defeat. Slimmer perhaps but as inventive as ever, they could even smuggle themselves across the partition-line to enjoy a Riviera holiday. The Czechs, until Germany reached the verge of collapse five years later, submitted almost without a protest to a harsh though tolerable existence. Just once did they feel the terrible whiplash of Nazism. It was in 1942, when 1,300 villagers of Lidice, men and women, were annihilated in retribution for the assassination of Reich 'Protector' Reinhard Heydrich, SS Obergruppenführer and head of Berlin's satanic Central Security Office. Two parachutists, serving with the British, flew in from London for the deed. Even then the Jews had to pay the greatest penalty: 3,000 of them sent to the Theresienstadt ghetto and then removed to a place of extermination.

Only Russian soldiers in captivity, besides known political opponents of Hitlerism, gypsies and such social misfits as homosexuals, shared a mass fate with the Jews. Already on 30 January 1939 Hitler had stated in an address to the Reichstag: 'If

Jewry should plot another world war to exterminate the Aryan peoples of Europe, it would not be the Aryan peoples which would be exterminated but Jewry.'[3] The Führer obligingly repeated the threat when, three years later, his troops stood poised at Stalingrad and El Alamein for an all-conquering pincer-snatch of the Caucasus and the Suez Canal. Triumphantly, he told his bewitched nation: 'At one time, the Jews of Germany laughed at my prophecies. I do not know whether they are still laughing or whether they have already lost all desire to laugh. But now I can only repeat that they will stop laughing everywhere, and I shall be right also in that prophecy.'[4]

These words leave little room for controversy regarding Hitler's possible ignorance of the 'Final Solution' of the Jewish problem until 1943, as argued by the historian David Irving,[5] or that he never personally gave an order to exterminate the Jews. By the end of 1942 approaching three million mainly East European Jews, according to German calculation, had already been done to death. Could this have occurred without the Führer's knowledge? And if he had not personally commanded their destruction why did he not issue an order to have it stopped? This man, described as Leader of the Nation, Supreme Commander of the Armed Forces, Head of Government, Supreme Justice and Leader of the Party, *was* the law, another Napoleon. And as for the unrelenting consistency of the policy, the last great deportation to Auschwitz took place on 8 July 1944. The German armies, desperately contesting every inch, were in their phase of retreat on all fronts, though one last counter-attack would yet occur, in the Ardennes salient. One might reasonably conclude that all effort would be concentrated on the defence of the fatherland, every capable individual brought into the struggle for the life or death of the Third Reich. The Army High Command, disgusted by the zeal of Heinrich Himmler's executioners, disclaimed any responsibility for them. Yet the killing proceeded, diverting manpower and transportation systems from operations

---

[3] *Voelkische Beobachter*, Munich edition, 1 February 1939, also cited in Nuremberg War Trials as ND 2663-PS.
[4] *New York Times*, 1 October 1942. Reproduced also in Raul Hilberg, *The Destruction of the European Jews*, London, 1961, p. 266.
[5] In *Hitler's War*, London, 1977.

against the advancing enemy. It continued virtually until Germany gasped its last breath of resistance and the victors opened the gates of the remaining concentration camps to release inmates who by the grace of God had survived, or to give burial to the tangled heaps of uncountable skeletons.

Nazism ultimately succeeded in wiping out two-thirds of the Jewish population of Europe west of Moscow because this continent was already psychologically prepared for their obliteration. As we have described, the 1930s saw Fascism germinate everywhere from the Atlantic to the Black Sea, not in its feeble British version but attracting strong support from people in all strata of society. Fascism in general, not Nazism alone, took racial homogeneity as the base from which to grow, or the condition to which it aspired. This exposed the Jews as rootless, superfluous and defenceless. Adolf Hitler thus formed the apex of an antisemitic pyramid erected by a great host of co-operative or acquiescent minions. Even Mussolini had to go against the Italian nature in the end, instituting racial laws while he was still his own master, and ultimately bowing to Jewish deportation in the northern rump of territory to which he was later reduced as puppet ruler. Had Hitler conquered Britain he would as surely have produced a puppet there, if not Mosley then another, to perform his Jewish policy. No doubt some Englishmen would have found the courage to protest, as some Germans and Poles and Frenchmen protested. A remnant of Jews, the old-established, the war veterans, the fully assimilated, might have been spared. This happened everywhere, including Germany. But transports carrying the victims away would have left the Channel ports for Auschwitz nevertheless, or perhaps for more convenient slaughterhouses located in the Outer Hebrides.

The ultimate disposal of the Jews by mass murder, hideously laborious to undertake and impossible to conceal, was made inevitable by the silence of those still free to speak, and the passivity of those free to act. In this regard the Vatican, with Pius XII as pontiff, failed at critical moments to use its mighty prerogative in the Catholic world to restrain the policy. Hitler, together with several of his immediate Nazi Party lieutenants, was born into a Catholic family. Some forty per cent of the population of Greater Germany belonged to the faith. Nazism was of course a creed of its own. The voice of Rome was unlikely to be heard with much deference in Berlin. But millions would not have dared to ignore it. And yet while the conscience of the Church relating to the Jews slept, another deep-rooted instinct remained alive in the Curia – Hitler was at war with Bolshevism, a philosophy with which it identified the Jews. God moves in a mysterious way, and the destruction of Bolshevism was holy work, no matter the instrument.

Representations made to the Vatican, by Jewish organisations, by a few bishops and not least by President Roosevelt through his representative in Rome, received ambiguous replies.[6] The Pope condemned race hatred, he cared for all God's children irrespective of denomination, he begged the protagonists in the war to conduct themselves with magnanimity. Never did he speak out against the 'Final Solution', nor did he once call upon the hierarchy in all countries to make particular efforts to save Jews. Lesser Catholics sometimes repaired the omission. Bernard Lichtenberg, Provost of St Hedwig's Cathedral in Berlin, insisted on praying publicly for persecuted Jews and went to prison for it. In 1943 the Dutch episcopate forbade Catholic policemen from helping to hunt them down, and similar examples of Catholic compassion occurred in Belgium and France. Hundreds of monasteries and convents, particularly in Poland, gave refuge to Jewish fugitives. It was a highly dangerous activity, but it saved thousands of lives. The Pope refrained from public utterance even when deportation to Auschwitz began from Rome itself, and a thousand were taken away on 18 October 1943, though many more, with the pontiff's approval, found refuge with the religious orders in the vicinity. Only when the tide had safely turned did the Vatican work for rescue, interceding on behalf of the Hungarian Jewish population in the middle of 1944. But by then it was mostly too late.

Paradoxically, the Soviet Union made the greatest contribution to Jewish rescue. It was a case of *fait accompli*. Until Hitler's break with Stalin in June 1941, 300,000 to 400,000 managed to flee the German zone of occupation in Poland into the Soviet sector or to Russia's lately acquired 'sphere of influence' in the

---

[6] See *Foreign Relations of United States*, Diplomatic Papers 1942, Vol. III.

Baltic states. Many of these Jews were dispatched to the Russian interior as forced labour. Their destiny wavered with Russia's war and Moscow's relations with the Polish government-in-exile in London. Eventually those of military age were conscripted to the flag of General Anders. A few, and they included Menahem Begin, a future Prime Minister of Israel, secreted themselves in the Siberian *taiga* and subsequently turned up in Polish uniform in Palestine. The rest suffered intense hardship but survived.

The conundrum as to Hitler's original intention towards the Jews, whether to banish them to the isolation of Madagascar or destroy them in Europe, became, as the war progressed to its frightful dimensions, empty of relevance. They could have no other fate than the one prescribed. The pathology of war induces a universal callousness towards death anyway. Normally compassionate men command bombers to wreak destruction upon cities filled with innocent inhabitants. Generals send their soldiers into an early grave at the drop of a brass hat. Ships sink with all hands. Blockade intends starvation. Mothers are sustained in the loss of a beloved son by the knowledge that other women, their neighbours, are likewise bereaved. But to compel the collaboration of a continent in a process of systematic annihilation encompassing millions! That requires a maniacal genius with an authority borrowed from the gods.

Hitler made himself the arbiter of who would live, who would die, soon after his lightning strike against Poland. In December 1939 he charged an immediate underling, Reichsleiter Philip Bouhler, head of the Führer's Chancellory, with the responsibility of ending by euthanasia the existence within Germany of all mental defectives and the incurably sick. It would be both a mercy killing and the purging of the Nordic race of its inferior genetic stock, to be painlessly achieved by either injection or asphyxiation.[7] Euphemism for unpublishable activities being the practice of the Nazi lexicon, the doctors who were nominated for this task camouflaged the project beneath the name Reich Committee for Scientific Research into Hereditary and Severe Constitutional Diseases. Bouhler was also appointed to command the Madagascar reservation in the event of that scheme's

[7] Hitler's order backdated to 1 September 1939, ND 630-PS.

materialisation – an association of ideas with horrendous resonance.

The number of mental defectives and others dispatched by euthanasia reached some 60,000 by August 1941, when the programme carelessly came into the open. The ensuing outcry, led by Cardinal Faulhaber, Archbishop of Munich, and Theophil Wurm, Protestant Bishop of Würtemberg, put a stop to it. So, interestingly, it was possible for public opinion in Germany, when moved, to exercise some restraint over Nazi brutalities. The two clerics are not known to have expressed indignation at what was happening to the Jews. Could they have been entirely ignorant of it?

People in Germany proper, that is the old Reich minus the Warthegau region lost to Poland at Versailles and now annexed (as opposed to the Polish area administered as the *Generalgouvernement* under Hans Frank), might not have perceived a great immediate difference. Jews were being moved across the country, but wartime, in Germany and elsewhere, customarily prompts heavy shifts of population in crowded trains. Ostensibly these were being directed to new places of work within the defence economy. However, German citizens visiting or resident in regained Posen or Lodz (Litzmannstadt) within the Warthegau and soldiers stationed in the East, not to mention the clergy serving the troops, would have observed something more: the methodical displacement of Jews from small towns and villages and their concentration in city ghettos. German contractors in the war industries eagerly employed them, at wages according wondrous profits. No one could fail to notice the arrival of many thousands of *Volksdeutsche*, ethnic Germans with a long history of residence in the old Baltic states, to fill the places vacated by these original inhabitants, Poles as well as Jews, who were being driven eastwards into the *Generalgouvernement*. The *Volksdeutsche*, slipping out of the Soviet net, came to reap the benefits of a richer life under the Swastika. Many would have preferred Sweden, but Hitler claimed them, and they had no option. They were resettled in Polish farms. They filled the many newly created vacancies in the factories, the police and town halls left by 100,000 Jews and 200,000 Poles now expelled. And the eyes of the many good Germans penetrating the *Generalgouvernement* in quest of easy gains from army business would have been greeted by a novel sight: the six-pointed Star of David emblem sewn on the garments of the Jews. It was decreed by Hans Frank for all over the age of ten in December 1939, as a badge of pariahdom long before it became mandatory in Germany proper.

From September 1941 the 'yellow star' was a requirement in Germany itself and in the 'Protectorate' of Bohemia-Moravia, to be followed at intervals in Belgium, Holland and France, and then wherever Nazism triumphed. It applied in Hungary only in April 1944. All Jews over the age of six in these countries wore the badge, including 'non-Aryan' apostates. Two Catholic churches existed in the Warsaw ghetto and one in the French concentration camp at Drancy, near Paris. Already before the war Jews remaining in Germany had been given a specific Nazi 'baptism' – males to include the name Israel with their signature, females Sarah, and the new-born to be registered according to an approved list of 'Jewish' names.

Such measures were the least of their trials. Persecution on a hitherto inconceivable scale began as German panzers crossed the demarcation line with Russia on 22 June 1941 and invaded along a thousand-mile front. Shadowing the military, four detachments of *Einsatzgruppen*, special action groups commanded by the SS élite, deployed themselves along the entire theatre with a mission to liquidate Jews, Polish and Russian intellectuals, Communist political leaders and any others likely, now or in the future, to make complications or offer resistance to the Nazi plan for the total enslavement of Europe. Civilians died almost in equal numbers with fighting troops, killed deliberately for the most part, but also in Luftwaffe raids or as they lay trapped within the fire of the all-conquering Wehrmacht. It was comparatively rare for ordinary members of the Slav races to be annihilated in cold blood, except in punishment. They were needed particularly to keep the war factories at full stretch and to harvest the huge grainlands of the Ukraine. Mass execution was reserved for the Jews. The *Einsatzgruppen* enlisted Slav help to do this, so that by the end of 1942 a German analysis prepared for police chief Heinrich Himmler could claim the destruction, at a conservative estimate, of two and a half millions.[8]

[8] Report of Richard Korherr dated 23 March 1943, ND NO5192–4.

Every step of the way is now more than adequately documented. The forty-two volumes of proceedings at the Nuremberg trials of major war criminals, and of subsequent trials, and the Nazi archives captured, together with the hundreds of personal diaries and testaments left in the ebb and flow of battle (many of those discovered yet to be examined), have rendered the terrible story into print: then from print to film and theatre, with fiction offered as fact and fact disputed as fiction, as much perhaps as any one generation can absorb. For the Jews themselves the Holocaust will forever burn in their collective memory, to give them an obsession to speak, and to write, and to put on display every aspect of their martyrdom. We have already had too much, yet still further material comes to light with more details of degradation, of apathy, of heroism. But indeed can there ever be enough?

Given that the Second World War claimed millions of innocent non-Jewish civilians too, and the chaos that supervened, with hunger and homelessness and civil war, this people fell within a genocidal process specific to themselves. Squads from the *Einsatzgruppen* trained machine-guns on men, women and children beside the ditches that would serve them as a common grave. They employed the forced labour of native populations to round up the living and dispose of the dead in these macabre operations. Jews co-operated too, in a vain bid for personal survival. One episode in particular has entered the canon of demonology, receiving poignant expression in the poetry of Yevgeny Yevtushenko, in a fictional epic by Anatoly Kuznetsov and also in the threnody of a Shostakovitch symphony. It occurred at Babi Yar, a ravine winding away from the edge of Kiev. The executioners required two days, 29–30 September 1941, to destroy 33,771 persons of all ages there, the great majority Jews, with units of the Ukrainian militia in Nazi service to help. Such triumphs, enacted also in the Baltic countries and the South-East, chronicled Hitler's progress. But they were judged too protracted, and no credit to German efficiency. Better use gas.

Jews could die also by neglect, starvation and torture in the concentration camps, some of them within the Reich itself, like Bergen-Belsen near Hanover, where Anne Frank of Amsterdam expired, and Dachau, just a bicycle ride from Munich and location of the first pseudo-scientific medical experiments on humans. Buchenwald, close to Weimar and constructed in a beech forest recalled as Goethe's favourite walk, was intended for 10,000 prisoners. When taken by the Americans in 1945 it held nearly 90,000 brought back from the East along with the retreating German armies, among them the seventeen-year-old Elie Wiesel, who would receive the Nobel peace prize in 1986.

Despite their horrors, these camps do not carry the apocalyptic ring in their names that we associate with Chelmno and Maidanek, Belzec, Sobibor and Treblinka, and especially Auschwitz-Birkenau. In their case murder was conducted by conveyor-belt through asphyxiation, and the destruction of the remains in crematoria, each of which consumed a thousand bodies every day.

Auschwitz, in what had once been Austrian Galicia, evoked associations for veteran Habsburg cavalrymen as the site of their barracks. The I. G. Farben Company selected the locality early in 1941 and established chemical works there, including the production in an adjacent area of synthetic rubber and coal-oil. Then old Gustav Krupp availed himself of the convenient slave labour to manufacture ignition fuses for his armaments. Auschwitz grew, with Polish prisoners its earliest inmates. After a personal inspection by Himmler in June 1941, to verify its suitability for Russian captives, Auschwitz with its outstations at Birkenau was converted for extermination. Hundreds of thousands of Russian POWs fell into German hands within a matter of weeks. They worked until exhaustion and were then killed. SS Obersturmbannführer (lieutenant-colonel) Rudolf Hoess, commander of Auschwitz, informed the British War Crimes Investigation Unit that during the thirty months of his control he supervised the extermination of two and a half million people there, while another half-million starved to death.[9] It was a delusion of executioner's grandeur; half that figure would be nearer the mark.[10] Some SS generals differed as to the most effective and 'humane' method of dispatch. Hoess preferred gassing because it was cleaner, though others considered shooting as the more

[9] Hoess affidavit, 5 April 1946, ND PS3868.
[10] Gerald Reitlinger, in The Final Solution, London, 1961, p. 500.

honourable. Adolf Eichmann, who held a rank similar to Hoess, witnessed a scene of execution by gunfire at first hand, and became sick. Scores of smaller labour camps existed, some of which were covered with soil for conversion into peaceful farmland and disappeared without trace during the German retreat. The grand total of death by gassing in the extermination centres specified above exceeded a multitude of five millions in all.

Transportation to Eastern Europe placed the irrevocability of the Day of Judgement upon the Jews as they were gathered in from every corner of the continent. In the process, they had first been expelled from their normal employment, then excluded from cultural life, from which their segregation in special neighbourhoods was but a short step. Jews mostly resided among their own anyway, so in the cities outside *Einsatzgruppen* territory they fondly believed they would be suffered to survive the war. They devised a bearable existence for themselves in the ghettos of Western and Central Europe through mutual support. In this way one, two, even three years might pass. But the death sentence of transportation could be defeated only if the Allies arrived in time.

In Poland, however, the ghettos were gated to control entry and exit, and in the case of Warsaw enclosed in a high brick wall. Into them were brought the Jews from all over Poland, with more 'resettled' there from Austria and the Protectorate portion of Czechoslovakia, and put to work. Other Jews, armed only with batons but often exceeding the Germans in their brutality, were enrolled to police them. It was from the ghettos, where the inmates enjoyed an eerie autonomy under an SS-appointed Jewish leader, that the most vivid, authentic records of the gradual death of the communities have come down to us. The Warsaw ghetto numbered 430,000 inhabitants in the middle of 1941, Lodz a quarter of a million.

The ghetto society miniaturised all human development from creation to decay. In the beginning it constituted a mass of beings crowded haphazardly together to serve an indefinite period for the criminal act of belonging to the lowest human race. Dislocation, loss of family life, sudden deprivation of purpose, close encounter with atrocities perpetrated by one person upon another, left them in a state of shock. The ghetto was an amorphous world condemned, it seemed, to perpetual darkness, its inhabitants obsessed only with survival of themselves and anyone dear to them. But quickly they brought order to the scene and a routine, with distribution of food, the establishment of hospitals and schools and regular burial of the numerous dead. Committees promoting cultural events and even entertainment came into existence. The ghetto would publish a newspaper strictly geared to matters of immediate concern. One luxury the Jews will apparently never surrender is politics. In the ghettos their divisions reproduced the pattern of East European groupings from their previous incarnation, offering a *raison d'être* to hopes that this ordeal would some day end. Activists joined the Bund, or the Communists, or one of the various groups of Zionists. Or they might detach themselves from the here and now by a strict regimen of prayer and Talmud study, in the conviction that the Nazi universe complied with God's design of catastrophe preceding Messianic salvation. Converts to Christianity kept clear of the rest.

All this surmounted a netherworld of smuggling, theft, betrayal and espionage. People escaped from the ghetto and passed as Nordic, a few even reaching the West to report its agonies and plead for intercession. Committees formed and reformed, while an aristocracy of sorts emerged at the behest of the Germans to implement their commands. Such was the *Judenrat*, or Council of Jews, which the mass of inhabitants regarded with a combination of envy, suspicion and hate. The leader himself, the *Aelteste*, or Eldest of the Jews, like Chaim Rumkowski of Lodz, could be a despot, perhaps a benevolent despot. Rumkowski has been portrayed by his fellow-inmates as a man posturing high above the other wretches, his likeness on the ghetto postage stamps, officiating at marriages and passing sentence of imprisonment on petty thieves and slackers.[11] Scholars and historians, notably Emanual Ringelblum and Chaim Kaplan in Warsaw, wrote everything down and buried their manuscripts for a future world.

Terror was the low cloud hanging over the ghetto. Kaplan's deportation to the gas chambers took place in 1942; Ringelblum

[11] See Lucjan Dobroszycki (ed.), *The Chronicle of the Lodz Ghetto, 1941–1944*, New Haven, Conn., 1984.

was murdered together with his entire family in 1944. Regular clearances, the victims mustered by a policeman of a *Judenrat* fearful of ignoring the order, decimated the population. The Germans eventually contracted the Warsaw ghetto to a quarter of its original area, though more and more Jews were deposited there, until every cellar and attic contained dozens of people in varying stages of disease and demoralisation. Lodz, under Rumkowski, fared the best and endured the longest, because of its importance to the war effort. When it was liberated by the Red Army in 1945 only 877 remained among the living, and they did not include the unlamented Rumkowski, for he too had been consigned to extermination.

Money talked loudest in the ghetto. The 'haves' could alleviate their plight by bribery, to which those in authority over the Jews, be they Poles, Ukrainians or Germans, were all susceptible. A gold wedding ring could buy extensive privileges, while lesser gifts took some inmates in and out of their prison almost at will. By a paradox, the American Jewish Joint Distribution Committee was enabled to keep representatives, US nationals and others, in Poland right until Pearl Harbor, when Hitler made the fatal decision to honour his promise to Japan and declare war on America. Aid from the American Joint, in the form of currency, food, blankets, artisans' tools, even letters of credit for redemption after the war, cast a lifeline from the 'Aryan' side of the cities to the Jews. The archives of the Joint tell of amazing transactions, and the circuitous routes by which resources reached the Jews of Poland. Saly Mayer, president of the Jewish community of Switzerland, devised the means to keep supplies flowing at great personal risk after Pearl Harbor. A little-known mission of the RAF was to drop 400,000 dollars in four packets into the Warsaw ghetto itself. Nearly all the money reached its underground destination.[12]

American dollars could also purchase false papers enabling Jews to travel from one ghetto to another, so information was quickly exchanged and plans for mutual help or rebellion discussed. Gratefully we record these highlights – the defiant will to live in the few, the struggle for self-respect by a minority, the succour from abroad. But they cannot brighten the picture of the vast

[12] Herbert Agar, in his officially sponsored history of the AJDC, *The Saving Remnant*, New York, 1960, p. 105.

mass in their stupor, the tyranny of a conspiratorial mafia of criminals and the eternal stench from funeral carts bearing the starved, the stillborn and the old to the ghetto cemeteries. And, finally, the SS line-up for the ultimate equaliser in the gas chambers. It would be left to the advancing Allied armies to discover Jewish habitations, if at all, spectrally occupied by both the living and the dead. Little wonder there are people today who insist that the numbers given of Jews exterminated were a gross exaggeration.

This had been so from the very start of hostilities. Reports charging Germany with bestiality – those Huns! – were a common propaganda ploy in the First World War, manufacturing lurid tales of children bayoneted by the Kaiser's troops in their advance across Belgium. It had a familiar ring. This time the scale of the atrocities as they leaked out appeared to exceed every limit of belief. The first news broke with an announcement by the Polish government-in-exile in London, via the Polish underground, a Home Army in the making, and through the ambassadors it maintained in neutral countries, Switzerland, Sweden and Turkey being the principal clearing-houses of intelligence.

The Polish authorities in London produced two 'black books', in June 1941 and April 1942, which detailed the burning of synagogues, the mass expulsions, the forced labour, camps and ghettos. Widely distributed in Britain and America, these illustrated publications gave the locations of mass executions and, where available, listed the names of the victims. They were sent also to the heads of Allied and neutral governments. But the information conveyed was received sceptically as grossly exaggerated horror stories. As early as March and April 1940, before the conquest in the West, the Polish envoy to the Holy See, Kasimierz Papée, besought the Vatican Secretary of State to intercede with Berlin to stop the persecutions, while simultaneously he begged the Superior General of the Jesuit Order, Wladimir Ledochowski, to devise ways of protecting the innocent in Poland.[13] General Sikorski, the Polish Prime Minister-in-Exile, visited America in April 1941 to enlist support over

[13] J. Ciechanowski, 'The Polish Government-in-Exile – Diplomatic Representations on behalf of Polish Jewry', paper submitted to the International Conference on Polish–Jewish Relations at Oxford, 1984.

there, only to experience an uncomfortable encounter with US Jewish leaders on the grounds of his country's traditional anti-semitism. (Sikorski promised his nation's atonement in the future.) He was speaking shortly before Germany's invasion of the Soviet zone of Poland and the capture of another million Jews there, not to mention those of Russian nationality about to enter the Nazi Gehenna.

Sikorski's confrontation with the Jews of the West, and his account of the plight of their co-religionists in Poland, produced some agonising ironies. The Polish leader found strong reluc-tance among his hearers to initiate a publicity campaign of their own. They contended that these reports, if true, revealed the failure of the Poles themselves in their elementary civilised oblig-ation to exert every effort for their fellow-citizens' protection.[14] It was a classic example of mutual incomprehension producing mutual hostility. The idea could not enter Sikorski's head that so influential an organism as American Jewry, which to the entire gentile world demonstrated its confident presence within the United States, shrank from making a stand lest it be stamped as a local warmongering element. America clung passionately to its neutrality. President Roosevelt intended to keep the country that way. By starting up a clamour on behalf of European Jews would not the general population read into it a message that this was specifically a Jewish war, and not one launched by Hitler against human freedom as a whole? Some US Jews may in their hearts have been hoping for American intervention, but they would die rather than admit it. Their country's fiercely isolationist mood had exposed itself, in its determination to admit no Jewish refugees, as the kissing-cousin of antisemitism. No less a national figure than Charles Lindbergh stood at the head of an influential body of vocal opinion arguing at that moment for friendship with Germany. The pusillanimous conduct of American Jewry, as we shall see, has stained the reputation of that community to this day.

Some validity attached to the charge of indifference on the part of Poland towards the Jewish fate. The Home Army was led by Polish officers of a class that had never before regarded, and

[14] Ibid.

would not now regard, the Jews as an integral segment of their nation. The Poles had assimilated much of the Nazi philosophy of race even though they were now the victims of it themselves. As Catholics of an ancient and proud tradition they in general truly desired the Jews out of the country. Couldn't their extermination, in the long perspective of history, prove a blessing in disguise?

If bitterness on this score coloured the reception by US Jews of Sikorski's mission then theirs was a cruelly simplistic view. Many Poles extended a hand to the Jews, providing them with food and shelter, even helping them to escape from the ghettos. And this despite the conqueror's law forbidding contact with Jews except for the requirements of the German war machine. Posters displayed throughout the *Generalgouvernement* warned that discovery meant execution. Polish agents of the Gestapo, well rewarded by their masters, betrayed their fellow-Poles every day. Yet aid was given, if not always for humanity's sake. To furnish a Jew with false papers entailed the forgery of a Polish identity card, a work certificate, a baptism certificate. Priests had to be enlisted in the conspiracy, and the only really safe hiding-places for Jewish women and children (grown men too on occasion) were the convents. It all required money, not only for bribes but to keep blackmailers quiet; and while this was mostly paid by the Jews themselves some of it came also from secret channels established by the government-in-exile in London. Jewish children clawed their way under the walls of the Warsaw ghetto every day, to beg for bread or to buy it with jewellery provided by their parents or stolen from others. At this writing, more than forty years after the end of the war, Poles of the different faiths continue to argue over the succour given, or withheld, from the less afflicted to the more.[15]

In 1986 a film of the Holocaust, *Shoah*, made by Claude Lanzmann with French governmental finance, angered the Poles to the degree of seeking its suppression. It is a nine-hour-long condemnation of Poland for having averted its eyes to the events taking place on its soil. The Poles countercharged France with

[15] See, e.g., the paper presented by Israel Guttman at the Oxford conference noted above.

resorting to an alibi for its own guilt towards the Jews. Nevertheless, the Polish leader, General Jaruzelski, endorsed the basic authenticity of the film, and it was screened on Polish television.[16]

Unhappily, the sombre recording of Polish–Jewish relations by no means exhausts the subject of Christendom's response to this, the worst catastrophe to beset the Jews since the Dispersion and the greatest crime in the history of Christian antisemitism. Nazi plans for the elimination of the Jewish people in Europe need not have proceeded virtually without interruption until Germany's defeat. The Poles could have done more, the French, the Dutch, the Czechs, the Vatican – a greater effort at rescue everywhere, or a significant concentration of protest, might have extricated large numbers from the jaws of death. But most of all, salvation lay within the capacity of the major Western powers: Great Britain and, before and after its entry in the war, the United States. They could have saved hundreds of thousands, perhaps more. And they could have achieved this without diverting resources from the admittedly supreme task of defeating the enemy at the earliest moment, though this became their automatic alibi for inaction. In the case of America, its neutrality until December 1941 precluded even this defence.

The occupation of Kiev in September 1941 was an early indication that the conquest of Russia, and with it mastery over half the world at least, would not be the easy victory Hitler had envisioned. The fate of Napoleon's Grand Army must surely have haunted the Wehrmacht as it captured the Ukrainian capital and demolished Marshal Budenny's numerous divisions just beyond. What happened next? The Germans settled in, and the Ukrainians, many of them doubtless breathing relief at the termination of Stalinist rule, appeared to take occupation in their stride. The Jews were marked out but for the moment remained in peace. Then, on 28 September, the crowded Kreshchatik, Kiev's main thoroughfare harbouring army headquarters and nerve-centre of the SS in the Ukraine, was blown to fragments by a series of explosions. Buildings came crashing down, shops, factories and dwellings went up in flames, the toll of casualties,

[16] Interview with Claude Lanzmann, *The Times*, London, 8 November 1986.

among the Germans as well as the native population, proved immense. Such was the Russian scorched earth policy, to warn the invaders of what was yet to come in a war Germany had not hitherto fought, in either Poland or the West. Grim-faced, the Germans responded with Babi Yar; to them a reprisal action against the Jews equated with action against the Bolsheviks.

Kiev had offered the Germans a swift military success but now bore a message of ultimate disaster. How did it appear to those devout isolationists, the Americans? As a whole, and despite Lindbergh, they sympathised with the Allied cause. Kiev now gave them reassurance that the war against Hitler could be won without their own active participation. American Jews shared this sentiment. They had no desire to disturb the climate with agitation for special intercession on behalf of their own people in Europe, for all would be well in the end. Furthermore, as Jews their emotions were additionally complicated by a factor wholly divorced from the local scene: Zionism. This movement, now being led with equal authority by Chaim Weizmann and David Ben-Gurion, was conducting a campaign for the creation of a Jewish army to fight beside the British but under its own flag. The claim carried strong validity. The Free Poles had such a force, the Free French, even that small complement, the Free Czechs. So why not the Jews? Enough of them now inhabited Palestine for the nucleus which, the Zionist leaders asserted, would expand greatly with transfers from the regular British army and Jewish volunteers from the rest of the world. It promised more soldiers than contributed by the Free Poles or the others. Britain did not absolutely decline the offer, but could not bring itself to a positive Yes.

The demand had been raised also in the First World War, and been reluctantly conceded – reluctantly because of its transparent political motive of strengthening the Jewish stake in Palestine. These representations, in the light of Hitler's persecutions, were now hardening into a demand for a Jewish state. Weizmann and Ben-Gurion crossed the Atlantic to stir up Jewish opinion there, in the knowledge that the British were heavily dependent on American material aid and needed all the goodwill they could muster in that country. Prudently, the Zionist leaders kept their fervent hope of American-Jewish volunteers in the contemplated army to a whisper, not welcoming the rebuff such a suggestion would inevitably receive if publicly made. But American Jewry, excluding itself, heartily endorsed the proposition in so far as it related to Palestine and the British Empire, and could safely lobby Washington to chastise Whitehall accordingly. Recruitment figures showed how the Jews in Palestine were already flocking to the colours in anonymous battalions, whereas the number of Arabs who cared enough about the outcome of the war to enrol was insignificant. Conscription did not apply to Palestine.

No harm ever befell Americans in voicing a grievance against the British, as the Irish community amply demonstrated, and the Jews took up the campaign for an identifiable Jewish army with a will. They had a further complaint to lodge against London. This concerned the Palestine White Paper of 1939. Here was a deliberate measure to restrict the flow of Jews to Palestine, and eventually to arrest it altogether. It held them prisoner in Hitler's Europe, almost certainly a condemnation to death. On this subject the British remained adamant, and consequently could be said to share some additional responsibility for the tragedy submerging the people. Once America found itself at war the Jewish leaders shed any previous inhibition, and grew still more strident in their criticism of Britain. Zionist representatives in New York passed a resolution calling for a Jewish state in the whole of Palestine,[17] something Weizmann himself had never demanded. They also felt able now to embrace the Jewish army cause as a virtue for the Western alliance as a whole, and with the cry 'Open the gates of Palestine!' they castigated the White Paper as a cynical betrayal of the Balfour Declaration of 1917. Still, they continued to refrain from calling upon Roosevelt to make an American contribution to the rescue of Jews from Europe. Obsessed with the fear of bringing antisemitism down on their heads, they failed to see a role for themselves in saving any of those people, many of whom numbered among their own close kin.

Field-Marshal Keitel committed a million soldiers through the long, pitiless Russian winter of 1941–2. He occupied an immense,

17 At the Biltmore Conference, May 1942.

heavily populated area, but still failed to reach Moscow, or to capture Leningrad, the city Hitler decreed should suffer a fate similar to Jerusalem in AD 70 and be erased from the map. Stalin's reserves seemed inexhaustible. He could replace an army complete immediately on its annihilation. In this theatre human life counted for so little on the battlefield that the ordeal of the civilian millions caught in the deadly crossfire barely drew anyone's attention, let alone concern. The deportation of Jews from all of conquered Europe to the East continued even while the strained German forces clamoured for supplies to be brought up in all the rolling stock available. Chelmno, in the annexed Warthegau, became an extermination centre late in 1941. Then followed Belzec, Auschwitz-Birkenau, Treblinka and Sobibor, and finally Maidanek in the autumn of 1942. The earliest gassing took place with carbon monoxide fed from their engines into specially constructed trucks, a process subsequently ruled out as too lengthy. Asphyxiation chambers, once properly installed, proved far more efficient. It was then the turn of the *Sonderkommandos* of prisoners, mostly Jews eventually doomed to die themselves, who shovelled the bodies into the incinerators, the ashes finally dispersed to obliterate the traces.

For a German schema of the extermination programme as it specifically affected the Jews we have the minutes of the secret conference of 20 January 1942 held in Wannsee, Berlin, convened by Heydrich on the orders of Field-Marshal Goering. This took place some weeks after the first experimental operations with gas vans were already in progress at Chelmno. The record survived for submission to the Nuremberg Trials as Document NG 2586, and was supplemented later from memory by Adolf Eichmann (he had provided a statistical brief for Heydrich's opening speech and also took the minutes) during his 1961 trial in Jerusalem. At Wannsee the expression 'Final Solution', encoding the total destruction of the Jews of Europe, entered the historical record.

Heydrich reviewed the demographic picture: approximately 537,000 Jews had fled the territories of Greater Germany (i.e. Germany proper, Austria and the Protectorate of Bohemia-Moravia) between Hitler's accession to power in 1933 and the end of October 1941. War conditions made further emigration unlikely – possibly the Madagascar idea was here inferred – and in any case had been forbidden by order of police chief Himmler. But the swift extension of German authority into Russia opened new possibilities for a settlement of the problem. Europe 'would be combed from west to east', eleven million Jews would be taken away, the sexes separated, utilised for labour and then dealt with in the Final Solution. Heydrich posited one small exception: those of former German citizenship over the age of sixty-five, together with severely wounded First World War veterans and holders of the Iron Cross First Class. To obviate tedious intercession on behalf of individual Jews, he stated, they would be consigned to the ghetto at Theresienstadt, formerly Terezin, in Bohemia.

Heydrich excluded no corner of the continent in his survey of the Jews marked for removal: not the Jews of England, nor European Turkey, nor Spain, nor even the four thousand estimated to reside in Ireland. The eleven million total was Eichmann's, but he had overestimated somewhat, having discovered no less than five millions in the USSR when the last Soviet census, of 1939, had produced only 3,010,000. For the rest, his population analysis indicated excellent homework by the Gestapo specialist in Jewish affairs. Undoubtedly problems would arise in some countries, Heydrich warned, enumerating Italy, Hungary and Romania. The ever-thorny subject of the *Mischlinge* first and second degree (half- and quarter-Jewish) required subtly balanced directives. Except in the case of second-degree persons married to Aryan Germans they would generally fall within the category of Jews. During his trial Eichmann was asked: 'The methods of killing – the systems of extermination – was not an important theme?' He replied: 'No, no. This of course was not put into the record.'[18]

As we have seen, efforts at concealment of the operation were in vain, detailed information on atrocities committed in the East since the beginning of hostilities being already in the hands of the Polish government-in-exile, which hastened to let the world know. The Soviet Foreign Minister, Vyacheslav Molotov, among others, advised the world of accumulating massacres as from November 1941. All these lacked one important endorsement,

[18] Raul Hilberg (ed.), *Documents of Destruction*, Chicago, 1971, p. 104.

the first-hand evidence of a German national. Who would have the courage and conscience to bring the intelligence out?

Such a man appeared: Eduard Reinhold Karl Schulte, whose business affairs took him on frequent trips to Switzerland. His identity remained unrevealed for over thirty years after the war. Schulte made the journey in July 1942 especially to advise a Jewish friend of the extermination programme. The information was then conveyed to Gerhard Riegner, of the World Jewish Congress office in Geneva, who immediately had this telegram transmitted through British and American diplomatic channels to his superiors in London and New York:

> Received alarming report stating that, in the Führer's headquarters, a plan has been discussed, and is under consideration, according to which all Jews in countries occupied or controlled by Germany numbering three and a half to four millions should, after deportation and concentration in the East, be at one blow exterminated in order to resolve, once and for all, the Jewish question in Europe. Action is reported to be planned for the autumn. Ways of execution are still being discussed including the use of prussic acid. We transmit this information with all the necessary reservation, as exactitude cannot be confirmed by us. Our informant is reported to have close connections with the highest German authorities, and his reports are generally reliable.[19]

The message reached Sydney Silverman, Member of Parliament and London head of the World Jewish Congress, with the postscript: 'Please inform and consult New York.' The one for New York was addressed via the State Department to Rabbi Stephen Wise, Silverman's opposite number there. But the State Department forwarded neither this communication to Wise nor another sent to the rabbi direct from the WJC in London. Thus the Anglo-Jewish community was promptly alerted, though not American Jewry.[20]

[19] Filed in Public Record Office, London, as FO 371/30917, C 7853/61/18, 10 August 1942.
[20] See David C. Wyman, *Abandonment of the Jews: America and the Holocaust, 1941–45*, New York, 1984, pp. 43–5.

Hence delaying tactics on the part of the State Department worked to withhold the news from the American public on the one hand, while the British government on its side refrained from any positive action. In the first place the information seemed an atrocity tale beyond credibility. More than this, both London and Washington had their own reasons for playing down the news. Agitation had at last begun in earnest for intervention to stop the persecution in so far as it was already known from earlier reports. Why shouldn't the Allies warn Germany of certain eventual punishment for its crimes? Why not threaten reprisals against German prisoners in Allied hands? Particularly, a strong plea was made for compelling Germany to release the Jews into neutral lands, and then bring them to America in the many troopships returning home empty. Indeed, Spanish and Portuguese vessels were regularly plying the Atlantic trade routes and were available for charter.

Washington was further asked to place America's tremendous weight behind the clamour for opening the gates of Palestine, to which Britain was still determined to remain deaf. But the administration closed its mind against all these proposals. It refused to embarrass the British, who already had loyalty problems with the Arabs in plenty – serious enough in 1942 to ring the palace of King Farouk in Cairo with tanks, as a warning against his intrigues with Italy and Germany. As for reprisals against German prisoners, who dared risk a cycle of inhuman executions that could envelop the innocents of all nations?

Neither the White House nor Congress was perceptibly troubled in the matter of rescue, even though the news from Europe, now doubly authenticated by neutral observers, began to focus on the public attention through great demonstrations of protest. The pressure was balanced by agitation of a contrary nature arising afresh in the United States against the entry of a single Jewish refugee. This now reared an undisguised antisemitism, and was not restricted to the average American. The Jews made little headway when they sought to enlist the help of the most prominent clerics, or the leaders of the many ethnic groups, be they Czech, Polish, Lithuanian or any other. No one seemed to read the newspaper accounts of persecutions in Europe, which the *New York Times*, Jewish owned and edited, never judged as worthy of front-page treatment. This indifference extended from the ordinary man in the street up through civic leaders to government agencies. Apart from a few notable exceptions, even Jews recognised for their independent stand on other issues, and they included the celebrated columnist Walter Lippmann, refrained from placing their influence behind the demand that America do *something*. Painful in the contrast, non-Jewish refugees were not abandoned in the same way. Several hundreds of them reached America in the early part of the war, along with such Jews privileged by their international fame as Marc Chagall and André Maurois. Hundreds are not many in a disaster of towering proportions, but they illustrate that America could move when it showed willing.

Although the ultimate result was the same, official British reaction revealed a different emphasis. There, a more powerful and more independent-minded Church espoused the Jewish cause, principally through the advocacy of William Temple, Archbishop of Canterbury, and Arthur Hinsley, Cardinal Archbishop of Westminster.[21] The Churchill government could not afford absolutely to ignore their voices. Upon verification of the mass murders it therefore proposed that the Allies make a formal declaration on punishment for war crimes. But Britain no longer wielded its influence of the inter-war years, and America showed reluctance. Washington would not go so far even as to endorse a general statement ascribing to the Germans an intention to exterminate the Jewish people in Europe, to be signed by all Allied governments, before it had emasculated the original British draft. It changed 'reports from Europe which leave no room for doubt' into 'numerous reports from Europe'. When finally the statement was issued, on 17 December 1942, the British Parliament stood in silence for two minutes. No parallel gesture took place on Capitol Hill.

General expressions of sympathy were all very fine, but the British refused to budge where they were still the paramount power: on immigration to Palestine. Winston Churchill liked to call himself a Zionist. In August 1942 he telegraphed a reproof to

---

[21] Gerhard Riegner stated later: 'The British, despite the official attitude, remained a beacon of light.' *Sunday Times*, London, 7 April 1985.

Roosevelt, who was making overtures to the Arabs intimating post-war independence for them all: 'I am strongly wedded to the Zionist policy, of which I was one of the authors.'[22] But he could not go against Anthony Eden, his Foreign Secretary, nor the Colonial Office, regarding a relaxation of the White Paper restrictions. Britain had enough Arab unrest to contend with as it was; and although the threat to the Middle East was thwarted by the end of 1942, the government bent over backwards lest a burst of violent Arab hostility, like the rebellion of 1936, keep army units employed as policemen when these would be needed for the assault upon Europe. The Mufti of Jerusalem had already arrived in Berlin to pledge the Muslim world's support to Hitler. The Arabs constituted an embarrassment for any British government rather greater than the Jews of America had become to any administration in Washington.

Apart from Roosevelt, Eden remained the most obdurate on the question of Jewish rescue. (Lesser men, notably the British Colonial Secretary, Lord Moyne, and the US Assistant Secretary of State, Breckenridge Long, equally held firm.) Aware, as he could not fail to be, that the United States had no intention of making a contribution, Eden realised that every discussion of the subject foisted the problem of refugee shelter upon the British, since the Zionist solution had emerged as the only practical option, with Palestine lying conveniently close to the stricken continent. Eden had his own pet dream for that country's future within the scheme of a great Arab League closely associated with Britain. A substantial increase in the Jewish population in Palestine could easily disrupt the plan. He therefore took recourse in the spectre of Hitler's exploiting Allied goodwill towards the Jews by disgorging the lot on to their laps. As he told a meeting in March 1943 with Roosevelt, Cordell Hull and Lord Halifax (British ambassador) in the context of Bulgaria's role in the deportation of Yugoslav and Greek Jews to Treblinka:

> The whole problem of the Jews in Europe is very difficult, and we should move very cautiously about offering to take them all out of a country like Bulgaria. If we do that,

---

[22] Quoted in F. L. Loewenstein (ed.), *Roosevelt and Churchill: Their Secret Wartime Correspondence*, London, 1975, p. 234.

then the Jews of the world will be wanting us to make similar offers in Poland and Germany. Hitler might well take us up on any such offer and there simply are not enough ships and means of transportation to handle them.[23]

In the thinking of militant Zionists, British apologetics on this score echoed as a declaration of war against the Jews. The White Paper had not come down from Sinai. Why not defy it? Volunteers prepared to risk their skins came forward to smuggle Jews into Palestine come what may. Illegal immigration to circumvent the regulations, already in operation before the outbreak of hostilities, now became doubly hazardous. The Zionists centred their activities in Romania, a country which had purchased a degree of independence from Nazism through association with it. The virulently antisemitic Iron Guard ruled Romania in uneasy alliance with the dictator, Ion Antonescu. The Iron Guard proposed to expel the Jews anyway. It made a start in August 1941 with the first of the transportations, ultimately comprising 200,000 Jews, to a region described as 'Transnistria', which was wrested from the Soviets in the early triumphant days of the Eastern Front. Perhaps half the Jews died before reaching that destination. So if the Zionists could smuggle any into Palestine, good riddance. Romania washed against the Black Sea, which joined the Mediterranean in the Turkish narrows and thus gave uninterrupted passage by ship to the Palestine coast. Uninterrupted, that is, but for the white ensign of the Royal Navy standing guard.

As early as November 1940 three ships in Zionist charter, carrying 3,500 would-be immigrants, all of whom lacked certificates guaranteeing entry, left Romanian ports en route for Haifa. The British made two of the ships captive and transferred their 1,900 passengers to the *Patria*, 11,700 tons, while awaiting the third vessel for similar treatment. The intention was to deport all of them to the Indian Ocean isle of Mauritius for the duration of the war. The Zionist Executive, at that time described as the Jewish Agency for Palestine, left security affairs in the hands of

[23] Harry Hopkins notes in *Foreign Relations of the United States*, Vol. III, p. 38, cited in Wyman, *Abandonment of the Jews*, p. 97.

its unofficial defence arm, the Haganah, and this body took steps to frustrate the operation. It sent frogmen to attach a mine and cripple the *Patria* as it lay anchored in the Haifa breakwater. But the daring sabotage went disastrously awry. The engine room blew up, the vessel keeled over and within minutes touched the harbour bottom. Some 260 passengers drowned. The rest were rescued by British naval personnel and harbour workers. As an act of mercy the survivors were allowed to remain in Palestine, though the passengers arriving in the third Zionist ship were dispatched to Mauritius as planned.[24]

The Jews' desperation to escape by any means from Europe forced them to pay outrageous rates on boats venturing into the Black Sea in such unseaworthy state as to render a voyage of any length perilous. Flags of convenience, profiteering captains and unscrupulous agents in Romania turned the scramble for life into a duel with fate. The determination of the Zionists, belonging to both the Haganah and its extremist 'competitor' the Irgun Zvai Leumi, sent the refugees into waters with the declared intention of throwing them on to the mercy of others to bring them to safety. Very few possessed British permits for Palestine. It became a battle of nerves in which their shocking plight confronted the conscience of the British Empire. Whitehall's local intelligence agents observed the gamble from start to finish. They were ostensibly watching for Nazi agents seeking to infiltrate Palestine under cover of innocent refugees – a meretricious argument, and no single Nazi was ever known to have reached Palestine. Less speciously, the British feared that any weakening in their application of the immigration quota system would send a fleet of refugee boats in a kind of Dunkirk evacuation across the Mediterranean. The policy brought fierce condemnation upon the British, not least within Britain itself. The Zionist Organisation naturally made the most of the cruel edict, particularly in America. As for Lord Moyne, Colonial Secretary of the period, it would one day cost him his life at the hands of Jewish terrorists.

And so the immigration blockade continued, to write a bizarre and poignant chapter in the maritime history of the Second

[24] The full story of the *Patria* in Munya M. Mardor, *Strictly Illegal*, London, 1964.

World War. On occasion the British would relent a margin, and allow the refugees to land and be taken into internment. Soon after the *Patria* affair, a Uruguayan sailing boat, the *Salvador*, carrying 350 Jews out of Bulgaria, though not citizens of that country, stood six days in Istanbul harbour awaiting a British verdict on their future. It was then turned away from Turkish waters and capsized. The survivors numbered 120, some of whom were returned to Bulgaria. The next vessel to reach Istanbul, the *Darien*, drifted with 793 of its own refugees plus a few left over from the *Salvador*. This miserable craft managed to limp into Haifa, where the plight of its passengers moved the British to bring them ashore.

Apportioning guilt in this tragic conflict can be facile. Here was Britain, the country which for a year stood alone as the solitary hope between Hitler and his domination of Europe; there the embittered Jewish people, the Führer's principal victims and thus the only Europeans whose loyalty Britain could really count upon as unquestioned until Russia was forced into the war in 1941. But the people of this island kingdom were themselves suffering painful casualties through German bombing raids, the war in the air and at sea. As German U-boats took their toll of Atlantic cargoes, food stocks diminished to crisis level, ironically necessitating rationing more stringent than in some parts of occupied Europe. No other nation joined that country's side militarily until circumstances dragged it there. Britain could lose a battleship with 3,000 hands drowned and still have no time to weep. In this fight for survival it regarded every complication – so many others besides the Jews' clamour for shelter – as impeding the all-transcending objective of crushing Germany. Taken as a whole, in the inglorious record of the world's indifference towards the Jewish martyrdom, the British came through as the least dishonourable.

Yet one old Danubian cattle-boat, the *Struma*, remains eternally enshrined in Jewish resentment as a pointless, hideous calamity summarising the blundering stolidity of Great Britain towards the Jews in their hour of deepest tragedy. The *Struma*, 240 tons, fifty feet in length, sailed from Romania weighted down with 769 Jews armed with nothing but their prayers to bring them salvation. This tiny craft ventured forth on 24 December

1941. Its passengers (if that is the correct term) trusted, once out to sea, that they could land somewhere along the Turkish coast while their future was debated. Whatever transpired, they would have eluded transportation to 'Transnistria', or perhaps some worse fate.

The *Struma*'s captain and crew, Bulgarian nationals, were receiving handsome compensation for the experience. Their boat, a barge really, had been fitted with a diesel engine and given a wooden superstructure of rough bunks, so that in order to breathe fresh air the passengers would stand on deck in ever-changing groups. It sailed under the Panamanian flag, and on the day following its departure that Central American republic, sucked into the wake of Pearl Harbor two weeks earlier, declared war upon the Axis. The usual fourteen-hour voyage to Istanbul took the *Struma* four days, in which the engine needed repair, the sick were *in extremis*, and the captain refused to navigate through waters policed by the Royal Navy. His own country had in fact just declared war on Britain and America, so he and his crew were duty bound to return home and join the colours. Whichever way the Turkish authorities looked at it, the *Struma* spelt bad news.

She stood outside Istanbul for nearly two months. On 10 February 1942 the Jewish Agency in Jerusalem received a quota of 3,000 certificates for Palestine, on account of the 75,000 allowed by the White Paper. The Agency offered to allocate the requisite number for *Struma* passengers, now reduced by eight, for five in fact already possessed certificates while three others were disembarked through the intervention of the American representative of Socony Oil in Istanbul. But the British High Commissioner in Palestine refused the Jewish request, since the refugees had left an enemy country before issuance of the 3,000 permits. However, he ultimately agreed as a gesture of humanity to take all children under the age of sixteen. They could travel overland.

This necessitated approval by the Turks. The delays had angered them, and they saw no profit in acting as intermediary between the British and the Jews, especially since the only official empowered to authorise disembarkation for the children's onward journey to Palestine was absent in distant Ankara and beyond contact. Wearying of the situation, the harbourmaster sent out tugs which, amid scenes of consternation and panic on the part of the passengers, pulled the *Struma* into the open roadstead. It drifted helplessly among the bobbing mines. And while the Jewish Agency and the British in Jerusalem continued to dispute the situation, a mysterious explosion occurred, sinking the 112-year-old vessel. The Bulgarian crew drowned with the rest – all 760 Jews except a youth of seventeen years.

Other nations watched uncomprehending. The Jewish world grieved. The British faced the music. Albert Einstein in America spoke of the disaster as 'striking at the heart of civilisation'. Eleanor Roosevelt, according to the *New York Times*, asked why technicalities should keep such people out of Palestine when the quota was not even filled – 'It just seems cruel beyond words.' Angry debates took place in both Houses of the British Parliament, where Harold Macmillan and Lord Cranborne inherited the invidious task of fending off the cataract of criticism from all sides.[25]

Expressions of disgust had their effect, so the sacrifice was not entirely in vain. Britain undertook, in the middle of 1943, to facilitate the onward journey of every refugee reaching Istanbul. But it insisted on the arrangement remaining secret, lest its leniency open the floodgates.[26] As it happened, the British had allowed non-Jewish Greeks, Yugoslavs and Poles fleeing the Nazis into Palestine and elsewhere in the Middle East throughout the war. The discrimination was not an example of deliberate antisemitism, except in so far as this was intrinsic to the Jewish condition. Those others, the British understood, would return to their homes after the war. What land could the Jews describe as their home?

Meanwhile the war turned against Germany, but the deportation trains rolled on eastward to their termini in the Polish necropolis. Stalingrad did not halt them, nor the German defeat in North Africa. By the summer of 1943 the greater part of the three and a half million Jews inhabiting Poland and the Baltic countries in 1939 were dust, together with another three million 'Aryan' Poles, Ukrainians and Russians. Partisan groups, now

[25] House of Lords debate, 11 March; House of Commons, 12 March 1942.
[26] Daphne Trevor, *Under the White Paper*, Jerusalem, 1948, p. 34.

actively embarrassing the German forces, assisted Polish agents to reach the West and tell the story. One of them, the intrepid courier of the underground Jan Karski, made the journey more than once, and was able to brief British cabinet ministers, including Eden, and, in America, President Roosevelt himself.[27] Their reaction to the atrocities left no room for doubt that they had already written off the Jews together with all other civilian victims of Hitler's paranoia.

Pessimistic by their nature the Germans might well be, but defeatist never. The Nazis had not abandoned their dream of fashioning a *judenrein* Europe cleansed of the Bolshevik menace and dominated by themselves. For civilisation to survive without a strong Germany was to them unthinkable, and this sustained their ruthlessness. Hence the extermination centres had to continue until war operations in the field brought them within identifiable range of the enemy. Sobibor, in the Lublin district, functioned until October 1943. In addition to 200,000 Jews from Czechoslovakia, Austria, Holland, Belgium and France, masses of others were consumed there, including Russian prisoners of war. Sobibor possessed no crematoria; the cadavers were burned in open ditches after gassing, when the ashes were removed and dispersed. There and elsewhere, labourers employed in the ghoulish work, being witnesses, could not themselves be allowed to survive. Such was the routine. Treblinka, situated in a pine forest sixty miles north-east of Warsaw, comprised two camps. Crematoria were located in the second Treblinka (TII), ten of them in fact, so disposal of the evidence was begun long before the closure of TI in July 1944. The Treblinka complex of structures occupied an area of thirty-two acres, and prisoners existed in varying propinquity to death – to the degree that it could boast two Jewish orchestras, for classical and jazz music. However, unlike Fania Fenelon, *chanteuse* in the Auschwitz orchestra,[28] none of the musicians survived. Himmler visited TII in February 1943. Six months later 300 inmates made a concerted escape, when some were concealed by Poles in the surrounding

---

[27] See Walter Laqueur, *The Terrible Secret*, London, 1980, pp. 229–35.
[28] Fania Fenelon (with Marcelle Routier), *The Musicians of Auschwitz*, London, 1977.

countryside, some betrayed. The Germans destroyed every trace of T II at the same time as Sobibor, in October 1943, ploughing up the land so that ordinary farming folk could endow a graveyard of 900,000 Jews, Poles, gypsies and homosexuals with all the paraphernalia of innocence.[29] A similar camouflage exercise was conducted at Belzec.

Initially, Belzec registered in the topography of this holocaust as a labour camp for Jews from Lublin and Warsaw. Encouraged along by horsewhips, they toiled until exhaustion in digging emplacements to mark the new frontier-line between the spheres of Germany and Russia while the two still posed as friends. Here the gas was piped into the chambers by diesel. Maidanek (method of extermination, Zyklon B made from prussic acid crystals) lay on the outskirts of Lublin. First intended as a Russian POW camp, it later took large numbers of Sephardic Jews deported from Salonika where, by a tradition two centuries old, many had worked as stevedores. Maidanek had its busiest day on 2 November 1943, when *Einsatzgruppen* of the SS machine-gunned 18,400 prisoners seized from the Warsaw ghetto, the victims being interred in ditches they themselves had dug.[30]

Wholesale murder at the four centres enumerated above brought Germany useful by-products. By order of SS Brigadeführer (brigadier-general) Odilo Globocnik, in overall command, women had their hair shorn off for industrial use, clothing was sorted for recycling, jewellery and other valuables salvaged and meticulously itemised. Little wonder Globocnik could not face the reckoning in 1945 and shot himself. At Babi Yar, reserved as an execution centre for two more years after the Jews were finished off there, peasants foraged and sifted through the soil long afterwards in an eerie gold-rush.

Globocnik's writ did not extend to Chelmno, on the Ner river thirty-five miles from Lodz, nor originally to Auschwitz in Galicia, the largest in the scale of monstrosity. He was a creature of Hans Frank's *Generalgouvernement*, while both these centres

---

[29] The Polish station-master at Treblinka, Franciszek Zabecki, who claimed to keep exact figures for each transport, stated that 1,000,200 were exterminated there. See article by Gitta Sereny in *The Times*, London, 14 February 1987.
[30] Edward Gryn and Zofia Murawska, *The Maidanek Concentration Camp* (in Polish), quoted in Ainsztein, *Jewish Resistance*, p. 235.

were located in the region juridically incorporated by Hitler within the Reich. Chelmno was closed down as early as the spring of 1943, apparently for ever, but subsequently reopened to take the 7,000 wretches surviving with Rumkowski in the latter's collapsed little empire, the Lodz ghetto. For the five months previous to January 1945, and with the Red Army just a few miles away, the activity in Chelmno was restricted to the feverish obliteration of the evidence. A German trial at Bonn estimated its liquidation statistics as 150,000 Jews and 20,000 Russians and gypsies.

Alone in the East, Auschwitz-Birkenau was captured undestroyed, except for the crematoria, and complete with its records and files. Many inmates survived to tell their tale, and so we know so much: the medical experiments on twins by Josef Mengele, the sterilisation practices of camp physicians Carl Clauberg and Horst Schumann, and the tattooing for number identification of 405,000, including children. Let us leave them to their evil designs still in 1943, while we resume the Jewish story from less cheerless perspectives.

The year 1943 was blessedly leading the conquered nations of Europe to thoughts of the dawn, though as we have already noted, the lesson still remained largely unlearnt in Germany itself. The Final Solution had not succeeded in keeping pace with the Nazi triumphs, and the eager, earlier co-operation of the puppet states was now faltering. Denmark, which had docilely surrendered in 1940 and jumped to the orders of SS Obergruppenführer Werner Best, now grew difficult and refused in September 1943 to hand over its 7,000 Jews. They were secretly ferried to Sweden, together with their 1,200 Aryan kin. Best could find only 400. These were dispatched to the ghetto at Theresienstadt, which has aptly been described, because of its 'light' regime, as a Potemkin village. It was the solitary place in the Nazi kingdom of death allowed to receive a visit from the Red Cross.

With the exception of Yugoslavia and Greece, neither of which conceded absolute victory to the conquerors, virtually no fighting on a perceptible scale occurred within the length and breadth of Europe by early 1943. The Germans had taken the precaution of consolidating their hold on Vichy France, achieved with the barest of protest. Partisan activity hardly reached any significant level even in Poland, where the underground Home Army would remain, for a long time yet, an infant force. The Nazis were nevertheless desperately anxious to be done with the Jews. They decided on the next stage while they still had time: liquidation of the ghettos. They would begin with Warsaw. There the Jews had only lately discovered that after the ghetto only one destination remained for them. The reign of terror applied to the Poles also, as we have seen; they too were burning in Auschwitz (half a million before the ovens went cold). But most of them could nevertheless exist, and hope to outlive the devil. Not so the Jews. Hence they determined to fight back.

For any Jewish revolt against the oppressor to attain more significance than a mere gesture, it could only occur in Warsaw. The ghetto had originally been established behind a perimeter wall nine feet high and eleven miles in extent, and was criss-crossed by public transport. On being reduced to one-quarter of this size its incarcerated 450,000 made the ghetto the most densely inhabited settlement in the pit of occupied Europe. Except for legitimate business in the service of their masters the Jews could leave it only in collusion with Poles and on risk of death. Warsaw beyond the walls concealed the headquarters of the Home Army, led by General Stefan Rowecki. This force possessed a considerable store of weapons salvaged from the collapse of Poland in 1939, and certain Jews were aware of it.

At its inception the ghetto presumed a continued existence, albeit in a form suggestive of the Middle Ages. The Jews arrived there with whatever of their property was movable – money, jewellery, even pianos – though radios were forbidden. Dentists brought their equipment, schools their books, printers their cases of type. Factories converted to German ownership turned out supplies under contract for the Wehrmacht. The *Judenrat* or Jewish Council worked with the zeal of frightened men painfully conscious of the penalty resulting from a command disobeyed. Illicit commerce in its fashion united those inside the ghetto to those outside. Guards traded with the Jews, even supplying the occasional pistol in exchange for cash or some article saleable on the black market. Poles could be 'bought' through the walls, to provide information, run messages to other ghettos, indicate escape routes along the sewers and send in luxuries for those able to afford them. Stronger inmates oppressed the weaker, teachers strained to give the community a reason for living, and while some Jews in Warsaw passed their monotonous evenings chatting in the cafés, others begged for food and sank into a state of demoralisation from which death might be termed a happy release. In April 1942 one case of cannibalism was discovered. This was duly reported to the ghetto historians engaged in what they regarded as a sacred obligation to record the times in all their agonising detail.[31] Six thousand of the people were classed as Jews only in the sense of the Nuremberg laws, and isolated themselves from the others except in the food queue. What hope of a revolt from all this human material? And yet each political cell – Bundist, Zionist, Communist – nurtured a military arm in the expectation of a signal from some risen Spartacus.

The Warsaw ghetto worried the SS Command intensely as a centre of potential sabotage and espionage, and as a breeding ground for infectious diseases that could engulf them all. Himmler required its liquidation already in the summer of 1942. The factories and workshops, employing several thousands, would close down, the people removed to Treblinka. The Wehrmacht protested, citing the necessary war material produced there for the armies in the East, and the general shortage of skilled labour. In the end the SS won. Ludwig Fischer, Warsaw police chief, summoned Adam Czerniakow, 'Eldest' of the Jews (head of the *Judenrat*), and notified him of a pending transfer of the Jewish population for 'resettlement' at a more suitable site further east. Czerniakow, in many ways a committed servant of his people who had in fact surrendered a permit to go to Palestine early in the war so as to remain with them, wished to believe Fischer when told that this would be healthier for the Jews, and earn them an increase in rations. Czerniakow informed the ghetto accordingly. The first transports left, carrying some 5,000 a day.

At this juncture the inmates learned of the ultimate purpose of the 'resettlement'. For a young member of the Bund, Zalman Frydrych, got himself smuggled out of the ghetto and, masquerading as an 'Aryan', managed with the help of a Polish

[31] B. Mark, *The Struggle and Annihilation of the Warsaw Ghetto* (in Polish), quoted in Ainsztein, *Jewish Resistance*, p. 554.

363

railwayman to follow a train-load to its destination, which transpired to be Treblinka's gas chambers. Discovering the deception, Czerniakow could not bear to face his people. He swallowed poison. The evacuation proceeded, block by block, their occupants driven to the *Umschlagplatz* (departure point) in Stavki Street by the truncheons of the Jewish police. Some resisted boarding the cattle-trucks, to be shot on the spot. By the autumn of 1942 two-thirds of the ghetto population was gone. Plans were then activated for rebellion. Every day counted, but each little fighting unit kept its own counsel.

At length the left-wing Zionists joined with the Communists to form the 'Jewish Combat Organisation' under the twenty-four-year-old Mordecai Anielewicz, whose mother and sister were among the earliest transported. His only training had been in the Zionist youth movement. The right-wing Zionists, the so-called 'Revisionists', stayed independent as the 'Jewish Military Union'. Eventually the Bundists joined the first body, while a few young people from the religious camp went over to the Revisionists: a motley force of 1,200 in all, among them a fair proportion of women. Their preparations extended to barely more than the digging of a labyrinth of underground passageways leading to the sewers, and the manufacture of Molotov cocktails or simply detonated grenades, together with a few rifles acquired from the Poles outside. Couriers maintained contact with Rowecki's Home Army, which was linked by radio to London. Immediately, problems of an unexpected kind arose. Urgent requests for assistance sent by Anielewicz to Rowecki put the latter in some difficulty. To his mind the revolt was premature; the Jews should not venture in a hopeless fight but await an order from the Home Army. Nevertheless he wished to help, but the Jews had formed exaggerated ideas of his arsenal. Some of his officers, of the old Polish élite, considered it a waste to give them precious weapons: who had ever heard of Jews with a will to fight?

Meanwhile, Rowecki could get no response from London on whether to pass some of his store into the ghetto. He sent a quantity of small arms notwithstanding, including two ancient machine-guns. In the end Sikorski ordered Rowecki from London to provide assistance rather to the Russian and other partisans gathering in the forests. In fact Free Polish and British air crews had for several months been flying missions to drop stocks to Rowecki for this purpose, but practically none of it reached the Jews.[32] It was now January 1943.

Himmler arrived with Globocnik to inspect what remained of the ghetto. By this time the anxieties of the Jewish fighting organisations centred on likelihood of betrayal. Intelligence was definitely reaching the Gestapo via Jews with connections over the wall, for armed German troops were entering the ghetto. This resulted in the execution by Anielewicz's men of one suspect, Alfred Nossig, formerly resident in Berlin as a Zionist colleague of Chaim Weizmann. Then, at long last, the two combat organisations united under the young man's command. They were not yet ready, but shots had been exchanged and this was enough to warn the Germans that the entire ghetto had better be eliminated at the earliest possible date. They selected SS Brigadeführer Juergen Stroop for the task.

It was intended to complete the evacuation in one swift operation. Stroop, a dedicated Nazi, enlisted armed Latvian and Ukrainian sections to flush the Jews out. He estimated just a day or two, and began the *Aktion* on 18 April 1943. Taking up their positions, the Jews thought it inconceivable now for the Home Army to stand idly by.

Unhappily, a few days previously Germany made an announcement of devastating impact upon the Poles: the discovery of a mass grave containing thousands of Polish officers in the forest of Katyn, near Smolensk – massacred, declared the Germans, by the Russians on taking over their share of Polish territory. Sikorski in London had long requested information from the Soviets on the disappearance of some 10,000 of his officers during that period. Russia however countercharged that the Germans were guilty. This statement Sikorski refused to accept pending investigation by the Red Cross. Stalin thereupon broke off relations with the government-in-exile, proclaiming it a Fascist body and no longer his ally. Sikorski, in response, forbade the Home Army from helping any Communists, with the consequence that no more assistance reached the ghetto Jews, a proportion of whom were indeed Communists.

[32] Ainsztein, *Jewish Resistance*, p. 603.

Brigadeführer Stroop kept a daily journal of his action against 'the subhumans and bandits', illustrated with photographs and grandiosely titled 'The Warsaw Ghetto Has Ceased to Exist'. This tells how a tenacious defence kept his soldiers in combat for twenty-eight days. They resorted to flame-throwers to burn every building to the rafters, then dynamited the bunkers and flooded the sewers to prevent escape. Jews not part of the Anielewicz organisation stepped into the positions of those who fell. As the SS force pressed forward, the Jewish Command occupied a strongly reinforced bunker at 18 Mila Street, previously the hide-out of the ghetto criminal fraternity. And there Anielewicz died, to be succeeded by Isaac Tsukerman. Some of those left still succeeded in escaping through the sewers. Tsukerman and his wife Sylvia Lubetkin lived to fight again with the partisans. After the war they reached Palestine and established a kibbutz there.

Virtually all resistance ended on 13 May, the night of a heavy Russian bombing raid on Warsaw. Incredibly, survivors continued to find their way out of the destroyed ghetto for the next two months. His work done, Stroop was posted back to Greece to resume his old anti-partisan command. His report on the destruction of the Warsaw ghetto turned up during his trial at Nuremberg. The American prosecutor there, Supreme Court Justice Robert Jackson, stated: 'I hold a report written with Teutonic devotion to detail, illustrated with photographs to authenticate its almost incredible text, and beautifully bound in leather with the loving care bestowed on a proud work ... It contains a day-by-day account of the killings.' Having been sentenced to death by the Americans, Stroop was handed over for retrial in Poland, and was hanged on 8 September 1951 at the scene of his iniquity.

While the titanic struggle proceeded in the East, and the Second Front still languished as a planner's blueprint, a million Jews beyond the battle lines lived with the hope of outwitting destiny. Some eluded deportation by concealment and masquerade, though most by the hesitant courtesy of those governments not completely under Nazi subjection and therefore enjoying a vestige of manoeuvrability. Germany's stampede of conquest and control had shifted to a strategy for its own survival. Time had also revised the ranking among the principal Allies, with America now the senior Anglo-Saxon partner and Russia demanding all the deference owing to an associate who did most of the fighting and suffered most of the sacrifice. The million Jews, domiciled in the main in Hungary and Romania, concerned the Soviets very little. But the Anglo-American leaders could no longer ignore them as hitherto, for they were now under heavy pressure from their own Jewish citizens to address themselves to the tyranny. Transportation to death could well befall the remnant of European Jewry before Germany was finally forced into surrender. Surely these at least could be saved?

It thus transpired that, during the battle for the Warsaw ghetto, a conference of Anglo-American representatives, wholly divorced from discussion relating to the prosecution of the war, took place in the sunshine of Bermuda. This conference was initiated by the British, public opinion on the need for Jewish rescue being far more vociferous in Great Britain than in the United States. Archbishop Temple told the House of Lords on 23 March 1943: 'We at this moment have upon us a tremendous responsibility. We stand at the bar of history, of humanity and of God.' Whitehall was persuaded.

Arrangements for the Bermuda Conference had proved peculiarly arduous in the making. The British invested the proposal with urgency, but at the State Department it came within the province of the antisemitic Breckenridge Long. He allowed it to repose in his files for five weeks without action. Ultimately Long agreed to a meeting, though in a location far removed from Jewish influence in London or New York. Hence Bermuda. Roosevelt himself was barely troubled in the matter. The State Department nominated a somewhat low-level delegation, which however included one Jew, Democratic Congressman Sol Bloom of New York. Their British opposite numbers comprised three senior members of government, men well briefed in the issues involved.

In the event, the conference became a replica of that futile earlier meeting at Evian (see page 321), another sop to the public conscience. It terminated in a conspiracy of inaction, based upon premises identical with those of its empty predecessor: not a word from the British on the United States stand against relaxing its immigration laws; not a sound from the Americans on

London's refusal to shelve, if only temporarily, its Palestine policy. And again, the mutual fear of releasing a flood. Incredibly, they found they could do virtually nothing about sending food into Europe (why feed the empty stomachs of untold millions on Hitler's behalf?). Although the two powers communicated regularly with Germany over exchanges of POWs and non-combatant civilians from their respective countries, to discuss the removal of Jews out of German hands would equate with negotiating with the enemy! They refrained from exploring the possibility of sheltering refugees temporarily in neutral countries against post-war financial reimbursement.[33] Indeed, the Bermuda Conference kept the Jewish situation well away from its concerns, for fear of the impression of this being a war fought for Jewry specifically and not for humanity as a whole – a subject upon which the American public was particularly sensitive.

Congressman Bloom proved more Catholic than the Pope in burying his stricken fellow-Jews beneath a mountain of excuses and alibis. All the delegates returned home without a solitary achievement of substance, though they arranged the evacuation of 630 refugees out of the 5,000 French Jews sheltering in Franco's Spain to a camp in North Africa – and that took another year to effect. A more demonstrative consequence was the self-immolation in London of Samuel Ziegelbaum, Jewish member of the Polish National Council (in fact the Bundist representative). Ziegelbaum escaped from Poland in January 1940, on instructions from his party. Before committing suicide two weeks after Bermuda he left a letter:

> The responsibility for this crime of murdering the entire Jewish population of Poland falls in the first instance on the perpetrators, but indirectly it is also a burden on the whole of humanity, the people and governments of the Allied states which thus far have made no effort towards concrete action for the purpose of curtailing this crime. By the passive observation of the murder of defenceless millions and of the maltreatment of children, women and old men, these countries have become the criminals'

[33] Report of Bermuda Conference in *Foreign Relations of United States*, 1943, Vol. V; Public Record Office, London, CO 733/449, 7620⁸/2.

associates. As I was unable to do anything during my life, perhaps by my death I shall contribute to breaking down the indifference.[34]

Ziegelbaum's wife and children, left behind when he escaped to London, had already been shot in Poland.

To some extent America succeeded in redeeming itself through the protests of an influential few, latterly made. The writer Dorothy Thompson published a Christmas manifesto against Hitler signed by fifty leading Americans of German descent. Christian notables, prominent among them the theologian Reinhold Niebuhr, spoke out against the shame of Bermuda. Thomas Mann, himself a privileged refugee, implored the United States to modify its entry laws and rescue what was left of European Jewry. Nevertheless the established Jewish leadership under Rabbi Stephen Wise (Roosevelt's 'friend Stevie') still hesitated from raising a clamour lest this might imply criticism of the man in the White House. However, much to the embarrassment of the official Jewish spokesmen, a small right-wing Zionist group, composed in the main of Palestinian citizens resident in the United States, came forward to fill the gap. It placed sensational full-page advertisements in the press (the copy sometimes written by playwright Ben Hecht) that turned the Jewish mood from 'respectable' agitation for a Jewish army to an aggressive demand for realistic American efforts at rescue. This novel form of press propaganda – later an American commonplace – stirred, among others, Secretary of the Treasury Henry Morgenthau Jr, scion of a family with a long tradition of Jewish service. Stepping from his own bailiwick, Morgenthau taxed the State Department for information. He then set out to investigate that department's record on the refugee question since the outbreak of war. His discovery that intelligence from Europe had been consistently played down or suppressed filled him with alarm. He put his own Treasury staff on the trail. In January 1944 they were able finally to produce their accusatory dossier: 'Report to the Secretary on the Acquiescence of this Government in the Murder of the Jews'. Morgenthau took this personally to the President. Incidentally

[34] *New York Times*, 22 May and 4 June 1943.

perhaps, 1944 was an election year. Morgenthau's intervention had an immediate effect. On 24 January, Roosevelt signed Executive Order 9417, creating the War Refugee Board. America had finally committed itself.

Gratifying it would indeed be to describe how the War Refugee Board succeeded, while Anglo-American troops moved up the Italian peninsula, Russian armies were across the old Polish frontier and Germany itself reeled under incessant air raids, in extricating a multitude of Jews from the mass executioner's axe. It didn't. Not only had the hour of salvation come too late; governmental initiative did not extend to financing such an agency. The WRB drew its budget mostly from Jewish sources (the American Joint Distribution Committee), signifying that its efforts would be vitiated through going largely unsupervised, in fact ignored, by official Washington. For all that Congress was concerned, it could have been a charity for the protection of superannuated cart-horses.

The best that could be said of the WRB's influence was its exploitation of the diminishing loyalty of Hitler's allies at the shrinking extremities of his authority. Romania, for example, repudiated an agreement with Eichmann to deport Jews to Lublin, and at WRB instigation brought home many thousands of survivors conscripted into slave labour in Transnistria. After the war Romania proclaimed, somewhat proudly but nevertheless disingenuously, that no Jew under its control died in the extermination centres.[35] In fact *force majeure* played its part. With the Russian recapture of Odessa and the approach of Soviet armies towards Romanian territory, the country hastened to switch sides. Earlier, it had willingly co-operated with the *Einsatzgruppen*.

Stalin had little patience with the War Refugee Board, which in his nose carried an aroma of treating with the enemy. He had borne the brunt of the war so far, by his calculation reprieving England from certain conquest. Who had intervened to save his own people during their long blood-letting? As for America, it

[35] See, e.g., statement by Ion Ratiu, a Romanian diplomat: 'Romania refused to deliver a single train for the gas chambers, despite tremendous pressure from Goebbels' minions. Only Denmark can say as much.' *Observer*, London, 15 March 1970.

had merely arrived in time for a European victory cheaply earned. Stalin could therefore be discounted now as a participant in the deliverance of what remained of Jewry in the East. The last great community whose fate hung in the balance, in Hungary, had so far escaped martyrdom. But extreme danger lay ahead.

At this stage of the extermination programme the Nazis doubtless felt their concept of a *judenfrei* Europe to be slipping from reality, along with their dream of a thousand-year Reich continent-wide. At Wannsee, Adolf Eichmann had been entrusted by Reinhard Heydrich with a mission of genocide, and so far he had discharged it well. Nowhere had he been completely successful, even in the case of Poland, but nowhere had his labours met with total failure. He had not betrayed his oath to his Führer. There could, however, have been an incipient flagging of his zeal. The last of the death camps, at Auschwitz-Birkenau, was due for closure and metamorphosis into pastureland. Eichmann could therefore make a virtue out of necessity. Why not spare the Hungarian Jews, together with others, and trade them against supplies of which Germany was now in dire need? This too could be a great service to Hitler. In the event of failure then clearly it would be revealed to posterity that Germany was not unique in regarding the lives of this people as of no consequence.

Eichmann arrived in Budapest and on 8 May 1944 made an astounding offer to a Jewish spokesman there, Joel Brand. He would release a million Jews in return for 10,000 trucks, to be used only on the Eastern Front. He also required 200 tons of tea, 200 tons of coffee, two million cases of soap and quantities of such scarce materials as tungsten.[36] Brand received the proposal in stunned silence as Eichmann invited him to fly to Istanbul and in that neutral territory initiate the Jewish Agency into the negotiations. Evidently some Nazi leaders were now seeking refuge in fantasy, for a similar *démarche*, made by Himmler himself, had reached the Jewish Agency the previous year. The police chief had proposed a meeting with Joseph Schwartz of the Joint Distribution Committee, preferably in Spain, to discuss the ransom of 100,000 Hungarian Jews in return for goods not at

[36] Statement of Rudolf Kastner, a Zionist colleague of Brand later assassinated in Israel, dated 13 September 1945, ND 2605-PS.

that time specified. Schwartz had wired his New York headquarters for instructions, to be told of a Washington veto on any meeting with the Germans for a discussion of what was palpably a blackmail device.[37] Now the Nazis, grown more desperate, were raising the stakes.

Admiral Horthy, Regent of Hungary and an early admirer of Adolf Hitler, had revealed himself as an uncertain wartime ally. He willingly poured his troops into Russia during the days of triumph, but the loss of half his army and most of his war equipment in the fierce battle on the Don south of Voronezh in January 1943 changed him into a man of peace, repeatedly sending out feelers to the Allies. Horthy refused to take his Fascist regime to the ultimate in antisemitic persecution as practised by the Nazis. He possessed 650,000 Jews, plus another 100,000 baptised 'non-Aryans' within his territory, one-third of them inherited with his acquisition (by courtesy of Hitler) of traditional Hungarian land from Slovakia, Romania and Yugoslavia. He had his scruples, except in the case of 11,000 refugees not regarded by Horthy as his responsibility; these he had driven across the frontier into the Ukraine, where, overtaken by Wehrmacht operations, they had been left to starve. The fluidity of the Hungarian situation gave the Jews considerable leeway for action. Joel Brand and others of the Zionist Organisation maintained good sources of information on the fate of the Jews in Poland, as well as underground contact with fellow-Zionists gathering intelligence in Istanbul and Geneva.

Following Mussolini's overthrow in Italy, Horthy decided to show still more independence from Germany, and spare his country, not to mention himself, the impending disaster. Too late. In March 1944 the SS moved in, installed a more pliant government and confined Horthy to his Budapest castle. As an immediate priority Eichmann placed the Jews under his close control and, on 15 May 1944, precisely while Brand prepared for that bizarre mission, he began deportation, at the rate of four train-loads per day. Auschwitz was soon crammed full of Hungarian Jews awaiting execution. Only 300,000 remained in Hungary, with some 200,000 of them in Budapest, all living in the

[37] Agar, *Saving Remnant*, p. 151.

most horrific conditions. The Russians had not yet crossed the Hungarian frontier. His family remaining behind, Brand arrived in Istanbul with a shadow, Andor ('Bandi') Grosz, a former Jew in Gestapo service, undertaking to return with a speedy reply. Brand failed to comprehend that a proposition such as he so urgently carried would not be settled to his satisfaction in a matter of days, if at all. To Brand's chagrin, he and Grosz were lured into Syria and taken into British military custody. Time passed.

But wasn't there another avenue of rescue, not dependent on German co-operation? Of course, the destruction of Auschwitz, and the railway lines leading into it, from the air! It was only a few weeks, in fact since late April 1944, that the exact location of Auschwitz-Birkenau had been defined. Two Slovak Jews had actually escaped from Birkenau after their gruesome employment there for some eighteen months. Until that moment this greatest extermination centre could be identified only as 'a location in Poland'. And so, while Brand was being debriefed in Cairo and he waited in vain for the Allies to open negotiations (Grosz having been 'eliminated' as a German agent), the two Jewish Agency leaders then in London, Weizmann and Moshe Shertok – the latter having just arrived after interrogating Brand – begged Anthony Eden to send in the RAF and bomb the Auschwitz installations. Brand had warned Shertok that every day lost meant thousands more Jews lost.

Eden readily agreed and, supported by Churchill himself, instructed Archibald Sinclair, the Air Minister, accordingly. Here the difficulties were raised: Auschwitz was beyond the range of night bombers, and daylight raids seemed too hazardous; such a diversion of air crews could not be justified at this critical juncture, the assault on 'Fortress Europe' having begun (6 June 1944) from England. Similar requests made in New York at the behest of the WRB likewise met with negative replies. Yet within weeks both American and Anglo-Polish air crews, based in Foggia, southern Italy, were flying over the vicinity of Auschwitz, refuelling on Russian soil, in the one case to bomb the synthetic rubber plants, in the other to supply the Polish Home Army now in action during a general insurrection in Warsaw. Some bombs, though by mistake, fell on the extermination camp itself, perhaps fifty yards from the gas chambers.[38] Sour paradoxes of this kind featured not infrequently in the conduct of the Second World War.

Meanwhile Joel Brand, held firmly in British hands, was dreading, as he justifiably might, every moment of delay. Understandably, the British assumed his mission to be a vehicle carrying overtures of peace to the Western Allies, primarily intended to divide them from Russia, a motive Bandi Grosz himself had taken little trouble to conceal under interrogation. Yet the Jews could not but feel the possibility within their grasp of saving a remnant of their people. No less an opponent than Lord Moyne, marked out for impending Jewish assassination, suffered a change of heart. He telegraphed home from Cairo that they 'should not impose a mere negative to any genuine proposal involving the rescue of Jewish victims'. Still, the known British attitude on the danger of 'flooding' Palestine with refugees cannot be discounted in their refusal to allow negotiations to proceed. Britain moreover was in no mood to quarrel with the Russians. Prudently, it communicated the Eichmann proposition to Moscow, fearing the consequences of a 'leak'. The Russians of course stamped it into the ground. In any event Horthy, in a last desperate move to rehabilitate himself with the Allies, risked a new challenge to his masters by halting further deportations from Hungary. Eichmann continued to feed Jews from other regions, including France, into the death machine. One who survived: the sixteen-year-old Simone Veil, of Nice, elected in 1979 as first President of the newly founded European Parliament.

In October, Horthy sued for peace. The Russians were closing in, but their enemy refused to acknowledge the loss of Hungary. The Nazis kidnapped the regent, brought him to Germany and installed an Arrow Cross government under the ultra-antisemitic Ferenc Szalasi as chief of state. It was a renewed period of torment for what remained of Jewry both within the capital and beyond. Deporting them to Poland was by this time out of the question, and transportation took place westward, mostly on foot, to the concentration camps nearer the Nazi heartland.

[38] For detailed accounts of discussions on the bombing of Auschwitz, see Martin Gilbert, *Auschwitz and the Allies*, London, 1981. Wyman, *Abandonment of the Jews*, more closely follows the American aspects, pp. 288–30[7].

Thousands died of hunger and exposure. When just 160,000 still survived, all compressed within a squalid Budapest ghetto, the WRB succeeded in intervening to interrupt this final episode of their anguish. Late though it might be, this was one of the few redemptive moments of European conduct towards the Jews during the Second World War. For the WRB obtained the practical intercession of the pope at last, and of the International Red Cross, together with the goodwill of Spain, Portugal, Switzerland and Sweden, all neutrals, in the task of rescue. While the Red Cross sent in food, these governments, and the Vatican, provided extraterritorial sanctuary with diplomatic cover to invest the Jews with their national protection.

History will forever connect the name of Raoul Wallenberg with the intergovernmental endeavour. The young Swede came to Budapest for this express purpose, placing the cloak of immunity against further persecution around some 20,000 Jews. When Soviet troops entered Budapest, in February 1945, 120,000 were found there, and Wallenberg was already a legend. In the confusion attending the city's capture he disappeared, never to be seen again—only 'sighted' in the USSR's own concentration camp system, the *Gulag*. The Russians may have suspected Wallenberg's credentials: his WRB contact in Sweden, Iver Olsen, was in fact a member of the American Office of Strategic Services, precursor of the CIA.[39] According to the Soviets, Wallenberg died of a heart attack during imprisonment in 1947, though this has by no means been established to Swedish satisfaction.

How to draw up a balance sheet of guilt and innocence in the destruction of European Jewry during the Second World War? On the one side Hitler and his Nazi fanatics constituted an absolute, bringing the doctrine of antisemitism to its inexorable conclusion in a holocaust of lives. Besides Hitlerism all Christendom became to a degree involved, shading off from active co-operation in the design to an existential hostility towards the Jew *per se*, and finally reaching indifference, which proves guilt by passive association. Free Jewry itself, because of its timidity, belongs in the equation.

The remorselessness of war breeds its inconsistencies, confus-

---

[39] Stated by William O'Dwyer, Washington chief of WRB, in 1945. See Wyman, *Abandonment of the Jews*, p. 243.

ing objectives. In taking up the struggle against Hitlerism, Great Britain naturally placed its own survival before any other consideration. Hence it acted out of thoughtlessness, apathy and panic when a spirit of understanding would have mitigated the Jewish ordeal somewhat. German-Jewish refugees in Britain found themselves behind barbed wire together with German Nazis in Britain. Others, hastily judged a security risk, were dispatched across the seas to drown in a U-boat attack. The United States, at war with Japan, took patriotic residents of Japanese descent into brutal internment. In the American South, German prisoners of war rode at the front in public vehicles, while black citizens, also *Untermenschen* of a kind, occupied the rear. The French under that old anti-Dreyfusard Marshal Pétain collaborated with their masters with a zeal in rounding up the Jews which even surprised the Germans, and great French writers, notably Robert Brasillach and Louis-Ferdinand Céline, loudly conducted the intellectuals' war against the Jews although French dignity might have impelled silence upon them. Germany never lacked for volunteers among the conquered nations in speeding the Final Solution forward. Stalinism, which was Fascism in reverse, condemned liberated Russian prisoners to a slow death in Siberia. The fortunate Jews of Sweden performed less honourably for their persecuted brethren sheltering in Stockholm than their gentile neighbours did.[40]

The Jews of Palestine, just half a million strong, conducted themselves at the opposite extreme. They were largely spared the rigours of war – no bombs, no food shortages, no conscription – but mourning for their European kin assumed the form of an ever-deepening bitterness against Britain. They alone, of the Jews living in freedom, took the law into their own hands in the cause of rescue. No illegal Jewish immigrants reached Sweden, or England, or the United States; but the Zionists, employing daring and cunning, saved whom they could by smuggling them into Palestine against all British efforts to frustrate them. A substitution of hostility resulted, the German enemy being remote, the harsh British administrators close by. It therefore transpired that in 1944, when the immigration of 75,000 was due to run out and

---

[40] Report of Iver Olsen, quoted by Wyman, *Abandonment of the Jews*, p. 230.

with the war at its pitch, a war which had to end in the destruction of Germany if it was to end at all, two Jewish groups in Palestine, the Irgun Zvai Leumi and the Stern Gang, launched their own private struggle against Britain. Their weapons were sabotage and terrorism. It was not as though the British had completely stopped all immigration in obedience to the White Paper: the war had put Palestine policy in flux once again, as everybody now recognised.

No national struggle is complete without its subsidiary conflict between moderates and militants, and so it happened in the case of the Irgun–Stern combination and their bitter rival, the official Jewish Agency. While the moderate leaders of the Agency pleaded in London for a specific Jewish military arm to fight Hitler, and for action to rescue the few still surviving in Europe, the others preyed upon the British from their safe positions in Tel Aviv and Jerusalem. The Zionists got their fighting force at last in August 1944, albeit in the stunted form of a brigade group, but the Irgun and the Stern Gang, led from the underground by Menahem Begin and Itzhak Shamir (each would later have his hour as Prime Minister of Israel), continued their own unrelenting battle. In the Stern Gang's case this extended to the point, as we have told, of assassinating Lord Moyne, Britain's political representative in the Middle East.

Thus we have reached the end of a war that began hesitantly with sporadic gunshots across the Franco-German border and terminated in a Promethean challenge to the elements with atomic blasts over Japan. Some nations had been more fortunate than others, but all were transformed. The Jewish people, having paid the greatest price, emerged from the war as the same constitutional nullity in which they entered it: without a land of their own, or a voice among the nations. Twelve years after Adolf Hitler seized the reins of control in Germany, the most catastrophic epoch in the history of antisemitism – one impossible to relate in its entirety – closed round the architect of Europe's graveyard in his bunker beneath the Chancellery building in Berlin. Of the many millions who perished, only the Jews were from the beginning intended to die. They were condemned by deliberate sentence, the others being the incidental casualties of Hitler's ambition to raise a nation purged of any genetic deficiency, a nation of Nordic supermen and women, to the summit of power. The exact arithmetic of extermination eludes us: five million, six million Jews destroyed? Some have calculated more, some less.[41] But a new geography of Europe bears the tale, and a scale of horrors ascending from the most western concentration camp at Drancy near Paris to the Babi Yar slaughterhouse outside Kiev.

While the victorious nations, if such they were, could inspire later generations with their triumphs at El Alamein, and Stalingrad, and Guadalcanal, Jewish history can tell only of tragedy superimposed upon tragedy, a story in which armies of ghosts stalk at Auschwitz, extermination capital of Europe; and at Bergen-Belsen, where an advance column of shocked British troops discovered thousands of unburied corpses; even after Belsen's liberation, 3,000 more were still destined to die.

It has often been said of the Jews that in constantly reminding Christendom of its greatest shame they have become vindictive. Why chase a fugitive like Adolf Eichmann out of his Buenos Aires obscurity and compel him to relive his demonic past at a show trial in Jerusalem fifteen years later? What purpose now to expend effort to establish whether Josef Mengele, the vivisector of humans, be alive or dead? Or to drag an elderly Ukrainian, presumed to be 'Ivan the Terrible' of Treblinka forty-four years earlier, from the USA? The German people themselves have displayed their contrition in countless ways: they continue to instruct their children in the agonising legacy of hate bequeathed to them, and have named 120 schools after Januscz Korczak, who could have saved himself yet chose to enter the gas chambers with the children in his care. Young German volunteers work to this day anonymously among the aged and infirm in Israel, neither demanding nor receiving recognition as they expiate the sins of their fathers. Germany has repaid its debt to society in the only way possible, by financial reparation to individuals fortunate enough to have survived, and to Israel collectively with subsidies keeping the young state from bankruptcy. Surely a moment must arrive when the appetite for retribution is sated!

[41] The figure of six million was the earliest rough computation. Reitlinger, a meticulous statistician of the Holocaust, gives, in *The Final Solution*, two estimates: low, 4,204,000; high, 4,575,400.

The argument carries its element of validity. But the world does not expect the Czechs to forgive and forget Lidice, the mining village totally destroyed in 1942 with its inhabitants massacred in retaliation for the murder of Reinhard Heydrich; nor the French Oradour, the little township set on fire in 1944 together with all 652 inhabitants by the SS division Das Reich for the crime of concealing, not using, explosives. Forty-five years after the discovery of Katyn the Poles were still demanding investigation of that crime. The Jews have suffered a thousand Katyns. How do they live with the memory?

They can face it only by a determination to become the masters, not the victims, of their destiny. Antisemitism may perhaps, like the common cold, never be cured. But the lesson the Jews have learned from the Holocaust is to ensure that it will never assume genocidal dimensions again.

12

End of Exile

Once the tumult and the shouting died, Europe gradually revived as a continent capable of living with itself. National grandeur was now a much depreciated commodity. Old-style antisemitism, seeded in religion, nourished on racial animosities and borne along by economic resentment, lapsed as a political expedient. It was not dead; it had spent itself for the time being because of its embrace by the man who had plunged the world into catastrophe. The Soviet Union now contained the largest Jewish population in Europe, but that country was a secretive world, observed only with difficulty from the outside and understood hardly at all. By a pre-arrangement on 'spheres of influence', the Yalta Conference of February 1945 sanctioned a virtual division of the continent between East and West as never before, with Russia, for the first time in its history, assuming the role of greatest European power. A huge legacy of unfinished business remained, at the centre of which stood the remnant of the Jews. What to do with them? Where should they go? Whose problem was it? A new item appeared on the international agenda: Displaced Persons. They belonged to various nationalities and were diverse in religion.

Streaming away from the devastation of the eastern war the Displaced Persons came to rest, most of them, under the umbrella of the Allied occupying forces in West Germany, Austria and Italy. Geographical frontiers were undefined and loosely guarded. Those who had found refuge in the Russian interior joined the flow while time allowed, until the Iron Curtain descended across the continent. From Germany's surrender in May 1945 to the end of 1946 eight million such DPs, uprooted by the hostilities, survivors of concentration camps, forced labourers, collaborators on the run, people spared through finding themselves at the lucky end of the long queues to the gas chambers, orphans and others from homes, families and neighbourhoods destroyed, the stragglers, the destitute and the demented, they turned up as a colossal responsibility of the victorious Western nations – to be fed, clothed and provided with accommodation. Where possible their identification was ascertained or verified, and family connections traced. When the sorting was done some seven millions secured repatriation to their former homelands. They included many thousands of Jews returning to France, as well as other deportees prepared to rebuild their lives in the Low Countries, Italy, Hungary and the Balkans.

Hardly any Jews of German or Austrian nationality, pitifully few as they were, could conceive of resuming where they had left off in those centres of their worst persecution. This applied to Poland too, and in any case that country proved deeply antagonistic to their return, emphasising its mood with a pogrom at Kielce in Lower Silesia that killed forty-two Jews in July 1946.[1] Manifestly, the solution to the problem of 'non-patriable' Jewish Displaced Persons would be found only in emigration. This should not have encountered difficulties. Barely a quarter of a million homeless Jews were now left. They waited in camps, in institutions for the young and disabled and in city dwellings commandeered by the occupying authorities for their use. But who would make the first move? England, the United States, Argentina, Australia? Empty space abounded on the world's surface.

The Jewish DPs vegetated in more senses than one. Without the spirit to help them rebuild and restore the past, they appeared as people deprived of their soul. Like the rocks swept along in a landslide they were components as well as victims of the collective European disaster. For them life fell into a series of negatives:

[1] Cause of the pogrom remains a mystery, though most likely it was born of resentment as Jews, returning from sanctuary in Moscow, sought to reclaim confiscated property. It started with a rumour that a local boy, who turned up two days later, had been abducted. During a subsequent enquiry the Soviet and Polish military authorities tried to implicate anti-Communist elements in the West. See Michael Checinski, *Poland: Communism, Nationalism, Antisemitism*, New York, 1982, pp. 21–34. Allegations were made of Jewish participation in the local black market. Eleven Poles found guilty of the pogrom were executed. *The Times*, London, 18 March 1987.

hatred of the soil on which they stood, and of the Christian world that had abandoned them; distrust of law; and an inability to plan, rebel or mend themselves. Their bitterness extended also to their brother-Jews across the seas, deemed guilty for having been spared. Such neurosis was of the kind suffered by survivors of an earthquake or, as in Japan, of an atom bomb. They received abundant assistance now, from the charity wholeheartedly bestowed by their more fortunate brethren, especially those in prosperous America. All the populations of ravaged Europe had to endure intense privation at that time, but the Jewish DPs suffered no hunger. They possessed coffee, cigarettes, dollars in profusion. This led some of them into a flourishing black market, to make one at least a millionaire without leaving the precincts of his Displaced Persons' camp constructed out of a cleansed Bergen-Belsen.

Thus months, and soon years, passed as this human material waited unwanted and in suspense. The United States, the globe's overriding power and still with three-quarters of its old immigration quotas unfilled (in 1945 by the accumulated total of 800,000), would not accept any but a thin trickle. Neither would Britain, nor the members of its spacious Commonwealth, nor the countries of Latin America. Their selfishness struck an ugly pre-war note. But this did not reckon with a new, aggressive element in one section of Jewry. As much by default as deliberate design, the Zionists proclaimed the Jewish Displaced Persons as their own. Out of that bruised humanity the Zionists knew they could build pioneers, and breed a majority in Palestine, and thus constitute themselves into a state. Inspired by David Ben-Gurion, a rugged leader of resistance in the making, skilled emissaries from Palestine arrived in Europe under the guise of social workers. They turned the DP camps into a Zionist domain of such thoroughness as to warrant their description as a colony of the Palestine community itself. The emissaries assured the drifting refugees that they were not only wanted in the homeland but needed, and this *because* they were Jews, not despite it. Moral pressure did the rest. Indeed, those preferring to await a visa for other destinations were branded as renegades. Youthful activists would parade in their camps with huge banners proclaiming 'No one leaves this place except for Palestine!'[2]

[2] Reported by Lord (Robert M.) Morrison in House of Lords, 31 July 1946.

But what of the 1939 White Paper? According to a logic understood by the British electorate alone Winston Churchill had sustained an overwhelming defeat at a general election, bringing the Socialist Clement Attlee, a calculating, unemotional politician, into office as Prime Minister. Attlee's party had regularly condemned the White Paper, describing it as a violation of both the Balfour Declaration and the Palestine Mandate.[3] The new Foreign Secretary, Ernest Bevin, had strongly supported the Zionists in his days as a trade union leader. Now he granted an allocation of 21,000 entry certificates to complete the 75,000 total laid down in the White Paper and, as though conceding the annulment of that edict, he offered the Zionists an additional monthly allocation of 1,500. Chaim Weizmann, still their principal spokesman and a statesman of the Jews respected throughout the world, demanded instead the abolition of the miserable system of periodic hand-outs to allow the Zionists to empty the camps. Rescue teams waited on the spot. They could begin with dispatching an immediate 100,000 to Palestine and continue from there. The only acceptable sequel to the European holocaust, Weizmann declared, was the Jews' own control of immigration in an independent Jewish state.

The first Foreign Secretary of a much weakened Britain obliged to wrestle with both the new Russia and an Arab world awakened to strong national feeling, Bevin gave open vent to his disappointment at what was revealed to him as Weizmann's failure to understand the facts of life. Did the Jewish leader expect him to embark upon a path entailing the military pacification of the Arabs? One day perhaps, after negotiations with that party, the request for 100,000 might be granted. For the present, as he stated at a press conference on 13 November 1945, 'Should the Jews want to get too much ahead of the queue you have the danger of another antisemitic reaction.' This observation, a fatal blunder on Bevin's part, rang round the world. The Jews wished to hear no more of queues, having been pushed to their head at Auschwitz and Treblinka.

That old docile resignation to the commands of others belonged to their past. Bevin's attitude indeed gave the British pacification problems in Palestine, but with the forces of Zionism in rebellion rather than with the Arabs. The Palestinian Jews

[3] E.g. in a Resolution of the Labour Party Conference at Southport, 1939.

contested London's right of jurisdiction over their affairs. They employed the conventional weaponry of battle – rifles and grenades against the soldiery and installations of the Mandatory authority – and established underground pathways of illegal immigration out of Europe and across the Mediterranean. The angry, co-ordinated voice of their people over the world functioned as a rearguard campaign. The unfortunate Bevin was himself labelled an antisemite, to burn in effigy in front of the British consulate-general in New York. Once again, the American Jews salved their conscience by generating passionate feeling against Whitehall while remaining passive towards Washington, as though their own country had no substantial contribution to make.

American Jewry had emerged from the war as a highly vocal element of transatlantic society, five million strong at least, organisationally bonded and politicised for action to a degree unequalled by any other of the country's many ethnic minorities. About ten times as many Jews lived in the United States as in Palestine, at least twice as many as in Russia, and in 1945 more than half of them inhabited metropolitan New York. They had ceased to travel hopefully; they had arrived, to constitute the strongest single unit Jewry had known since the Dispersion. And although New York was not America, it radiated its cosmopolitanism and cultural radicalism over the country as a whole. Zionism worked no personal attraction upon the American Jew, but he espoused the doctrine totally on behalf of his less endowed brethren elsewhere. He knew the strength of his political clout. So did the United States Congress. It was no accident, therefore, that in 1945 President Truman challenged Britain by placing the authority of his office behind the Zionist demand for the immediate intake of 100,000 refugees to Palestine.

In the meantime, the disorders in that country assumed a triangular pattern, British, Jews and Arabs all in conflict with each other. The Jews proved more than merely troublesome. Their Haganah (self-defence arm of the Jewish Agency) contained a highly skilled, whole-time militia now undertaking operations in association with the Irgun Zvai Leumi and the Stern Gang, both of which it had previously outlawed as terrorist. Each of these groups used New York as its shop-window and supply centre. The ships approaching Palestine with illegal immigrants scored immense capital for Zionism in other countries too, especially since British destroyers mostly intercepted the vessels and put the Jews in camps (barbed wire again!) first in Palestine and later in Cyprus. Attlee (incidentally, he had twenty-six Jews on his parliamentary benches to the Conservatives' one) became enraged.

He deeply resented Truman's identification with the Zionist agitation for the 100,000. Its hollowness as anything but a pandering to the President's domestic Jewish constituency became manifest in a public statement, made in August 1945, that 'I have no desire to send half a million American soldiers there to make peace in Palestine.'[4] Evidently, his partisan stand eschewed any responsibility for the consequences. This was unacceptable to Attlee. In an astute move the British Prime Minister secured American participation in an enquiry into the problem of the Jewish DPs and their bearing on the Palestine impasse. This Anglo-American Committee of Inquiry heard evidence in Washington, in Europe and in Palestine itself: twelve men with their ears bent in different directions. The Americans listened more attentively to the Jews, the British to the Arabs. Of the Washington hearings, Richard Crossman, a left-wing intellectual nominated by Bevin to serve on the committee, wrote: 'The Zionists are passionately anti-British and have obviously organised nearly all the American Jews and all the press. The case for the Arabs, and indeed the difficulty of putting a million Jews suddenly into Palestine, simply goes by default here.'[5]

The irony of the situation appeared at times to approach the level of gallows humour. The Jews had their champions everywhere, deeply sympathetic to a people whose ordeal but a year or two earlier could hardly be absorbed in human comprehension. Anxious to atone for the sins of Christendom, the civilised world was one in execrating antisemitism. It grieved for those left to rot in their DP camps yet balked at a contribution towards solving the problem. While Truman endorsed the plea for the 100,000, it took him two laborious years, 1946–7, to secure the entry of

[4] *The Truman Memoirs*, London, 1956, Vol. II, p. 144.
[5] R. H. S. Crossman, *Palestine Mission*, London, 1947, p. 47.

39,000 homeless Jews to his own country. This miserable concession almost exactly equalled the number admitted by the British
to Palestine in the same period. Bevin told Parliament of a visit
from the veteran South African Prime Minister Jan Smuts
(unnamed, but referred to as 'a great statesman in the British
Commonwealth') and adored by South African Jewry. Smuts
had added his petition on behalf of the 100,000, whereupon Bevin
asked: 'How many will you take? I will get a ship and send them
to you tomorrow.' The response was silence.[6] And a South
African Jewish leader, Simon Kuper, president of that country's
Board of Deputies, unblushingly testified to the Anglo-American
Committee of Inquiry that they had taken 260 Jews in five years,
but this had caused antisemitism, so the prospect of further
immigration was practically nil.[7]

Painfully effecting a compromise of views, the Anglo-
American Committee reported in its conclusions that Palestine
should have neither a Jewish nor an Arab state (deferring to
British desires), but the 100,000 should be allowed in at once (the
American judgement).[8] The report, to say the least, displeased
Attlee. He equivocated, announcing his acceptance of the
findings but contingent upon America's sharing the military and
financial burdens incurred. A further pre-condition applied to
the Jews directly. They must disband the militias which kept the
British army so busy in policing Palestine. Those militias also
protected the Jews from the Arabs, and the Zionists rejected the
terms. So did the Arabs themselves, who clamoured for an independent Arab Palestine. The Anglo-American report, along with
the Peel Commission's pre-war investigation of the same problem in 1937, stayed on the shelf. The deadlock continued. The
situation deteriorated.

Hungry for international attention, the Jews seized every
opportunity to humiliate their traditional friend Britain. Iron
entered into the determination of a people whom the world
habitually overlooked. Amidst the misgivings of the Jewish
Agency leadership, Menahem Begin's Irgun now assumed an

[6] House of Commons Report, 25 February 1947.
[7] Hearings of Anglo-American Committee of Inquiry, *New Judaea*, London,
March–April 1946.
[8] Cmd 6808, London 1946.

independent initiative for direct operations against the British. On 22 July 1946 they blew up the wing of the King David Hotel in Jerusalem housing the headquarters of the Mandatory administration. This resulted in ninety-one Arab, British and Jewish dead and many injured. Before long martial law was imposed. Then, bowing to pressure both at home and abroad, Ernest Bevin conceded defeat. He could no longer conduct a policy that brought Britain the contempt, unuttered but by no means unregistered, of friendly governments everywhere. London was about to hand independence to an India partitioned between Hindus and Muslims. A parallel of sorts existed in Palestine, though paramount power there legally resided in the international community. Bevin therefore passed the problem over to the United Nations, heir to the League of Nations which had conferred the Mandate, and confident no doubt that its members, so eager to criticise, would not succeed where he had failed. A UN Special Commission on Palestine set to work.

British rule in Palestine had not been conducted with total insensitivity towards the Jews; nor had it, in the thirty years of its duration, been without achievements. A substantial degree of autonomy for the pioneer community had been theirs from the beginning; the Arabs could have had it too, had they not expressed their opposition to Zionism in consistent non-co-operation with the country's rulers. An ambience of dignified beauty spread over the land, from Jerusalem whose spoliation by uncontrolled building the British prevented, to the stately port of Haifa which they had constructed, and to the inspiring land reclamation schemes they had encouraged. Jewish colonial officials, British born, ranked high in the Mandatory administration, but of Arabs there were few. And it was a British declaration of state which had made a beginning possible. Yet British rule is retained in the memory as though epitomised by one old immigrant vessel, *Exodus 1947*, acquired in America, refitted at La Spezia under the tolerant eyes of the Italians and loaded to the scuppers with refugees through the courtesy of France. It limped across the Mediterranean towards Haifa. Then, while the UN's investigators watched from the harbour shore, *Exodus* was boarded by the Royal Navy – England's pride – and its passengers, after harsh deprivations, returned in three floating prisons to DP camps in the country reponsible for their supreme misfortune: Germany.

So ended an epoch. The thoughts uppermost in every mind except the British government's were finally voiced by the UN's Special Committee on Palestine. A majority of seven members (Canada, Czechoslovakia, Guatemala, the Netherlands, Peru, Sweden and Uruguay) proposed the division of the Holy Land into two independent states, with Jerusalem a separate province under international trusteeship. India, its thoughts upon its own large Muslim population, Iran for a similar reason and Yugoslavia, which expressed a Communist view of Zionism, together signed a minority report favouring a solution on the basis of an Arab–Jewish federal state, but in which Jewish immigration would cease after the two communities achieved numerical parity. Australia, which had managed to find asylum for a shameful sprinkling of homeless Jews since the end of the war, stood on the sidelines, uncommitted to either solution.[9]

The Zionists were thus awarded all they could hope for when the majority report, with slight modification, was adopted by resolution of the UN General Assembly on 29 November 1947. They danced the night away in the streets of Tel Aviv and Jerusalem. On the other hand, Arabs of all nationalities rejected the decision as an affront to themselves and the UN Charter. This major diplomatic defeat for Britain was made even more ignominious by its sour, mischief-making exit from Palestine. More blood would flow before the end, and more attempts by illegal immigrants to run the blockade. In view of the Arab reaction, and the threat by their various governments to invade the Jewish area so as to forestall the establishment of an independent state there, and the immediate proclamation of a general strike by Arab leaders within the country, Britain condemned the United Nations solution as unworkable. It would not be party to its implementation. Nevertheless it announced its own intention to terminate the Mandate on 15 May 1948, come what may, and evacuate Palestine by the date specified in the United Nations Resolution – 1 August.

Overall governmental authority promptly ceased to exist, and

[9] Report to the UN General Assembly, A/364, London, 1947.

the anticipated civil war between Arab and Jew took its place. In another classic miscalculation of where the strength lay, the Foreign Office intensified its wooing of the League of Arab States whose birth Anthony Eden had inspired, in the fond belief that this grouping would end up in control of the situation.

The Zionists had overturned every traditional preconception of the Jews' political impotence. They had demonstrated their ability to conduct a successful crusade on the basis of a series of unprovable hypotheses: that only with a state of their own could they defeat antisemitism and put an end to what had always been termed the 'Jewish problem'; that statehood, had it been granted them years before, would have enabled them to save the millions who perished in Europe; that their people everywhere would hasten to share in the blessings of Jewish citizenship; and that Jewish independence would benefit the Arabs equally with themselves.

Had they been correct in all these assumptions then this account could have mercifully terminated with the establishment of the State of Israel in 1948. Unhappily, the Jewish question emerged where previously it had rarely been perceived. Antisemitism burst out in new directions, and at once. Following the UN Resolution the virus spread, for the first time in many decades, to countries where the Jews, enjoying communal autonomy, resided in peaceful neighbourliness with the Arabs. The disease doubtless required description by another name, both races being Semitic, but the effect was the same. From Casablanca on the Atlantic coast of North Africa to Baghdad in the heart of the Middle East the Jews felt a change of relationship: in some places merely a stony hostility, in others an anti-Jewish hysteria erupting into violence. The change occurred well before Israel declared itself an independent state; a difficult road, both diplomatic and military, had still to be traversed until that consummation. In all the capitals of the West, Jews anticipated the forthcoming Jewish state with enthusiasm. Multitudes of Christians endorsed their joy. To Muslims everywhere it foretold tragedy. They now affirmed their brotherhood with the Arabs of Palestine where such an instinct had not hitherto been strongly demonstrated, though the British, old colonial Arabophile realists as they were, had long been warning of its existence.

Consequently Jews in the Muslim countries dared not rejoice. They had played an imperceptible part in political Zionism, which was specifically a European national movement of the Ashkenazim. The Mediterranean divided the Ashkenazim from the bulk of the Sephardic branch, the latter having crystallised in the mass with a profile largely Orientalised and Arabised. This had resulted from their extended epoch as a tolerated minority embedded within the civilisation of the Koran, where nationalism lagged at least a century behind, and economic development had been paced out at the discretion of distant masters, first in Constantinople and subsequently in empires ruled from London, Paris or Rome. Not all Sephardim belonged to the type, of course, but it was exclusive to them. The Zionist dream of statehood, once expressed by Theodor Herzl in a simplistic though revealing novel,[10] leaned towards the establishment of a Switzerland on the Jordan. He prophesied a nation secular, democratic, liberal and technologically advanced – concepts remote from what had once been a great Islamic civilisation but was now in eclipse, it seemed forever. The Jews of this region were in the main wretchedly poor, but so were the Arabs. However, they did not live in universal dejection. In Algeria the Jews enjoyed the privileges of French citizenship, in Morocco they were protected *dhimmi* of the sultan, in Egypt they controlled the banks, while in Baghdad, where they exceeded a third of the city's population, Jews were conspicuous in commerce, teaching, artisanry and petty trade as in pre-war Warsaw. As a group they remained impervious to the ideals of European Judaism, just as they were largely untouched by European culture. In Palestine, Ashkenazim and Sephardim lived side by side, but spoke different languages and looked in opposite directions.[11]

Few Sephardi Jews had ever attended a Zionist Congress; not one of them had sat on the Jewish Agency Executive. Neither they nor the Ashkenazim appeared inordinately bothered. But human behaviour rarely falls into absolute categories. As in the case of their Muslim neighbours, religion ruled a large part of Sephardi lives. And the religion of Judaism promised the arrival

---

[10] *Altneuland*, 1902; English edition tr. as *Old-New Land* by Lotte Levensohn, New York, 1941.

[11] See, e.g., Elie Eliachar, *Living with Jews*, London, 1983.

of the Messiah, be he ever so far away or just round the next corner, to restore the people to their never-forgotten homeland. So how could they not regard the UN Resolution as a signal of divine intercession in their affairs? Not surprisingly, therefore, the Jews located within the Muslim world noted the prospective revival of the nation with a compound of exhilaration and apprehension. We speak here of fewer than a million altogether, and of the eleven million Jews left throughout the world at the end of the Second World War they were the least assimilated and the least articulate. Now, with Nazism destroyed and Arab nationalist feeling given a focus of resentment, they also became the most vulnerable.

Thus the earliest casualties of the UN decision lived remote from Palestine. Disorders first broke out in two British possessions, Aden and Bahrain, with the loss of seventy-six lives. Those responsible for inciting the mobs made no distinction between apolitical Jews and Zionists; for that matter they detected hardly any between Jews and Europeans as a whole, for the latter protected the former and were extracting from the Arabs retribution for their own antisemitic crimes by stealing Palestine and presenting it to the afflicted race in compensation. Zionism was nominated the handmaiden of imperialism, and the Jews situated in their *mellah* (ghetto) beside the kasbah were an easy target through which to attack those kindred evils. Ugly incidents occurred in cities where Jews and Arabs were closely intertwined in their interests, even united in business partnership as in Beirut and Aleppo.

The sands of British rule were running out in Palestine, with tension increasing, so that the country was now rarely absent from the preoccupations of the United Nations in New York. Jews felt the chill of pogrom more and more frequently in the Muslim countries. Rioting in Morocco, despite the exhortation of restraint upon his subjects by the sultan, led to forty-four deaths. In Cairo, 250 non-Muslims died through indiscriminate killing of Jews and Europeans in general, though the news broke through official censorship only when a journalist travelled to Istanbul to report the massacre.

The Arab states clearly intended to fulfil their threat and invade – unless the clock was stopped in Palestine. In Iraq all

Jews would shortly be declared enemy aliens, and their venerable chief rabbi, Sassoon Kadourie, sent to jail. If the Jewish state were to survive it could register the end of a Sephardic diaspora dating back six centuries before Christ. Such a possibility was not lost upon the Jews preparing for independence in Tel Aviv, the world's only all-Jewish city. They told themselves that once they had emptied the DP camps in Europe, another rescue operation would await them in the Muslim world. This great reservoir of Jewry, now under threat for the first time, could well provide the immigration necessary for the country's future. In the meantime, as foreign Arab irregulars poured into the vacuum created by the vanishing British to help their local Palestinian brothers assume control, Ben-Gurion determined that this territory would be defended to the end. The last time the Jews had fought independently of others and exclusively on their own behalf had been the Bar Kochba revolt of AD 135, and that war they had lost. This time the Jews were strongest in the coastal plain while the Arabs enjoyed concealment by spreading themselves over the hills.

The relative strength of the two sides foretold a grim and costly struggle ahead. The Jews were now 650,000 in Palestine, a population of disconnected elements (some not even Zionists) and just one-quarter their number in New York City. Valour was unevenly distributed. The enemy comprised 1,200,000 Arabs in Palestine supported by a limitless mass organised on national lines at their rear. Within five weeks of the November UN Resolution to partition this land into two states, and before the Arab governments sent their troops in, rival armies came into the open and fought out possession of hill and roadway. The retreating British watched from the cover of their tanks as six hundred Jews and Arabs perished. Ben-Gurion's military situation looked hopeless. He had once served in the Royal Fusiliers but had never tasted action. Not every Jew offered him allegiance; the Irgun and the Stern Gang took up independent positions and fought their own way.

At their forum in New York the United Nations observed the results of their good intentions in consternation. Russia smelt a capitalist rat and accused Britain of fanning the disorders by its attitude of aloof non-co-operation in the partition scheme. Refugees were still being turned away from Palestine, while

Jerusalem, planned by the UN to have a supranational regime surrounded by a *cordon sanitaire*, changed from a city of religious calm into a beleaguered nexus of fortified strong-points, short of water and down to basic rations.

Washington feared that the chaos ensuing from the British departure would necessitate a policing operation on international lines. James Forrestal, President Truman's Secretary of Defense, shared the State Department's displeasure at the administration's benevolence towards Zionism, which he regarded as unwarranted provocation of the Arab countries of the Middle East. He testified before the House Armed Services Committee in January 1948 that the 'unworkable partition scheme' would cost America the oil supplied by that region. The United States must therefore take steps without delay to disembarrass itself of the proposal and secure its withdrawal.[12] The Army Chief of Staff, General Eisenhower, expressed another anxiety: if they were compelled to send troops to Palestine to police the country they might well have to reintroduce the draft, and the American public would not tolerate such an eventuality. Then again, American strategy in the Middle East not only worried about the Arabs. It feared the intrusion of the Soviet Union into an arena traditionally the preserve of the Western powers. Russia supported Arab and Jewish independence with suspicious ardour. Did the partition plan conceal a sinister Kremlin trap to get its foot in the door?

Under the force of these arguments Truman attempted a political somersault: indefinite postponement of partition and the transfer of Palestine to the aegis of the UN Trusteeship Council. Infuriated, the Zionists foresaw a complete sell-out of their interests, perhaps the brazen continuance of Great Britain in the new, unholy guise of 'Trustee'. This put Truman in a quandary. He was due for re-election in 1948, and his chances of return to the White House were rated very poor should he lose New York State, and impossible should he forfeit also the Jewish vote expanding in California. Truman could not count on the unswerving loyalty of the American Jews to quite the same

[12] Special Sub-Committee on Petroleum, *Hearings*, 80th Congress, Second Session.

degree as had Roosevelt. Indeed, their most energetic Zionist leader now, a turbulent priest out of Cleveland, Ohio, named Rabbi Hillel Silver, was a Republican. He loomed as a threatening force in politics. The President's advisers in the Democratic Party, particularly his counsel Clark Clifford, warned of the perils of crossing American Jewry. They had been Jews of silence during the war and would not now repeat that shame. Truman later wrote: 'The White House was subjected to a constant barrage. I do not think I ever had as much pressure and propaganda aimed at the White House as I had in this instance. The persistence of a few of the extreme Zionist leaders – actuated by political motives and engaging in political threats – disturbed and annoyed me.'[13]

Truman could not but worry for his future. Despite giving an instruction to his staff to allow no more Zionists into his presence, he consented to receive the now venerable Chaim Weizmann, never an 'extreme' Zionist, and made him a promise: no matter what the American delegate might state to the United Nations in public, he, the President, would honour America's word. Should the Jews proclaim their state he would grant it recognition.

The question went before a special session of the General Assembly late in April 1948, and heard the American delegate's proposal for Trusteeship. The nations in New York were still fumbling over their next move weeks later, on 14 May. It was twilight, near to the sabbath in Tel Aviv. British rule would formally end the next day and, in anticipation, Ben-Gurion convened a meeting in the city museum and announced to the world the creation of an independent Jewish state, to be called Israel. Within the space of minutes the United States accorded it recognition, followed swiftly by the Soviet Union. No Arab state was declared.

The first measure adopted by this youngest nation abolished the 1939 British White Paper on Palestine. It opened its gates to the immigration of Jews from all corners of the Dispersion. It undertook to develop the country for the benefit of all its inhabitants without distinction of religion, race or sex. It would

---

[13] *Truman Memoirs*, pp. 168–9.

uphold the rule of the United Nations and be guided by the principles of liberty, justice and peace as conceived by the Prophets. The signatures on the Proclamation of Independence, thirty-seven names constituting the Provisional State Council, were barely dry when Egyptian planes flew over Tel Aviv to bomb the city's tiny airfield. At first light five countries of the Middle East – Egypt, Transjordan, Syria, Lebanon and Iraq – crossed the frontiers to reverse the decision and bring Palestine back into the Arab fold.

That 15 May the Jews will always recall, and the world with them, as a defiance of history and a challenge to destiny: the end of Exile. Whether they would keep their tiny state no one could be sure. Many were doubtful, for the people were untested in making laws, or in electing governments, levying taxes or negotiating treaties. Jews were known to be clever at trade, excellent musicians, talented in science and the arts. Such qualities were important, but a nation also needed builders, soldiers, self-discipline. Democracy was achieved with experience through evolution; it had rarely succeeded when imposed.

The Arabs recall the first stirrings of this people reborn in another event – a pogrom. That word traditionally applied to assault by gentiles upon defenceless Jews, innocent victims of a lust for blood. It now appropriately described the fate which befell an Arab village on the outskirts of Jerusalem on 10 April, weeks before Ben-Gurion called his state into being. The modern portion of Jerusalem, almost completely Jewish, was isolated and surrounded by the enemy based upon the Old City, Arab though not so completely. From Suleiman the Magnificent's sixteenth-century walls the Arab Legion, belonging to Britain's nominee Emir of Transjordan and commanded by British officers, dominated the scene. In Jerusalem Menahem Begin's Irgun refused to acknowledge Ben-Gurion's leadership and fought how and where it chose. In association with the Stern Gang, the Irgun determined to take the village of Deir Yassin and thus ease a Jewish opening from the land-locked Holy City to the coast. Begin's force encountered unexpected resistance. It called for help, to be answered by a small detachment of the Haganah's crack troops. Soon the place was pacified, and the Haganah men left. What then ensued adds a dark and disfiguring episode to this story, clouding the heroism earned by the Jews in the defence of a homeland legalised by the supreme international authority of the United Nations. The Irgun called through loudspeaker upon the inhabitants of Deir Yassin to surrender. There was no response. Perhaps the non-combatant villagers, out working in their fields, did not hear the call. Perhaps they were afraid. However, the next move of the Irgun was to slaughter 240 to 250 men, women and children, bringing some corpses back to Jerusalem to vaunt their capabilities.

Deir Yassin undoubtedly marked the original savage stroke in the cycle of violence that has characterised Arab–Jewish relations in the Middle East from that day to this, and is still without prospect of termination. An Arab band retaliated three days later by intercepting a Jewish convoy on its way to the Hebrew University and the Hadassah Hospital situated on Mount Scopus. It left the bodies of seventy-seven doctors, nurses and university faculty staff lying on the road. And another consequence of Deir Yassin: the flight in panic of Arabs from all parts of the contested ground. Zionist history has written of their departure as being completely of their own volition, in the conviction that they would return to a rich prize once the Jews were pressed to the coast and perhaps driven into the sea. The truth resides rather in their fear of a repeat of Deir Yassin. Frequently, noise proved adequate as a weapon to drive the Arabs away. They fled from Jaffa, Safed, Tiberias, and many from the mixed city of Haifa. They rushed into Lebanon, into Transjordan and south to Gaza. The 'official' war with the Arab states had not yet been launched, but it was already tragically apparent that the Jews would be solving their refugee problem by the creation of an Arab refugee problem. Though with this significant difference: the Arabs became refugees among people of their own race and faith.

Hostilities lasted sixty-one days. An arms embargo, imposed upon all the warring factions by the Security Council despite Soviet opposition, had little force and was easily circumvented. Israel procured its weapons, flown in by Jewish volunteer air crews of British, American and South African nationality, from France and Czechoslovakia (the latter covering for Russia). The earliest arrivals from the European DP camps were quickly put into uniform and enrolled as a second-line reserve, the brunt of the fighting being carried by young men from the old settler class reinforced again by 5,000 volunteers mainly from English-speaking countries. In the early skirmishes preceding the establishment of the state the Jews had fared badly, but they now demonstrated that no fighting force in the Middle East, organised or irregular, confronted piecemeal or taken together, was a match for them. They secured the area of Palestine allotted to them in the UN decision and a great deal more besides. Egypt occupied a strip of territory around Gaza, but its best troops remained encircled and could retreat across the frontier only consequent upon an armistice with Israel. The Emir Abdulla of Transjordan annexed a huge enclave west of the Jordan, retained his hold on the Old City of Jerusalem and changed the name of his country to the Kingdom of Jordan to emphasise his rule on both sides of the river. Thus Palestine was cleared to give Israel the entire coastal plain as far as Lebanon, all the Negev and Galilee. Jerusalem, bespoken for internationalisation, became a prize divided, but the Jews won a broad corridor through the Judean Hills enabling them to strengthen their hold upon their half of the city. The Palestinian Arabs lost everything, including their spirit. Just 160,000 of them, Muslim and Christian, remained to enter Israeli jurisdiction as a sullen, leaderless minority whose future would stay a question mark. Yasser Arafat, born in Jerusalem, kinsman of the first Palestinian revolutionary the Grand Mufti, was eighteen years old. Now he drifted from Gaza to Cairo to Kuwait, awaiting his day. Thirty years later it had still not dawned.

The consequences of calamity fell upon the five invading Arab countries. Their lacklustre performance in the harsh realities of war brought their governments into disrepute at home and disregard abroad. One by one they came to grief. Abdulla, once in the pay of the Zionists,[14] always a British pensioner, alone emerged with his position intact; but only until 1951, when the discovery of his secret negotiations with Israel cost him his life at the hands of an assassin in Jerusalem.

Israel's casualties included some 6,000 killed, a third of them civilians. The cream of the tiny nation's youth died – the first

[14] See Weizmann, *Letters and Papers*, Vol. X, 1977, p. 338.

generation of pioneers actually born in the country. Within eighteen months a half-million immigrants replaced them: the residue in the camps and remnants unwilling to reside in East European countries, now under Communist regimes, which formed the landscape of their wartime sorrows; then almost the entire Jewish population from primitive Yemen, 35,000 people transported by air; and substantial groups from Turkey, Morocco, Libya, Egypt. This gave Israel 110,000 Arabic-speaking Jewish citizens, with still more on the way. The rest of the world contributed few. Israel declared those others would surely come to their senses and arrive in the end, if not induced by antisemitism then spontaneously, because here, and here alone, could the Jew live unfettered by gentile restraints. Some Israeli spokesmen dropped their guard on the subject, almost betraying a vested interest in antisemitism. But in regard to 'idealistic' immigration the country would always experience disappointment.

Although there would be no peace, the establishment of the state placed the Jews as a whole in a uniquely favourable position among the world's peoples. For it gave them two complementary sources of strength, Israel itself and Diaspora Jewry. Sometimes their attitudes would conflict. Occasions arose when Israel adopted policies discomforting, even frightening, to many Jews beyond its shores. Israel in its turn resented advice from outsiders who scorned its proffered citizenship. But the combination in general brought benefits to both sides. Independence won for Israel a seat at the United Nations, ambassadors in the major capitals of the world, the right in fact to be heard whenever Jewish interests seemed threatened – no need any more to resort to intermediaries, or enter through back doors, as in the past. Particularly, American Jewry helped the process of Israel's development by functioning as a supplementary exchequer for the state. Israel would eternally lament that the Diaspora did not contribute enough funds to speed the absorption of immigrants; the Jews outside would caution the state against going too fast, or being too ambitious and adventurous. But such differences are in the nature of partnership. When raised on the homeland's behalf, the ubiquitous Jewish voice gave added potency, denied to other nations, to the spread of Israel's message. In New York,

London, Paris, Geneva, Johannesburg and elsewhere that voice penetrated to parliaments and the press, to commercial centres and the faculty rooms of universities. Wherever members of the tribe concentrated they would speak out on Israel's achievements and its desire for peace with the Arabs. Years needed to elapse before the Arabs would enjoy the assistance of a supportive voice of equal, if not superior, force. The oil revolution would work that miracle, but it was not to be foretold, and it came too tardily to redeem the Palestinian cause.

On their side of the balance sheet, the Jews of the world gained enormous psychological capital. Israel heralded the destruction of one old stereotype of antisemitism, the unproductive, pusillanimous ghetto Jew. Now they too could exult in the glory of a victorious war, such as nourished the morale of races throughout history but of which they were previously deprived. Israel's other achievements filled them all with pride: newcomers of diverse origins and characteristics welded into a nation; a soil reclaimed to make the desert blossom; industries and cultural institutions of Western standard in a region not yet properly awakened to the twentieth century. All these, and in addition the redemption of Zion giving reality to the Psalmist's dream. Closely following upon their recent European experience, a resurgent confidence transformed Jewish thought and action. Even the most irreligious, assimilated Jew felt closer to Israel than did the Boston Irishman to the Emerald Isle, or the Chicago teamster to Poland, or the Australian to his ancestral motherland Great Britain. The state bestowed a vicarious citizenship upon him. That much he did not welcome, for he had no wish to complicate his allegiance to his own nationality. Yet it was his nevertheless. What, then, were the repercussions in the Soviet Union?

On the morning following the UN Resolution of 29 November 1947 Chaim Weizmann had telegraphed the delegation of the USSR: 'You have placed our people under an eternal debt of gratitude by your noble action during these days of stress and strain.'[15] And in 1948, on the anniversary of the Russian Revolution, Ben-Gurion's message of congratulation to Josef Stalin included these words: 'We shall never forget the assistance that

---

[15] Ibid., Vol. XXIII, 1980, pp. 51–2.

the Soviet Union extended to the Jews, victims of Nazism, and her consistent support for the people of Israel in their war for freedom and independence in their historic homeland.'[16] Most of Ben-Gurion's Cabinet, born in the tsarist empire, spoke Russian. It should have augured well for future relations between the two peoples.

In the event things were developing differently. The Communists had no objection to Zionism when applied to refugees, but could not tolerate the creed as a global epidemic infecting the Jews of their own country. Their ideology taught that Zionism exploited religious feeling for retrograde national purposes, and as endorsed by America was a naked tool of imperialism. Disconcertingly, the Russian Jews, far from obliterating such sentiments, had greeted the arrival of Israel with the same fervour as their people elsewhere. This new state showed every sign of reviving ideas of interrelationship of a kind that denied working-class solidarity in favour of racial and religious criteria. The tendency of the Jews within Stalin's empire to enthuse over Israel indicated, in Marxist eyes, a loyalty to a foreign capitalist country. Ben-Gurion had issued an open invitation to Jews everywhere to return to the fold. Did this not include, by implication or directly, the minority within the Soviet Union? For proof positive, Golda Meir, minister plenipotentiary of the new government accredited to the USSR, brought crowds into the streets in a rapturous welcome when she attended the Moscow synagogue on the Jewish New Year. Such a demonstration was merited in this closed society only by Stalin himself.

It horrified the Russian dictator to perceive that a dissenting Jewish spirit, despite a generation of atheistic education and official decrees, continued as a pernicious survival from the bad old days before the revolution. Yet the Soviet constitution outlawed antisemitism. Stalin had wooed the Jews as best he could, by granting those desirous for ethnic self-expression an autonomous *oblast* in Biro-Bidzhan, on Russia's Far Eastern border. True, this Jewish region ostracised the Hebrew language, which was declared a subtle Zionist instrument, but it fostered Yiddish instead, as the recognised tongue of a secular community taking

---

[16] David Ben-Gurion, *Israel: A Personal History*, London, 1971, p. 305.

equal place with other ethnic minorities in the Communist system. Biro-Bidzhan promised elevation, if sufficient Jews settled there, to the status of a full republic within the Soviet Union. Thus they could have their own kind of life and still remain within the Soviet fold. But the experiment proved a dismal failure, as unattractive as Siberian exile.[17]

Not that Jews without exception had repudiated Communism in consequence of the cynical pact between Stalin and Hitler, precipitating war, signed in 1939. Many clung to Marxism in New York, Paris and London (where one of only two Communists in Parliament won a largely working-class Jewish constituency at the 1945 general election). Moscow-trained Jews, riding on the upheaval following Germany's defeat, numbered prominently among the leaders of the Communist regimes established in Eastern Europe. Nevertheless an obstinate Jewish solidarity, forged, according to Communist thinking, from the legends of a spurious work, the Bible, and rooted in the mists of time, continued to expose the people as their own worst enemy. This astonished and irked the Communists. Was it possible for the Jews to be fired by such an event as the establishment, by half a million of them, of a petty state in the Middle East whose strength was no match for its arrogance? Indeed they could. Stalin decided to punish them for it. He now launched a campaign to warn his Jews that, whatever the reasons prompting his

[17] A revealing exchange at Yalta between Roosevelt and Stalin, not recorded in the official report, included a reference to Biro-Bidzhan. It is described by Charles Bohlen, an adviser to the American President at that meeting, as follows: 'After dinner at Yalta on February 10, Roosevelt had asked Stalin if he was for the Zionists. Stalin had answered warily: yes, in principle, but he recognised the difficulty of solving the Jewish problem. The Soviet attempt to establish a Jewish home at Biro-Bidzhan had failed because the Jews scattered to other cities. Some small groups had been successful at farming, he said. Roosevelt then mentioned that he was going to see Ibn Saud right after the Yalta conference. Stalin asked what he was going to give the king. The president replied, with a smile, that there was only one concession that he thought he might offer and that was to give Ibn Saud the six million Jews in the United States. Stalin said again that the solution of the Jewish problem was difficult. He called the Jews "middlemen, profiteers and parasites" and joked, "No Jew could live in Yaroslav" – a city noted for the sharpness of its merchants. Roosevelt smiled, but did not reply.' See Bohlen, *Witness to History*, New York, 1971, p. 203.

support of Israel's birth, the Zionist message would not be allowed to infiltrate the USSR or its satellites.

That eminent survivor of successive Moscow purges, Ilya Ehrenburg, was assigned the task of eradicating the disease. One of the great war correspondents during the recent struggle for Europe, Ehrenburg had tasted the Jews' cosmopolitan instincts as both a participant and a witness during the heady Popular Front days in pre-war Paris. He now proved more than equal to his Communist task. Ehrenburg's first attack upon Israel and Zionism appeared in *Pravda* on 22 September 1948, three weeks before Golda Meir's attendance at the synagogue and five days after she had formally approached the Soviet foreign ministry to 'let my people go'. His article denied the existence of bonds of solidarity between Jews of different countries. Israel might warrant support as a provisional refuge where Jews from reactionary states might shelter until the evil of antisemitism waned and the Jewish question was solved by the world-wide victory of the working class. But they should not be deluded: Israel was a capitalist country governed not by the people but by exploiters. Its rulers, under the pressure of Anglo-American capital, were liable to betray national interests for the sake of the dollar. Such a country could have no relevance for Jews in Russia, where antisemitism was a punishable offence. Newspapers throughout the USSR reproduced the article.

This was warning enough for any Russian Jew cherishing thoughts of a cultural-national renaissance inspired by Israel. Such beliefs were prudently to be kept under his hat. Perhaps also Ehrenburg's assault was the earliest lesson in international politics learnt by Israel, a nation born with the cold war between East and West reaching a climax. Perils attended every move of a small country in taking sides, and Israel had opted for association with the West. It desperately needed American friendship, both to safeguard the financial aid generously granted under the Truman Doctrine, and to maintain close ties with the multitudinous Jewish community in that country. Their official bodies passionately expressed their Americanism by yielding to none in their detestation of Communism – in fact it was loudly whispered that the powerful American Jewish Committee, whose well-endowed leaders conducted the affairs of the Joint Distribution

Committee, was a tool of the State Department disguised in Hebrew camouflage. The Kremlin certainly thought so. Consequently, as Israel drew closer into the American orbit Moscow became progressively disenchanted.

Russia had anticipated friendship from Israel in appreciation of the support tendered during the young state's early critical days. Russia lacked a foothold in the Middle East. On the other hand, the Anglo-American partnership, which owned and operated the oil fields, regarded this entire region as its own preserve. Israel was therefore fully aware of the significance of Western rather than Russian influence in persuading the Arabs towards a readiness for peace.

During the Second World War, when the Soviet Union was eagerly embraced by Churchill as an ally, and Stalin the despot achieved transmogrification into the benevolent 'Uncle Joe', Russia had relaxed its earlier persecution of religion. After all, weren't the clergy potent war propagandists in England and the United States? A zealous Soviet instrument, the League of Militant Atheists, was dissolved. Bishops appeared at Kremlin receptions. The Orthodox Patriarch, newly recognised as a Soviet stalwart, was graciously permitted to conduct a public service of intercession for the success of Russian arms. The Jews of Russia took their place in this new atmosphere of tolerance. They formed a Jewish Anti-Fascist Committee of writers and artists (Ehrenburg among them) which dispatched missions overseas and proclaimed from Moscow the inauguration of an age of 'world Jewish solidarity'. Alas, this benign policy disappeared as a casualty of the peace. Organisational religion survived, but only to limp along. Believers daring to challenge the official creed of godlessness suffered persecution and exile. Jews were singled out for special attention; unlike Christianity, Judaism implied a culture as well as a faith, and those who professed the religion were making an unacceptable political statement encouraging separatism. Thus Ehrenburg's article inaugurated not merely a campaign against Zionism but the elimination of all Jewish self-expression within the Soviet Union. It developed into a ruthless operation and coincided with the last paranoid years of a dictator haunted to the end by the ghost of his arch-rival of yore, the Jew Trotsky.

Historians refer to them as the 'Black Years'. Virtually every leading figure in Jewish cultural life, all ardently professing Communism, all piously 'Yiddishist' as opposed to Hebraist – poets, novelists, theatre directors, artists, musicians – they received that notorious 'knock on the door' and were rarely heard of again.[18] Many died in Siberian deportation, but twenty-four intellectuals faced a firing-squad in the cellars of the Lubyanka prison in Moscow. A celebrated actor and head of the defunct Jewish Anti-Fascist Committee, Solomon Mikhoels, encountered death in a staged motor-car accident. The victims included bearers of the Order of Lenin and officers decorated at the front. In this, the last great purge conducted by the NKVD's executioner-in-chief, Lavrenti Beria, few Jewish public figures slept secure, and none identified with national self-expression, even if ever so slightly.[19] Information on the removal of persons guilty of 'cosmopolitanism' reached the average citizen, but only in doctored instalments. The ruthless Beria himself fell victim to the process he commanded. No sooner had his fellow-Georgian Stalin died than the secret police received orders to execute him too. A convenient opportunity presented itself within the year.

Parallel with the purge came the systematic excision of all Jewish references from the Soviet hagiography, while the so-called complete edition of Maxim Gorky's writings, a thirty-volume venture which had taken years to produce, excluded all the writer's many references to Jews, Zionism and antisemitism. It was estimated that, of all those summarily disposed of, two-thirds were Jews guilty, in the words of the ideologist Konstantin Simonov, of 'the desire to undermine the roots of our national pride and ... liable to be suborned by American imperialism'.[20] Stalinist loyalty seemed recognisable by its metaphysical quality, for Lazar Kaganovitch, veteran of the revolution, held his place in the Politbureau, while Maxim Litvinov, celebrated in the 1930s as Foreign Minister, died in tranquil retirement. Ehrenburg wrote on, adjusting to the later Khrushchev thaw as if he had never besmirched himself as a Stalinist hack. Boris Pasternak too;

---

[18] Joel Cang, in *The Silent Millions*, London, 1969, pp. 225–8, lists 431 such Jewish intellectuals by name.
[19] For the terror in progress, see, e.g., *American Jewish Year Book*, 1950–4; Yehoshua A. Gilboa, *The Black Years of Soviet Jewry*, Boston, 1971.
[20] *Pravda*, 27 February 1949.

but then, the author of *Doctor Zhivago* was not known, even once, to shed a tear or write a line in any Jewish cause. In this way the identity crisis of Soviet Jewry was solved by the virtual eradication of its identity altogether. Fate was performing one of its balancing acts: Arabism dissolved in Israel, Jewishness obliterated in Russia. In neither case would it meet with total success.

As with all matters conditioning America's stance towards the USSR, controversy raged in the disputatious New York atmosphere over the veracity of reports of a Stalinist terror. The storm crossed also to the relaxed social climate on the West Coast, where Los Angeles had expanded into a metropolis with a large concentration of second-generation Jewish intellectuals. Corroboration of the reports coming out of Russia existed in the dispatches of disinterested newspaper correspondents, though the isolation enforced upon foreigners in that country necessarily limited their sources. Proof in abundance became available only after the death of Stalin in 1953. Meanwhile, Communist and anti-Communist Jews in America argued with a passion and assurance as though each was uniquely qualified to pronounce on the subject.

'Middle America', not just the far Right, feared Communism as the ideology seeking to poison the arteries of the nation, and diagnosed its seditious progress among the liberal intelligentsia of the large northern cities, where Jews were conspicuous both as 'nigger-lovers' and as agitators in the civil rights movement. The first DPs allowed into the country by special Act of Congress in 1948 gave preference to ethnic Germans and Baltic farmers, thus safely guaranteeing a preponderance of newcomers who were conservative in politics and Protestant by religion. Besides Communists, America pin-pointed 'fellow-travellers', hence widening the net to include thousands of people suspected on the slightest grounds. Modern Europe had a precedent for the crusade against 'heretics' in the Dreyfus Affair, which hung like a curse over French public life for decades. Witch-hunting in America, shocked into nervous activity by the Alger Hiss case,[21]

[21] Hiss, president of the Carnegie Endowment for International Peace and a former foreign service officer, denied he was a Communist before the House Un-American Activities Committee in 1948, and was subsequently sent to prison for perjury.

undermined the nation's confidence in itself, virtually mutilating its democracy. It split families, tore through the motion-picture industry and sent talented progressives into European exile. One episode in 1949 fomented an antisemitic, anti-Negro riot at Peekskill, Westchester County, when the pro-Soviet Negro singer Paul Robeson (his wife Jewish) ventured to fulfil an engagement at a fund-raising concert there in aid of the Harlem Chapter of the Civil Rights Congress. Robeson was supported on the platform by the Jewish writer (and Communist Party member) Howard Fast. Then the ultra-patriotic American Legion moved in, and at least 150 people, described as 'niggers and kikes', sustained injuries.

Investigation of Hollywood by the House Un-American Activities Committee – a body inconceivable in other democratic countries – embellished the campaign to provide a spectacle for popular entertainment and sent the Jews, so prominent in the film capital, into a mood of panic. A fair approximation would divide Hollywood into preponderately Jewish 'liberals' and the rest, when the term 'liberal' denoted close sailing, at some period of one's life, to the radical wind. This might have been during one's student days, doubtless at City College of New York, that noisy citadel of pro-Soviet sentiment in the years before the war. Of nineteen film colony personalities – writers, directors, actors – regarded by the HUAC as 'unfriendly witnesses', thirteen were Jews. Some broke under the strain, recanted and named others. From this group the celebrated 'Hollywood Ten' went to jail rather than cringe to a Star Chamber.[22] The Hollywood film magnates, mainly elderly Jewish immigrants, saw their country as a terrestrial paradise, automatically on the side of the angels. They had tackled the theme of antisemitism in 1947 with *Crossfire* and *Gentleman's Agreement*. Then came *Home of the Brave* and *Lost Boundaries* to demonstrate the irrationality of colour prejudice. We were all alike under the skin, their stories told, especially in the United States. Now they drove the point home by conducting their own purge of the film colony.

Jewish equanimity in the United States, delicately poised be-

---

[22] See David Caute, *The Great Fear: The Anti-Communist Purge under Truman and Eisenhower*, London, 1978, pp. 164–6, 487–520.

tween self-confidence and insecurity, was therefore to receive a crippling blow in 1950 with the arrest of Esther and Julius Rosenberg. This husband and wife team were convicted of conveying atomic secrets to the Soviets. They died in the electric chair in 1953, the first executions for espionage in peacetime America. Protestation was world-wide, while the drawing-rooms of Beverly Hills and New York's Riverside Drive felt a shudder of unease. How could American Jewry harbour such enemies of the beloved country in its midst? Atonement became the order of the day. The community reacted with a demonstration of patriotism that placed this people in the vanguard of the anti-Russian crusade. Support for Israel, entailing annual fund-raising campaigns of superb dexterity, was vaunted as a blow struck for American interests in the Middle East, since Israel stood in the way of Russian penetration there. In this regard the Soviet Union's onslaught upon Zionism appeared as an opportune development. And to cleanse the household stable the magazine *Commentary*, owned by the American Jewish Committee and largely dependent upon the philanthropy of Jacob Blaustein, an oil millionaire, pursued a relentless anti-Communist line. In the way of such phenomena, the campaign was led by a coterie of New York writers formerly known for their strict Trotskyite convictions. Soon America as a whole would learn to relax its anti-Communist obsessions, for by 1954 Senator McCarthy took the witch-hunt to such absurdity as to instigate its self-destruction. *Commentary*, on its part, would grow more and more conservative through the years, and would eventually qualify as required reading in Richard Nixon's White House.

But in the early 1950s the Jews in their global situation represented a two-headed monster to their detractors: distrusted in America on grounds of their addiction to the political Left; and simultaneously the foe of the bourgeois, reactionary Right of Stalin's twilight years. The Soviet tyrant could search out Zionist conspiracy in the most unexpected places: practising their sinister surgery in the operating theatres of Moscow hospitals; in American intelligence; among the officials administering the charity of the Joint Distribution Committee. But most directly Stalin detected treachery wherever Jews occupied high positions of state in the Communist countries within his orbit of Eastern Europe. These 'People's Democracies' formed the Soviet Union's first line of defence against the assault he anticipated at any moment from the capitalist world.

If the Marxism of the People's Democracies – Czechoslovakia, Hungary, Poland and the rest – could be distinguished in any significant aspect from the fifteen Soviet republics within Russia itself, it lay in their greater tolerance of religious life. They readily obeyed Moscow directives in all else: economic and foreign policy, the denial of a free press, single-party rule. They all voted with their master to assure the UN Resolution for Arab and Jewish independence its necessary two-thirds majority in 1947. Russia had struggled to eliminate God since 1917, though in vain. On the other hand, the Communist regimes constructed upon the ruins of the old capitalist societies following the Second World War were not disposed to begin their new existence by precipitating conflict where none need arise. The people were therefore allowed to worship as they chose, the Jews equally with other denominations.

By government consent (never officially given in Hungary) they largely availed themselves of the welcome extended by Israel to emigrate there. In 1950 the United States at last liberalised its entry laws a fraction, and some took that road. Of the great population of Jews inhabiting Eastern Europe before the Nazi holocaust, who then remained? Perhaps a half-million outside the USSR all told, and the large majority of them in Hungary and Romania. These survivors included dedicated Communists, veteran leaders of the movement from the period between the wars. They had fled to the safety of Russia on the German advance and had returned with the liberating armies of Marshal Stalin on its retreat. They now occupied a privileged place in the new Marxist hierarchies: as government and party officials, ambassadors, film-makers, journalists and professors; truly, a revolution in Jewish status in that part of the world.

However, such people did not regard themselves as Jews, and anyway by their thinking this was a new age. The Socialist system in the making presumed the annulment of ethnic particularism and with it the death of antisemitism. In rejecting the metaphysical Jew, they also overlooked his definition according to the celebrated phrase of Jean-Paul Sartre: 'A person who is regarded as such by the community in which he lives.'[23] Anna Pauker, Romanian Foreign Minister, and Rudolf Slansky, a vice-premier of Czechoslovakia, came within this category. Comrades of the same origin numbered among the leading lights of Hungary and Poland.

Stalin could not abide this situation. While he ruled in the Kremlin the purge undertaken in Russia would be incomplete without extension to his satellites. These people too must surely carry the virus of Zionism in their blood, thus forcing a connection with anti-Communist Israel and reaching to the reactionary Jewish elements in the USA, a country overtly bent upon the destruction of the Soviet empire. Stalin caught them in his liquidation net. Anna Pauker of Romania was deprived of her office, expelled from the party and placed under house arrest in 1952.

Under the pressure of Moscow's campaign against 'rootless cosmopolitanism' most of the Jews prominent in the party structure of Czechoslovakia and other organs of the state were removed from their positions in 1951 and taken into custody. While in prison they were subjected to the classic, relentless interrogation that rarely failed to secure confessions in totalitarian systems. Rudolf Slansky, probably the most powerful man in Czechoslovakia and a former secretary-general of the party, was among those arraigned. At an elaborate Kafkaesque show trial the following year he took his place in the dock with thirteen other defendants, ten of them Jewish like himself, and all dominant on the national scene as deputy ministers – of National Defence, State Security, Foreign Trade, Finance. Czechoslovakia, it will be recalled, had provided Israel with arms vital in the fight for independence. It had done so in defiance of the UN embargo and in collusion with the Soviet Union. Slansky had apparently helped the Zionists to arm themselves, though Ben-Gurion later affirmed that Slansky was so against Zionism as to violently oppose the sale.[24] Now the final note of unreality: for a key witness in the man's condemnation the prosecution produced a left-wing member of the Israeli parliament, Mordecai

23 Jean-Paul Sartre, *Réflexions sur la question juive*, Paris, 1946, p. 93.
24 Ben-Gurion, *Personal History*, p. 268.

Oren, who had been arrested while on a mission to a 'peace congress' in Berlin sponsored by the Comintern. He had been broken during a year's isolation and interrogation under torture.

Oren's friends at home tuned their radios to Prague and to their horror heard him denounce Zionism as one of the seven deadly sins of imperialism against the international working class. Slansky, with the other defendants, refused to plead for mercy and, except for three, they were all executed. One of the accused, deputy Foreign Minister Artur London, sentenced to life imprisonment, suffered an experience similar to Oren's. He was released in 1956 and described in a book, subsequently filmed, the twenty months of torture that extracted his confession at the trial.[25] All the accused were rehabilitated together with London, as innocent victims of the Stalinist terror. They included Oren, who returned to his kibbutz in Upper Galilee a loyal Socialist-Zionist still, though somewhat wiser in the ways of his ideological world.

Among the offences for which Slansky paid with his life was one of engaging a physician to kill the Czech President, Klement Gottwald. This charge arose again in the even more surrealist 'Doctors' Plot' in Moscow. Nine senior physicians, six of them Jews, faced allegations of membership of a terrorist cell connected with Western intelligence and assigned to assassinate the entire body of civil and military leaders in the Soviet Union. The state prosecutor claimed that Andrei Zhdanov, party chief in Leningrad and Politbureau spokesman for cultural ideology, had died as a result of this organisation's activities in 1948.

According to the indictment, the doctors' conspiracy embraced the operations of the American Joint in Russia and other countries since the First World War. *Pravda* 'exposed' the plot, with its ramifications in international Zionism, in January 1953, implicating Dean Acheson, Henry Morgenthau, David Ben-Gurion and British intelligence. The 'criminals' were shown to be linked with the wartime Jewish Anti-Fascist Committee, for one of the accused doctors was a close relative of Solomon Mikhoels. How all this can be explained remains a mystery, except in the context of a duel between rivalling aspirants to the

[25] *On Trial*, London, 1970.

succession in Communist Russia against the background of the cold war. In the persecution of Jews, together with others in upper-echelon employment, hundreds of additional doctors were summarily tried and executed along with the principal suspects, on grounds of professional neglect, of falsely acquiring their degrees and of staffing research institutions with their friends. The term 'Jew' was rarely employed in the denunciation of any individual, but their Jewish names, often long discarded, were invariably emphasised to testify to their murky origins. The USSR broke off diplomatic relations with Israel in February 1953. Would Stalin's next step be the deportation of all Russian Jews to Siberia? So it was strongly rumoured at the time,[26] but the following month the tyrant mercifully died – of a stroke.

Beria then promptly exonerated himself from complicity in staging the Doctors' Plot. It had been pure fabrication, he declared, on Stalin's orders. There existed an anti-Beria group in the secret police, and soon both the pros and the antis were put to death, twisting the mystery into an enigma. Anna Pauker was now allowed to live out her life in peaceful obscurity. Khrushchev's famous 1956 disclosures at the Twentieth Party Congress on life in Stalin's Kremlin referred to the Doctors' Plot, and although he refrained from specifying the Jews as the particular target of his old chief's obsessions – Russian leaders spoke about this people only when driven to do so by foreign critics – all the victims, dead or alive, were officially rehabilitated and their families awarded compensation.

We cannot however leave this subject with simple dismissal of the excesses as an index of the irrational fury engendered by struggles only within the Soviet power structure. In the West, democracy encourages investigative journalism, not to mention loose talk, and since those days we have been made better aware how the cold war lacked the restraints, on all sides, of a conflict fought under Queensberry Rules. Though long obscured from the public gaze, political murders were actively planned also by the West, sufficiently at least to necessitate a six months' sitting in 1975 of the US Intelligence Committee on CIA plots to

[26] Peter Grose, in Harrison Salisbury (ed.), *Anatomy of the Soviet Union*, London, 1967, p. 428.

assassinate foreign heads of state. The names of Patrice Lumumba, Fidel Castro, Rafael Trujillo *et al.* rolled off witnesses' tongues. These referred to events beginning in 1960. Thus we are no longer convulsed in immediate disbelief at reports of assassination attempts upon national leaders. Nevertheless, both Khrushchev and, as late as November 1987, Gorbachev spoke of their predecessor's paranoia.[27] It is now common knowledge that in 1953 an Anglo-American plot succeeded in toppling another enemy of the West, Muhammad Mossadegh, from the premiership of Iran, while the murder of President Abdul Nasser of Egypt was under active consideration by the British in 1956.

Israel functioned as a nation-state without a memory. It produced a new generation which was both ignorant of the Diaspora and profoundly sceptical of its virtues. It matured with the conviction that in this land the Jew was different, a complete being rather than a warped product of the minority psychology, and its self-confidence was limitless so that it accepted Jewish help from outside while despising it. For these younger Israelis the Jewish world had experienced a rebirth in 1948: they had emerged from a trial of strength, intelligence and courage with a victory of priceless worth – a territory entirely their own. In their calculation the Arab refusal to sit down to a formal peace conference intimated a second round, perhaps a third, for which Israel had to maintain absolute preparedness. Therefore they assessed their situation only in terms of survival or disappearance. The test came suddenly, but Israel's army was ready.

The moment arrived when Britain and France, two Western powers still clinging where feasible to their imperial inheritance, decided to eliminate Abdul Nasser, President of Egypt and leader of the Arab world. Nasser accepted Soviet aid in building the Aswan Dam and in equipping his forces. He nationalised the Suez Canal, property of the Franco-British partnership. These

---

[27] According to an article in the London *Jewish Chronicle*, discussing the close co-operation between American and Israeli intelligence, and quoting American reports including *Newsweek*, the Jewish contacts of Mossad (Israel's counter-intelligence agency) in the Soviet Union and Eastern Europe were among the CIA's most valuable sources. Khrushchev's speech denouncing Stalin at the secret session of the Twentieth Party Congress in January 1956, *Newsweek* affirmed, was obtained by a Mossad agent. *Jewish Chronicle*, 13 December 1985.

steps could only lead to the introduction of Soviet influence in the Middle East, an eventuality as unwelcome to Israel as to the others, even though it was the only country in the area where the Communist Party was legal. Furthermore, Egypt still considered itself in a state of war with Israel and kept the Red Sea port of Elath under blockade, for Nasser was committed to the restoration of his brother-Arabs in Palestine.

When, in 1956, the Anglo-French alliance laid its plans to invade Egypt and restore the status quo, Israel accepted an invitation to participate in the operation. Ben-Gurion was tempted to believe that an Egyptian defeat could win for Israel possession of Sinai and the Gaza strip, bases of regular Arab sorties harassing the Jews' outlying Negev settlements, with women and children among the killed.

The role allocated to Israel was as *shabbos goy*. The Yiddish expression denotes the employment of a gentile to light the kitchen fire on the sabbath, whereby the Jew might enjoy warmth and cooked food without transgressing the Commandment of complete seventh-day rest from labour. In this case the Jew would act the gentile. Israel was to light the fire by sending its troops against Egypt so that the other two might virtuously descend upon the scene, separate the antagonists, put the fire out, retrieve the Suez Canal, dispose of Nasser and remain in occupation. Anthony Eden, the British Prime Minister, saw himself delivering one hell of a lesson to an upstart Egyptian who ought to know his place. Israel, a necessary element to ensure speed, had been brought in by the French. Eden himself had never evinced enthusiasm for Zionism. Israel's part, begun 29 October 1956, went perfectly to plan; its armour smashed through the Egyptian defences and all but reached the Suez Canal within the week. The Franco-British operation stumbled. The overall design of all three powers ended in catastrophe, Russia and the USA uniting in condemnation of the entire episode.

In the reckoning, Israel emerged with its reputation badly tarnished. This democratic state, ruled by a Labour premier whose every speech quoted the Bible, a state commanding admiration throughout the world for the idealism of its collective settlements, the kibbutzim, and which by Herculean effort had given a home to a million Jews, most of them refugees, now forfeited the esteem of large groups of erstwhile supporters. To be condemned equally by America and Russia was no light affair for a small country in desperate need of friends. Liberal opinion everywhere, while recognising the skill demonstrated in Israel's Sinai operation, denounced the motive: rude *Machtpolitik*. The Arabs of course had fresh fuel to add to their detestation of Zionism, and Nasser seized this as an excuse to expropriate and expel the large community of Jews still domiciled in Egypt. More, the advantages Israel gained through removal of the blockade of Elath, and the ending of frontier incursions, proved transitory. What became permanent was the crippling arms race in the Middle East, retarding the country's urgent development programme and thereby delaying the smooth absorption of immigrants. With substantial assistance from his newly acquired patron in Moscow, Nasser gathered immense prestige as a spokesman and defender of a young, emerging world embattled against the cynical colonialism of the old.

Israel, defining its independence by claiming freedom of action whenever it felt its security impinged, evinced only small concern for the loss of external goodwill. It weathered the storm also because the Christian nations saw its leader Ben-Gurion as an extraordinarily reassuring figure on the world stage – the embodiment of Jewish forgiveness for the crimes of past antisemitism. The man refused to wear the aching Jewish heart on his sleeve. So far as he was concerned the attachment of the people to their historic soil had been a revolution, normalising their psychology. Some Jews, obsessed by their grievance against Christendom, could not follow the argument. His political enemy Menahem Begin made the woes of their Diaspora history the strongest article of his Zionist faith, and preached glorification of might as the only weapon available to the Jews against the constant of persecution. Begin's inability to transcend Germany's guilt, or Russia's, or Britain's, determined his attitude towards every gesture of disapproval made towards his country's policies.

This caused Begin to bring insurrection near when Ben-Gurion, early in the national life, agreed to accept reparations from Konrad Adenauer, Federal Germany's Chancellor, in indemnification for the deeds of Nazism. Begin recoiled from dealing with Germany. He would not personally touch the money, and he considered Israel defiled by accepting it. Money could not of course heal the wounds, nor bring back the millions of dead, nor redress the suffering and humiliation visited upon those caught in the Nazi horror but who had survived. Nor could it purchase redemption for Germany. But reparations were not intended, by either donor or recipient, to wipe the slate clean. Manifestly, West Germany dearly wished for rehabilitation in the eyes of the world, with entry into the comity of nations. The first step in the process must necessarily be reconciliation with Jewry. Begin, and those who thought like him, relegated Germany to the condition of a leper nation, to endure for all eternity.

Israel did not take part officially in the negotiations for financial restitution. Negotiations were conducted principally by Nahum Goldmann, president of the World Jewish Congress. He represented those whose property had been confiscated, or were the trustees of synagogues and other institutions destroyed, as well as the bereaved, and spoke in the name of those unknown who had perished together with their entire families. How to assess the catastrophe in material terms, except by making Israel the central element in the arrangement? The state had risen phoenix-like over the ashes of Jewish Europe; it had resettled the greatest number of survivors, it stood in direct historical sequence to the effects of Nazism. In another category, individual payments would be made to claimants now displaced across the world. What could not be distributed would be taken as endowment to sponsor the revival of a culture Hitler had gone far to eliminate at its historic source.

Over the space of thirty years some 36 billion dollars was paid out, in the form of goods and services to the State of Israel, pensions to many thousands of individuals, to committees building old people's homes and hospitals for the mentally and physically damaged. The rest went to an instrument, the Memorial Foundation for Jewish Culture, supporting academic research and religious endowments so as to replenish the intellectual and spiritual resources of the Jewish collectivity.[28] A formal

[28] See S. J. Roth, *West German Recompense for Nazi Wrongs* (Institute of Jewish Affairs, Research Report No. 16), London, 1982.

agreement was signed only in September 1952, but when Ben-Gurion announced his government's stake in the negotiations earlier that year, and opened a debate in the Jerusalem parliament, the Knesset, Begin led his followers from the chamber and turned nearby Zion Square into a battlefield. Tear-gas could not disperse the demonstrators. Knesset windows were smashed, and stones hurtled over the heads of those within.

Begin knew how to inflame the crowd: 'The police have gas grenades containing gas manufactured in Germany, that very gas used to kill your fathers and mothers. We shall suffer any torture they may think up for us to prevent a decision to deal with Germany!' He then returned to the rostrum within the chamber, and warned the government: 'We shall go to the barricades, we are ready to die, drag us to concentration camps if you will, but some issues are dearer than life!' The words were taken by some to threaten the return of the underground Irgun, presaging resistance against Israel as against Britain in the days of the Mandate. The man could do it; who had forgotten the King David Hotel? Ben-Gurion replied: 'We have sufficient will, strength and means to prevent any terrorism designed to destroy our democracy ... I can guarantee to the nation which dwells in Zion, to the Jewish people abroad and public opinion throughout the world, that terror against the sovereignty and the freedom of the State of Israel will be unhesitatingly uprooted.'[29]

Even then, a government motion succeeded only with difficulty, by 61 votes against 50 with five abstentions. Feeling ran high against accepting 'blood money' from Germany not only in the ranks of Begin's party, but on the Socialist far Left and among prominent citizens unidentified politically. Incidentally, this indicated where power was located in Israel; with the old pioneers, few in number, born in pre-revolutionary Russia, and not with those mainly Polish Jews, whether of the Left or Right, personally touched by Nazism. As the heat receded, and the country managed the more easily to pay its bills, it seemed that little more would be heard from Begin or his pretensions to national leadership. But this man of recklessness and blinkered

[29] For the Knesset debate in detail, and the disorders outside, see B. Litvinoff, *Ben-Gurion of Israel*, London, 1955, pp. 236–9.

vision was simultaneously a monument to patience, upon which might have been inscribed *Resurgam*.

Another kind of restitution took place in Rome. The Vatican did not accord diplomatic recognition to the young state. It had not welcomed the Zionist Organisation since the very birth of the national movement. Theodor Herzl was received by Pius X in 1904, to be told:

> We cannot give approval to this movement. We cannot prevent the Jews from going to Jerusalem but we could never sanction it. The soil of Jerusalem, if it was not always sacred, has been sanctified by the life of Jesus Christ. As head of the Church I cannot tell you otherwise. The Jews have not recognised the Lord, therefore we cannot recognise the Jewish people.[30]

The UN had voted for the separation and internationalisation of Jerusalem, but a war had superseded, leaving the Holy City a place where Jew and Arab warily confronted each other across a barricade. Ben-Gurion had expressly challenged world opinion and embittered the Church of Rome by declaring Jerusalem his capital. Yet the Vatican knew also how severely history would judge its resounding silence during Hitler's persecutions. Actuated by contrition, it began to examine its responsibility also for the evil of antisemitism across the centuries: the stigmatising of the Jews as agents of the Antichrist by the founding fathers of the Church, the enforced baptisms of the Middle Ages, the Inquisition, the modern catechism inciting the innocent to racial hatred. The curse laid upon this people had never been lifted. It was time for better coexistence. How to achieve it?

Doctrinal change in the Roman Catholic Church is by its nature an arduous process. To improve in one direction involved offence in another. For its part, the psychology of Orthodox Jewry allowed no coming together with what the Talmud branded as a mortal enemy, and every syllable in the Talmud remained sacrosanct, making anathema of Christianity. So nothing could be said by the Church that might betoken an assault upon the rock of Judaic teaching. Moreover, gestures

[30] Raphael Patai (ed.), *Complete Diaries of Theodor Herzl*, Vol. IV, pp. 1602–3.

towards the people of Israel implied, in the Arab world, gestures towards the State of Israel, and thus hostility in the direction of Islam. The pontificate realised, further, that in the conscience of many of its bishops revision of their vocabulary repudiated the meaning of the Gospel regarding Hebrew perfidy: literally understood, revision would pass a verdict of sin upon a long succession of scholars and saints beginning with the Apostles.

An initiative was nevertheless undertaken by two men, a Jew and a Catholic, united in their conviction that the account as given in the Testament of the trial and crucifixion of Jesus had sown the seed from which antisemitism had flourished from that day to the present. Jules Isaac, the eminent French historian and practically a household name in his own country (his textbooks studied by every schoolchild), had in former days barely considered himself a Jew. But the transportation of his wife and daughter to their death inspired him to devote the remainder of his life to the study of Judeo-Christian relationships. The German Jesuit Cardinal Augustin Bea, confessor to Pius XII and subsequently appointed by John XXIII to head the Secretariat for the Promotion of Christian Unity, began drafting with Isaac a new interpretation of the Christian message. It would be submitted to the Second Vatican Council, due in 1962, and open a way towards dialogue between the faiths. In 1959 Pope John, in a measured step of reconciliation, invested the Israeli ambassador to Italy with the Grand Cross of Sylvester. A year later he received an American-Jewish group with the greeting, 'I am Joseph your brother.' He then ordered deletion of the epithets *perfidis* (*Judaeis*) and (*Judaicam*) *perfidiam* from the Good Friday liturgy.

Insignificant as these gestures might be, they brought a cataract of abuse upon Cardinal Bea. He was subjected to violent attacks from the die-hards among his brother bishops. When the Council convened, all its members received presentation of a book, *Conspiracy against the Church*, edited by Maurice Pinay, a determined enemy of ecumenism. Its main thesis demonstrated that 'the centuries-long struggle of the Holy Church against the Jewish religion and its rites was due, not as falsely claimed, to the religious intolerance of the Catholics but to the utter infamy of the Jewish religion, which constitutes a deadly threat to Christianity'.[31] Pinay brought accusations before the Council against certain cardinals, and they included Bea, as being in fact secret Communists, even disguised Jews. 'They defend Jews with far more fanaticism than they have ever shown in the cause of the Holy Church.' The liberalisation of Church teaching was assailed as a plot instigated by 'Judeo-Masonic infiltrations of the Jesuit orders', while the 'Nazis did only what the Holy Catholic Church had commanded during the last 14 centuries'.[32]

Pope John died in 1963, before the Vatican Council's work was completed. In the meantime, the Curia was shaken by the reception accorded to the drama *Der Stellvertreter* ('The Representative') at its first production in West Berlin. Written by Rolf Hochhuth, the play revived controversy over the wartime pontiff's failure to protest loudly enough against the Nazi measures. Its staging throughout the world brought agonised searching to Catholic hearts. Pope John's successor, Paul VI, determined to continue along his predecessor's hazardous path, and during an interlude undertook a pilgrimage to what he judiciously designated 'the Holy Land', with one day spent within the Jews' territory of Israel, and one in the Jordanian portion of Jerusalem. Ultimately, on 28 October 1965, a formula, not as forthright as Cardinal Bea's original draft, was agreed as the papal declaration *Nostra Aetate*. Apart from expressing esteem for Islam, Hinduism, Buddhism and other advanced religions, this spoke of ties between Jews and Christians through the Old Testament, and continued:

> Although the Jewish authorities and those who followed their lead pressed for the death of Christ, still, what happened in his Passion cannot be charged against all the Jews without distinction then alive, nor against the Jews of today. Although the Church is the new people of God, the Jews should not be presented as rejected or accursed as if this followed from the Holy Scriptures. All should take pains then, that in catechetical work or in preaching the word of God they do not teach anything that does not conform to the truth of the Gospel and the spirit of Christ ... As the Church has always held, and holds now, Christ

[31] Cited in Heer, *God's First Love*, p. 1.
[32] Ibid., p. 388.

underwent his passion and death freely, because of the sins of men and out of infinite love, in order that all may reach salvation.

The document could have been composed in identical terms if the Holocaust had not occurred, or a revived Jewish state not been created on biblical soil as before. It referred to neither of the two great happenings that concluded one kind of Jewish existence and inaugurated another. Be that as it may, *Nostra Aetate* brought Christian–Jewish relations into a fresh atmosphere, to clear away the incense of religious superstitition and give human tolerance a chance to prevail.

On the Christian sabbath, 13 April 1986, the spiritual head of the world's 700 million Catholics, Pope John Paul II, recited Psalm 113 within the precincts of a synagogue situated in the old ghetto of Rome. The congregation responded with Psalm 150. This gesture of reconciliation, unprecedented in the history of the pontificate, may well have drawn a line under centuries of conflict and mutual recrimination. History cannot be rewritten; however, much has been achieved that may prevent its repetition.

13

Conflicts of Identity

With the concluding chapter of this historical survey we have reached the stage, in the early 1960s, when the Jews could relegate antisemitism to that part of the subconscious where fact and fantasy mingle. The result could, at times, feed the imagination with grotesque apparitions.

Those who searched for antisemitism could find it, in all conditions of men, for no true definition existed of the thing they sought. A candidate defeated in a competition for employment might ascribe his failure to racial prejudice rather than to his personal inadequacies. Sporting and social clubs were known to restrict membership to their own kind, excluding Jews. Groups continued to appear on the fringes of political life to denounce 'alien influence' and hearken nostalgically to the good old pre-war days when Fascism was respectable. An insensitive or contemptuous remark dropped from the unguarded lips of a public figure, a swastika daubed on a tombstone by a lone neurotic during a nocturnal spasm of paranoia, a gratuitous insult – perhaps never intended – in a book or television programme, and lo! some Jews would observe the shade of Hitler stalking the earth anew.

They squirmed from every hostile reminder that they were not quite like everyone else, imagining the growth of a cancer from an insect sting. 'Twas ever thus for the outsider. Deviants from the norm, whether by colour, religion, sexual mores or physical disability, have suffered since time immemorial (until quite recently in silence) from such indignities. We are all deviants of a sort: a man or woman, even a child, must be fortunate indeed never to have experienced the sensation of the despised and rejected Jew in a world of gentiles.

Against all this, ethnic consciousness decreased as a

dominating component of this people's mentality during the second half of the twentieth century. Zionism, once a quantifiable index of national commitment, weakened perceptibly as the ideological cement binding Jewry to the State of Israel. That country gave every impression of going its own way, more and more detached from the assimilating Diaspora. Such was the situation until the six days of June 1967, when Israel, its existence challenged by every one of its neighbours (and some not so near), delivered another overwhelming defeat upon a great Arab alliance and emerged from the test as a world power in minuscule.

That almost instantaneous victory, so unpredictable, followed a crisis week during which the world almost despaired of the Jewish state's future. The odds seemed insurmountable. Egypt had received up-to-date Russian weaponry during the decade following the Suez War of 1956 to recoup the losses incurred, and now had 80,000 men bristling in their tanks in Sinai. The other Arab countries had enjoyed a respite of nineteen years since their 1948 débâcle and yearned to wipe that humiliation from the memory. A UN Emergency Force, ostensibly posted to prevent President Nasser's interference with Israeli shipping in the Gulf of Akaba, had been withdrawn. General de Gaulle, cooler towards Israel than any previous French leader, adopted an ambivalent position and warned its Foreign Minister, Abba Eban, not to fire the first shot. The Soviet Union, adopting the view that no crisis existed, opposed external intervention.[1] Washington felt time allowed for the UN to stage a Middle East debate before Nasser moved. On 30 May, Jordan signed a military pact with Egypt under a joint command. And finally, Israel itself felt leaderless with a Prime Minister, Levi Eshkol, who lacked the determination, authority and martial competence of his predecessor Ben-Gurion.

The Arab refugees were a running sore. They could easily have been absorbed by Israel's neighbours, but to do so would imply recognition of the Zionists' right to stay as a nation in their midst, and this they would not countenance. Israel might have allowed the return of at least a part of them, and recompensed the rest,

---

[1] Abba Eban, *Autobiography*, London, 1977, pp. 339–46.

but refused to move in that direction until its legitimacy was formally accepted in the area. Arab hostility and Jewish obstinacy had therefore reached an impasse: without superpower intervention another clash of arms became inevitable. The Arabs would survive defeat, doubtless to fight yet another day, but defeat for Israel would bring the infant state's annihilation.

Nasser said as much. He told his people on 26 May 1967:

> What we see today in the Arab masses everywhere is their desire to fight, to regain the rights of the people in Palestine ... There is complete co-ordination of military action between us and Syria. We shall operate as one army fighting a single battle ... The battle will be a general one and our basic objective will be to destroy Israel ... Iraq has sent its troops into Syria, Algeria will send troops, Kuwait too. This is Arab power, the true resurrection of the Arab nation.[2]

Thus the Israelis were in an agony of suspense, realising they stood on the brink. A clamour arose for the return of Moshe Dayan, hero of Sinai, to the Eshkol Cabinet as Minister of Defence. Eshkol could not abide the man, but the government could fall on the issue. Dayan was sworn in on 1 June, together with the rebel Menahem Begin in a balancing act to reassure the nation that the hour had produced statesmanship and national conciliation. Three days later Israel struck. By 9 June all was over. Israel held the whole of Palestine, including the Old City of Jerusalem, as far as the Jordan. It expelled the Egyptians from the Sinai peninsula, seized the east bank of the Suez Canal and occupied the heights of the richly watered Golan within Syria. This was victory indeed, dazzling by its completeness, the textbook strategy of crushing blitzkrieg.

Of significance equal to this military accomplishment was the victory of Israel over the Jews dispersed across the continents. Overnight they rediscovered themselves as a single, united people. For the Jews everywhere found that the nation whose existence they had grown to take for granted was too important to them to be allowed to disappear. History before statehood had

---

[2] Quoted in Walter Laqueur, *The Road to War 1967*, London, 1968, pp. 294, 296.

terminated in a holocaust, its wounds still unhealed. And so, in the last days of May and the early days of June, men and women pleaded at Israel's embassies to be sent to the country's aid. Wild scrambles took place at airports to secure aeroplane seats. Demonstrations of support, convened only by word of mouth, attracted many thousands. Letters on behalf of Israel's cause appeared in the world's press from intellectuals who hitherto refused to be burdened with Jewish preoccupations and were remote from Zionist sentiment. In the parliaments of the democracies 'Jewish' parties made their appearance. Money flowed to Israel in torrents: workers gave their life savings, and one famous Jewish family sold its racing stable.

The Israelis themselves were taken by surprise. They had felt betrayed by the Jewish Diaspora, for it had disappointed their expectation of spontaneous immigration from the West; in general, the only Jews to come were those with nowhere else to go. Without an ally among the nations Israel had been prepared to fight this war alone. Dayan insisted, at a press conference televised throughout the world, that he did not want American or British boys to die in Israel's battles. They came nevertheless, elderly Jews protesting they were under forty years of age.

This tidal wave of emotion in response to Israel's crisis appeared perfectly comprehensible to other nations, no more remarkable than the flocking to Great Britain's colours by those 'colonials' from the older Commonwealth when the mother country found itself in danger. And in many quarters Israel's pre-emptive action echoed as the only one possible in that desperate situation. It would undoubtedly lead at last to a final peace in the Middle East, with Israel's withdrawal from 'territories occupied in the recent conflict and the right of every state in the area to live in peace within secure and recognised borders free from threats and acts of force'. The words come from Resolution No. 242 of the UN Security Council, passed 22 November 1967.

However, Israel did not withdraw. Much to the victor's indignation, the Arab states refused to sign the treaties expected of defeated nations. Gradually, the ceasefire lines assumed the permanence of frontiers. Israel's armour held down a further 1,200,000 Arabs in a mini-empire three times its own area. Beneath the surface calm their impotent discontent bred a hatred that lumped all Jews together as the authors of their plight.

Israel explained its case for non-withdrawal in a public relations campaign so formidably scaled as to warrant the description of an industry: mountains of paper in documentation, miles
and miles of film, the sending forth of regiments of speakers
briefed on every episode of Zionist history. Jewish personalities,
not all of them nationalistic by any means, for even the most
detached was now a willing captive, retailed the arguments in
their diverse centres of influence. When their efforts proved
without result, except in those localities where Jewish support
was necessary to a politician's electoral interests – this did not
solely apply to the United States – loud complaints were heard
about the deficiencies of Israel's spokesmen in conveying the
message. Or was it, the Jews said, that the general anti-Israel,
even antisemitic, bias had turned the world deaf to reason?[3]

Alas, Israel had achieved its triumph in a wholly justifiable
campaign during a period when the conclusion of wars at the
peace table, with absolute victors and obedient losers, had
become an anachronistic rarity. Although the Vietnam War had
still a long way to go before the morass into which the United
States was immersed began teaching its moral, nations were
generally aware that occupation of another's soil now reacted
disastrously upon themselves, for which the cure lay only in
retreat. The great powers feared the Middle East situation as a
time-bomb with dire consequences inherent for them all, and
impatiently awaited a surrender of the conquests. But the government in Jerusalem succumbed to the error of convincing itself
that the Arabs would eternally remain insignificant, divided and
confused: time was therefore on the victor's side.

'The difference after this war from 1948 and 1956', wrote a
correspondent reporting for the London *Times*,

> is that Israel's victory is so complete that the nation is not
> under pressure to settle for anything less than a full peace.
> In a way the Israeli attitude is naïve: as pushful, argumen-
> tative, but basically reasonable people they seem to
> believe that the Arab leaders should respond, sit down

[3] See, e.g., *So Sorry We Won*, London, 1967, by the Israeli satirist Ephraim
Kishon.

with them and talk equally reasonably. A senior member of *Mapai*, the main government party, put it this way: 'We are prepared to stay on in the occupied territories for a year, two years, five years, a generation if necessary. We shall not move until we get a settlement.'[4]

According to the map, the Jewish state had at last achieved the security it had always craved. A blanket of desert sand now kept the Egyptians at a healthy distance. The River Jordan was an ideal, natural eastern border where formerly the country was cramped into a wasp-waist and the Hashemite Kingdom of Jordan threatened just eleven miles away. Through possession of the Golan Heights, Israel towered over the road to Syria's capital. Let the Arabs know: Israel could, if necessary, seize Cairo, Beirut, Damascus, Amman, at a thrust. King Solomon himself had not commanded more authority over the lands of the Eastern Mediterranean. The children of the Auschwitz generation had transformed themselves into a new Sparta.

Maps, however, tell a deceptive story. Effective borders may hold enemies at bay from without. What of the enemy within? When Israel moved to deliver a crippling blow upon its neighbours, the Arabs already under its control had not stirred. They lived as a subject minority deprived of the right of free movement inside the country, though with every encouragement to emigrate. Israeli Arabs were restricted to employment among their own, being disqualified from civil service posts higher than the rank of assistant district commissioner. Forbidden to bear arms, separated from the Jews by a language and culture which the latter did not consider worthy of study, these Arabs were economically secure and equal before the law, but they knew they were untrusted and unwanted. As late as twenty years after the Six-Day War their children's schools were described by the Jews themselves as 'an affront to the conscience of our country'.[5] By the year 1967 these Israeli Arabs had grown, from a high birth rate and family reunions, to 286,000 souls (excluding Bedouin), a quarter of them Christian. If the Israelis would only admit it, this minority enjoyed fewer rights and received less consideration

---

[4] *The Times*, 15 September 1967.
[5] *Jerusalem Post*, 7 December 1986.

than Jews in the nineteenth-century Pale of Settlement when the tsar appointed antisemitic governments termed by more civilised nations a moral disgrace.

The government of Israel justified its conduct by the steadfast hostility of the Arab states. The minority would receive the same rights as all others, it promised, once the danger of an internal fifth column in some future war was removed. Security considerations alone, not racial prejudice, rendered the Arabs second-class citizens. In the meantime they freely elected their own municipal councils and sent Arab members to the Knesset (parliament) who addressed the assembly in their own language. Some were Communists, and where in the Muslim world was such a party tolerated?

The Israeli Arabs, it may fairly be assumed, felt no fanatical loyalty to the Jewish state. But they gave no trouble on the three occasions, in 1948, 1956 and 1967, when the country fought their brothers over the border. The Jews were not persuaded that this would have been the case had the wars lasted longer, or gone badly for Israel.

Now the new acquisitions increased the Arab element under Jewish control five times over. Pending a binding settlement these could not enjoy the few privileges granted to their kin within Israel proper. Let those desirous of departing do so (as some did, to a better life elsewhere or to join the homeless Arab population in the refugee camps). If Israel had to wait a generation before the enemy adjusted to peaceful coexistence, those living in what were officially designated 'administered territories' must accept their fate. According to an official publication of the Ministry of Foreign Affairs, 'on the whole the population has shown itself law-abiding, reasonably co-operative and at times even appreciative'.[6]

Perhaps the Israelis had forgotten their own rebellious temper during the British Mandate, and remained in ignorance of the difficulties in keeping resentment under indefinite control, as the scattering throughout modern history of such horrors as the Amritsar massacre of 1919 in India, or the Sharpeville calamity of 1960 in South Africa, or even the more recent sectarian violence

[6] *Facts About Israel*, Jerusalem, 1970.

in Northern Ireland, amply illustrated. Perhaps again, they underestimated Arab potential for martyrdom when driven to desperation in a cause. Plainly, they failed to foresee how their conquests must inevitably lead them into a trap. Disaffection among the Arabs grew, first in the form of sullen demonstrations, then in acts of terrorism against innocent Israeli civilians at home and abroad. This shattered many Zionist illusions and gave rise to punitive reprisals by Israeli commandos operating on land, in the air and at sea. Such actions aroused widespread condemnation in the international arena, just as invariably befell Britain, South Africa, Russia and any other nation dependent upon armed force to police subject peoples. Traditional friends overseas, notably in the churches and the liberal camp, became aware that the Israel of their sentimental imagination was remote from reality, while its level of retaliation disturbed even large numbers among its own. But most Jewish leaders abroad remained silent, and were therefore seen as endorsing every Israeli retaliatory action as legitimate and necessary.

We have arrived at the crux. Were Israel a nation-state like any other, it would develop in its own way, winning approval for those of its policies considered reasonable for its consolidation and security while attracting criticism for those regarded as cruel, unjust or intransigent. The mid-twentieth century witnessed the emergence of many independent countries newly organised in the ebb of empire, and these were measured by such criteria. But Israel fell into a category unique to itself. Its very birth offended the entire Muslim world. It was nursed into existence by Jews everywhere, and asserted an association with them that could not be denied. Only world Jewry shared the state's official religion and prehistory, and registered that connection with subventions over and above normal taxation in its lands of domicile. Through the Law of Return, a specific Israeli decree passed without consultation with the dispersed people, Jews everywhere enjoyed the right of its citizenship automatically on request.

The Israelis in general regarded residence in their state as a Jewish duty, fulfilling a religious precept and responding to a national instinct; certainly, the bond between the two halves of the Jewish world heartened the spirit of the partners outside. Yet it also created complications. A government does not as a rule consult non-citizens on its politics, and Israel was no exception. Nevertheless the Jews overseas, in claiming a share in Israel's glory, had also to respond by shouldering some of the responsibility. This made for a curious relationship divorced from exact demarcation lines, so that in the course of time the terms Israel, Zionism and Judaism all became intermingled in the gentile mind as in some way corresponding with each other.

Anomalous though this situation might appear, it barely troubled the Jews in the early, uncontentious years of Israel's existence. Independence was a legitimate and worthy aim, an act of historic justice and consequent upon a catastrophe without modern parallel that had caused the loss of a third of their people through being deprived of a territorial base. Now, however, they had relinquished the role of universal scapegoat. They walked with heads high. In all the countries of the Western world they scaled the economic, social and cultural heights unobstructed, while Israel sprang out of the small area originally allocated to it and emerged in the Middle East as a military power reducing each of its neighbours to a state of fear.

Circumstances favoured them. The bulk of the people were concentrated in the democratic West, which granted them equality of entry into its parliaments, in its courts of justice, in its commerce. Jews held executive positions in great newspapers, in the academic world and in the entertainment industry. Their writers were widely read in many languages and regularly won the most prestigious awards. Jews were the most affluent group in the United States, the most bountiful of nations.[7] Of course, many remained poor, but in so far as the word has any meaning, this people were prominently ensconced in the establishment, owning property in the most desirable residential locations and exchanging their old radical convictions for more conservative politics. On their side the Israelis enjoyed a high standard of living (it was a mystery how, for the country seemed perennially on the verge of bankruptcy), while their government was among the world's leading arms suppliers, frequently acting as

---

[7] Of the 400 richest people in the United States since 1982, as listed in *Forbes Magazine*, at least one-quarter have been Jews, who constituted only 2.7 per cent of the country's total population. In 1986 there was one black, no Hispanics.

America's surrogate in this regard. It invested heavily in nuclear research and forged reciprocal relations with many right-wing, dictatorial regimes which acquired arms where they could. It therefore transpired that Israel lost its reputation as the liberal, humanitarian, democratic baby among the nations and looked rather as just another state obsessed with the banality of power. Adverse votes at the United Nations, now dominated by Third World countries supported by the Communist bloc, followed each other in swift succession. A climax was reached at the General Assembly in November 1975, when a resolution condemning Zionism as 'a form of racism and racial domination' was carried by 72 votes to 35, with 32 abstentions. The US delegate, Daniel P. Moynihan, declared the vote to be 'an infamous act'. Nervously, many Jews reacted by castigating opposition to Zionism, and to Israeli policies, as classic antisemitism come again – that is, discrimination based upon historic prejudice and kept alive by racial hatred for this people as a whole.

Not that criticism was restricted to Israel's acknowledged ideological enemies. In the West, both press and television reached similar adverse conclusions when reporting flashpoints in the Middle East conflict. The Jews challenged the information media's impartiality, as though an unseen hand directed correspondents of different nationalities and tongues to speak in unison, describing only the negative side. Again, the Jews charged antisemitism.[8] But this was a *reductio ad absurdum*. The media employed Jews equally with other correspondents: even Israeli reporters were accused of a pro-Arab bias.

Could it have been, rather, that Zionism now expanded in meaning to embrace what had become a collective Jewish position towards the depressing Middle East situation? As we have seen, the Diaspora had been sufficiently affected by the Six-Day War to form Israel's second line of defence. That dramatic triumph, coinciding with America's enduring agony in the Vietnam War, introduced a mutation in world forces. Linked as two aspects of the same oppression, these two conflicts forged a solidarity among the coloured races as a whole and ranged them

[8] See, e.g., Stephen Karetsky and Peter E. Goldman (eds.), *The Media's War Against Israel*, New York, 1986.

frontally against 'white supremacy', which they saw as colonialism without the flag. Because the Jews were numerous and strong in America, that country, already grievously divided over Vietnam, became also the scene of a dangerous polarisation between the Jews and the blacks, for their traditional alliance had turned sour.

During the first half of this century the Negro–Jewish relationship expressed the common aspirations of two minorities thrown together in the big cities of America. Together they voted solidly Democrat and stood side by side in the struggle against race prejudice. In identifying with the Negro claim to equality of opportunity and an end to their discrimination in education, employment and housing, the Jews elevated their sympathies to the character of a hallowed principle. Did they not share a persecuted past with the Negro, for which Christendom was largely to blame?

The American Jewish Committee, that organisation of the old-established German-Jewish 'aristocracy', occupied an active role in creating the National Association for the Advancement of Colored People (NAACP) in 1909 and then kept it supplied with funds. Another body, the American Jewish Congress, largely emerging from the East European immigration, marched in the streets together with the blacks, where the committee remained the somewhat aloof, rich benefactor. Jews and blacks addressed each other's conferences and preached in each other's houses of worship. Particularly, the congress filed supporting briefs when the NAACP came to the courts, providing the lawyers because in those days successful black lawyers remained apathetic towards the struggles of their own people. The Jews created a university, Brandeis, which specifically invited blacks to study Jewish civilisation. James Baldwin cut his literary teeth in that influential Jewish organ, *Commentary* magazine. This happy association reached consummation in the black victory against educational discrimination through the historic Supreme Court ruling of 1954 in *Brown* v. *Board of Education of Topeka*, which condemned compulsory racial segregation in state-supported schools as a violation of the Fourteenth Amendment of the Constitution.

Apparently, the two minority races would, in the United

States, forever hold each other in mutual esteem. No Italian- or Irish-American organisation had so completely espoused the cause of the oppressed Afro-American, but during the 'freedom rallies' of 1964 nineteen rabbis flew down to Birmingham, Alabama, to participate in them, while two Jewish youths were lynched by whites in Philadelphia, Mississippi, for their part in Negro demonstrations. A Black Muslim movement had existed since 1930, but the Jews did not regard it as inimical to themselves. It was born as a non-white, not anti-white, gesture of particularism, seemingly far-fetched, without a substantial following and, like the equally minute Black Jews, not to be taken seriously.

However, the blacks had now grown impatient at their slow progress towards economic as opposed to legalistic equality. Fifty years arm in arm with the Jews and here they languished at the bottom of the pile where manifestly the Jews lived at the top. Vietnam vividly epitomised the injustice. More blacks of military age were sent to fight there because they were either unemployed or in menial labour. Many whites, Jews among them, gained exemption so as not to interrupt their studies. Suddenly, advocates of 'Black Power' usurped the leadership from the traditional, moderate civil rights movements of the race. They spurned co-operation offered by the 'New Left', which was white, middle-class at its core and passionately embraced by young Jews enacting their generational revolt.

The new black leaders perceived the Jews not as friends but as their most immediate oppressors. The ones they knew best through daily contact were the profiteering store-keepers in Harlem, the slum landlords, the supervisors of the public schools that gave black children the worst education. 'If you happen to be an uneducated, poorly trained Negro living in a ghetto', stated Bayard Rustin, himself a moderate black spokesman, 'you see only four kinds of white people – the policeman, the businessman, the teacher and the welfare worker. In many cities, three of those four are Jewish.'[9]

The eruption of black militancy, particularly in an environment so endemically violent as New York City, brought the

[9] *Time* magazine, 31 January 1969.

confrontation out in the open at all times of civic unrest: during a teachers' strike, for example, when Jewish teachers felt victimised by a local school board composed of blacks (an experiment) in an East Side slum once inhabited by Jewish workers; and when the lower middle-class district of Canarsie in Brooklyn, mainly Jewish and Italian, resisted black occupancy of some neighbourhood housing. The conflict destroyed the promising political career of Mayor John Lindsay, the white Protestant liberal whose impartiality cost him the support of both sides. Antisemitism was taking root in what had become the city with the largest Jewish and Negro populations in the world.

The blacks were not slow in hurling Zionism into the fray. One of their most respected authors, Harold Cruse, aligned Israel with an international conspiracy against the blacks. 'The emergence of Israel as a world power in minuscule', he wrote, 'meant that the Jewish question was no longer a purely domestic problem. A great proportion of American Jews began to function as an organic part of a distant nation-state.'[10] In rejecting Anglo-Saxon civilisation some American blacks likewise rejected its semantic restraints. They did not hesitate to describe themselves as antisemites in their attitude to the Jews, where mankind in general, since Hitler, recoiled from such a stamp. Zionism assumed a connotation, borrowed from the Arabs and the Communist bloc, as synonymous with evil, and the term was employed as such. Conversions to Islam grew apace, not only to register the blacks' abdication from the Christian way of life but also as a direct challenge to a specifically Jewish doctrine. Meanwhile, in 1964 Arab frustration in the Middle East had given birth to an armed irredentist movement, the Palestine Liberation Organisation (PLO) under whose umbrella opposition to Israel, through a combination of political agitation and violent outrage, found release. At its head stood Yasser Arafat, the first nationalist leader of stature to emerge from Palestine since the Mufti of Jerusalem, ally of Hitler and Mussolini before 1945.

Soon after the Six-Day War the PLO recruited young volunteers from the refugee camps around Israel's frontiers, renamed

[10] *The Crisis of the Negro Intellectual*, as quoted in *Time*, 31 January 1969.

them guerrilla fighters and trained them to sow terror across the border, deliberately choosing civilian prey. They were split into factions of varying aggressive intensity, and secured reinforcements from ultra-left sympathisers of other races. Israeli planes swept all frontiers on the look-out, so that barely a day passed tranquilly in the spiral of reprisals plunging Arab and Israeli into a continuous war of revenge. As early as 1970 Cairo was placing anti-aircraft missiles within easy reach of Israeli targets and, with the help of Russian pilots and technicians, adopted a menacing position diagnosed by Israeli intelligence (correctly, it transpired) as preparation for a renewal of hostilities on a major scale. Israeli aircraft, on reconnaissance over the Suez ceasefire lines, accidentally bombed an Egyptian industrial plant during which eighty workers died. On another occasion they spotted an installation which they recognised as a military target, and struck at it. It happened to be a school, and thirty children perished. Such exploits indicated the trigger-happy mood of the Israelis. The PLO responded from Lebanon, killing eight Jews. Israel then came back with a massive reprisal raid in Lebanon. So the Arabs returned to ambush a school bus in which the dozen dead included nine children below the age of eight. Between times, an Israeli-bound aircraft with forty-seven passengers from Switzerland exploded in mid-air, an extremist wing of the PLO admitting responsibility.

Violence met by violence assumed so commonplace a character as to receive only incidental mention in the world's press. However, hundreds of millions witnessed the scene on their television screens when the Black September unit of the PLO held eleven Israeli athletes captive during the Olympic Games in 1972. The Arabs demanded the release of 200 of their comrades in Israeli jails, plus Andreas Baader and Ulrike Meinhof, leaders of the anarchist-terrorist 'Red Army Faction', held in West Germany. Negotiators played for time, but when at length orders were given to shoot, the Arabs used hand grenades and machine-guns to kill the eleven. The horror occurred in Munich, a city already bearing a curse as the birthplace of Nazism.

The Israelis, then being led by Golda Meir, the Prime Minister whose international reputation subsequently rested on one unforgivable phrase, 'Who are the Palestinians?', replied in the fashion expected of them: with a succession of air raids upon PLO nests embedded in refugee camps in Syria and Lebanon, leaving a toll of some 200 dead. Simultaneously, Israeli agents of the Mossad counter-intelligence service scoured Europe on a mission to execute Arabs believed to define the strategy of the terrorist campaign. So far as Israel interpreted the situation, this was the only appropriate response. As others saw it, the Palestinian resistance had succeeded better than it hoped, by reducing the Jewish government to its own level of conduct. But worse was to come: the Yom Kippur War of October 1973. As a side-effect, governments everywhere were brought to a state of economic crisis because the Arabs realised they possessed a powerful weapon indeed to punish the nations for allowing Israel to come into existence: oil. Arab nations controlled sixty per cent of the world's proven resources of the fuel. Led by King Faisal of Saudi Arabia, they now sent the price rocketing by slowing down production overall, and cutting off supplies to the United States altogether. Oil as a political instrument wrecked the disposition of international power at a stroke. The Jewish state, announced the Arabs, must return to its 1967 borders and either allow the refugees back or recompense them. No one dared ignore the financial strength behind the voice – except Israel.

Had Israel deigned to listen, this amounted to recognition of the state as it existed before the Six-Day War. Previously, official Arab League policy had rested on the Khartoum Agreement of September 1967. This declared, 'No peace, no recognition, no negotiations with Israel.' Indeed, King Hussein of Jordan was now more than ready – he had been secretly negotiating with Israel for years. Syria and Lebanon would likewise have come round; both countries ardently desired riddance of that focus of internal discontent, the Arab refugees, whose militant elements were parading jauntily with their rifles through the streets of Damascus and Beirut like the janissaries of old. Arafat was riding a crest, but would have to bow to a compromise peace. His every penny came from the sheikhs, now so rich they could buy their way into Buckingham Palace.

But Israel had hardened. The Yom Kippur War traumatised the nation. Egypt and Syria had launched a surprise attack, on the Jews' sacred Day of Atonement, and had fought better than ever before, bringing revelations of slackness and blunder that tarnished the reputation of a body hitherto deemed infallible – the Israel Defence Force. The war, ended under pressure of US–Soviet superpower diplomacy, had lasted just eighteen days, but too long for the casualties to be regarded as tolerable in so small a country. Disengagement returned the eastern shore of the Suez Canal, and an encircled army, to Egypt, enabling the Arabs to mark up the clash of arms as a glorious victory, restoring their morale. In the reckoning, Golda Meir, weeping for the nation's dead, bowed to popular clamour and resigned from office. Never again would Israel have an administration automatically dominated by *Mapai*, the Labour Party.

In the new mood, the people took little convincing that their security required permanent retention of the West Bank of the Jordan, together with all other conquests. God was now enlisted to sanctify Jewish settlement of those territories which, except for East Jerusalem (the Old City), had been held in suspense pending an absolute, binding peace treaty. Thus strictly Orthodox Jews, frequently American-born, intoned passages from the Bible as they began establishing villages, first near Hebron, then throughout the West Bank.[11] A creeping annexation of the conquered territory was now in train. The process was accelerated with no regard for world opinion by Menaham Begin when that man unexpectedly won a general election in 1977. But many Jews across the world, prominent intellectuals among them, described this policy, which presumed to swallow a region populated by well over a million Arabs (and growing fast), as morally unacceptable.[12]

World Jewry's attitude, profoundly affected by the mutually developing adversarial stance in the Arab–Israel conflict, therefore disqualifies attempts at generalisation. The relationship brought joy and apprehension to the Diaspora, a feeling of pride in the state's calibre when *in extremis* tinged with fear of its 'Samson complex'. While accepting the need for strength in a struggle for survival, many Jews simultaneously looked with

[11] In fact, the villages were built by local Arab contractors employing their own.
[12] As, e.g., in open letters to Prime Minister Begin, quoted in *Time*, 23 July 1979, and the London *Jewish Chronicle*, 2 November 1979.

dismay upon Israel's level of retaliation against terrorism. The policy exposed its own futility time and again. But the Arabs and their sympathisers (principally on the Left) might well regard Jewry collectively as an extension of statehood, since every official Jewish organisation, including university student unions, indubitably spoke with an Israeli voice, or docilely responded to an Israeli command.

Arafat nevertheless won a loyal Jewish friend: Bruno Kreisky, first Socialist Chancellor of Austria. During the 1970s the two met frequently in Europe and on Arab soil, Kreisky being the first European democratic statesman to embrace the PLO leader as champion of a righteous cause. Israel naturally raged at the 'traitor', a charge dismissed by Kreisky as nonsensical. He was not alone. The American most popular in Arab countries, and with their leaders personally, was Henry Kissinger, appointed US Secretary of State while President Nixon hung on the rack of the Watergate scandal late in 1973, and himself a German-born Jew who had lost thirteen relatives in Nazi concentration camps. Kissinger's 'shuttle diplomacy' achieved the disengagement of forces in Sinai and on the Golan Heights after the Yom Kippur War, a step which justified President Sadat of Egypt's courageous visit to Jerusalem in 1977 in a dramatic bid for peace. Kissinger was warmly received as an honest broker by the Arabs while some Israelis taunted him with 'Jewboy', thus stigmatising him as an obsequious product of the Diaspora mentality. The irony of Jews resorting to an antisemitic jibe! Yet the peace treaty signed between Egypt and Israel in 1979 owed much to Kissinger's patient mediation on the spot.

That treaty, agreed by a country which the Jews had frequently insisted would *never* recognise Israel, did not bring a queue of Arab leaders to the peace table behind Sadat. The Egyptian had attained his heart's desire in wringing all of the Sinai peninsula from Prime Minister Begin's grasp, though as regards release of the West Bank, Sadat found himself addressing the Rock of Gibraltar. This so-called West Bank, claimed Begin, connoted biblical Judea and Samaria. The Arabs living there could have administrative autonomy – a sort of regional district council – but the land was indissolubly part of Israel. Sadat had bought peace for Egypt at the price of postponing the Palestinians' claim to self-determination and he paid, heavily, first with Egypt's expulsion from the Arab League and ultimately with his life.

In the event, the situation in the Middle East took a still uglier turn. PLO terrorists operating from bases in Lebanon increased hostility to such a dimension as to prompt Israel's invasion of that country, and to ally itself with Christian Arab elements locked in a savage civil war with the Muslims. Soon Begin's air force was pouring destruction into Arafat's stronghold in West Beirut. His Defence Minister Ariel Sharon exceeded the instructions of his right-wing chief, so before long the tragic country on the Jews' northern border, victim of its own fanatical religious conflicts, turned into a proxy battleground between Israel and Syria. Each of them supported one or other of the little private armies as they fought cruelly for a portion of turf.

Begin had arrived in 1977 to the Israeli leadership amidst disquiet approaching consternation in the Jewish world. His strength rested on a voting bloc largely composed of Oriental Jews with a hatred of the Arabs which was born of their treatment since Israel's birth, when they were still neighbours in North Africa. It outstripped the emotions of European-born Jews. Begin suited the Orthodox parties too, for he encouraged their fundamentalist perception of the Holy Land. World Jewish opinion as a whole could not abide the idea of a 'superhawk' with an avowed terrorist past as Prime Minister of Israel. But Begin had been democratically elected by the country's citizens, so the Jews, though thoroughly discomforted, felt bound to sacrifice their scruples and put the best gloss on his policies. They stretched credence for an argument to defend his Lebanese operation. Indisputably, the terrorists (now universally raised in status by the media as guerrillas) had been rendering life miserable and dangerous for all Jews in Upper Galilee and for the population elsewhere through seaborne forays that were virtually suicide raids.

Israel had numerous supporters among the general American population, true. In parts of that country, as we have seen, a politician could hardly survive without the Jewish vote. Moreover Russia, Syria's paymaster, remained consistently hostile to the Jewish state. Few people in America, convinced of Russia's ambition to usurp their own country's influence in the

Middle East, trusted the Kremlin's pretensions to disinterestedness. Israel was an ally, as it were holding the fort for the West. Newspaper and television correspondents, however, reported what they saw. It was rarely favourable to Israel. The Jews continued to condemn their reportage as selective, to say the least. It concentrated on the severity of Israeli action, they maintained, while practically ignoring the atrocities committed by Syria, either directly or through its local accomplices.

Of all the American groups opposed to Israeli policy – the (non-fundamentalist) churches, the liberals, the far Left – the blacks made the loudest noise. They cared nothing for America's preoccupation with Soviet policies in the Middle East. Washington and the white American establishment, rather, were their enemy, just as they were the arch-oppressor of all coloured races. Seen from the blacks' perspective Arafat, engaged in a struggle similar to their own, looked heroic.

Some of their outstanding sons had reached the establishment too, though hardly to compare with the Jews. But the black vote was also an important factor upon which the Democrats relied and before which the Republicans had to make obeisance. President Jimmy Carter brought one of them, the dynamic but somewhat loose-tongued Andrew Young, into his administration as ambassador to the United Nations. Young and Carter, both southerners, were friends. The ambassador, however, made a gesture in 1979 that the Jews deemed unspeakable: he met secretly with a PLO representative in New York. America had long assured Israel that it would never legitimise the PLO by negotiating with it until the PLO formally recognised the Jewish state's right to exist. Now, in Jewish eyes, Ambassador Young had betrayed that pledge. In the consequent uproar he was forced into resignation, to be hailed by his black brothers as a fearless champion of human rights and a martyr to Jewish power in America. It was a blow to Carter, who had stalwartly covered up for his friend in many a gaffe, such as when Young compared the Israeli bombing of Lebanon with the American bombing of Vietnam.

The Andrew Young affair demolished whatever hope remained for a restoration of the old coalition of blacks and Jews. Even members of the moderate NAACP stated that their allies of yore had long ceased to believe in civil rights, but had become apologists for the racial status quo. A Baptist preacher in Harlem described the Palestinians as 'the niggers of the Middle East'. This was too much for the Jewish leadership. Black anti-semitism, it asserted, had arrived with a vengeance. Picture the Jews' unease, therefore, as another black spokesman, the Reverend Jesse Jackson, emerged in the preliminaries to the presidential election of 1984 as a likely vice-president should the Democrats win.

Jesse Jackson placed the chosen presidential candidate, Walter Mondale, in a quandary. On the one hand, what greater tribute to the American way of life, where the humblest could rise to the highest, than for a descendant of Negro slaves to be his deputy in the White House? Ronald Reagan, the incumbent, was also cultivating the black vote, but could he trump such a card? Yet the Jews did not stand alone in fearing Jackson's adoption. Almost all white America saw his people as moving too fast. Unspoken was the dread of some mishap to send a successful Mondale into the next world, putting Jackson into office as Chief Executive. But Jackson spared them the agony (as indeed did Mondale, for he lost by a landslide). He perpetrated enough insults – called in Americanese 'ethnic slurs' – to indicate that the Jews of America would not have him at any price. Disparaging name-calling had long been inadmissible in America, to the degree that 'black' reached the language because 'Negro' or 'coloured person' had begun to give offence. No one in his right mind, except a rabid antisemite, would speak of the Jews as 'Yids'. Jackson, however, transgressed the taboo by referring to them in an aside (published as it happened by a black reporter) as 'Hymies', and to New York as 'Hymie-town'.

Struggling to recapture lost ground, Jackson later recanted. He failed. Mondale decided he could still make history by choosing his running-mate from another 'discriminated' sector of the population who simultaneously responded to the desirability of ethnicity: a woman, Geraldine Ferraro, descended from Italian immigrants. Mondale needed the Jews not only for their vote; he needed their money too, for campaign expenses. Individuals could no longer give huge personal contributions as hitherto, Congress having made this illegal, but they could circumvent the law through the device known as Political Action Committees. And via this channel, Jews endowed their favoured candidates royally. Joan Rivers, the star comedienne, endorsed a fund-raising circular addressed to Jewish America on this score, stating that the relevant PAC had contributed 779,000 dollars in 1984 to candidates of both parties 'who recognise Israel as a strategic asset to America and our only reliable ally in the Middle East'. Contrariwise, a black pro-Jackson organisation had received 100,000 dollars from the Arab League in 1981.

Jackson had only tardily repudiated the support of Louis Farrakhan, high priest of the 'Nation of Islam'. This separatist movement, starting from the back streets of Chicago, was fast converting a significant element of the black population to the Koran. Until Farrakhan was given his *congé*, at Mondale's insistence, the man stood at Jackson's elbow at many of his meetings. He was wont to describe Judaism as 'a dirty religion'. That he dared openly to enunciate such a phrase gave him national prominence. Farrakhan kept the press on its toes to record his every antisemitic observation, as when he told a UN correspondents' meeting in August 1984 that 'President Reagan and Walter Mondale absolutely bow down to the strength of the Jewish lobby' and, on another occasion, 'There seems to be an unwritten law that Israel and Jews cannot be criticised, particularly by blacks.' One publication of the Nation of Islam, *The Final Call*, declared in a 1984 issue: 'Two thousand years have not changed the Jews, nor has it changed God's condemnation of them from the mouth of one of his righteous servants. Then it was Jesus, today it is Minister Farrakhan.' Jackson successfully re-established his credibility as an authentic Democratic Party leader, and received substantial endorsement as presidential material in 1988 against that other 'ethnic' Michael Dukakis, who was ultimately preferred.

Nowhere in the world today does an overtly antisemitic force exist (and they never cease to be born) with so great a following as black nationalism in America. Argentina and the Soviet Union have been guilty of persecuting Jews not on religious or racial grounds, but because of their identification with movements vocally dissenting from their authoritarian regimes. This might be left-wing agitation as in Argentina, or cultural separatism (in

Jewish terms, Zionism) in the USSR. Jews numbered excessively among the *desaparecidos*, the 'disappeared', brutally disposed of during the long night of military rule in Argentine. And they of course constituted the most numerous of 'refuseniks' in the USSR, bravely asserting their right to exit visas when this commonly entailed dismissal from employment, and on occasion imprisonment, internal exile or confinement in mental institutions. But average citizens of those two countries were uninvolved. Only in America, however, has antisemitism developed from a base in populist mythology, and it has arrived there as a tributary to the stream of fundamentalism found in all religions today, and flowing counter to the Western world's ecumenical tendencies hastening to heal spiritual conflict. White Christian fundamentalism in the United States performs uniquely: it despairs of Judaism as a religion yet glorifies Israel as a state – the right-wing, anti-Soviet reflex.

How has Judaism itself succumbed? Menahem Begin seemed a frustrated leader in the fundamentalist mould until restrained by the responsibilities of high office. But a Jewish equivalent of the Shi'ite ayatollahs emerged in the form of Rabbi Meir Kahane. He arrived in the late 1960s as an extreme practitioner of racial hatred when he founded the Jewish Defense League in the United States and authored the slogan 'Never Again!'. Born in New York, Kahane's career flowered with his distorted response to the Holocaust, so injecting a neo-Fascist ingredient into Jewish public life. He first came into prominence through a policy of aggressive vigilantism against the blacks. For a while he commuted between New York and Jerusalem. Then in 1984 he gained a seat in the Israel parliament, signifying that at least 26,000 voters saw Kahane as the people's saviour.

Kahane is a mirror image of Farrakhan: an American in Israel, largely dependent upon a constituency of anti-Arab Zionist 'ultras', many of them religious with a Messianic obsession. So the man expresses, in the most extreme sense, the Jews' peculiar location in the Western as well as the Eastern world. His followers in America, young toughs, adopted the tactics of violence, including arson and death threats, to harass Soviet UN officials and their families night and day, to the acute embarrassment of the US government and the displeasure of Jewish bodies quietly working to increase emigration permits for Jewish refuseniks. Yet Kahane won many supporters in New York, including folk-singer Bob Dylan (born Robert Zimmerman). In his Israeli persona Kahane mounted a fanatical campaign with the object of driving every Arab out of the enlarged territory. Generating waves of disgust whenever he appeared in public, he has served time in Israeli prisons for incitement against the Arabs. But Kahane admits of no containment, and has earned the distinction of turning the Zionist dream of hope into a recurring possibility of nightmare. In and out of Israel, Jews are working towards an accommodation with the Arabs, a people whom Kahane has publicly addressed as 'dogs'. To a small section of the Oriental Jewish community such insults come over as inspired.

Kahane has applauded each explosion of Jewish violence with some grotesquerie of his own. In 1982 an American-born serviceman opened fire to kill two young Arabs on the Dome of the Rock, the site most sacred to Islam in Jerusalem, and Kahane described the murder as the act of a 'hero who tried to liberate the Temple Mount from the foreigners' hands'. He planned an 'emigration office' in an Arab village, purporting to initiate the Arab evacuation of the country, only to be frustrated by a group of rabbis spending their sabbath in peaceful commune with the local inhabitants of the village. Every people has its lunatic politicians. They arouse derision rather than fear. The menace of Kahane resides in his success among maximalist hard-liners whose solitary approach to the Arabs is to meet terror with terror.

That Kahane won his malignant spurs in America as a rabble-rouser on behalf of the Jews of the USSR damaged what became, after Israel, the prime unifying cause in Jewish life. It is a cause riddled with contradictions in any case, demanding re-examination of the term 'antisemitism' when applied to post-Stalinist Russia. Dispassionate students of the Jewish situation in that country require to assess motivation on all sides: that of the Soviet Union in periodically opening and then closing its gates; that of Israel in orchestrating a vociferous international campaign on their behalf; and that of the Soviet Jews themselves, who began by gratefully proceeding to Israel as though in realisation of a long-cherished dream and then, in the large majority, choosing other destinations.

Self-evidently, the freedoms all men and women take for granted in democratic countries have never obtained in Russia, tsarist or Communist, though at this writing Mikhail Gorbachev, with his modest reforms and more open government, appears to have embarked on a new course. But expressions of views opposed to official Communist doctrine continue to invite action by the KGB. Emigration is not allowed, nor overseas visits, while refusal to perform military service on grounds of conscience is just one of the 'crimes' which can earn long terms of imprisonment, confinement to a labour camp or internal exile. Although officially an atheistic state, Russia sanctions the existence of churches, synagogues and mosques formally registered as such, but they may be used only for purposes of prayer. The Orthodox Church alone, having made peace with the regime and been rendered an obedient tool, is allowed links overseas, through the World Council of Churches. Indeed, the Orthodox Church received observer status at the Second Vatican Council. But the others may not join with followers of the same confession in international organisations, nor share their objectives. Jews wishing to follow their religion are penalised because all the literature involved is in Hebrew, a language virtually proscribed. Devotional books and religious calendars may not be published, and the manufacture of phylacteries and prayer shawls is forbidden. Rabbinical replacements for the few synagogues in existence are hard to find.

Where does this leave individuals and groups who fail to bow to such laws? They are marked out as dissidents. In exceptional cases they will be left alone, but if judged troublesome or dangerous, punishments can be harsh. So far as can be discovered, there are no rigid rules. Were Russia only to permit foreign correspondents to travel easily across its vast expanse and interview its citizens, doubtless many happy people would be observed, softer application of the regulations would be reported, life would not appear so bleak, and the country might receive a better press. But Russia chooses to keep its citizens and the foreign media apart. As a consequence, information comes mostly from those brave enough to challenge the rules, in fact from dissident sources, and it speaks of persecution, tyranny and a Soviet justice which, like the Slansky trials in Czechoslovakia, rightly belongs to Kafka.

Organisations closely monitoring Soviet religious persecution, such as Keston College and Amnesty International in England, long estimated a figure of approximately 10,000 prisoners of conscience in Russian jails and labour camps, or banished to internal exile. Of these, some 2,000 were said to be religious believers, the majority of them Baptists, undergoing punishment for failing to register their congregations and conducting Bible classes and seminars, or for publishing material without prior submission to the official censor. Beginning with 1986, the figures were radically scaled down. The Soviets themselves announced the release of several hundred during 1987, and the number actually known for certain as remaining in detention was fewer than 300. The world spoke little of such religious dissidents. It focused attention rather on the plight of the most renowned: the scientist and Nobel laureate Andrei Sakharov, for example, various writers and the Jewish dissident Anatoli Sharansky, who was sentenced to thirteen years for treason in 1977. Benjamin Levich, the distinguished physicist, lost his Chair of Chemical Mechanics at the Moscow State University in 1972 on announcing his desire to emigrate to Israel. He was condemned to unskilled employment until 1977, when protests by fellow-scientists throughout the world secured his exit visa.

In mid-1987, not one known Jew was still undergoing penal sentence, but the number so far refused permission to emigrate could be in the neighbourhood of 11,000, some of whom have been awaiting exit visas for at least ten years. This by no means exhausts the total of Jews hoping to leave, which to Western knowledge could exceed a third of a million. World Jewry, in response to a lead from Israel, has conducted a large-scale campaign on their behalf for many years, elevating Russia's treatment of its Jews to an urgent international issue with repercussions on Soviet relations with the United States, other democratic countries and the Jews in general. In a striking reversal of circumstances, Jews now have places to go to but they cannot leave Russia; before the Second World War, Europe wanted them out but no one would take them.

Russian Jews, it will be recalled, flocked to the Bolshevik ranks during the early revolutionary days. They constituted a highly visible element in the Communist Party apparatus, though Stalin's successive purges dislodged them from their peak of influence. This decline continued in the Khrushchev and Brezhnev periods. There is a pattern in the functioning of Jewish natural laws and it must apply to the Soviet Union as elsewhere. Assimilation, since the nineteenth century a tendency in Russian Jewry, was fast eroding the community into disappearance on its fringes, a process which the Second World War of course encouraged. This was taking place in more recent times precisely as educational opportunities spread through the country to strengthen the flow of adequately trained 'real' Russians to the commanding cultural and administrative heights of the hierarchy. The Soviets ardently desired the change and assisted it. Ekaterina Furtseva, Minister of Culture in the Khrushchev era, once stated in defence of removal of Jews that they constituted ten per cent of members of the Soviet Academy of Sciences and thirty-four per cent of personnel in the film industry.[13] A new intelligentsia was arising in all the Soviet republics and it was time to thin the proportion out.

Perhaps Jewish identity was diminishing into nothingness in the USSR. It had happened in earlier civilisations. Then, as we have told in the preceding chapter, the birth of the State of Israel disturbed the Jews' acquiescent temper towards Soviet Communism. Formerly they had in the main accepted the Russian realities, which gave all other nationalities opportunities for cultural fulfilment on a homeland basis – Ukrainians in the Ukraine, Armenians in Armenia and so on – while the Jews, not possessing their own republic (and declining the invitation to establish one in Biro-Bidhzan), remained a nationality without a territory. As far as could be discovered, they had no yearning for one. But the sense of national deprivation born in 1948 received dramatic impetus with the Six-Day War of 1967. Russian Jews too wanted their homeland now. There it stood, in a blaze of glory, though outside the Soviet Union. Traitorously as it were they pointed themselves towards Israel, a capitalist society

[13] Lionel Kochan (ed.), *The Jews in Soviet Russia since 1917*, London, 1970, p. 36.

withal, and heavily committed to Russia's rival superpower America. Zionism, to be fulfilled by emigration, was born again in the country of its fifty years' prohibition. But who could distinguish Zionists and those suddenly embracing the doctrine as a pretext simply to escape the regime?

From the day of its establishment Israel had not abandoned hope of persuading Russia to permit them to leave. The young state hungered for European immigrants. It owed its life source to Russian Jews, those founding fathers imbued with a Tolstoyan faith in the healing qualities of work on the land. Instead, most newcomers since 1948 were of Oriental (Sephardic) stock, and the fear was openly expressed that they were not of the mettle out of which nations aspiring to Western standards are forged. Hence the propaganda mounted on behalf of Soviet Jews.

This was a truly hazardous step. Conventional wisdom had it that *everyone* would, if he could, bid farewell to the Soviet Union; from what the world understood of the place, life there was dreary, harsh and regimented, a month's salary going into a new pair of shoes. Give the Jews exit permits and they would start a landslide. Keep them locked in and the USSR was guilty of denying this people something the system respected and all other Russians rightfully enjoyed, a national culture of their own. The Jews alone in the USSR were deprived even of a national language. Yiddish was a recognised folk language of the Jews – well, some Jews – but it lacked the stature of Hebrew, to which the people had clung as their sacred and literary tongue during 3,000 years, and which had achieved a renaissance in the nineteenth century to become again a spoken language in the twentieth. Propagating Zionism was a crime, and it seemed that the only reliable Jew by the standards of the USSR would be an anti-religious party member in some insignificant employment who had no relatives abroad and spent his free time exposing those of his kin illicitly engaged in singing Hebrew songs and favouring Israel in that country's conflict with the Arabs.

A Jewish resistance took root, alongside demonstrations against official policy on other grounds: armed intervention in Czechoslovakia (1968), persecution of dissidents, denial of human rights. Sharansky belonged to both groups, while his friend Andrei Sakharov, during his exile to Gorky, and while at liberty, spoke out fearlessly as a 'pure' Russian on behalf of freedom to emigrate. Jews publicly renounced their citizenship, returned war medals and circulated illegal (*samisdat*) literature. They claimed the right to reunion with their families already domiciled in Israel. The communal leadership in America, haunted by the guilt of its Holocaust silence during the war, made this so pressing a cause as to embarrass President Nixon in his moves for détente with the Kremlin.

Nixon entertained hopes of wooing the Jews away from the Democratic Party to support his re-election in 1972, especially since the Democratic candidate (George McGovern) was known to be lukewarm towards Israel. Nixon's Jewish confidant, his party benefactor Max Fisher, informed the President this would have greater prospects of success if he exerted pressure upon the Russians to release their Jews. Nixon took up the cause with a will. He accorded Russian Jews right of automatic entry into the USA to a limit of 30,000 per year, as political refugees, over and above the existing immigration quota (preference by national origin had been abolished since 1965). This infuriated the Kremlin all the more. Jews had no cause to describe themselves as political refugees, it contended, for they were not being persecuted. Nor should the USA interfere in the domestic affairs of another country, and decidedly not when its own record on human rights was by no means unblemished.

Relations between the two countries suffered further deterioration as Henry Jackson, Democratic Senator for Washington State, agitated from 1972 onward to make the granting of most-favoured-nation status to Russia in new trade negotiations dependent upon the release of Soviet Jews. Senator Jackson doubtless acted out of humanitarian motives, but it was not lost on the White House that he too nursed presidential ambitions and therefore had his own reasons for making the Jews his special concern. He pressed the issue for three years, until he succeeded in attaching his amendment prohibiting most-favoured-nation status to any country limiting rights of emigration.[14] It was left to Kissinger, who fought the amendment all the

[14] Freedom of Emigration Amendment to the Trade Reform Act (known as the Jackson–Vanik Amendment) signed into law by President Gerald Ford, 3 January 1975.

way, to carry the message to Moscow. This particular display of American Jewry's political muscle so angered the Russians that they repudiated their trade agreements with America and for a period turned a deaf ear to any talk of détente emerging from Washington.

In all the agitation on behalf of Russian Jewry one man, Andrew Young, remained singularly unimpressed. While President Carter's UN ambassador during Sharansky's trial in 1977, and precisely as his chief placed human rights in the centre of a foreign policy directed warningly at Moscow, the black leader commented that 'hundreds, maybe thousands, of people I would categorise as political prisoners are in American jails'. To the blacks the entire Soviet Jewry campaign was studded with hypocrisy: the Jews felt no concern for the Palestinian Arabs aching to return to their homeland but supported their exclusion by Israel. Yet that same country had houses and jobs ready for Jews out of Russia, in any number, and excoriated Soviet obstruction as a policy of antisemitism.

In some Jewish quarters cries of antisemitism have a way of arousing feverish action, with crisis meetings, pamphleteering and urgent fund-raising campaigns in the way that signs of the death-watch beetle in the roof of a church will excite its congregation. Bowing before the storm as early as 1970, Russia relented. The Israelis stared in admiration as a thousand highly skilled European newcomers, some speaking perfect Hebrew, adapted swiftly to the capitalist system, assumed posts at the universities, established orchestras and brought an infusion of much-needed skill into the plumbing trade. Before long these Russians were so completely at home in Israel that their complaints against the bureaucracy exceeded those of old-established citizens. In 1971, 13,000 arrived, one year later 31,000, then 35,000. Then in 1974 the flow decreased. Anxiety spread that the Kremlin was about to shut it off completely, but in 1979 no fewer than 51,000 left the USSR. Much of this success rate had to do with the raising of the agitational temper, more of it from a desire of the Soviets to demonstrate renewed goodwill in the interests of an accommodation with the West. It seemed a miracle. Along with the Jews, many hundreds of Soviet Germans, Armenians and Christian religious dissidents were allowed out.

Unhappily for Israel, the exodus took an unexpected turn –
away from the Holy Land, not towards it. Political refugee
status, conferred by America as a blessing, transpired as a grievous wound inflicted upon the self-esteem of the Jewish state. The
call for reunion of families now sounded hollow, the Russian
Jews were criticised for cheating, while the cause of Zionism
received a rebuff as Jews seemed to hasten not only to America
but almost anywhere except to Israel. This set off an unedifying
tug-of-war between Zionist and non-Zionist welfare bodies over
the 'stealing' of Jewish souls. Russia co-operated with the fiction
of 'return to their homeland' for a time, then openly declared its
hand. The emigration, it contended, had manifestly absorbed all
those professing an attachment to Israel. Those now applying for
exit permits were prompted purely by a desire to put their own
country behind them. This could not be tolerated. Emigration
decreased once more, to a trickle. The Jews were refused exit
visas on the pretext that their work, or their military service, had
made them privy to knowledge vital to the security of the state,
even when they had engaged in no such occupation for a decade
or more. Emigration was also refused on the grounds of not
satisfying the requirement of close kinship with a relative abroad.

Sharansky – that intrepid computer programmer whose final
words at his trial had been, 'To my wife and my people, I can only
say, "Next year in Jerusalem". To this court, which decided my
fate in advance, I say nothing' – was freed in 1986 after nine
years, in a prisoner exchange with America. It was as though he
had been a spy. One of the most awkward, surely the most
celebrated, of Russia's prisoners of conscience, he received a
hero's welcome in the country he had regarded as his motherland
for so long. But few others came to Israel. The emigration had
virtually drawn to a halt. In December 1986, seventy-seven Jews
departed, seventy of them to lands other than Israel.

Despite a perceptible relaxation of rules in 1987, with
increased departures, the Jews of the world, speaking through *ad*
hoc bodies, would not accept the situation. They viewed it as one
aspect of Russia's anti-Jewish posture where its condemnation of
Israel's policies towards the Arabs was another. Israel preferred
to believe the brakes were imposed because the Jews spurned
their true home. In its indignation it demanded direct flights from

Moscow to bring them to Israel, as it were avoiding the temptation of stop-overs in Vienna and Rome by which they customarily dropped out. Russia declined. It had again broken diplomatic contact with Israel during the Six-Day War, and was not yet in the mood to heal relations. In refusing to grant exit visas to Jews and others requesting them, the USSR was in breach of the Universal Declaration of Human Rights (Article 13) as ratified by the USSR in 1973. It also infringed the spirit, if not the letter, of the thirty-five-nation conference that adjourned in 1975 with the Helsinki Final Act. Then, in 1988, Moscow allowed direct flights to Bucharest, thus creating a Communist-controlled emigration 'funnel' to Israel.

Discussion of the formidable pressure mounted against the Soviet Union over its conduct towards its Jewish minority would be incomplete without noting the absence of such pressure in the case of Argentina. During the years of junta rule in that country, 1976–83, some 9,000 people, mostly young men and women but also on occasion their near relatives, were kidnapped from their homes and in the streets, never to be heard of again. This is the official figure produced by an investigatory commission appointed after the Falklands War by the junta's democratic successor, President Raul Alfonsin.[15] Of the names listed, about 800 could be identified as Jews. More, the commission specifically reported that 'antisemitism must be seen against the backdrop of the ruling regime's totalitarian view of society'. We are concerned here not with mere incarceration. Torture, rape and other unspeakable atrocities accompanied the imprisonment, mostly ending in death for the victims.

Argentina's rigid Catholic tradition lent itself to Fascist dictatorship as easily as Italy and Spain, so with a considerable Jewish population, 450,000 (a maximum estimate), antisemitism has rarely been absent from the social and political atmosphere. The Jews constitute less than two per cent of the total population, though nine per cent of the *desaparecidos*, on whose behalf the black-sashed Mothers of the Plaza de Mayo movingly demonstrated every Thursday. One body notably silent over this

---

[15] *Nunca Mas* ('Never Again'), Report by Argentina's National Commission on Disappeared People, Buenos Aires, 1984; Published in London, 1986.

situation, never enquiring why Jews were carried off five times as frequently as their numbers would justify, was the elected Jewish representative council, Delegación de Asociaciones Israelitas Argentinas (DAIA). Further, this body discouraged international Jewish condemnation of the persecutions. Such was the degree of fear under which the organisation laboured, as obedient to the ruling camarilla as was the Russian Orthodox Church to the Kremlin.

Discretion may in this case have been the better part of Latin-American valour. But the question arises notwithstanding: should not their brethren overseas, generally so passionate in defence of Jewish causes, have joined in the general outcry against the junta's brutality as it was known abroad? Their leaders in the United States and England, frequently welcome in the White House and Downing Street for discussions on Israel, and Russian Jewry, refrained from protest. The Israeli government, professing to champion Jewish rights everywhere, remained silent. The editor of the London *Jewish Chronicle* visited Argentina in 1979 and years later admitted that he was urged 'not to make an issue of the disappeared'.[16]

This conspiracy of silence was broken by Jacobo Timerman, editor of *La Opinión*, who was tortured for months, kept in solitary confinement and then sentenced to two years' house arrest before his expulsion from Argentina in 1979. He fell foul of Jewish spokesmen in his own country and abroad with his devastating exposure, *Prisoner Without a Name, Cell Without a Number*.[17] He was arrested, he asserts there, purely as a Jew, a liberal and a Zionist, though others claimed he had connections through a banker friend, also a Jew, with left-wing terrorists. Whatever the reason for his incarceration – and his denial of the terrorist link was accepted by the authorities – his story is harrowing in the extreme. Timerman's principal purpose was to attack the passivity, indeed complicity, of the DAIA and world Jewry in the face of the barbaric military rule. Hand on heart, the DAIA retorted that it had only a few Jewish names, notified by their parents, among the disappeared. These were individuals

[16] *Jewish Chronicle*, 25 May 1984.
[17] New York, 1981.

punished for acts of violence in a dangerous period while the country rocked in civil strife. Jews certainly belonged to the Left and took part in such acts to overthrow the regime, during what had become known as 'the dirty war'. But parents too had been abducted. Grounds therefore existed in plenty to mount a campaign similar in scale to the one proceeding on the Russo-Jewish question. The Latin American representative of the influential American Jewish Committee was forced to flee Buenos Aires in 1977 after right-wing guerrillas threatened his life, and those of his wife and children. Meekly, and silently, the AJC closed its office in Argentina.

The contrasting Jewish attitudes in fact suggest another explanation: the exigencies of the cold war, which find the Jews wholly committed to the West. For an indication we have the judgement of Irving Kristol, once on the editorial staff of *Commentary*, subsequently a leading expositor of America's neo-conservative Right. He described Timerman as just another 'Solzhenitsyn of the Left'. Argentina was a friendly 'authoritarian' regime, Kristol wrote, not a hostile 'totalitarian' regime like the Soviet Union.[18] There we have it: a distinction without a difference. Jewish energies in the struggle against antisemitism were making their own selection. Argentina lay in the Western camp. It enjoyed close ties approaching alliance not only with the United States but with Israel also, and therefore was not to be harried, neither on the Jewish nor any other human rights issue.

Avoiding this only possible but unpalatable conclusion, the Jewish leadership everywhere followed the example set by its American flag-bearers in ascribing its reticence to the DAIA's fear of further repression should the regime come under attack. Perhaps. But the argument should apply even more strongly to the USSR. There the Jews were more vulnerable because they had no representation properly speaking, and no Jewish leaders; sometimes a Russian Jew (for example, General David Dragunski) would speak out to tell the world community to shut up, only to be derided as a government stooge. And nothing prevented foreign Jews, in pre-war days, from raising their voice, and launching a trade embargo, against Nazi Germany despite

[18] *Wall Street Journal*, 29 May 1981.

pleadings by the community within that country to leave it alone to deal with its plight.

*   *   *

The current of Jewish thought and practice, as we have seen, frequently moves in opposite directions. Against the instinct for self-renewal, most vitally expressed in the birth of Israel immediately following the Holocaust, Jews readily discard their particularities of religion and manners so as to embrace the majority society in which they are located. The substitution can be total. As they confront the twenty-first century, Jews therefore ask themselves whether the recurring tensions of two thousand years, with which this book has been concerned, will extend into the next millennium. Will antisemitism never cease?

An answer based upon the guidance of historical criteria eludes us. The Jews are not the people they were. The social revolution ensuing from the Second World War effected in them a transition more complete perhaps than in most others. They no longer form so clearly a defined sect in their Diaspora, while independence in Israel has reshaped them as a nation both physically and psychologically, opening up a road they have never travelled before. In considering their future, the Jews might well enquire whether external forces will allow their survival as an individual people – not because of violence, but as a consequence of tranquillity.

Since the 1960s societies universally have undergone radical change, from the smallest unit, the family, to the largest, the nation. In the case of the Jews the family once constituted the strongest instrument of stability. It bound the people to monogamy, their women to chastity, their children to obedience within the home, and the whole interconnecting with other families by a sense of community. All this was altered by libertarian doctrines, by the dramatic spread of university education and not least by the birth control pill. Such inroads into the age-old social pattern befell other peoples too, of course, but to a lesser degree. None has progressed so wholly and so swiftly into the middle class, and higher, because no others were so completely identified with those great cities which inaugurated the change. Thus the Jews were drawn out of themselves and into a wider world, which itself was being transformed so thoroughly as to render traditional class and national structures obsolete. The Jews seized all the opportunities suddenly available. The younger generation broadened its experience with travel, and deserted its faith as never before. Daughters, released from gender restraints, now seek out careers, achieve economic independence and marry, or cohabit, with whom they will. For a paradigm, think of Judith Resnik, the professional astronaut who died in the explosion of the space shuttle *Challenger* in January 1986. The process is irreversible, despite the penetration of fundamentalist beliefs in Judaism in common with other religions.

As a corollary, familiarity with the Jew in all walks of life has shorn him of his mystique, which in the past caused distaste and suspicion, if not worse. The bearded Jew, once universally caricatured by the antisemite, is lost in the profusion of other men with beards. His traditional caftan, badge of piety, is now confined to the few, and is more frequently encountered among persons of other races less self-conscious about their attire. Where differences of colour become commonplace, differences of religion wane in significance. Our new world is composed of multiracial societies, with the introduction of black, brown and yellow peoples into Europe and North America in great number. Yet the clearest division of mankind passes along a line between North and South, alienating the Third World from the First. A conflict exists here, and we don't know how it will end, except to eliminate the older divisions that kept the white man in perpetual war against his own. We have now entered the uncharted territory of genetic engineering, semen banks and surrogacy. The consequences are likely to overturn all our existing assumptions concerning heredity and culture. Call a man a Jew in the twenty-first century and you may well be addressing an Eskimo.

The prospect turns us back to our present-day civilisation, which allocates a specific role to the Jew if only because the United States has conquered the world politically through economic power and culturally because of the saturation spread of film and television. In this regard nothing in the Jew's history equals the function he has achieved through his establishment in that country. One-half of the Jewish world is concentrated between New York and California, whereas the rest are dispersed in smaller settlements, including Israel, across the globe. He is ensconced with such authority in the entertainment industry and its ancillary activities that he can deliver a face and a theme effortlessly before a billion pairs of eyes. Frequently the face is Jewish, and proclaims itself so. In Woody Allen, born Allen Konigsberg, the world observes the Jew in all the guises of rejected man – flawed physique, unsuccessful lover, failed businessman, frustrated intellectual – and ever engaged in a hopeless search for a spiritual anchor. His plethora of Jewish symbols, so characteristic of American humour, betray a certain arrogance: understand them if you can.

Woody Allen belongs to a cinematic school that translated the traditional Jewish stereotype into a weapon of satire, thus defeating antisemitism by ridicule. Others have appropriated Jewish culture of the more conventional kind for purposes of mass communication. The musical play *Fiddler on the Roof*, sketchily drawn from the Yiddish tales of Sholem Aleichem, dresses dozens of English amateur opera companies in the costume of the Hassidim, yet audiences find this as legitimate for the stage as *The Merry Widow*. American Jewry has still not accustomed itself to the sensation of complete acceptance. It regularly takes its own temperature, and commissions surveys to measure others' attitudes towards the people (what percentage of the population of Nebraska dislikes us?) as if periodically digging up a plant to examine its growth. Barbra Streisand had a message for them, should the community wish to hear it. She adapted a short story by Nobel laureate Isaac Bashevis Singer, *Yentl*, and made its uncompromisingly Jewish theme, other-worldly in itself, a *succès d'estime* on the international screen.

The people have by no means totally released themselves from their obsession with being a marked race. France in the 1980s nominated two baptised Jews as Prime Minister and Archbishop of Paris. The community there couldn't decide whether to be flattered or distressed. Financial scandals affecting Jews, such as the one associated in 1986 with Ivan Boesky, the notorious Wall Street arbitrageur, sent tremors of apprehension among them in America. Boesky and his associates were an uncomfortable reminder that the late nineteenth-century manipulator of the money market, personifying greed and so damaging to Jewish self-esteem, was with us still. Margaret Thatcher appointed five Jews to her Conservative government in 1983. One of them resigned three years later in a political argument (along with a purely gentile Cabinet minister, it transpired), and some British Jews actually fell to wondering whether he was a victim of antisemitism!

Better to contemplate the new world preparing to face the next century with its more realistic anxieties. The Bible speaks of the man Moses who defected from his people, intending to disappear among the gentiles, when the Burning Bush reminded him of his origins and induced his return as their leader and teacher. If there is a moral to conclude this account of antisemitism in the context of world history, it lies perhaps in the futility of man's struggle to elude his destiny. The Jew's future demands a stronger awareness of his own capacities to affect his relationship with his fellow-men. He must relinquish that archaic conception of being a victim tossed in the storms of other peoples' development.

The challenge is awesome, for with this awareness he will discover a greater role for himself in bringing a new atmosphere to one of the world's most painful of international problems, the quest for a just peace where his people are still at war in the Middle East. Until this is achieved he will be unable to enjoy that harmony with Islam that now pervades his relations with Christendom. Middle East peace will moreover render him better equipped also to work towards true equality for those other racial minorities suffering, to this day, the cruel discrimination which the Jews have at last put behind them.

BIBLIOGRAPHY

GENERAL

American Jewish Year Book, editions from 1939, Philadelphia, 1939–86.

Baron, Salo W., *A Social and Religious History of the Jews*, 3 vols., Philadelphia, 1937.

The Cambridge Ancient History, Vols. IX–XII, 1970–84.

The Cambridge History of Islam, 2 vols., 1970.

The Cambridge Medieval History, 8 vols., 1911–64.

Dubnov, Simon, *History of the Jews*, 5 vols., tr. Moshe Spiegel, London, 1967–73.

Encyclopaedia Judaica, 16 vols. plus supps., New York, 1972.

Graetz, Heinrich, *History of the Jews*, 6 vols., Philadelphia, 1956.

Heer, Friedrich, *God's First Love*, London, 1970.

The Jewish Encyclopaedia, 12 vols., New York, 1901–6.

The New Cambridge Modern History, 11 vols., 1962–71.

The New Catholic Encyclopaedia, 15 vols. plus supps., Washington, 1967.

Poliakov, Léon, *The History of Antisemitism*, 4 vols. to 1933, London, 1974–85.

1 ROME AGAINST JERUSALEM

Aberbach, Moses, *The Roman–Jewish War*, London, 1966.

Bentwich, Norman, *Philo-Judaeus of Alexandria*, Philadelphia, 1910.

Brandon, S. G. E., *Jesus and the Zealots*, Manchester, 1967.

——, *The Trial of Jesus of Nazareth*, London, 1969.

Cohn, Haim, *The Trial and Death of Jesus*, London, 1972.

Eusebius, *Ecclesiastical History*, London, 1927.

Gibbon, Edward, *The Decline and Fall of the Roman Empire* (Chs. 15 and 16, publ. as *Gibbon on Christianity*), London, 1957.

Grant, Michael, *The Jews in the Roman World*, London, 1973.

Herford, R. Travers, *Christianity in Talmud and Midrash*, Clifton, NJ, 1966.

——, *The Ethics of the Talmud*, New York, 1966.

Josephus, *Works*, tr. W. Whiston, London, 1906.

Juster, Jean, *Les Juifs dans l'Empire romain*, 2 vols., Paris, 1914.

Luibheid, Colm (ed.), *The Essential Eusebius*, New York, 1966.

Maccoby, Hyam, *Revolution in Judaea*, London, 1973.

Millar, Fergus, *A Study of Cassius Dio*, Oxford, 1964.

Reinach, Theodore, *Textes d'auteurs grecs et romains relatifs au judaïsme*, Paris, 1895.

Renan, Ernest, *The Life of Jesus*, London, 1891.

Schürer, Emil, *The History of the Jewish People in the Age of Jesus Christ*, 2 vols., revised and ed. by Geza Vermes *et al.*, Edinburgh, 1973, 1979.

Vermes, Geza, *The Dead Sea Scrolls in English*, London, 1962.

Yadin, Yigael, *Massada: Herod's Fortress and the Zealots' Last Stand*, London, 1966.

2 BETWEEN THE CRESCENT AND THE CROSS

Augustine, *City of God*, tr. Henry Betterson, ed. David Knowles, London, 1972.

Baer, Yitzhak, *A History of the Jews in Christian Spain*, Vol. I, Philadelphia, 1966.

Caplan, Samuel, and Ribalow, Harold U. (eds.), *The Great Jewish Books*, New York, 1952.

Dunlop, D. M., *The History of the Jewish Khazars*, Princeton, NJ, 1954.

Goldstein, David, *Hebrew Poems of Spain*, London, 1965.

Gregory of Tours, *History of the Franks*, tr. O. M. Dalton, Oxford, 1927.

Hitti, P. K., *History of the Arabs*, London, 1943.

Katz, Solomon, *The Jews in the Visigothic and Frankish Kingdoms of Spain and Gaul*, Cambridge, Mass., 1937.

Koestler, Arthur, *The Thirteenth Tribe*, London, 1976.

Parkes, James, *The Conflict of the Church and the Synagogue*, London, 1934.

Southern, R. W., *The Making of the Middle Ages*, London, 1968.

3 HOMELANDS IN THE WILDERNESS

Adler, A. (ed.), *The Itinerary of Benjamin of Tudela*, New York, 1927.

Adler, Michael, *Jews of Medieval England*, London, 1939.

Anchel, Robert, *Les Juifs de France*, Paris, 1947.

Baer, Yitzhak, *A History of the Jews in Christian Spain*, 2 vols., Philadelphia, 1966, 1971.

Blumenkrantz, Bernhard, *Le Juif médiéval au miroir de l'art chrétien*, Paris, 1966.

——, 'Les Auteurs latins chrétiens du Moyen Age sur les Juifs et le Judaïsme', *Revue des études juives*, Vol. 10⁹, Paris, 1948.

Coulton, G. G., *Medieval Panorama*, Cambridge, 1938.

Holinshed, Raphael, *Chronicles of England, Scotland and Ireland*, 6 vols., London, 1807–8.

Jacobs, Joseph, *The Jews of Angevin England*, London, 1893.

Lea, Henry C., *A History of the Inquisition in Spain*, 3 vols., New York, 1922.

Lehrman, Charles, *The Jewish Element in French Literature*, Cranbury, NJ, 1971.

Le Strange, Guy, *Palestine under the Moslems, 650–1500*, London, 1890.

Llorente, Juan A., *The History of the Inquisition of Spain*, London, 1826.

Murray, Albert V., *Abelard and St Bernard: A Study in Twelfth Century Modernism*, Manchester, 1967.

Rabinowitz, L., *The Social Life of the Jews of Northern France in the 12th–14th Centuries*, New York, 1973.

Roth, Cecil, *A Short History of the Jewish People*, London, 1959.

Routh, C. R. N., *They Saw it Happen in Europe*, Oxford, 1965.

Runciman, Steven, *A History of the Crusades*, 3 vols., Cambridge, 1951–4.

Tuchman, Barbara W., *A Distant Mirror: The Calamitous 14th Century*, New York, 1978.

Ziegler, Philip, *The Black Death*, London, 1969.

4 OUTCASTS OF EUROPE

Abrahams, Beth-Zion (tr. and ed.), *The Life of Glückel of Hameln, Written by Herself*, London, 1962.

Altmann, Alexander, *Moses Mendelssohn*, London, 1973.

Besterman, Theodore, *Voltaire*, London, 1969.

Birmingham, Stephen, *The Grandees*, New York, 1971.

Bossuet, Jacques Bénigne, *Oeuvres Complètes*, Paris, 1863.

Braudel, Fernand, *The Mediterranean and the Mediterranean World in the Age of Philip II*, 2 vols., London, 1972–3.

——, *Civilisation and Capitalism, 15th–18th Centuries*, 3 vols., London, 1979.

Clarke, G. N., *The Seventeenth Century*, Oxford, 1947.

Ehrenberg, R., *Capital and Finance in the Age of the Renaissance*, London, 1928.

Fiedler, Leslie, *The Stranger in Shakespeare*, New York, 1972.

Fisch, Harold, *The Dual Image: A Study of the Jew in English Literature*, London, 1971.

Hyamson, Albert M., *The Sephardim of England*, London, 1951.

Israel, Jonathan I., *European Jewry in the Age of Mercantilism, 1550–1750*, Oxford, 1985.

Kobler, Franz, *Letters of Jews Through the Ages*, 2 vols., New York, 1978.

Lehrmann, Charles, *The Jewish Element in French Literature*, Cranbury, NJ, 1971.

Levin, Harry, *Christopher Marlowe*, London, 1961.

Litvinoff, Barnet, *Another Time, Another Voice* (fiction), London, 1971.

Ogg, David, *Europe in the Seventeenth Century*, London, 1965.

Pascal, Blaise, *Pensées*, ed. L. Brunschvig, Paris, 1925.

Pullen, Brian, *The Jews of Europe and the Inquisition of Venice, 1550–1670*, Oxford, 1985.

Roth, Cecil, *The House of Nasi*, Philadelphia, 1947–8.

—— (ed.), *Essays in Jewish History*, London, 1934.

Rousseau, Jean-Jacques, *Émile*, tr. Barbara Foxley, London, 1955.

Sholem, Gershom, *Sabbetai Sevi: The Mystical Messiah*, London, 1973.

Sombart, Werner, *The Jews and Modern Ca'italism*, London, 1913.

Tanner, J. R., *English Constitutional Conflicts of the Seventeenth Century*, Cambridge, 1962.

Tawney, R. H., *Religion and the Rise of Capitalism*, London, 1938.

Walter, H., *Moses Mendelssohn*, New York, 1930.

5 STEPS TOWARDS THE RACIAL DIVIDE

Anchel, Robert, *Napoléon et les Juifs*, Paris, 1928.

Arendt, Hannah, *Rahel Varnhagen*, London, 1957.

——, *The Origins of Totalitarianism*, New York, 1973.

——, 'Privileged Jews', *Jewish Social Studies*, New York, January 1946.

Boerne, Ludwig, *Gesammelte Schriften*, Stuttgart, 1840.

Brandes, Georg, *Main Currents in Nineteenth Century German Literature*, Vol. VI, London, 1896.

Brod, Max, *Heine, the Artist in Revolt*, London, 1956.

The Cambridge Economic History of Europe, Vol. V, Cambridge, 1977.

Carlyle, Thomas, *Miscellaneous Essays*, London, 1904.

Corti, Count, *The Rise of the House of Rothschild*, London, 1928.

Goethe, J. W. von, *Wilhelm Meister's Travels*, tr. Thomas Carlyle, London, 1904.

Hertzberg, Arthur, *The French Enlightenment and the Jews*, New York, 1968.

Herz, Henriette, *Ihr Leben und ihre Erinnerungen*, Berlin, 1850.

Key, Ellen, *Rahel Varnhagen*, New York, 1913.

Kober, Adolf, 'The French Revolution and the Jews of Germany', *Jewish Social Studies*, New York, October 1945.

Litvinoff, Barnet, 'Rahel Levin: The Apex of a Triangle', in *German Life and Letters*, Vol. 1, Oxford, July 1948.

Mahler, Raphael, *A History of Modern Jewry 1780–1815*, London, 1971.

Sachar, Howard M., *The Course of Modern Jewish History*, London, 1958.

Schwartzfuchs, Simon, *Napoleon, the Jews and the Sanhedrin*, London, 1979.

Szakowski, Zosa, *The Economic Status of the Jews in Alsace, Metz and Lorraine, 1648–1789*, New York, 1954.

Tama, D. *Transactions of the Parisian Sanhedrim (sic)*, London, 180⁷.

Untermeyer, Louis, *Heinrich Heine, Paradox and Poet*, New York, 1937.

Weldler-Steinberg, Augusta (ed.), *Rahel Varnhagen, Ein Frauenleben in Briefen*, Weimar, 1912.

Yogef, Gedalia, *Diamonds and Coral: Anglo-Dutch Jews and Eighteenth Century Trade*, Leicester, 1978.

6 PERILS OF EMANCIPATION

Berlin, Isaiah, *Against the Current: Essays in the History of Ideas*, London, 1979.

Blake, Robert, *Disraeli*, London, 1966.

Bouvier, Jean, *Les Rothschild*, Paris, 1970.

Carlebach, Julius, *Karl Marx and the Radical Critique of Judaism*, London, 1978.

Charvet, P. E. (ed.), *A Literary History of France*, 6 vols., London, 1964–74.

Chouraqui, André, *L'Alliance Israélite Universelle et la renaissance Juive contemporaine*, Paris, 1965.

Hess, Moses, *Rome and Jerusalem*, New York, 1958.

Lipman, Sonia and V. D., *The Century of Moses Montefiore*, Oxford, 1985.

Marx, Karl, *Early Writings*, tr. Rodney Livingstone and Gregor Benton, London, 1975.

McLellan, David, *Marx*, London, 1975.

Posener, S., *Adolphe Crémieux*, Paris, 1934.

Rabi (Wladimir Rabinovitch), *Anatomie du judaïsme français*, Paris, 1962.

Schulman, Mary, *Moses Hess: Prophet of Zionism*, New York, 1963.

Sholem, Gershom, *Major Trends in Jewish Mysticism*, London, 1955.

Stanislawski, Michael, *Tsar Nicholas I and the Jews*, New York, 1983.

Syrop, Konrad, *Poland in Perspective*, London, 1982.

Talmon, J. L., 'Social Prophetism in Nineteenth Century France', *Commentary*, New York, August 1958.

Weill, Georges, 'Les Juifs et le Saint-Simonisme', *Revue des études juives*, Paris, Nos. 30–1, 1895.

Weinreich, Max, *History of the Yiddish Language*, Chicago, 1973.

Wilson, Edmund, *To the Finland Station*, London, 1960.

7 WAGNER, DREYFUS AND THE LIBERAL PARADOX

Biale, David, *Power and Powerlessness in Jewish History*, New York, 1986.

Bloch, Jean-Richard,—*And Co.* (fiction), tr. C. K. Scott-Moncrieff, London, 1930.

Bouvier, Jean, *Le Krach de l'Union Générale*, Paris, 1960.

Brogan, Denis, *The Development of Modern France, 1870–1939*, London, 1967.

Chamberlain, Houston S., *Foundations of the Nineteenth Century*, London, 1910

Chouraqui, André, *L'Alliance Israélite Universelle et la renaissance juive contemporaine*, Paris, 1965.

Encyclopaedia Judaica, articles 'Music', Vol. 12, and 'Historiography', Vol. 8, New York, 1972.

Fraenkel, Joseph (ed.), *The Jews of Austria*, London, 1982.

Gobineau, Arthur de, *Essay on the Inequality of Races*, London, 1867.

Goldman, Albert, and Sprinchorn, Evert (eds.), *Wagner on Music and Drama*, London, 1977.

Gregor-Dellin, Martin, *Richard Wagner, His Life, His Work, His Century*, London, 1983.

Lestschinsky, Jacob, 'The Economic and Social Development of the Jewish People', in *The Jewish People, Past and Present*, New York, 1946.

Mann, Thomas, *Pro and Contra Wagner*, tr. Allen Blunden, London, 1985.

Manning, P. W., *Rehearsal for Destruction*, London, 1949.

Marrus, Michael R., *The Politics of Assimilation: The French Jewish Community at the Time of the Dreyfus Affair*, Oxford, 1971.

Newman, Ernest, *Richard Wagner*, 4 vols., London, 1933–47.

Pulzer, P. G. H., *The Rise of Political Antisemitism in Germany and Austria*, London, 1969.

Renan, Ernest, *Histoire générale et système comparé des langues sémitiques*, Paris, 1855.

Rabi (Wladimir Rabinovitch), *Anatomie du judaïsme français*, Paris, 1962.

Szakowski, Zosa, *Poverty and Social Welfare among French Jews, 1800–1880*, New York, 1954.

Wilson, Nelly, *Bernard-Lazare*, Cambridge, 1978.

Wilson, Stephen, *Ideology and Experience: Antisemitism in France at the Time of the Dreyfus Affair*, London, 1982.

Zweig, Stefan, *The World of Yesterday*, New York, 1943.

8 POGROM: THE JEWISH RESPONSE

Adler, Cyrus (ed.), *Jacob H. Schiff, His Life and Letters*, 2 vols., New York, 1928.

Baron, Salo, *Russian Jews under Tsars and Soviets*, New York, 1964.

Cahan, Abraham, *The Rise of David Levinsky* (fiction), New York, 1960.

Fuks, Marian, *et al.*, *Polish Jewry: History and Culture*, Warsaw, 1982.

Greenberg, Louis, *The Jews in Russia*, 2 vols., New Haven, Conn., 1951.

Howe, Irving, *World of Our Fathers* (publ. in London as *The Immigrant Jews of New York*), New York, 1976.

Jewish Encyclopedia, article 'Universities', Vol. XII, New York, 1906.

The Jewish Question in the Duma, speeches by Deputies, London, 1915.

Joselit, Jenna, *Our Gang*, Bloomington, Ind., 1984.

Kerensky, Alexander, *Russia and History's Turning Point*, New York, 1965.

Kunitz, Joshua, *Russian Literature and the Jew*, New York, 1929.

Leftwich, Joseph (ed.), *Yisröel: The First Jewish Omnibus* (anthology), London, 1954.

Levin, Shmarya, *Forward from Exile* (autobiography), tr. and ed. Maurice Samuel, Philadelphia, 1967.

Low, Charles, *Alexander III of Russia*, London, 1895.

Mendelsohn, E., *Class Struggle in the Pale: The Formative Years of the Jewish Workers' Movement in Tsarist Russia*, Cambridge, 1970.

Motzkin, Leo, *Die Judenpogrome in Russland*, Cologne, 1909.

Osofsky, Gilbert, *Harlem, the Making of a Ghetto: Negro New York 1890–1930*, New York, 1966.

Patai, Raphael (ed.), *The Complete Diaries of Theodor Herzl*, New York and London, 1960.

Patkin, A. L., *The Origins of the Russian-Jewish Labour Movement*,

Melbourne, 1947.

Pipes, Richard, *Russia under the Old Régime*, New York, 1964.

Samuel, Maurice, *Blood Accusation: The Strange History of the Beilis Case*, London, 1966.

——, *The World of Shalom Aleichem*, New York, 1943.

Seton-Watson, Hugh, *The Russian Empire 1801–1917*, London, 1967.

Shapiro, Harry L., *The Jewish People, a Biological History*, Paris, 1960.

Silberman, Charles E., *A Certain People*, New York, 1985.

Stone, Norman, *Europe Transformed, 1878–1919*, London, 1983.

Waxman, Meyer, *History of Jewish Literature*, 5 vols., New York, 1960.

Weisgal, Meyer W., *et al.* (eds.), *The Letters and Papers of Chaim Weizmann*, Vol. II, Oxford, 1971.

Wischnitzer, Mark, *To Dwell in Safety*, Philadelphia, 1948.

Zipperstein, Steven, *The Jews of Odessa: A Cultural History, 1794–1881*, Stanford, Calif., 1986.

9 IN QUEST OF THE ELDERS OF ZION

Agar, Herbert, *The United States: The Presidents, the Parties and the Constitution*, London, 1950.

Antonius, George, *The Arab Awakening*, London, 1938.

Belloc, Hilaire, *The Jews*, London, 1922.

Birmingham, Stephen, *Our Crowd: The Great Jewish Families of New York*, New York, 1967.

Bowle, John, *Viscount Samuel*, London, 1957.

British Statement of Policy, 'Churchill White Paper', Cmd 1700, London, 1922.

Chesterton, G. K., *What I Saw in America*, London, 1922.

Cohn, Norman, *Warrant for Genocide*, London, 1967.

Davis, David Brion, *Slavery and Human Progress*, New York, 1984.

Deutscher, Isaac, *The Prophet Armed, Trotsky 1879–1921*, London, 1965.

Documents of British Foreign Policy, 1918–1939, Vols. IV, VII, VIII, London, 1952, 1958.

Fishman, William J., *East End Jewish Radicals 1875–1914*, London, 1975.

Ford, Henry, *The International Jew*, London, 1920.

Friedman, Isaiah, *Germany, Turkey and Zionism*, Oxford, 1977.

Garrard, John A., *The English and Immigration, 1880–1910*, Oxford, 1971.

Gartner, Ll. P., *The Jewish Immigrant in England 1870–1914*, London, 1960.

Griffiths, Richard, *Fellow-Travellers of the Right*, London, 1980.
Grunberger, Richard, *A Social History of the Third Reich*, London, 1971.
Holmes, Colin, *Antisemitism in British Society 1876–1939*, London, 1979.
Herberg, Will, *Protestant – Catholic – Jew*, New York, 1960.
Hyman, Paula, *From Dreyfus to Vichy: The Remaking of French Jewry, 1906–1939*, New York, 1979.
Lipman, V. D., *Social History of the Jews in England, 1850–1950*, London, 1954.
Litvinoff, Barnet (ed.), *The Essential Chaim Weizmann*, London, 1982.
Oren, Dan A., *Joining the Club*, New Haven, Conn., 1986.
Stein, Leonard, *The Balfour Declaration*, London, 1961.
Weisgal, Meyer W., *et al.* (eds.), *The Letters and Papers of Chaim Weizmann*, Vols. I–VII, Oxford, 1968–75.
Weizmann, Chaim, *Trial and Error* (autobiography), London, 1949.

10 FASCISM TRIUMPHANT

Abrahamsen, D., *The Mind and Death of a Genius*, New York, 1946.
Arendt, Hannah, *The Origins of Totalitarianism*, New York, 1973.
Baynes, Norman H. (ed.), *The Speeches of Adolf Hitler, April 1922–August 1939*, London, 1942.
Bentwich, Norman, *They Found Refuge*, London, 1956.
British Statement of Policy, 'MacDonald White Paper', Cmd 6019, London, 1939.
Bullock, Alan, *Hitler: A Study in Tyranny*, London, 1952.
Conquest, Robert, *The Great Terror: Stalin's Purge of the Thirties*, London, 1968.
Dawidowicz, Lucy, *The War against the Jews 1933–45*, London, 1977.
Diamant, David, *Combattants juifs dans l'Armé républicaine espagnole*, Paris, 1979.
Fairgold, Henry, *The Politics of Rescue*, New Brunswick, NJ, 1970.
Freud, Sigmund, *Moses and Monotheism*, London, 1939.
Griffiths, Richard, *Fellow-Travellers of the Right*, London, 1980.
Grunberger, Richard, *A Social History of the Third Reich*, London, 1971.
Hitler, Adolf, *Mein Kampf*, tr. Ralph Manheim, Boston, 1943, and London, 1974.
Jay, Martin, *Adorno*, London, 1984.
Kochan, Lionel (ed.), *The Jews in Soviet Russia since 1917*, London, 1970.
——, *Pogrom: 10 November 1938*, London, 1957.

Liptzin, Solomon, *Germany's Stepchildren*, Philadelphia, 1944.

Lottman, Herbert, *The Left Bank: Writers in Paris from Popular Front to Cold War*, London, 1982.

Mack Smith, Denis, *Mussolini*, London, 1981.

Marcus, Joseph, *Social and Political History of the Jews in Poland 1919–1939*, New York, 1983.

Mosley, Oswald, *My Life*, London, 1968.

Palestine Royal Commission, *Report* (Peel Report), Cmd 5479, London, 1937.

Parkes, James, *Antisemitism*, London, 1963.

Rezzori, Gregor von, *Memoirs of an Antisemite* (fiction), London, 1983.

Roth, Cecil, *The Jewish Contribution to Civilisation*, London, 1956.

Seton-Watson, R. W., *Britain and the Dictators*, Cambridge, 1938.

Shirer, William L., *The Rise and Fall of the Third Reich*, London, 1964.

Skidelsky, Robert, *Oswald Mosley*, London, 1975.

Wischnitzer, Mark, *To Dwell in Safety*, Philadelphia, 1948.

Wyman, David C., *Paper Walls; America and the Refugee Crisis 1938–41*, Amherst, Mass., 1968.

11 HOLOCAUST

Agar, Herbert, *The Saving Remnant*, New York, 1960.

Ainsztein, Reuben, *Jewish Resistance in Nazi Occupied Europe*, London, 1974.

Amoureux, Henri, *La Vie des Français sous l'Occupation*, Paris, 1965.

Arendt, Hannah, *Eichmann in Jerusalem*, London, 1963.

Bauer, Yehuda, *American Jewry and the Holocaust*, Detroit, 1981.

——, *A History of the Holocaust*, New York, 1982.

—— with Rotenstreich, Natan (eds.), *The Holocaust as Historical Experience*, New York, 1981.

Beauvoir, Simone de, *La Force de l'âge*, Paris, 1960.

Blum, John M., *Roosevelt and Morgenthau* (revision and condensation of *From the Morgenthau Diaries*), Boston, 1970.

Bullock, Alan, *Hitler: A Study in Tyranny*, London, 1962.

Dawidowicz, Lucy, *The War against the Jews 1933–45*, London, 1975.

Dobroszycki, Lucjan (ed.), *The Chronicle of the Lodz Ghetto, 1941–1944*, New Haven, Conn., 1984.

Fenelon, Fania, with Routier, Marcelle, *The Musicians of Auschwitz*, London, 1977.

Fleming, Gerald, *Hitler and the Final Solution*, London, 1985.

Gilbert, Martin, *Auschwitz and the Allies*, London, 1981.

——, *Atlas of the Holocaust*, London, 1982.

——, *The Holocaust: The Jewish Tragedy*, London, 1986.

Hersey, John, *The Wall* (fiction), New York, 1950.

Hilberg, Raul, *The Destruction of the European Jews*, London, 1961.

—— (ed.), *Documents of Destruction: Germany and Jewry 1933–45*, Chicago, 1971.

Hoess, Rudolf, *Commandant of Auschwitz* (autobiography), tr. Constantine FitzGibbon, New York, 1960.

International Military Tribunal, *Trial of the Major War Criminals*, 42 vols., Nuremberg, 1947–9.

Irving, David, *Hitler's War*, 2 vols., London, 1977.

Kaplan, Chaim A., *Scroll of Agony: The Warsaw Diary*, tr. Abraham Kotch, London, 1966.

Keneally, Thomas, *Schindler's Ark* (fiction), London, 1982.

Kuznetsov, Anatoly, *Babi Yar* (fiction), tr. David Floyd, London, 1970.

Laqueur, Walter, *The Terrible Secret*, London, 1980.

Litvinoff, Barnet, *et al.* (eds.), *The Letters and Papers of Chaim Weizmann*, Vols. XIX–XXI, New Brunswick, NJ, 1979.

Loewenstein, F. L. (ed.), *Roosevelt and Churchill: Their Secret Wartime Correspondence*, London, 1975.

Mardor, Munya M., *Strictly Illegal*, London, 1964.

Marrus, Michael R., and Paxton, Robert O., *Vichy France and the Jews*, New York, 1981.

Morse, Arthur D., *While Six Million Died*, New York, 1968.

Nuernberg Military Tribunals, *Trials of War Criminals under Control Council Law*, 15 vols., Washington, 1949–53.

Pearlman, Moshe, *The Capture and Trial of Adolf Eichmann*, London, 1964.

Reitlinger, Gerald R., *The Final Solution*, London, 1961.

Ringelblum, Emanuel, *Notes from the Warsaw Ghetto*, ed. Jacob Sloan, New York, 1958.

Shirer, William L., *The Rise and Fall of the Third Reich*, London, 1964.

Trevor, Daphne, *Under the White Paper*, Jerusalem, 1948.

Wasserstein, Bernard, *Britain and the Jews of Europe, 1939–1945*, Oxford, 1979.

Weissberg, Alex, *Desperate Mission: The Joel Brand Story* (publ. in London as *Advocate of the Dead*), New York, 1958.

Wyman, David C., *Abandonment of the Jews: America and the Holocaust, 1941–45*, New York, 1984.

Zylberberg, Michael, *A Warsaw Diary 1939–1945*, London, 1969.

12 END OF EXILE

Anglo-American Committee of Inquiry Regarding Problems of European Jewry and Palestine, *Report*, Cmd 6808, London, 1946.

Bar-Zohar, Michael, *Ben-Gurion*, London, 1978.

Beaufre, André, *L'Expédition de Suez*, Paris, 1967.

Ben-Gurion, David, *Israel: A Personal History*, London, 1971.

Bohlen, Charles, *Witness to History*, New York, 1971.

Cang, Joel, *The Silent Millions: A History of the Jews in the Soviet Union*, London, 1969.

Caute, David, *The Great Fear: The Anti-Communist Purge under Truman and Eisenhower*, London, 1978.

Checinski, Michael, *Poland: Communism, Nationalism, Antisemitism*, New York, 1982.

Crossman, Richard H. S., *Palestine Mission*, London, 1947.

Dayan, Moshe, *Diary of the Sinai Campaign*, London, 1967.

Eliachar, Elie, *Living with Jews*, London, 1983.

Forrestal, James, *Diaries*, ed. Walter Millar, New York, 1951.

Gilboa, Yehoshua A., *The Black Years of Soviet Jewry*, Boston, 1971.

Goldberg, Anatol, *Ilya Ehrenburg: Writings, Politics and the Art of Survival*, London, 1984.

Goldmann, Nahum, *Memories*, London, 1969.

Goodman, Walter, *The Committee: The Extraordinary Career of the House Committee on Un-American Activities*, Baltimore, 1969.

Heer, Friedrich, *God's First Love*, London, 1961.

Heikal, Mohammed J., *Cutting the Lion's Tail*, London, 1986.

Herzl, Theodor, *Old-New Land* (fiction), tr. Lotte Levensohn, New York, 1941.

Kimche, Jon and David, *The Secret Roads*, London, 1954.

Kochan, Lionel (ed.), *The Jews in Soviet Russia since 1917*, Oxford, 1970.

Litvinoff, Barnet, *Ben-Gurion of Israel*, London, 1955.

—— *et al.* (eds.), *Letters and Papers of Chaim Weizmann*, Vols. XXII–XXIII, and *Papers*, Vol. II, New Brunswick, NJ, 1979–84.

London, Artur, *On Trial*, London, 1970.

Oren, Mordecai, *Prisonnier politique à Prague 1951–1956*, Paris, 1960.

Radosh, Ronald, and Milton, Joyce, *The Rosenberg File*, New York, 1983.

Rhodes James, Robert, *Anthony Eden*, London, 1986.

Robinson, Nehemiah (ed.), *European Jewry Ten Years after the War*, New York, 1956.

Sartre, Jean-Paul, *Réflexions sur la question juive*, Paris, 1946.

Shuckburgh, Evelyn, *Descent to Suez*, London, 1986.

Stone, I. F., *Underground to Palestine*, New York, 1946.

Truman, Harry S., *The Truman Memoirs*, Vol. II, London, 1956.

United Nations Special Committee on Palestine, *Report*, A/364, London, 1947.

Wistrich, Robert S. (ed.), *The Left Against Zion*, London, 1979.

13 CONFLICTS OF IDENTITY

Adams, Michael (ed.), *The Middle East: A Handbook*, London, 1971.

Argentina's National Commission on Disappeared People, *Nunca Mas*, Buenos Aires, 1984, and London, 1986.

Dayan, Moshe, *Break-Through*, London, 1981.

Eban, Abba, *Autobiography*, London, 1977.

Gilbert, Martin, *Sharansky, Hero of Our Time*, London, 1986.

Hart, Alan, *Arafat − Terrorist or Peacemaker?*, London, 1984.

Kaminskaya, Dina, *Final Judgement: My Life as a Soviet Defence Lawyer*, London, 1983.

Karetsky, Stephen, and Goldman, Peter E. (eds.), *The Media's War Against Israel*, New York, 1986.

Kishon, Ephraim, *So Sorry We Won*, London, 1967.

Kissinger, Henry, *Memoirs* (Vol. I, *The White House Years*; Vol. II, *Years of Upheaval*), New York, 1979, 1982.

Laqueur, Walter, *The Road to War 1967*, London, 1968.

Litvinoff, Barnet, *A Peculiar People: Inside World Jewry Today*, London, 1969.

Orbach, William W., *The American Movement to Aid Soviet Jews*, Amherst, Mass., 1979.

Prittie, Terence, *Eshkol of Israel*, London, 1969.

Quinley, Harold E., and Glock, Charles Y., *Antisemitism in America*, New Brunswick, NJ, 1984.

Rabin, Yitzhak, *The Rabin Memoirs*, London, 1979.

Rafael, Gideon, *Destination Peace: Three Decades of Israeli Foreign Policy*, London, 1981.

Rieder, Jonathan, *Canarsie: The Jews and Italians of Brooklyn against Liberalism*, Boston, 1985.

Sakharov, Andrei, *My Country and the World*, New York, 1975.

Silver, Eric, *Begin*, London, 1984.

Timerman, Jacobo, *Prisoner Without a Name, Cell Without a Number*, New York, 1981.

Weizman, Ezer, *The Battle for Peace*, New York, 1981.

Wilson, Harold, *The Chariot of Israel: Britain, America and the State of Israel*, London, 1981.

INDEX

Aaron of Lincoln, 59
Abd-ar-Rahman, Sultan, 50
Abdulla, Emir of Transjordan, 395, 397
Abelard, Peter, 57–8
Abrabanel, Isaac, 81
Abraham, 57
Abraham of Bristol, 68
Abrahamsen, D., *cit.*, 288n
Abulafia, Samuel Halevi, 73
Acheson, Dean, 410
Acre, capture of, 62
Action Française, 213, 272, 310, 312
Acts of the Apostles, 16
Adams, Henry, 247–8
Aden, disorders, 391
Adenauer, Konrad, 414
Adler, Cyrus, *cit.*, 237n
Adler, Jankel, 286
Adler, Michael, *cit.*, 68n
Adler, Victor, 197n
Adorno, Theodor, 10, 289
Agar, Herbert, *cit.*, 341n, 372n
Agnon, Samuel, 152
Agobard, Archbishop, his epistles,
   46–7
Ainsztein, Reuben, *cit.*, 329n, 360n,
   363n, 365n
Akiva, Rabbi, 22, 24
Albigensians, 67, 77
Aleichem, Sholem, 456
Alexander I, Tsar, 137, 143
Alexander II, Tsar, 221–3, 230
Alexander III, Tsar, 204, 224, 225n
Alexander of Alexandria, 22
Alexander, Tiberius Julius, 22
Alfonsin, Raul, 451
Alfonso VI, of Castile, 54, 73
Alfonso XI, of Castile, 71
Algeria, and Jews there, 203; anti-Jewish
   riots, 213
Aliens Commission, 253–5; its Report,
   254n; Aliens Act, 255, 273
Allen, Woody, 456

Allenby, Gen. Edmund, 270
Alliance Israélite Universelle, 164, 205,
   214, 225, 263, 267–8
Alsace, situation of Jews, 71, 123, 130; as
   French possession, 120n; French
   Revolution, 125–8; Franco–Prussian
   War, 202–3; Nazi Germany, 304
America (USA), independence, 121;
   immigrants to, 198, 225–6, 228, 241–52
   passim, 273–4; Negro slaves, 251; and
   WWI, 252–3, 258–61, 269; and Balfour
   Declaration, 268–9; and Bolshevik
   Revolution, 268–70; 'Jewish peril',
   273–6; immigration quota, 276–8,
   367–8; and Fascism, 300–1; European
   Jewry, visas for, 301, 316–17, 319,
   321–3, 343; *St Louis* refugees, 323–5;
   neutralism in, 343, 345, 350n–2; and
   Jewish rescue, 345, 350–4, 367–70;
   disclosure of 'Final Solution', 350–1;
   and WWII, 341–6 *passim*, 366–7, 376;
   Sikorski's visit, 342–3; campaign for
   Jewish army, 346–7, 369–70; demand
   for Jewish state, 347; and war crimes,
   352; and Arabs, 352–3; and
   immigration quota to Palestine, 358,
   384–6; Bermuda Conference, 367–9;
   War Refugee Board, 370–1, 373, 375;
   and Holocaust, 376–7; Displaced
   Persons, 382, 385–6, 405–6; Palestine
   partition scheme, 393–4; recognition of
   Israel, 394; and financial aid, 402–3;
   and Communism, 405–9; Central
   Intelligence Agency, 411–12; and Suez
   War, 413; and Six-Day War, 422;
   Vietnam War, 425, 430; Black–Jewish
   relations, 430–3, 439–41, 449; oil crisis,
   435; Yom Kippur War, 436–7; Israel
   invasion of Lebanon, 438; and PLO,
   439; Black nationalism, 440–1;
   'refuseniks', 447–50; and Argentinian
   atrocities, 451–2
American Civil War, 250–1, 275

471